Italian Trans Geographies

SUNY series in Italian/American Culture

Fred L. Gardaphé, editor

Italian Trans Geographies

Edited by

DANILA CANNAMELA, MARZIA MAURIELLO, and SUMMER MINERVA

Cover photo by © Lina Pallotta

Published by State University of New York Press, Albany

© 2023 State University of New York

All rights reserved

Printed in the United States of America

No part of this book may be used or reproduced in any manner whatsoever without written permission. No part of this book may be stored in a retrieval system or transmitted in any form or by any means including electronic, electrostatic, magnetic tape, mechanical, photocopying, recording, or otherwise without the prior permission in writing of the publisher.

For information, contact State University of New York Press, Albany, NY
www.sunypress.edu

Library of Congress Cataloging-in-Publication Data

Names: Cannamela, Danila, 1983– editor. | Mauriello, Marzia, editor. | Minerva, Summer, 1987– editor.
Title: Italian trans geographies / edited by Danila Cannamela, Marzia Mauriello, and Summer Minerva.
Description: Albany, NY : State University of New York Press, [2023] | Series: SUNY series in Italian/American culture | Includes bibliographical references and index.
Identifiers: LCCN 2022059335 | ISBN 9781438494586 (hardcover : alk. paper) | ISBN 9781438494593 (ebook)
Subjects: LCSH: Transgender people—Italy. | Gender-nonconforming people—Italy.
Classification: LCC HQ77.95.I8 I835 2023 | DDC 306.76/80945—dc23/eng/20230324
LC record available at https://lccn.loc.gov/2022059335

10 9 8 7 6 5 4 3 2 1

Contents

List of Illustrations   xi

Acknowledgments   xiii

Timeline of Key Events   xv

Introduction   1
Italian Trans Geographies: Retracing Trans/Cultural Narratives of People and Places
   Danila Cannamela

SOUTH

Part 1. Memories of Transitions

Chapter 1
From *AntoloGaia: Vivere sognando e non sognando di vivere; I miei anni settanta* (*AntholoGay: Living Dreaming and Not Dreaming of Living; My Seventies*)   29
   Porpora Marcasciano

Chapter 2
From *L'aurora delle trans cattive: Storie, sguardi e vissuti della mia generazione transgender* (*The Dawn of the Bad Trans Women: Stories, Fragments, and Lives of My Transgender Generation*)   41
   Porpora Marcasciano

Chapter 3
From *Tra le rose e le viole: La storia e le storie di transessuali e travestiti* (Among Roses and Violets: The Story and the Stories of Transsexuals and Transvestites)   47
   Porpora Marcasciano

Chapter 4
From *Dolore minimo* (Minimum Pain) and *Dove non siamo stati* (Where We Haven't Been)   61
   Giovanna Cristina Vivinetto

Part 2. The *Femminielli*: A Gender-Variant Community between Past and Present

Chapter 5
"Et io ne viddi uno in Napoli." I femminielli: Ricognizione storica e mitografica; Spunti per una riflessione sull'identità di genere ("And I saw one of them in Naples." *Femminielli*: Historical and Mythographic Recognition; Starting Points for a Reflection on Gender Identity)   77
   Eugenio Zito, Paolo Valerio, and Nicola Sisci

Chapter 6
From *Altri transiti: Corpi, pratiche, rappresentazioni di femminielli e transessuali* (Other Transitions: Bodies, Practices, Representations of Femminielli and Transsexuals)   103
   Maria Carolina Vesce

Chapter 7
Two Real-Life Perspectives on the *Femminielli*: A Conversation with Loredana Rossi and Ciro Cascina   117
   Marzia Mauriello

CENTER

Part 3. A Felliniesque Dolce Vita

Chapter 8
From *L'aurora delle trans cattive*   127
   Porpora Marcasciano

CHAPTER 9
From *Io, la "Romanina": Perché sono diventato donna* (*I, "Romanina": Why I Became a Woman*)   135
    Romina Cecconi

Part 4. Narrating Trans History as a Meaningful Experience

CHAPTER 10
From *Elementi di critica trans* (*Elements of Trans Critique*)   161
    Edited by Laurella Arietti, Christian Ballarin, Giorgio Cuccio, and Porpora Marcasciano

CHAPTER 11
Non siamo nat@ ieri (We Weren't Born Yesterday)   183
    Egon Botteghi

NORTH

Part 5. Stories of Trans Identity and Activism

CHAPTER 12
From *AntoloGaia*   197
    Porpora Marcasciano

CHAPTER 13
From *Favolose narranti: Storie di transessuali* (*Fabulous Narrators: Stories of Transsexuals*)   201
    Porpora Marcasciano

CHAPTER 14
From *Camminavo rasente i muri: Autobiografia tascabile di un transessuale* (*I Was Walking Along the Walls: Pocket Autobiography of a Transsexual Man*)   213
    Massimo D'Aquino

CHAPTER 15
Three Stories of Activism in Italy: Conversations with Christian Ballarin, Giorgio Cuccio, and Mazen Masoud   225
    Marzia Mauriello

viii | Contents

Part 6. Testifying to Voices and Images of Transness

CHAPTER 16
Perverse Polymorphs Proto T* at the Dawn of 1980s Italian *Riflusso*   245
   Helena Velena

CHAPTER 17
A Trans Revolution and Its Contradictions: An Interview with
Simone Cangelosi   263
   Danila Cannamela

CHAPTER 18
Lina Pallotta's Portrait of Porpora: "Snapshots of a Moment" and
Geographies of Friendship   275
   Danila Cannamela and Stella Gonzalez

TRANSITIONS ACROSS THE OCEAN

Part 7. Italian Migration and Queer Roots

CHAPTER 19
Michela Griffo: "Io sono sangue"; I Am Blood, or the Stonewall
Story from the Perspective of an Italian American Lesbian   287
   Summer Minerva

CHAPTER 20
What Does It Mean for the Italian American Community to
be Trans?   293
   *Frances Rose Subbiondo, Erin Ferrentino, Liz Mariani,
   Summer Minerva, and Liana Cusmano*

Part 8. New Italian American Migrations: Back to Italy

CHAPTER 21
Summer Within: A Journey of Migration and Reconnection   319
   Danila Cannamela

CHAPTER 22
A Queer 'Talian Pilgrimage   331
   Summer Minerva

CONCLUSION
Paths for Future Exploration: Language, Situatedness, and
Glocal Paths   339
  Danila Cannamela and Marzia Mauriello

LIST OF CONTRIBUTORS   353

INDEX   361

Illustrations

Figure 5.1 "Ballo di Tarantella del'Affeminati di Napoli" [Dance of the Tarantella by the Affeminati of Naples]. 182

Figure 18.1 Porpora Marcasciano in Rome, 1990. 277

Figure 18.2 Porpora Marcasciano and Marcella Di Folco in Modena, ca. 1999. 279

Figure 18.3 Roberta, Lucrezia, and Porpora in Rome, 1990. 280

Figure 18.4 Lina and Porpora in New York, 1996. 282

Acknowledgments

We would like to express eternal gratitude to our contributors who responded to our call with great enthusiasm. It is because of your strength, wisdom, and life force that this volume exists. The gift of your words will be appreciated for generations to come and will be a guidepost for so many future generations of trans and LGBTQ+ people struggling to see themselves reflected in our global culture. In particular, we would like to thank Porpora Marcasciano for her willingness to help us bring together many of these voices, with utmost integrity, care, and humor. Thank you to the Center for the Arts and Humanities at Colby College for its generous financial support, and to the Generations Project and Adam Golub for their support in raising the voices of LGBTQ+ Italian America.

The introduction is derived in part from an article published by Danila Cannamela in *Journal of Modern Italian Studies* 27, vol. 4 (2022): 600–22. https://doi.org/10.1080/1354571X.2021.1965753.

An earlier version of "The Dawn of our 'Wonderful Adventure,'" featured in chapter 2, was originally published in *TSQ: Transgender Studies Quarterly* 6, no. 1 (2019): 124–31.

An earlier version of Helena Velena's essay, "Perverse Polymorphs Proto T* at the Dawn of 1980s Italian *Riflusso*," included in chapter 16, was originally published in the volume *T**, edited by Ilaria Bombelli (Milan: Mousse Publishing, 2020).

The photos in chapter 18 are reproduced with Lina Pallotta's permission.

Liana Cusmano's "Boyfriend," featured in chapter 20, first appeared in *Transformations: The Italian Canadian Experience*, a project by the Toronto Catholic District School Board (TCDSB) and the National Congress of Italian Canadians (NCIC).

Unless otherwise indicated, all of the explanatory footnotes were added while the anthology was being translated and compiled, to offer additional explanations about historical contexts and terminologies. For the texts that featured footnotes in the original Italian, we used the abbreviations "t/n" (translator's note) or "ed./n" (editor's note) to distinguish our explanatory notes from those of the authors.

Timeline of Key Events

This is a timeline of global and local events that have shaped the history of Italian trans activism and that are referenced throughout the volume.[1]

1949   Sexologist David Oliver Cauldwell coins the term "transsexual" to designate those who have a gender orientation not aligned with their biological sex.

1952   American trans woman Christine Jorgensen is the first person to become widely known for undergoing gender reassignment surgery.[2]

1966   German American endocrinologist and sexologist Harry Benjamin publishes *The Transsexual Phenomenon*. The text treats transsexualism as a medical condition and sets the standards for trans care.

1967   Romina Cecconi, called Romanina, undergoes gender reassignment surgery in Switzerland. She represents the first case recognized in Italy.

1968–1971   Romina Cecconi is sent to confinement because she is considered a socially and morally dangerous person. The obligatory residence takes place in Volturino, a small village in the province of Foggia (in the southern Italian region of Puglia).

1969   On the night of June 28, in New York, a series of riots start in the aftermath of a police raid on a Greenwich Village gay bar, the Stonewall Inn. This protest, led by street transvestites and homeless youth, marks the birth of the global LGBT+ liberation movement.

1972   On April 5, Mario Mieli and a group of gay activists gather in front of Sanremo Casino to protest the International Congress of

Sexology, which was discussing deviant sexual behaviors, including homosexuality. Their public protest is seen as the Italian Stonewall.

1979   In August, in a crowded swimming pool in Milan, a group of transsexual women led by Pina Bonanno demonstrate for the recognition of their identity, exposing their breasts in public.

1979   Foundation of the Harry Benjamin International Gender Dysphoria Association (HBIGDA) in the US.

1981   Official foundation of MIT (Movimento Italiano Transessuale [Italian Transsexual Movement]). The Movement had been active since 1979.

1982   On April 14, the Italian Parliament approves Law 164, which permits and recognizes sex change. Italy is the second European country, after Germany, to pass a law on this matter.

1982   In Bologna, Circolo di Cultura Omosessuale 28 Giugno (an LGBT+ association that originated from the Collettivo Frocialista) obtains a space from the municipal government: the so-called Cassero in Porta Saragozza. The official inauguration takes place on December 19, and trans activist Valérie Taccarelli is the one who cuts the ribbon.

1988   Foundation of MIT Emilia-Romagna; this regional section would take the lead in the national association. Marcella Di Folco is the president.

1990   Lazio is the first Italian region to approve a law to implement Law 164. Its signatory is Pietro Mastrantoni, from whom the law takes its name.

1994   MIT opens a health center. This is the first public service completely run by trans people.

1995   Di Folco is elected city councilor in Bologna. She is the first trans woman to hold political office in Italy and most likely in the world.

1997   The first "Sportello Trans CGIL" (job help desk for trans people) opens in Bologna.

1998   Foundation of ONIG (Osservatorio Nazionale sull'identità di genere [National Observatory of Gender Identity]). In connection with HBIGDA, this Italian center aims at fostering dialogue and collaborations, to reach a deeper understanding of trans experiences from a scientific and social perspective and promote the freedom of expression of transgender people.

1999 On November 20, the Transgender Day of Remembrance (TDOR) is celebrated for the first time. This annual observance honors the memory of the transgender people whose lives were lost in acts of anti-transgender violence.

1999 In the same year, MIT, Movimento Italiano Transessuale, becomes Movimento Identità Transessuale (Transsexual Identity Movement).

2000 From June 28 to July 2, Bologna hosts Transiti (Transitions), a week of trans culture featuring films, photographic exhibitions, entertainment, and an international conference with the major experts of transsexuality and gender identity. American trans activist Sylvia Rivera is the guest of honor.

2000 July 8, Rome hosts World Pride. MIT succeeds in allowing Rivera to address the crowd, even if her speech had not been arranged.

2003 Foundation of Libellula. This association, based in Rome, is engaged in protecting LGBTQIA+ people and educating the public opinion on gender identity in the city and across the Italian national territory.

2004 American transgender activist and writer Leslie Feinberg visits MIT.

2004 On May 17: Inaugural year of the International Day Against Homophobia, Transphobia, and Biphobia.

2005 In April, Bologna hosts the fourteenth world meeting of HBIGDA, which in 2007 becomes WPATH (World Professional Association for Transgender Health).

2006 Foundation of the Coordinamento Trans Sylvia Rivera (Trans Steering Committee Sylvia Rivera), which gathers the main Italian trans associations.

2007 Trans activist Vladimir Luxuria is elected deputy with the leftist party Rifondazione Comunista.

2007 Foundation of ATN (Associazione Transessuale Napoli [Transsexual Association Naples]). Its mission is to defend the rights of trans

	people against discrimination and to provide support and legal advice during the transition phase.
2008	The seminar "Elementi di critica trans" (Elements of Trans Critique) takes place in Tuscany. The meeting is an occasion to discuss and elaborate on trans issues from the perspective of trans subjectivities. The conference proceedings are published in 2010.
2008	Inaugural year of Divergenti (Divergent), the international festival of trans cinema—the first in Italy and the second in Europe.
2010	Marcella Di Folco dies in Bologna at the age of sixty-seven.
2011	On July 11, Euro Pride takes place. Lady Gaga is the guest of honor. MIT holds the vice presidency of the organizing committee.
2015	In July a ruling of the Court of Cassation recognizes the possibility of name change without gender reassignment surgery. In November, the Constitutional Court also recognizes this right.
2016	In June, the meeting of TGEU (Transgender Europe) takes place in Bologna. Three hundred international delegations participate. TGEU is a network of different organizations working to combat discrimination against trans people and support trans rights. It was founded in 2005 in Vienna.
2016	MIT joins the steering committee of TGEU.
2017	MIT again changes the name behind its acronym to Movimento Identità Trans (Trans Identity Movement). The name change is meant to acknowledge the wide range of different gender-variant experiences represented by the association.
2020	In November, Legge Zan (Zan Law), a law against homo- and transphobia, is approved by the Camera (the Italian House of Representatives), but in 2021 the Senate votes against it. The goal of this law was to modify clauses 604-bis and 604-ter of the Italian Penal Code, regarding violence or discrimination due to sexual orientation or gender identity. Since its proposal, Legge Zan has generated a heated debate among political parties and the general public.
2021	In October, trans activist and former president of MIT Porpora Marcasciano is elected city counselor in Bologna, and in November

she is appointed president of the Commissione Pari Opportunità del Comune di Bologna (Commission for Equal Opportunities of the City of Bologna).

Introduction

Italian Trans Geographies: Retracing Trans/Cultural Narratives of People and Places

Danila Cannamela

In the documentary film *Comizi d'amore* (*Love Talks*, 1965), director Pier Paolo Pasolini travels across the Italian peninsula like "a sort of traveling salesman" to interview Italians about their opinions on gender and sexuality.[3] Throughout his journey, Pasolini discusses love and sex with people of all ages and different socioeconomic backgrounds: children and the elderly, male chauvinists and emancipated women, northern factory workers and southern peasants, families vacationing at the beach and young people having fun in a dance hall, illiterates and intellectuals. By gathering so many voices, *Comizi d'amore* succeeded in showing a multifaceted—though often reticent and rather conformist—perspective on questions that are still relevant more than fifty years later, including sexuality, marriage, gender roles, and sex work. However, if one considers that while making this film Pasolini was keeping his homosexuality hidden from his audience, it seems paradoxical—and certainly ironic—that the only voices that remained completely unheard in *Comizi d'amore* are those of sexual and gender minorities. Still, despite being excluded, these underrepresented people and their narratives become a central object of discussion in the movie: indeed, all Pasolini's interviewees, when asked about "sexual abnormality," rush to distance themselves from what they regard as a disgusting abomination or a pitiful illness, and promptly condemn those *invertiti* (inverts)[4] who transgress from the norm. Nevertheless, this patriarchal and androcentric view, while demonstrating a repulsion for any form of sexual and gender diversity, at least acknowledges the existence of "deviant" men; conversely, the possibility that *invertite* (literally, "female inverts") might exist is not even remotely recognized in the film.[5]

Italian Trans Geographies is modeled after Pasolini's thought-provoking "love talks" but changes the narrative point of view from the cisgender crowd to trans people and expands the inquiry beyond the Italian peninsula, interrogating members of the Italian American diaspora as well as trans migrants who moved to Italy.[6] In giving voice and visibility to this alternative perspective, we—myself and the two other editors of this book, Marzia Mauriello and Summer Minerva—have drawn especially on the practice and poetics of Porpora Marcasciano. Marcasciano is a sociologist, human-rights activist, and leading figure of the Italian trans movement who since the 1980s has been at the forefront of struggles for gender self-determination and civil rights in Italy. In conjunction with her LGBT+ activism, she has engaged in extensive documentation, combining her commitment to trans liberation with her passion for storytelling. Her accounts of grassroots trans history include memoirs, essays, and collections of interviews, among which are *AntoloGaia: Vivere sognando e non sognando di vivere; I miei anni settanta* (*AntholoGay: Living Dreaming and Not Dreaming of Living; My Seventies*, 2007; 2nd ed. 2016), *Favolose narranti: Storie di transessuali* (*Fabulous Narrator: Stories of Transsexuals*, 2008), *L'aurora delle trans cattive: Storie, sguardi e vissuti della mia generazione trans* (*The Dawn of the Bad Trans Women: Stories, Fragments, and Experiences of My Trans Generation*, 2018), and *Tra le rose e le viole: La storia e le storie di transessuali e travestiti* (*Among Roses and Violets: The Story and the Stories of Transsexuals and Transvestites*, 2002; 2nd ed. 2020). As she stated in her introduction to *Elementi di critica trans* (*Elements of Trans Critique*, 2010), a volume that resulted from a seminar organized by Marcasciano and other trans activists, a key component of the trans movement resides in an ongoing process of self-recognition and narration. That process, much like the 1970s feminist engagement with self-discovery and collective sharing,[7] has its roots in the nexus between gaining individual awareness (the practice of starting from oneself) and participating in a movement, an idea that Marcasciano expands upon: "Reflecting and thinking about one's path means reappropriating it; it means becoming writers of *our own* history and, by writing it, giving *our own* meaning to it."[8] By contrast, if people are unable to retell their history in their own terms, it will be impossible to build a new future and envision different paths that can challenge those generated by the words of patriarchal—and explicitly as well as implicitly transphobic—narratives. This is why storytelling can serve as a personal and political instrument of transformation.

But what is the storytelling strategy that has the potential to change dominant narratives and reframe the expectations of the cisgender audience? The revolution, Marcasciano has contended, is achieved through laughter;[9] in fact, her use of humor has been a successful strategy to "make space where there is no space"[10] and win over a non-trans audience that might be inherently biased or simply unequipped to comprehend gender diversity. Likewise, the adoption of comedic or ironic elements is a storytelling device to which other gender nonconforming authors anthologized in this volume have similarly resorted, in order to create an immediate, and perhaps unexpected, connection with their audience.[11] Ultimately, for Marcasciano, performing the role of contemporary bard of the trans movement is a constructive form of activism.[12] Words have a world-making function, she has maintained, and giving voice to experiences has the potential to foster future geographies, perhaps even dreamlike, joyful ones, by opening new cognitive and affective routes across gendered spaces and gender identities.[13]

Inspired by Marcasciano's poetics—a poetics in which storytelling, entertainment, political action, and fanciful visions are intertwined—this volume charts overlooked sites of Italian culture through narratives of gender nonconforming people. The overarching goal is to generate new cultural spaces of memorialization, critical reflection, and opportunities for interaction in the present. Playing on the interpretative potential of the word "trans" ("across" and "beyond"), *Italian Trans Geographies* shows how trans people have been shaped by the places they have traversed and, in turn, have contributed in shaping those places. The book illustrates how documenting stories of gender transition is not solely a question of LGBTQ+ civil rights; it is a much broader matter that involves diving into the centuries-old syncretism of Italian culture, venturing into migration journeys, challenging white monoculturalism, and moving across issues of class, race, and gender inequality. In the accounts in this volume, Italy functions both as a place for the investigation of the trans experience in its relation to a specific territory and as a larger "identity factor" that contributes to the construction of one's subjectivity. If the geographic focus of our investigation is on Italy, this geography does not remain within the country's borders: Italy becomes simultaneously a magnifying lens and an enlarged context, filled with identity symbolisms. In the trans narratives of people and places featured in this collection, the Italian peninsula represents a multifaceted space of transitions: an ancient Mediterranean landscape where cultures have mingled for centuries; the land of the economic miracle, in which the influence of American cultural and economic models has been pivotal; a diasporic land, abandoned and idealized. This is particularly visible in the narratives of Italian American trans people, whose ethnic background interacts with their trans identity, embodying the multidimensionality of the identity experience and arising from their inherent, and incessant, crossing of borders.

There are two key terms in this volume: "trans" and "geographies." "Trans" is adopted here as an umbrella term that, in providing a unifying label for gender variance, cannot encompass all the many specific diversities and concerns expressed by gender nonconforming individuals. This aspect is effectively stated in the aforementioned book *Elementi di critica trans*; there, Nicoletta Poidimani maintains that trans experiences have been grouped together in an all-encompassing category in order to be socially represented but notes that this category is difficult to map with precision, as "it constantly pushes its borders further and further, reaching the point of subverting itself."[14] Areas of inner subversion include, on the one hand, trans-normativity tendencies—people who try to erase their transition path to exclusively affirm their post-surgical identity[15]—and, on the other, the acritical adoption of a queer fluidity that might misrepresent the experience of trans subjectivities (e.g., transsexual or intersex people) and generate a "globalized indifference" for the specificity of their struggles.[16] Poidimani's view is in line with trans studies scholars who have warned of the risk of exclusively identifying trans individuals with narratives of gender transition, "as if certain concrete somethings could be characterized as 'crossers,' while everything else could be characterized by boundedness and fixity."[17] The many stories in this book contribute to charting the diversity inherent to trans identities and the contradictions underlying the unifying trans category. Some authors can hardly position themselves within the notion of gender and might agree with Marcasciano's assertion that "among heterosexuals I felt gay, among gay men I felt like a trans woman, and among trans women I felt I was something else or, better yet, somewhere else."[18] Others have embraced a masculine or feminine identity without modifying their bodily appearance; still others have decided to modify their bodies or go through gender reassignment surgery to better express their gender identities. And yet, for the majority of them, coming out and transitioning did not represent a final destination but rather marked an important milestone in a path made by and opened to many other experiences. Touching on this point, LGBTQ+ activist, performer, and educator Egon Botteghi has made clear that it would be too confining to use his trans identity as the only measure of his engagement. Botteghi goes on to explain that, as an environmentalist, he has participated in numerous projects in his hometown, Livorno, in Tuscany. For example, since 2015, he has been involved in the collective reappropriation of an abandoned green area that was converted into an urban garden. As Botteghi concludes: "Trans people can carry on very important struggles in their territory, and the complexity of their identities cannot be exhausted by their being trans, so that their engagement and their whole existence are seemingly flattened on this one thing."[19] To summarize, a crucial point raised by Botteghi is that while identities inevitably create gendered spaces, those spaces should never become places of stalemate and self-confinement.

Regarding the second key term, "geographies": the exploration of the relationships between trans bodies and their surrounding spaces is certainly not novel to this book. Indeed, the nexus between sense of place and gender identity has been investigated by a variety of studies, which all predicate their arguments and assessments on feminist, queer, and critical race theories and practices that have demonstrated the ways in which "social differences are the effects of how bodies inhabit spaces with others."[20] There are, however, some discipline-specific aspects of this research that should be noted.[21]

Since the 1980s, geographers of gender and sexualities have shown that "space is fundamental to the ideological and material production of the dominant and normative," and this interconnection might indeed explain why LGBTQ+ communities initially developed in marginalized areas—"gay ghettos"—at the periphery of heteronormative desires and behaviors.

More recent research has reframed the stark divide between normative and transgressive spaces to articulate how geographies are constantly defined and redefined by the interplay between the material and the figurative, the corporeal and the imaginative.[22] Spaces are not intrinsically straight or gay, and people who identify as LGBTQ+ embody multiple diversities that go beyond attempts to assimilate "on the basis of largely capitalist and heteronormative values" or confining themselves to transgressive spaces.[23] In light of this reframing, studies in the emerging subfield of trans geographies have been focusing instead on the "importance and distinctiveness of trans* and intersex people,"[24] giving consideration to how different "bodies and spaces . . . revolve around, resist, and live in-between and beyond binary gender."[25] Trans people have indeed generated new social codes and modes of interactions in places perceived as ordinary (e.g., workplaces, public restrooms, or sports venues).

Geographies of "r/existence"—Marcasciano's term[26]—can be located everywhere, yet, historically, urban settings have been a particular arena for the rise of LGBTQ+ groups. "Rainbow cities" across the world represent "a milieu of political, economic, cultural, urban and social aspects [that have been] crucial for LGBT inclusiveness."[27] Cities have put forward political agendas centered on "the issue of the equality of citizens," becoming sounding boards for the need for legislative action at the national level.[28] In the case of Italy, the proposal of a law against homo-transphobia in 2020 (the Zan Law)[29] and the introduction of same-sex civil unions in 2016 demonstrates how Rome, Bologna, Naples, and other Italian cities have been a driving force in modeling inclusive local legislations that have typically resulted from the "virtuous triangulation [of] mayors–associationism–cities."[30]

Therefore, it comes as no surprise that the academic field of trans studies originally developed from the reconstruction of subaltern geographies—bars, clubs, hotels—in cities such as San Francisco and New York, where, in the 1960s, police repression, criminal exploitation, and LGBTQ+ activism reached a turning point.[31] This is indeed the setting of Leslie Feinberg's autobiographical novel *Stone Butch Blues* (1993), the bildungsroman of a young factory worker who finds themselves fighting for gender self-determination and workers' rights, first in Buffalo and then in New York City. Moreover, it is important to recall that the Stonewall Inn—the bar where, on June 28, 1969, the most monumental civil rights uprising took place in New York City's Greenwich Village—is one of those urban sites in which diasporic geographies contributed to the construction of a subversive North American landscape during the following decades. Those at the heart of this rebellion were not just Sylvia Rivera, an American activist of Latinx descent, who is believed to have started the protest, and Marsha P. Johnson, one of the first Black icons of the trans movement in the US.[32] The exploration in this volume draws attention to the intricate gendered and cultural geographies that developed within gay bars. In these establishments run by the local mafia (which illegally served alcohol to the transgender and homosexual clientele), the Italian American mobsters' exoticized masculinity converged with queer expressions of sexuality and gender. Yet, for some, having a shared Italian ancestry with the mafiosi bar owners helped activists fighting for equal rights as LGBTQ+ to break through certain identity barriers.[33]

However, also these niche spaces outside mainstream culture ended up reproducing geographies of exclusion that reinstated hierarchical binaries. As Renato Busarello recalls in *Elementi di critica trans*, in the late 1970s, the rising Italian LGBT+ movement eventually rejected the performativity of "the fairy, [or] the transvestite" to embrace a mainstream path that identified the sole subject of fights for civil rights with the masculine gay.[34] This shift mirrors what happened in the post-Stonewall epoch in the US, when it became clear that racialized street queens and sex workers like Rivera and Johnson remained isolated. While they were still participating in groups like GAA (Gay Activists Alliance) and GLF (Gay Liberation Front), their struggle for survival was at odds with the assimilationist politics of the movement.[35] Indeed, in 1986, when the New York City Council finally approved a homosexual rights bill, there was no mention of trans people. Furthermore, both in Italy and in the US, trans women were often antagonized by feminist groups, who felt that trans women were reproducing sexist stereotypes and, despite wearing female clothes, still benefited from their male privilege.[36] As these inner conflicts show, even the outposts of sexual liberation and gender equality ultimately generated problematic inner geographies of oppression and inequity.

The type of academic research developed by the aforementioned studies on gender and space finds an obvious "geographic" limitation in its narrow circulation, typically within academia. *Italian Trans Geographies* seeks to reach a broader audience by mapping the intersections of space, place, culture, and gender variance, through texts authored by either trans people or by allies who have closely collaborated with trans individuals and respected their authorship. If one were to categorize the nonfiction works anthologized in this volume—memoirs, interviews, scholarly essays, poems, documentary films, songs, performances, and photographs—within a particular genre, it might be within the tradition of the transition memoir. One of its pioneering voices was Jan Morris, a renowned travel journalist who recounted her personal journey across genders through "variable construction[s] of gender relations in different local-cultural space/places."[37] Yet, if in the 1970s Morris's influential autobiography *Conundrum* (1974) helped debunk taboos about transsexualism and reposition trans identities within social spaces, it also served as a generator of recognizable clichés (e.g., the trope of being trapped in the wrong body or the idea of gender reassignment surgery as a lifelong destination) that made trans narratives acceptable to a cisgender audience.[38] Addressing these fixed conventions, Julia Serano, in the opening of *Whipping Girl* (2015; first ed. 2007) candidly admits that her book was going to disappoint "non-trans" readers who were expecting another "confessional tell-all . . . one that begins with my insistence that I have been a 'woman trapped inside a man's body' . . . one that explains the ins and outs of sex reassignment surgery."[39]

Undoubtedly Romina Cecconi's autobiography, *Io, la "Romanina": Perché sono diventato donna* (1976), the first book authored by a transsexual person in Italy, fits the script mocked by Serano. Romanina describes surgery as "the crowning achievement of [a] lifetime" and the final overcoming of a mistake of nature.[40] Still, her book testifies to the possibility for gender nonconforming people to gain agency as narrators of their own story, a story that dominant narratives have either medicalized or criminalized. *Io, la "Romanina"* provides a valuable testimony of everyday life as a gender-variant and low-income person in 1960s Florence, at a time when cross-dressing was considered a crime, laws against homophobia and transphobia were nonexistent, and local institutions exerted the power to define "what bodies [were] allowed to do, when and where."[41] In her hometown, Romanina had been incarcerated and repeatedly fined by the police for her "socially dangerous" behavior and for soliciting on the Lungarno (the streets right next to the river Arno); as a punishment, she was eventually sentenced to staying confined to the remote village of Volturino, in southern Italy.[42] Cecconi's path to gender transition was dotted with migration journeys: initially, she traveled with an itinerant circus, il Gratta, doing an impersonation of Brigitte Bardot. She then moved to Paris to work as a burlesque dancer at Madame Arthur, a drag cabaret in the Rue des Martyrs, and she finally relocated in Switzerland to undergo surgery.

Io, la "Romanina", in its twofold process of storytelling and reappropriation, demonstrates how, in Italy, literature has offered an important venue for gender-variant people to speak for themselves and shift normative perspectives. Another notable, but radically different, case is the seminal work of Mario Mieli, comprising his masterpiece *Elementi di critica omosessuale* (1977, translated as *Towards a Gay Communism: Elements of a Homosexual Critique*, 1980, rev. ed. 2018), numerous articles, and his autobiographical memoir, *Il risveglio dei faraoni* (*The Pharaohs' Awakening*, posthumous publication in 1994). Mieli never exclusively identified as trans; rather, he embodied a type of polysexual and polymorphous gender fluidity that today could be defined as pansexual or genderqueer but that he dubbed "transsexual."[43] His idiosyncratic view of "transsexualism" constituted a driving force in the Italian and international discourse of gender liberation. Through his activism and literary work, Mieli was one of the protagonists of 1970s counterculture, at a time when (proto-)LGBTQ+ collectives began spreading across the peninsula and challenging heteronormative conventions.[44] One of the most significant developments during those tumultuous years was the 1977 movement, a sociopolitical laboratory that loosely joined a constellation of collectives, groups, and individuals (students, unemployed youth, workers, gender minorities) who shared the need to experiment with forms of life that were alternative (or "oblique") to the rigid order and stifling institutions of both capitalist society and leftist organizations, including the Communist Party and trade unions.[45] In her memoir *AntoloGaia*, Marcasciano situates Mieli within a broader historical geography of LGBTQ+ liberation: "Three years earlier [Stonewall, June 28, 1969,] Sylvia Rivera had launched the bottle at the cops; a year earlier [April 5, 1972,] Mario Mieli and Alfredo Cohen, together with others, had organized a sit-in in Sanremo against a conference of sexologists who still considered homosexuality an illness."[46] The protest against the Congresso internazionale di sessuologia su comportamenti devianti della sessualità umana (Sexology International Congress on Deviant Behaviors of Human Sexuality) resulted in the birth of FUORI! (Fronte Unitario Omosessuale Rivoluzionario Italiano [United Italian Homosexual Revolutionary Front]), a group officially founded in Turin in 1971, which constituted the Italian Gay Liberation Front.[47]

For Mieli, liberating sexual desires was the first step toward the creation of an alternative communist society beyond gender polarities, a society radically different from heteropatriarchal capitalism, which either represses or exploits sexual desire.[48] His activism traced a "geography of experiences" across places and cultures, spanning Italy, England, France, Germany, the Netherlands, Morocco, the US, and India.[49] Unapologetically cross-dressed, he queered a myriad of private and public spaces, ranging from his family's bourgeois house, which became the first seat of FUORI!, to convention centers, squares, and museums, where he improvised scandalous performances. Mieli proclaimed that it was possible to turn ordinary places into revolutionary geographies: "Factories, occupied manufacture plants, feminist spaces—or female homosexuality—and supermarkets, trams, cinemas, public restrooms can turn from ghettos into places where we make love."[50] In 1974, he left FUORI! because cofounder Angelo Pezzana and other members of the group had joined the Partito Radicale (Radical Party).[51] Mieli then created a new autonomous collective, Collettivo Autonomo di Milano (Autonomous Collective of Milan), which rejected the possibility of using parliamentary politics as a forum to achieve revolutionary ideals.[52] Still, the Collective led to the dissemination of a grassroots LGBTQ+ movement across Italy, which generated the formation of other groups, such as the Collettivo Frocialista in Bologna and the Collettivo Narciso in Rome. Marcasciano was a cofounder of the latter, which was eventually renamed Circolo Mario Mieli. However, unlike FUORI!, the goal of Collettivo Narciso was to situate the process of

LGBTQ+ liberation within an all-encompassing narrative that could unite all the oppressed of the world around common objectives and one shared enemy: bourgeois capitalist society.[53]

The 1977 liberation movement was the epicenter of the rising LGBTQ+ discourse in Italy, and more specifically, of trans liberation; the movement acted as a catalyst for new demands: first and foremost, the need to give voice to creativity, corporeality, and stigmatized desires and to locate these forms of life outside the space-time of wage labor. A site that particularly testifies to the aftermath of 1977 is the so-called Cassero, in Bologna, a historical building in Porta Saragozza, one of the city's ancient gates. In 1982, after a period of heated debates and negotiations, the city of Bologna assigned it to house Circolo 28 Giugno (an LGBTQ+ association that was the successor to Collettivo Frocialista during the social turmoil of the 1970s).[54] This was the first time an Italian LGBTQ+ community was officially granted the use of a public space by a municipal government in Italy, and its trans component, as Marcasciano recalls in *AntoloGaia*, had a fundamental role in the "storming of Cassero": trans activists were among the people who marched at the forefront and cut the ribbon during the inauguration.[55]

However, even before the creation of an iconic space like the Bolognese Cassero, a trans protest took place at a public swimming pool in Milan in 1979. A group of transsexuals, wearing men's swimming trunks so as to expose their naked breasts, expressed their dissent for not being "recognized as such by the state, and recognized even less as women."[56] From that moment, according to Stefania Voli's historical reconstruction, transsexual activist groups began to proliferate in many Italian cities, organizing to claim their civil rights, protesting against discrimination, and advocating for a law allowing "them to change their sex and name in accordance with their chosen gender identity."[57] Such mobilization led to the creation of the Italian Transsexual Movement (Movimento Italiano Transessuale [MIT]), formally founded in 1981. This national association fostered the creation of regional branches in major cities across the peninsula. A crucial year for trans rights was 1982, when the "Italian parliament approved Law 164: Rules Concerning the Rectification of Sex-Attribution, [a] law [that] made it possible for transsexuals to proceed with the surgical adjustment of sex characteristics and change of registered name."[58]

Since the late 1980s, the city of Bologna has become the most important hub of the trans movement, with the founding, in 1988, of MIT Bologna (which in 1999 became Movimento Identità Transessuale [Transsexual Identity Movement], and then, in 2017, Movimento Identità Trans [Trans

Identity Movement]). This separate regional section became the new de facto leading group in Italy, causing a sort of schism within the national trans movement.[59] In 1994, after obtaining its headquarters in via Polese 22 and funds from the Emilia-Romagna region, MIT established a health center (a *consultorio*), after which many other community-based projects took off, including Progetto Moonlight (to reduce the risks associated with prostitution), "lo sportello Cgil" (to help trans people find jobs), welcome centers for gender nonconforming homeless people, and services for trans inmates at Carcere della Dozza.[60] In addition, MIT has organized cultural events open to the greater community; one of these is Divergenti (Divergent), an international film festival of trans cinema, which in 2020 celebrated its tenth year. Finally, the process of documentation that Marcasciano has promoted as a narrator and public figure led to important archival projects in Bologna: the Centro documentazione Sylvia Rivera (which houses Marcasciano's personal archive and a special collection of materials donated by Cecconi) and, more recently, the audiovisual Out-Takes Archive.

This brief overview of key places and events that have shaped the Italian political geography of the trans movement is certainly important from an historical perspective. However, it raises a question that this volume tries to address: Would it be possible to map personal journeys of gender self-determination and liberation without exclusively tracing the history of "places out of place," such as streets where demonstrations took place, gender reassignment clinics, gay bars, police stations, legal courts, and seats of national LGBTQ+ associations? Put differently, can a map that only relies on these places of transgression actually reframe the typical expectations of the non-trans audience, involve this audience in appreciating and understanding trans people's voicing personal and political concerns, and ultimately create new shared venues of dialogue and mutual interaction?[61] The trans narratives of people and places gathered here, besides serving as examples of the historical geography sketched above, testify to surprising—and at times problematic—sites of Italian trans/culturalism that have often been omitted from geographies of anti-normativity: religious festivals in Naples, everyday life in Roman working-class neighborhoods, traditional family gatherings in Brooklyn, extravagant Italian families and matriarchs who recall the houses and the "house mothers" of *Paris Is Burning* (1990), friends' reunions in New York, pilgrimages across the Atlantic Ocean, and political activism in Northern Africa.[62] Exploring these places implies, first of all, repositioning trans people within history and social spaces but also reflecting on the shifting relationships among bodies, genders, and places; entering into a dialogue with cisgender allies; and respecting the diversity that informs individual trans experiences. What emerges from this remapping is a complex web of interrelated stories that are simultaneously personal and collective, both memories and testimonies. These trans narratives neither attempt to make trans people "pass" nor exclusively celebrate them as champions of a subversive movement. Overall, these accounts succeed in recounting anti-normative movements as well as what Andrea Long Chu has called "nonnormative attempts at normativity," by embracing a perspective that "refuses . . . the pomp of antinormativity . . . for something slower, smaller, more tuned in to the ways in which ordinary life fails to measure up to the political analyses we thrust upon it."[63] Finally, the stories in *Italian Trans Geographies* call into question the current LGBTQ+ macro-narrative of inclusion and dominant Anglophone gender discourses by asking: What if retracing Italian cultural and historical geographies could unsettle taken-for-granted Western notions of places, boundaries, and borders? And, finally, how can mapping overlooked geographies reshape the Anglo-American globalized understanding of LGBTQ+ movements or academic concepts of queer antinormativity?

The eight parts of this volume are arranged in four sections representing the three large geographic areas within the borders of the Italian peninsula—southern Italy, central Italy, and northern Italy—and beyond its borders across the Atlantic. Included in each section are a variety of creative works and scholarly essays, which analyze key issues emerging from the self-narratives.

The journey begins in southern Italy. Part 1, "Memories of Transitions," presents excerpts from Marcasciano's memoirs (*AntoloGaia*, *L'aurora delle trans cattive*, and *Tra le rose e le viole*) and a selection of poems by Giovanna Cristina Vivinetto—a "living archive" of the trans movement and an emerging poetic voice of trans liberation. Marcasciano and Vivinetto, in very different styles and literary mediums, have chronicled their personal coming outs and the peculiar sociocultural dynamics of acceptance and machoistic denial surrounding gender variance in the south of Italy.

Part 2 focuses on the *femminielli* (or as they often refer to themselves, using the feminine form, *femmenelle* or *femminelle*), an archaic gender-variant community rooted in the city of Naples and nearby areas.[64] Their unique theatricality has informed Neapolitan folklore, inspired countless creative works, and generated iconic characters such as "la Tarantina."[65] This section's opening chapter, by Eugenio Zito, Paolo Valerio, and Nicola Sisci, locates the *femminielli* in the context of Neapolitan cultural history, providing an in-depth analysis of the first written documents that testify to the existence of this community and of the myths and traditions tied to these sacred figures across genders. The *femminielli* were, and in certain niche areas still are, the undisputed protagonists of performative rituals that have involved the entire Neapolitan *popolino* (the local underclass), such as playing the game of *tombola* (similar to bingo) and participating in re-enactments of weddings and births. The contribution of anthropologist Maria Carolina Vesce, from her 2017 book *Altri transiti* (*Other Transitions*), discusses how the *femminielli* have resiliently survived in the contemporary world. Vesce advances the hypothesis that highbrow culture has attempted to transform these local figures—their rituals, folklore, religiosity—into a Neapolitan cultural heritage. On the one hand, this process has implied a revalorization of their traditions, while on the other it has fueled the assumption that the *femminielli* no longer exist and therefore need to be memorialized as an extinct culture. The chapter ends with an interview with two Neapolitan activists, Ciro Cascina and Loredana Rossi, who have both embraced and personally reinterpreted the gender identity of *femminielli*.

Part 3, "A Felliniesque Dolce Vita," reveals the hidden party life in which trans people in central Italy participated from the 1960s to the 1980s. The section begins with Marcasciano's description of downtown Rome in the 1970s and early 1980s. In the area around Termini Station, southern migrants, trans sex workers, and "misfits," as well as writers, poets, eccentric divas, beauticians, and "*bombardere*,"[66] created the syncretic landscape of a unique Roman *dolce vita*, where Felliniesque fantasy and Pasolinian subaltern reality clashed. This part also includes a few excerpts from Cecconi's biography, including her narrations of nightlife in Florence's Lungarno, her picaresque adventures across Europe and then back to Italy, and her time confined to the village of Volturino.

Part 4, "Narrating Trans History as a Meaningful Experience," presents more recent retellings of trans experiences, which have contributed to generating new narratives about gender variance. Chapter 10 is from the anthology *Elementi di critica trans*, which deliberately echoes Mieli's cult classic *Elementi di critica omosessuale*. In the opening conversation—which took place in 2008, at a Tuscan *agriturismo* (a farmhouse resort)—a group of trans scholars and activists discuss the importance and the challenges of recasting a meaningful trans (hi)story that can feel simultaneously personal and collective. Chapter 11 is the script of Egon Botteghi's performative workshop "Non siamo nat@ ieri" ("We Were Not Born Yesterday"), which debuted in 2019 at the Centro Donna (Women's Center), in Livorno. The performance mixes verbal and visual narration with various actions/events around town. In this work, Botteghi resuscitated two stories from the past known only through legal and medical documents: the life of Giovanni Bordoni, a man who, in 1743, died in the hospital of Santa Maria della Scala in Siena and was discovered to be a woman and the journey of Harry Crawford (named Eugenia Falleni at birth), an Italian migrant, native of Livorno, who moved to New Zealand in 1877. While effectively retracing overlooked geographies of transition and belonging, Botteghi's project also maps experiences of class, gender, religious beliefs, and race discrimination.

The northern Italy section opens with part 5, "Stories of Trans Identity and Activism," which features different trans experiences united by a similar commitment to activism. This part begins with two chapters showcasing Marcasciano's memoirs, both set in the Emilia-Romagna region. Chapter 12 narrates the historical "conquest" of the Bolognese Cassero (the first LGBT center in Italy) from the perspective of trans activists; chapter 13 is an interview with Lisa, a Brazilian trans woman fighting for civil rights and a residency permit in a highly touristic beach area on the coast of the Adriatic, the Riviera Romagnola. The section proceeds with an excerpt from Massimo D'Aquino's autobiographical novel, *Camminavo rasente i muri: Autobiografia tascabile di un transessuale* (*I Was Walking Close to the Walls: Pocket Autobiography of a Transsexual Man*, 2019). Here D'Aquino, who has been involved in the trans association Libellula Italia, recounts his path to "conquer his place in the world" as a trans man and a migrant from the south to the north of the Italian peninsula. The last text of part 5 is a conversation with three LGBTQ+ activists—Christian Ballarin, Giorgio Cuccio, and Libyan refugee Mazen Masoud—who are currently all based in northern Italy. They talk about their stories of FtM transitions; their engagement in support groups and transfeminist collectives; and their reflections on Italian language, a binary gendered language that poses obvious linguistic challenges to nonbinary identities.

Part 6, "Testifying to Voices and Images of Transness," explores how artists have experimented with a variety of mediums—music, cinema, and photography—to retell personal stories of transness. Musician Helena Velena, in "Perverse Polymorphs Proto T* at the Dawn of 1980s Italian *Riflusso*," contextualizes the emergence of a discourse of trans liberation in Bologna and analyzes the role that the music scene played, both in Italy and the US, in fostering alternative models of masculinity and femininity. Chapter 17, "A Trans Revolution and Its Contradictions," is an interview that Danila Cannamela conducted with filmmaker Simone Cangelosi. The conversation focuses on the central role that Marcella Di Folco—a leading figure of the Bolognese MIT, with a rich experience in acting—has played in Cangelosi's work and on his current project of creating an archive in Bologna that would preserve the history of Italian trans and queer people. Chapter 18, coauthored by Danila Cannamela and Stella Gonzalez, examines a selection of photographs from Lina Pallotta's portrait of Marcasciano. This photographic work—an intimate visual journey traversing Naples, Bologna, Rome, and New York—is a reflection on Pallotta's nomadic friendship with Porpora, which has succeeded in crossing places, genders, and sociocultural revolutions.

Part 7, "Transitions across the Ocean," brings to the fore understudied connections between Italian heritage and LGBTQ+ activism in the US. This chapter opens with the personal testimony of Michela Griffo, collected by Summer Minerva. Griffo's story, "Io sono sangue" ("I Am Blood"), sheds light on the unforeseeable intersections between Italian American LGBTQ+ protesters and the gangsters who ran gay bars, which developed from their shared knowledge of southern Italian dialects. Chapter 20—"What Does It Mean for the Italian American Community to Be Trans?"—features writings by Italian American and Italian Canadian trans activists and artists who have elaborated on their Italianness and gender identity through short stories and poems.

Part 8, "New Italian American Migrations: Back to Italy," returns to the south of Italy, the epicenter of the Italian diaspora and starting place of this geographic inquiry. Chapter 21, "Summer Within: A Journey of Migration and Reconnection," authored by Danila Cannamela, is an analysis of Minerva's film *Summer Within* (forthcoming in 2023).[67] The movie recounts a counter-migration journey from New York to Naples, in search of roots and a sense of belonging. The chapter discusses the different levels of identity that have contributed to Italian American constructs of home and displacement, and how the film explores these unresolved contradictions. Chapter 22, "A Queer 'Talian Pilgrimage," retells the experience of a group of Italian American trans people who, in 2019, visited Naples for la Candelora (Candlemas) a sacred festival greatly attended by the *femminielli*. The piece includes the transcript from a community conversation with queer Italian American pilgrims who express their longing for a cultural identity that can encompass simultaneously their Italian roots and queer/transness.

The volume ends by suggesting, in its conclusion, several possible paths and directions for current and future research in the emerging field of Italian and Italian American trans studies. What all of them have in common is the idea of "starting from ourselves"—that is, from the acknowledgment of our disparate points of view and research interests—and together we might envision how this interdisciplinary field can lay the foundations for new routes of collaborative inquiry, teaching, and learning, while creating more diverse and inclusive curricula across disciplines.

Ultimately, the geographic approach of this book underscores the notion that trans narratives, in retracing diasporic movements, liminal identities, and a precarious sense of belonging, can reorient our understanding of the slippery concept of Italianness. "What is the real Italy? The one that people see in my investigation or the one that nobody sees?," Pasolini asks writer Alberto Moravia, in *Comizi d'amore*, venting his frustration with the answers of his interviewees, which do not even scratch the surface of sexual and gendered taboos. Pasolini's question can be considered the point of departure of this journey, which delves into blind spots in Italian and Italian American culture while highlighting overlooked points of junction and friction between LGBTQ+ global discourse and local realities. The 2020 Netflix documentary *Disclosure: Trans Lives on Screen* offers an example of how, in North America, the debate over transgender identities and their representation has gained great visibility, beyond academia. However, *Disclosure*, like many scholarly works produced in the US, employs umbrella terms and constructs of race, class, and gender that do not exhaust the complexity of trans embodied experiences in Western societies. The narrators gathered in this volume "queer," or "reorient," the comforting notion that Western cultures share a homogeneous Anglo-American discourse and language of LGBTQ+ liberation. These voices suggest that switching the focus on the Italianness that still remains unseen or misrepresented can turn invisible and silenced spaces into what Marcasciano has affirmed are "meaningful experiences."[68]

Notes

1. This timeline is based on a private document that Porpora Marcasciano shared with us. We have edited and expanded her timeline to better fit the purposes of this volume.

2. Jorgensen was not the first to undergo gender reassignment surgery. In 1931, Magnus Hirschfeld, neurologist and pioneer of modern sexology, had performed the operation that turned the Danish painter Einar Wegener into Lili Elbe—the first transsexual woman of history. For more on this, see Maria Carolina Vesce, *Altri transiti: Corpi, pratiche, rappresentazioni di femminielli e transessuali* (Sesto San Giovanni: Mimesis, 2017), 91–95.

3. Acknowledgment: This introduction is derived in part from an article published by Danila Cannamela in *Journal of Modern Italian Studies* 27, no. 4 (2022): 600–22, available online: https://doi.org/10.1080/1354571X.2021.1965753.

4. "Invert" is an outdated, often derogatory, term used to designate homosexuals and, more generally, any form of sexual and gender diversity; it is no longer in use in English. When Sigmund Freud spoke of inversion, in the first of his *Three Essays on the Theory of Sexuality* (1905)—"The Sexual Aberrations"—he was not speaking of gender inversion but rather same-sex. However, generally speaking, the term "invert" came to refer to behaviors that fell outside the traditional categories of male and female within a two-gender system and conflated same-sex desire with gender variance, positing homosexual men as women trapped in men's bodies and homosexual women as men trapped in women's bodies. This reversal of gender traits, called "sexual inversion," was believed to be inborn; male inverts were thought to be inclined, to a greater or lesser degree, to traditionally female pursuits and dress, and vice versa. The term persisted in the US as late as the 1960s. On this, see in particular Umberto Grassi, Vincenzo Lagioia, Gian Paolo Romagnani, eds., *Tribadi, sodomiti, invertite e invertiti, pederasti, femminelle, ermafroditi: Per una storia dell'omosessualità, della bisessualità e delle trasgressioni di genere in Italia* (Pisa: ETS, 2017). For an historical perspective see also Richard von Krafft-Ebing, *Psychopathia Sexualis: Eine Klinisch-Forensische Studie* (*Sexual Psychopathy: A Clinical-Forensic Study*) (Stuttgart: Enke, 1886); and Genny Beemyn, "A Presence in the Past: A Transgender Historiography," *Journal of Women's History* 25, no. 4 (2013), 113–21.

5. On lesbianism and gender nonconforming women in Italy, see Paolo Pedote and Nicoletta Poidimani, eds., *We Will Survive: Storia del Movimento LGBTIQ+ in Italia* (Sesto San Giovanni: Mimesis, 2020); and the work of Laura Schettini, in particular, *Il gioco delle parti: Travestimenti e paure sociali tra Otto e Novecento* (Milan: Mondadori, 2011).

6. We are adopting the term "trans" to indicate subjectivities whose gender identities do not align with the sex assigned at birth, or, more generally, individuals who do not exclusively self-identify using binary and heteronormative gender constructs. Further clarifications on our use of LGBTQ+ terminology are provided throughout this introductory chapter.

7. On Italian feminism and its focus on language and narrative agency, see Linda Zerilli, *Feminism and the Abyss of Freedom* (Chicago: University of Chicago Press, 2005); Graziella Parati and Rebecca West, eds., *Italian Feminist Theory and Practice: Equality and Sexual Difference* (Teaneck, NJ: Fairleigh Dickinson University Press, 2002); Milan Women's Bookstore Collective, *Sexual Difference: A Theory of Social-Symbolic Practice*, ed. Teresa de Lauretis (Bloomington: University of Indiana Press, 1990); and Cesare Casarino and Andrea Righi, eds., *Another Mother: Diotima and the Symbolic Order of Italian Feminism* (Minneapolis: University of Minnesota Press, 2018).

8. When not otherwise indicated, translations from the Italian original are our own. Porpora Marcasciano, *Elementi di critica trans*, eds., Laurella Arietti,

Christian Ballarin, Giorgio Cuccio, and Porpora Marcasciano (Rome: Manifesto-Libri, 2010), 17. Excerpts from the opening day of this seminar are translated in chapter 10 of this volume.

9. She made this statement in the documentary short *Divieto di transito* (*No Trespassing*) directed by Roberto Cannavò (Humanreels, 2020).

10. We are borrowing the reflection about humourism and space from Paola Mieli, *Figures of Space: Subject, Body, Place*, trans. Jacques Houis (New York: Agincourt Press, 2017), 76.

11. On the use of humor and irony, see in particular the essay by Helena Velena (chap. 16) and the interview with Simone Cangelosi (chap. 17), as well as the reflections shared by Ciro Cascina and Loredana Rossi (chap. 7) and our conversation with Christian Ballarin, Giorgio Cuccio, and Mazen Masoud (chap. 15).

12. The use of the term "bard" came from a personal phone conversation of Cannamela with Marcasciano (March 4, 2021). It is important to mention that, in her role of bard, Marcasciano has also collaborated on, and inspired, several projects included in this volume: Lina Pallotta's photographic portrait "Porpora," exhibited at Officine Fotografiche in Rome, in 2019; Simone Cangelosi's documentary *Una nobile rivoluzione* (*A Noble Revolution*, 2014) about trans activist Marcella Di Folco; Roberto Cannavò's 2021 film, *Porpora*, and Roberta Torre's 2022 film *Le Favolose* (*The Fabulous Ones*).

13. On this, see Marcasciano *AntoloGaia* and *Elementi di critica trans*. See also Serena Bassi, "Excerpts from *The Dawn of the Bad Trans Women: Stories, Fragments, and Lives of My Transgender Generation* by Porpora Marcasciano—Translation," *TSQ: Transgender Studies Quarterly* 6, no. 1 (2019): 124–31. Generally speaking, all Italian 1970s liberation movements engaged in a recasting of dominant language as a political counteraction; on this practice, see Andrea Hajek, *Negotiating Memories of Protest in Western Europe: The Case of Italy* (New York: Palgrave Macmillan, 2013); and Andrea Righi, *Biopolitics and Social Change in Italy: From Gramsci to Pasolini to Negri* (New York: Palgrave Macmillan, 2011).

14. Arietti et al., eds., *Elementi di critica trans*, 127.

15. Arietti et al., eds., 93, 99.

16. Arietti et al., eds., 118.

17. Susan Stryker, Paisley Currah, and Lisa Jean Moore, "Introduction: Trans-, Trans, or Transgender?" *WSQ: Women's Studies Quarterly* 36, no. 3–4 (2008): 11.

18. Marcasciano, *AntoloGaia*, "Le tracce dei sogni" ("The Traces of Dreams"). This passage is translated in chapter 1.

19. Personal conversation with Cannamela (via Messenger), November 18, 2019.

20. Sara Ahmed, *Queer Phenomenology: Orientations, Objects, Others* (Durham, NC: Duke University Press, 2006), 5.

21. It is outside our scope to provide an exhaustive overview of queer theories that conversate with our geographic approach. However, a few publications partic-

ularly resonate with, or complement, our focus on space and trans identities; see Elizabeth Freeman's exploration of temporal and sexual dissonance in *Time Binds: Queer Temporalities, Queer Histories* (Durham, NC: Duke University Press, 2010); Susan Stryker's revised version of *Transgender History*, rev. ed. (New York: Seal Press, 2017); Jack Halberstam's "low theory" and the critique to heteronormative definitions of success in *The Queer Art of Failure* (Durham, NC: Duke University Press, 2011); and Heather Love's investigation of the sociological origins of queer theory, in *Underdogs: Social Deviance and Queer Theory* (Chicago: University of Chicago Press, 2021).

22. On this, see Kath Browne and Jason Lim, eds., *Geographies of Sexualities: Theory, Practices and Politics* (New York: Routledge, 2007); Kath Browne and Leela Bakshi, "We Are Here to Party? Lesbian, Gay, Bisexual and Trans Leisurescapes beyond Commercial Gay Scenes," *Leisure Studies* 30, no. 2 (2011): 179–96; Johnston Lynda, "Gender and Sexuality I: Genderqueer Geographies?" *Progress in Human Geography* 40, no. 5 (2016): 668–78.

23. Brown, Browne, and Lim, introduction to *Geographies of Sexualities*, 12.

24. Some scholars and activists use "trans*" (with an asterisk) to designate the many different identities gathered within the umbrella term trans. However, as editors, we decided to go with "trans."

25. Johnston, "Gender and Sexuality I," 674.

26. Marcasciano, *L'aurora delle trans cattive*, appendix.

27. Fabio Corbisiero, *Over the Rainbow City: Towards a New LGBT Citizenship in Italy* (Milan: McGraw-Hill Education, 2015), 8.

28. Corbisiero, *Over the Rainbow City*, 8.

29. The law was approved by the Camera (the Italian House of Representatives) in November 2020, but, in October 2021, the Senate voted against it.

30. Fabio Corbisiero and Salvatore Monaco, *Città arcobaleno: Una mappa della vita omosessuale nell'Italia di oggi* (Rome: Donzelli, 2017), 7.

31. See Stryker, *Gay by the Bay: A History of Queer Culture in the San Francisco Bay Area* (San Francisco: Chronicle Books, 1996); Stryker, *Transgender History*, rev. ed. (New York: Seal Press, 2017); and Stryker and Stephen Whittle, eds., *The Transgender Studies Reader* (New York: Routledge, 2006).

32. Lorenzo Bernini offers a more detailed explanation of the legendary role of Rivera during the Stonewall riots: "As the story goes, it was a transgender activist of Puerto Rican and Venezuelan origin, Sylvia Rivera, who started the clashes by throwing an empty bottle of gin at a policeman—most probably, it was Stormé DeLarverie, a butch lesbian and drag king, born of a black mother and a white father, who stirred up the crowd to fight. In any case, in the years following, Rivera went on to found STAR (Street Transvestite Action Revolutionaries)"; see Bernini, *Queer Theories: An Introduction; From Mario Mieli to the Antisocial Turn* (New York: Routledge, 2020), 106.

33. On this, see in particular the story of Michela Griffo in chapter 19.

34. Arietti et al., eds., *Elementi di critica trans*, 43–44. See also Mario Mieli, *La gaia critica: Politica e liberazione sessuale negli anni settanta. Scritti (1972–1983)*, eds. P. Mieli and Prearo (Venice: Marsilio, 2019); Gianni Rossi Barilli, *Il movimento gay in Italia* (Milan: Feltrinelli, 1999); and Maya De Leo, *Queer: Storia culturale della comunità LGBT+* (Turin: Einaudi: 2021).

35. On the discrimination issues within LGBT+ groups, see in particular Martin Duberman, *Stonewall* (New York: Dutton, 1993), 235–39; and Stephan L. Cohen, *The Gay Liberation Youth Movement in New York: "An Army of Lovers Cannot Fail"* (New York: Routledge, 2008), 89–94.

36. On the debate between trans activists and feminists, see the interviews with Giorgio Cuccio and Simone Cangelosi in chapters 15 and 17 of this volume; see also Marcasciano, *L'aurora delle trans cattive* (the chap. "La Scapigliatura trans" ["The Trans Bohème"]).

37. Here we are adapting an observation of Doreen Massey in *Space, Place, and Gender* (Minneapolis: University of Minnesota Press, 1994), 178.

38. Juliet Jacques, "Forms of Resistance: Uses of Memoir, Theory, and Fiction in Trans Life Writing," *Life Writing* 14, no. 3 (2017): 357–70.

39. Julia Serano, *Whipping Girl: A Transsexual Woman on Sexism and the Scapegoating of Femininity* (New York: Seal Press, 2015), 1.

40. Romina Cecconi, *Io, la "Romanina": Perché sono diventato donna* (Florence: Vallecchi, 1976), 159. On the notion of the error of nature, see also 172–73. The excerpt "In Switzerland" is translated in chapter 9 of this volume.

41. Brown, Browne, Lim, "Introduction," 4. As Laura Schettini clarifies in her introduction to Marcasciano's *AntoloGaia*, gender transgressions in Italy were handled by the police, in line with the norms of *Testo Unico di Pubblica Sicurezza* (Tups), in 1926, and later on, with the laws of the so-called Codice Rocco, a new penal code adopted in 1931.

42. See Cecconi, *Io, la "Romanina"*, 182–203; Marco Luceri, "Le mie notti da Romanina" ("My nights as Romanina"), *Corriere fiorentino*, November 11, 2015. https://corrierefiorentino.corriere.it/firenze/notizie/arte_e_cultura/15_novembre_11/mie-notti-romanina-46c8c89c-885d-11e5-b112-d5532a056ec2.shtml; Stefania Voli, "Broadening the Gendered *Polis*: Italian Feminist and Transsexual Movements, 1979–1982," *TSQ: Transgender Studies Quarterly* 3, no. 1–2 (2016): 237–47; and Paolo Pazzi, "Romanina, la donna pipistrello" ("Romanina, the Batwoman"), *Orlando Magazine.it*. April 13, 2019: https://www.orlandomagazine.it/2019/04/13/romanina-la-donna-pipistrello/.

43. Mario Mieli, *Towards a Gay Communism: Elements of a Homosexual Critique*, trans. David Fernbach and Evan Calder Williams (London: Pluto Press, 2018), 254; and Bernini, *Queer Theories*, 116.

44. See Rossi Barilli, *Il movimento gay in Italia*; Voli, "Broadening the Gendered *Polis*"; and Bernini, *Queer Theories*.

45. See Michael Hardt and Paolo Virno, eds., *Radical Thought in Italy: A Potential Politics* (Minneapolis: University of Minnesota Press, 1996); Hajek,

Negotiating Memories of Protest in Western Europe; and Righi, *Biopolitics and Social Change in Italy*.

46. Marcasciano, *AntoloGaia*, "La fonte della coscienza" ("The Awakening of Self-Awareness"). The excerpt is translated in chapter 1 of this volume.

47. Paola Mieli and Massimo Prearo, "Biografia critica," in Mario Mieli, *La gaia critica*, 331.

48. Mieli, *Towards a Gay Communism*, 254; and Bernini, *Queer Theories*, 118.

49. Mieli and Prearo, introduction to Mieli, *La gaia critica*, 13.

50. Mieli, *La gaia critica*, 338.

51. Rossi Barilli, *Il movimento gay in Italia*, 98.

52. Mieli and Prearo, "Biografia critica," 334.

53. See Marcasciano, *AntoloGaia*, "Narciso."

54. For a detailed chronology, see the website of Cassero: https://www.cassero.it/chi-siamo/storia/.

55. See chapter 12 in this volume.

56. Voli, "Broadening the Gendered *Polis*," 237.

57. Voli, 237.

58. Voli, 238.

59. See Voli and the website of MIT: https://mit-italia.it/.

60. See Marcasciano, *L'aurora delle trans cattive*, "Marcellona" ("Big Marcella").

61. Here, we are paraphrasing Jacques, "Forms of Resistance," 365.

62. *Paris Is Burning* is a documentary on ballroom culture in queer communities (or houses) in New York City. The film is centered on five "house mothers": Dorian Corey (House of Corey), Pepper LaBeija (House of Labeija), Angie Xtravaganza (House of Xtravaganza), Willi Ninja (House of Ninja), and Paris Dupree (House of Dupree).

63. Andrea Long Chu and Emmett Harsin Drager, "After Trans Studies," *Transgender Studies Quarterly* 6, no. 1 (2019): 107, 113.

64. In a few instances Marcasciano has also used the feminine forms *femminiella* (singular)/*femminielle* (plural).

65. On "la Tarantina," see the biography by Gabriella Romano and see also Fortunato Calvino's documentary. More broadly, among the works inspired by the figure of the Neapolitan *femminiello*, there are theatrical plays, like Roberto De Simone's *La gatta cenerentola* (*The Cat Cinderella*, which premiered in 1976 at the Festival dei due Mondi in Spoleto) and Annibale Ruccello's *Le cinque rose di Jennifer* (*The Five Roses of Jennifer*, which premiered at the Na Babele Theatre in Naples in 1980); Giuseppe Patroni Griffi's novel *Scende giù per Toledo* (*Comes down along Toledo*, 1975); and films, including *Cerasella, ovvero l'estinzione della femminella* (*Cerasella, or the Extinction of the Femminella*, 2007) and *Mater Natura* (2005), both directed by Massimo Andrei.

66. *Bombardera* is the Italianized form of the Brazilian Portuguese term *bombaidera*. In trans communities, a *bombaidera* is a person trained to inject silicon and who typically performs this service (illegally) in private houses. On this figure,

see Marcasciano, *L'aurora delle trans cattive*, "Roma" ("Rome"), and her interview with a Brazilian trans woman, Lisa, translated in chapter 13 of this volume. On this topic, see also Don Kulick, *Travesti: Sex, Gender, and Culture among Brazilian Transgendered Prostitutes* (Chicago: University of Chicago Press, 1998).

    67. For updates on this documentary film, see https://www.summerwithinfilm.net/trailer.

    68. Marcasciano has often used the expression "esperienza umana significativa" ("meaningful human experience") to define the process of the re-signification of the experience that trans people have embraced both individually and collectively. An all-encompassing definition of this concept can be found in the conclusion of the chapter "Napoli" ("Naples") in *L'aurora delle trans cattive*.

References

Ahmed, Sara. *Queer Phenomenology: Orientations, Objects, Others*. Durham, NC: Duke University Press, 2006.

Andrei, Massimo, director. *Cerasella: Ovvero l'estinzione della femminella*. Università degli studi di Napoli "Federico II" and Mater Produzioni, 2007.

———. *Mater Natura*. Intramovies, 2005.

Arietti, Laurella, Christian Ballarin, Giorgio Cuccio, and Porpora Marcasciano, eds. *Elementi di critica trans*. Rome: ManifestoLibri, 2010.

Bassi, Serena. "Excerpts from *The Dawn of the Bad Trans Women: Stories, Fragments, and Lives of My Transgender Generation* by Porpora Marcasciano—Translation." *TSQ: Transgender Studies Quarterly* 6, no. 1 (2019): 124–31.

Beemyn, Genny. "A Presence in the Past: A Transgender Historiography." *Journal of Women's History* 25 no. 4 (2013): 113–21.

Belais, Francesco, and Matteo Tortora, directors. *La donna pipistrello*. Documentary film, 2015.

Bernini, Lorenzo. *Queer Theories: An Introduction; From Mario Mieli to the Antisocial Turn*. Translated by Michela Baldo and Elena Basile. New York: Routledge, 2020.

Bolognini, Mauro, director. *C'era una volta un ragazzo lucchese: La vita di Romina Cecconi*. Rai TV, 1978.

Brown, Gavin, Kath Browne, and Jason Lim. "Introduction, or Why Have a Book on Geographies of Sexualities?" In *Geographies of Sexualities: Theory, Practices and Politics*, edited by Kath Browne and Jason Lim, 1–18. New York: Routledge, 2007.

Browne, Kath, and Leela Bakshi. "We Are Here to Party? Lesbian, Gay, Bisexual and Trans Leisurescapes beyond Commercial Gay Scenes." *Leisure Studies* 30, no. 2 (2011): 179–96. doi: 10.1080/02614367.2010.506651.

Calvino, Fortunato, director. *La Tarantina*. Università degli Studi di Napoli, 2016.
Cangelosi, Simone, director. *Una nobile rivoluzione*. Kiné, 2014.
Cannamela, Danila. "Italian Trans Geographies: Retracing Trans/Cultural Narratives of People and Places." *Journal of Modern Italian Studies* 27, no. 4 (2022): 600–22. doi: 10.1080/1354571X.2021.1965753.
Cannavò, Roberto, director. *Divieto di transito*. Humanreels, 2020.
———. *Porpora*. Humanreels, 2021.
Casarino, Cesare, and Andrea Righi, eds. *Another Mother: Diotima and the Symbolic Order of Italian Feminism*. Minneapolis: University of Minnesota Press, 2018.
Caudwell, Jayne, and Kath Browne. "Sexy Spaces: Geography and Leisure Intersectionalities." *Leisure Studies* 30, no. 2 (2011): 117–22. doi: 10.1080/02614367.2011.561977.
Cecconi, Romina. *Io, la "Romanina": Perchè sono diventato donna*. Florence: Vallecchi, 1976.
Cohen, Stephan. *The Gay Liberation Youth Movement in New York: "An Army of Lovers Cannot Fail."* New York, London: Routledge, 2008.
Corbisiero, Fabio. *Over the Rainbow City: Towards a New LGBT Citizenship in Italy*. Milan: McGraw-Hill, 2015.
Corbisiero, Fabio, and Salvatore Monaco. *Città arcobaleno: Una mappa della vita omosessuale nell'Italia di oggi*. Rome: Donzelli, 2017.
De Leo, Maya. *Queer: Storia culturale della comunità LGBT+*. Turin: Einaudi: 2021.
De Simone, Roberto. *La gatta cenerentola*. Turin: Einaudi, 1977.
Duberman, Martin. *Stonewall*. New York: Dutton, 1993.
Feder, Sam, director. *Disclosure: Trans Lives on Screen*. Netflix, 2020.
Fellini, Federico, director. *La dolce vita*. Film. Riama, Pathé Consortium Cinéma, Grey Film, 1960.
Freeman, Elizabeth. *Time Binds: Queer Temporalities, Queer Histories*. Durham, NC: Duke University Press, 2010.
Freud, Sigmund. *Three Essays on the Theory of Sexuality (1905)*. Translated by James Strachey. New York: Basic Books, 1975.
Grassi, Umberto, Vincenzo Lagioia, and Gian Paolo Romagnani, eds. *Tribadi, sodomiti, invertite e invertiti, pederasti, femminelle, ermafroditi: Per una storia dell'omosessualità, della bisessualità e delle trasgressioni di genere in Italia*. Pisa: ETS, 2017.
Guerrieri, Giovanni, director. *Romanina*. Script by Anna Meacci and Luca Scarlini. Performed October 3, 2015. Milan: Teatro Filodrammatici.
Hajek, Andrea. *Negotiating Memories of Protest in Western Europe: The Case of Italy*. New York: Palgrave Macmillan, 2013.
Halberstam, Jack. *The Queer Art of Failure*. Durham, NC: Duke University Press, 2011.
Hardt, Michael, and Paolo Virno, eds. *Radical Thought in Italy: A Potential Politics*. Minneapolis: University of Minnesota Press, 1996.

Jacques, Juliet. "Forms of Resistance: Uses of Memoir, Theory, and Fiction in Trans Life Writing." *Life Writing* 14, no. 3 (2017): 357–70. doi: 10.1080/14484528.2017.1328301.

Jacques, Juliet. *Trans: A Memoir*. London: Verso, 2015.

Johnston, Lynda. "Gender and Sexuality I: Genderqueer Geographies?" *Progress in Human Geography* 40, no. 5 (2016): 668–78. doi: 10.1177/0309132515592109.

Kulick, Don. *Travesti: Sex, Gender, and Culture among Brazilian Transgendered Prostitutes*. Chicago: University of Chicago Press, 1998.

Livingston, Jennie, director. *Paris Is Burning*. Miramax, 1990.

Long Chu, Andrea, and Emmett Harsin Drager. "After Trans Studies." *Transgender Studies Quarterly* 6, no. 1 (2019): 103–16.

Love, Heather. *Underdogs: Social Deviance and Queer Theory*. Chicago: University of Chicago Press, 2021.

Luceri, Marco. "Le mie notti da Romanina." *Corriere fiorentino*. November 11, 2015. https://corrierefiorentino.corriere.it/firenze/notizie/arte_e_cultura/15_novembre_11/mie-notti-romanina-46c8c89c-885d-11e5-b112-d5532a056ec2.shtml.

Marcasciano, Porpora. Afterword to *Altri Transiti* by Maria Carolina Vesce, 195–98. Sesto San Giovanni: Mimesis, 2017.

———. *AntoloGaia: Vivere sognando e non sognando di vivere; I miei anni settanta* (2007). Rome: Alegre, 2016. iBooks.

———. *Favolose narranti: Storie di transessuali*. Rome, ManifestoLibri, 2008.

———. *Il sogno e l'utopia*. Performed November 9, 2019. Ferrara: Teatro Ferrara Off.

———. Introduction to *Elementi di critica trans*, edited by Laurella Arietti et al., 9–16. Rome: ManifestoLibri, 2010.

———. *L'aurora delle trans cattive: Storie, sguardi e vissuti della mia generazione transgender*. Rome: Alegre, 2018. iBooks.

———. *Tra le rose e le viole: La storia e le storie di transessuali e travestiti* (2002). Rome: Alegre, 2020. iBooks.

Massey, Doreen. *Space, Place, and Gender*. Minneapolis: University of Minnesota Press, 1994.

Mieli, Mario. *La gaia critica: Politica e liberazione sessuale negli anni settanta. Scritti (1972–1983)*, edited by Paola Mieli and Massimo Prearo. Venice: Marsilio, 2019.

———. *Towards a Gay Communism: Elements of a Homosexual Critique*. Translated by David Fernbach and Evan Calder Williams. London: Pluto Press, 2018.

Mieli, Paola. *Figures of Space: Subject, Body, Place*. Translated by Jacques Houis. New York: Agincourt Press, 2017.

Mieli, Paola, and Massimo Prearo. Introduction to *La gaia critica: Politica e liberazione sessuale negli anni settanta. Scritti (1972–1983)*, edited by Paola Mieli and Massimo Prearo, 9–30. Venice: Marsilio, 2019.

Pallotta, Lina. "Porpora." Rome: Officine Fotografiche, 2019.

Parati, Graziella, and Rebecca West, eds. *Italian Feminist Theory and Practice: Equality and Sexual Difference*. Teaneck, NJ: Fairleigh Dickinson University Press, 2002.

Pasolini, Pierpaolo, director. *Comizi d'amore*. Film. Arco Film, 1965.
Patroni Griffi, Giuseppe. *Scende giù per Toledo*. Milan: Garzanti, 1975.
Pazzi, Paolo. "Romanina, la donna pipistrello." *OrlandoMagazine.it*, April 13, 2019. https://www.orlandomagazine.it/2019/04/13/romanina-la-donna-pipistrello/.
Pedote, Paolo, and Nicoletta Poidimani, eds., *We Will Survive: Storia del Movimento LGBTIQ+ in Italia*. Sesto San Giovanni: Mimesis, 2020.
Righi, Andrea. *Biopolitics and Social Change in Italy: From Gramsci to Pasolini to Negri*. New York: Palgrave Macmillan, 2011.
Romano, Gabriella. *La Tarantina e la sua dolce vita: Racconto autobiografico di un femminiello napoletano*. Verona: Ombre Corte, 2013.
Rossi Barilli, Gianni. *Il movimento gay in Italia*. Milan: Feltrinelli, 1999.
Ruccello, Annibale. *Le cinque rose di Jennifer*. Rome: Ubulibri, 2005.
Schettini, Laura. *Il gioco delle parti: Travestimenti e paure sociali tra Otto e Novecento*. Milan: Mondadori, 2011.
———. "L'insostenibile leggerezza del genere tra storia e biografia." Preface to Porpora Marcasciano, *AntoloGaia*. Rome: Alegre, 2016. iBooks.
Sera, Fabio. *In un corpo differente*. Bologna: Comma 22, 2011.
Serano, Julia. *Whipping Girl: A Transsexual Woman on Sexism and the Scapegoating of Femininity*, 2nd ed. New York: Seal Press, 2015.
Sisci, Nicola, Paolo Valerio, and Eugenio Zito. "*Et io ne viddi uno in Napoli*. I *femminielli*, ricognizione storica e mitografica: Spunti per una riflessione sull'identità di genere." In *Femminielli: Corpo, Genere, Cultura*, 37–68, edited by Paolo Valerio and Eugenio Zito. Naples: Libreria Dante and Descartes, 2019.
Stryker, Susan. *Gay by the Bay: A History of Queer Culture in the San Francisco Bay Area*. San Francisco: Chronicle Books, 1996.
———. *Transgender History*. Rev. ed. New York: Seal Press, 2017.
Stryker, Susan, Paisley Currah, and Lisa Jean Moore. "Introduction: Trans-, Trans, or Transgender?" *WSQ: Women's Studies Quarterly* 36, no. 3–4 (2008): 11–22.
Stryker, Susan, and Stephen Whittle, eds. *The Transgender Studies Reader*. New York: Routledge, 2006.
Torre, Roberta, director. *Le Favolose (The Fabulous Ones)*. Europictures, 2022.
Valerio, Paolo, and Eugenio Zito, eds. *Femminielli: Corpo, Genere, Cultura*. Naples: Libreria Dante and Descartes, 2019.
Vesce, Maria Carolina. *Altri transiti: Corpi, pratiche, rappresentazioni di femminielli e transessuali*. Sesto San Giovanni: Mimesis, 2017.
Voli, Stefania. "Broadening the Gendered *Polis*: Italian Feminist and Transsexual Movements, 1979–1982." *TSQ: Transgender Studies Quarterly* 3, no. 1–2 (2016): 237–47.
———. Introduction to *L'aurora delle trans cattive* by Porpora Marcasciano. Rome: Alegre, 2018. iBooks.
von Krafft-Ebing, Richard. *Psychopathia Sexualis: Eine Klinisch-Forensische Studie (Sexual Psychopathy: A Clinical-Forensic Study)*. Stuttgart: Enke, 1886.

Women's Bookstore Collective. *Sexual Difference: A Theory of Social-Symbolic Practice*, edited by Teresa de Lauretis. Bloomington: University of Indiana Press, 1990.

Zerilli, Linda. *Feminism and the Abyss of Freedom.* Chicago: University of Chicago Press, 2005.

SOUTH

PART 1
MEMORIES OF TRANSITIONS

Chapter 1

From *AntoloGaia*

*Vivere sognando e non sognando di vivere;
I miei anni settanta (AntholoGay: Living Dreaming
and Not Dreaming of Living; My Seventies)*

Porpora Marcasciano

In *AntoloGaia*, Marcasciano recounts her experience in the 1970s: the turmoil of those years, which deeply transformed Italian society, serves as the setting and sounding board of the protagonist's personal quest.[1] While the external world is changing, the autobiographical narrator is challenging a male identity that his biological sex and birth name have seemingly imposed on him. Initially, the narrating voice speaks only in the masculine, but as the story continues, the narrator also starts to use feminine forms. This constant shift between masculine and feminine is a fascinating idiosyncrasy of Marcasciano's language, which the English translation can hardly render.

The style of *AntoloGaia* is vibrant and empathic, humorous and light-hearted. In this selection the protagonist describes the excitement of witnessing a world in transition: the music, the daring fashion, the pop icons, the new cultural debates. The narration juxtaposes milestone events of LGBT+ history—for example the Stonewall riots and Mario Mieli's protest in Sanremo—with a close-up view of everyday life in a southern Italian village, where being gay is one of the biggest taboos. The narrator's coming out during a school assembly marks the beginning of a liberation path that Marcasciano would culminate in her college years.

Le début (1973–1976)

> Writing always means hiding something in such a way that it then is discovered.
>
> —Italo Calvino

Somewhere in the West

There are many beginnings—all of those life events that move us, that make an impression. Every beginning is contained in one moment, one situation, one time! So, what better beginning than "Once upon a time"?!

Once upon a time in Italy, as in many other parts of the world, a reality existed that was a bit different from what we know and imagine today, a reality in which trans and gay people, lesbians, women, and others were revolutionizing their lives and, in turn, the life of the world. It was a whole new scene yet to be created—before others could create it for us. We had to give meaning, form, and, most of all, substance to our liberation. Had I been forced to hew to the rules of writing—of scholarly writing—I could not have chronicled the accounts of a very important time in LGBT history. I would have recounted it in verse if I could, because poetry—better than any other means—would be able to describe that scene inhabited by artists and dreamers, vagabonds and intellectuals, creatives and revolutionaries, witches and wizards, Martians and happy wanderers. It was an intense time, rich in happenings, in ideas, embodied by those figures whom I define as *pioniere* (I'm using the feminine word here because it better conveys the idea).[2] A stream of exhilarating and life-changing new experiences was creating a new reality, inventing it. Then, little by little, these all flowed down towards an abyss that, in the 1980s, would swallow everything and everyone: AIDS, the so-called plague of the third millennium, which marked the end of an era and the beginning of a new one.

As I wrote in *Tra le rose e le viole*, "*pas de document pas d'histoire*" ("without documents, there is no history"),[3] because, if we don't know our own history, the journey that led us to where we are today, we cannot build our future. To fill in a gap in gay literature, a wholly Italian lacuna, I will begin with myself, using storytelling as a powerful tool for reclaiming that world from which we have always been excluded [ed./n in Italian, "*esclus**," where the asterisk can stand in for any possible gender ending].[4] I will start over, specifically from that asterisk!

In the 1970s, you could often see written on walls, "Live as if you are dreaming and don't dream of living." Those are the words that best express the desire that came over me to transform my life and the entire world around me. It might have been down to the sun, the hot weather, or the thing that was burning inside of me, but the summer of 1973 was crucial to my transformation. It may be that the planets in my horoscope were in a particular configuration in the sky, one that predisposed me to change, to seek, to revolutionize, because that was when my exodus—my "trip," as people used to say back then, or "transition," as people say today—from alienation to self-fulfillment, began. Seen from Earth, on the other hand, closer to that terra firma where I struggled along, the sky was roiling and heavy with clouds. I was wracking my brain to find a way to survive within a reality that felt deeply hostile, in a world where I felt out of place, ill-suited, wrong—let's go ahead and say it, "different." I felt confined in a closed-off space, one that was sharply defined and finite, and it gave me a suffocating sense of social and cultural claustrophobia.

That was the summer when Mia Martini released "*Minuetto*" ("Minuet") and Patty Pravo was all the rage with her super-fag "*Pazza idea*" ("Crazy Idea"), songs that made me—and thousands of budding young fairies like myself—absolutely lose our minds. In those years the world seemed to be exploding, like a meadow bursting into flower in spring, and the colors, scents and sounds of that explosion set my imagination healthily ablaze. Enraptured, I would read and reread articles I had cut from my mother's magazines: in Amsterdam, thousands of happy hippies in deconsecrated churches and public parks; in London, Mick Jagger releasing millions of butterflies, while his incredibly sensual mouth sang "Sympathy for the Devil"; in San Francisco, music and free love in the streets of California; in Paris, transvestites, artists, and rebels in the streets of the Latin Quarter. From those clippings and what I was hearing on TV, I grasped that something was happening. Meanwhile, I was striving to imagine myself out of that rusty world I felt confined in—whose rust threatened to cover my life, but luckily not my imagination! Judging from what was going on in the world, it truly seemed that the imagination was rising to power, and it acted as a beacon to light the way for my transition. All around me, that which Mario Mieli had dubbed "educastration" still hung on.[5] It drew its lifeblood from a cultural system capable of circumscribing the universe and nature inside frameworks, boundaries, laws, codes—within which everyone sooner or later feels cramped or even imprisoned. It is a system that today, after many years, has come back to threaten us, thanks to a body of laws aligned with the preservation of society—or rather, of a specific society. Multiplicity is never even taken into account, because that society posits itself as the one and only: the Western one! Its "vetero-sexual"[6] order to quote Nicoletta Poidimani, or "straight mind," as Monique Wittig put it, generates suffering. So much disharmony, such malaise, so much violence justified simply to uphold and safeguard its order! However, within that West that posits itself in the singular, that sees itself as the only and the irreplaceable, other places and other stories do exist that give the lie to the singular nature it claims, contaminate its rank purity, and tell us something different!

Once upon a time, there was a fairy! Somewhere, in one of the many Western spheres, my deviant, scandalous, degenerate experience flowered, to my delight and to the disapproval of others. It imbued with color a history that for centuries had flowed by silently, sweeping away countless other histories, or "stories of others," depriving them of their color, their words, their life, their "fairy-tale" nature. My life, seen as going against nature, started to flow—first like a stream and then like a river in flood—on September 15, 1957. However, I am going to tell you just a piece of it, my "pride," which began sixteen years later, in September 1973, to be precise.

Traces of Dreams

I have never felt like a man, but neither have I ever felt like a woman. Even my name I never felt to be truly mine. Among heterosexuals I felt gay, among gay men I felt like a trans woman, and among trans women I felt I was something else or, better yet, somewhere else—"beyond!" As our beloved friend Aracne, who left us in 2007, used to say, "Onwards!" Moving, journeying, transitioning, passing through. To encourage and cheer me up, my mother used to say, "Buck up! Life is just passing through!" I have never felt male and I've never seen myself as a man, but that has never caused me to think of myself as a woman or think that I was born in the wrong body—it's more like the wrong world. I have never been very masculine, and perhaps I've been more feminine, but in a world where the prevailing logic is "six of one or a half dozen of the other," if I wasn't one thing, then I must have been the other. The entire male universe has always irritated, embarrassed, and frightened me, but at the same time attracted and unsettled me—in the good sense of the word.

The village where I was born and lived until I was nineteen is one of those places that people wind up leaving, sooner or later. They flee because it's small, because it's in the south, because it's poor, because it's in the mountains, because it's isolated. It's a village where nobody is even born anymore—not recently, anyway—because people go elsewhere to give birth, far away from home in hospitals in the city. It's a village on the routes of nomadic shepherds who migrate with their charges across the mountains of Abruzzo and the plains of Apulia and Campania—a borderland village that never gave me a precise sense of belonging, of being from one region or another. Whenever people asked me where I was from, I usually hesitated before responding, because, since no one knew my village, I had to say "from Campania"—an answer that was geographically accurate but barely relevant to the culture of the place. Similarly, to say Molise or Puglia was right in some ways and wrong in others. Later, I came to understand that the best definition for my origins was Samnite, because Samnium is a land that straddles all three of those regions and it is the one that best represents me: it's a land of anarchists and bandits, of peasant uprisings and union movements, a land that resisted the Romans until the bitter end and never surrendered. Mine is a land that straddles borders, just as my sex and gender do. There is a tendency toward movement, transition, and therefore travel, towards making the "trip," as people used to say.

Even my name never belonged to me. My given name, the one written on documents, I inherited from my maternal grandfather, but since it's bizarre and rather uncommon, my parents decided to pair it with the name of my other grandfather, but they forgot to record that at the registry office. They kept on calling me by my middle name, forgetting about my first one—the official one. When I started middle school, I learned that my actual name was my first name, not my middle name, although that was the one everyone knew me by. There was no proof that I had attended elementary school. After a series of corrections and bureaucratic steps, I had to begin signing things with a new name, which was actually my old one. It was an issue I resolved only later on, when I chose the name that I felt was my own. I therefore have different names: one for the registry office, one for relatives and acquaintances, one for friends, and one for lovers. Borders, mixing and melding, uncertainty, hybridization, exodus—for years these were causes of insecurity, but today they are my poetics, my exploration and construction of meaning, my personality, and the way I view the world. I feel that I am a nomad, a transversalist, a hybrid, an outsider. The only thing I'm sure of remains my body—roughly five feet, six inches tall and weighing 155 pounds, the hub of my happiness, because it is the starting point and the end point of all my needs and desires.

The Awakening of Self-Awareness

At the beginning of my third year of high school, I attended a packed student assembly at my school about the coup in Chile and the violent repression that had followed. I listened to seniors talk about fascism and torture, repression and freedom, revolution and justice. These new words and new topics made an impact because they opened a breach inside of me that went on to become a chasm—and later, self-awareness, struggle, and lived experience. My story begins at this moment because this is where my liberation began.

For some time I had been in the throes of a profound crisis. I was a teenager living in a village in the south in the early 1970s, and I was homosexual. In whom could I confide what was, at that time, a terrible truth?

Back then, as was the case in most little towns, the only person designated to listen was the priest—by no means capable of understanding things that were considered mortal sins but capable of arousing the worst feelings of guilt. After years of pointless and repetitive confessions, I was sick to death of having him ask me, "With whom did you do it? How did you do it? How many times did you do it? Where did you put your hand?" Those questions made me feel embarrassed, guilty, and even stranger than I was. Repeating in confession that I had committed impure acts with my friends—and therefore with other boys—explaining how far I had dared to go, was exhausting and, above all, excruciating. After the confession, I would feel released from my feelings of guilt, but all it took was a touch or even just a glance to make me fall into temptation again.

From an early age, I should have been playing with toy cars or guns, but I preferred dolls. I should have been aggressive, gotten into fights, joined in communal pissing with the other boys, and flirted with the girls, but instead I was quiet. I didn't piss with others. I liked to be flirted with, but not by the girls—who were my friends—but rather by the boys, for whom my personality just didn't add up. Many aspects of me were hard for them to understand then, and, to be honest, I couldn't really understand them either.

I was a teenager and, like everyone at that age, I was trying to figure out my place in the world—a world that felt deeply hostile to me, and by which I felt neither accepted nor understood. The students who had threatened to have me thrown out of school for being homosexual a few months earlier belonged to that world. Paradoxically, those who had suggested I should be expelled were the same ones with whom I used to engage in pleasant bouts of necking.

Necking and much more—which I, living in solitude and isolation, believed to be part of an experience that was unique, isolated. Later in life, when I confided these things to my fairy girlfriends, I realized that the world is just one big village, as they say. Every fairy, in her own closed environment, had had her flings and flirtations. That famous saying, "Do, but don't tell," typified (and still does a fair job of typifying) Italian culture. It was a way of doing things that puzzled me. How come all of them played along—or even sought me out, actually—and then refused to accept my homosexuality? Why, I wondered, if last night I was making out with that guy in a wheat field, is he saying today that if I'm really a faggot, it would be better if I dropped out of school? The only logic was, in fact, that of the do-but-don't-tell mindset, because if you do tell, the facades crumble. Some people felt exposed, others regretted what they'd done, others had a guilty conscience, but despite all that, they continued to seek me out. I was "wanted." As often happens, and as I have had the opportunity to verify through my own experience, the most intolerant and violent people are those who have a guilty conscience, or "a tail made of straw,"[7] as it's called. I believe that social control, with its related mechanisms of repression, has always worked through self-censorship—by exorcizing and demolishing that part of one's self that one cannot accept and likewise destroying it in others. To be clear, given how widespread the homophobia was, I'm convinced that there really were a whole lot of closeted faggots back then! In an interview, Dario Bellezza—a famous gay poet and writer I had a chance to spend time with thanks to an odd romantic entanglement with my dearest sweetheart, Marco—would maintain that sexual intercourse between men fell off during the era of sexual liberation, especially—and I use his words—"since women had started to give it away." However, I believe that the reason the frequency fell was because, in the past, men either could not or were unable to bring themselves to come out as gay, so they all looked male and what we saw was a world split into two: boys on the one side and girls on the other. There were a lot of faggots, but on the outside everybody had to be masculine because you "do, but don't tell"!

When the accusations and threats against me started, my world came crashing down. I was frightened. I felt like a fox being chased by a pack of dogs. This was a situation that, unfortunately, did not apply only to me and my tiny little village but to the whole of Italy and, we can suppose, the entire world. In the early 1970s, the gay liberation had just begun, but it wasn't yet universally shared. Something had happened—was happening—but I knew nothing about it. Sylvia Rivera had thrown *the* bottle at the cops three years earlier,[8] and then [ed./n in 1972, just one year before my story begins], Mario Mieli, Alfredo Cohen, and others had organized their sit-in in Sanremo to protest a conference of sexologists who still considered homosexuality an illness.[9] That was the first gay protest in Italy, but I knew nothing about it. Two years earlier, Romanina had finished serving two years in internal exile, in a village near mine, for being transsexual.[10] I remember that people in town were talking about this strange person, half-man and half-woman, a transvestite who had moved to Volturino, in the province of Foggia (roughly six miles from my village). I couldn't understand exactly who this person was or what it was all about. It was Romina Cecconi, now a dear friend of mine. She was sent into internal exile there because she was considered a socially and morally dangerous individual. She had been living in Florence and hadn't concealed her identity at all—on the contrary, she'd flaunted it. Her ostentatiousness, so provocative for the times, gave Pier Luigi Vigna[11] the bright idea of sending her into internal exile in a tiny village a million miles away from Florence. She had to be put under surveillance and punished because she was a trans woman, or rather, a transvestite.

I use the term "transvestite" because, at the time, the term "transsexual" did not yet exist—or, if it did, I wasn't aware of it. I had already seen a few transvestites on the streets of Naples. My sister had pointed them out to me. Otherwise, naive as I was, I would have never imagined that there could be men dressed like women—despite the fact that cross-dressing was my favorite pastime. I dressed up as the Madonna, as Saint Awestruck and Saint Genuflected, as absurd queens of imaginary countries, using veils, turbans, feathers, laces, and various pieces of costume jewelry I would scrape together from the belongings of the women in my family. After my religious phase, I started mimicking Sandy Show, who sang barefoot, and Patty Pravo, who was kicking off her career with "*Oggi qui domani là*" ("Today Here, Tomorrow There"), "*Ragazzo triste*" ("Sad Boy"), and "*La bambola*" ("The Doll"). Both of them flaunted the first shockingly short and scandalous miniskirts. I'd do a sort of karaoke, fashioning myself a miniskirt out of a towel, and for me and my family all of this remained a simple and innocent game. The first miniskirts generated a huge sensation, upset morality, and aroused the imagination—boys' imaginations for some reasons, women's for others, and mine because of the amazing fabulousness that I felt inside and for which I still had no name. The miniskirt, together with long hair for men, not to mention the numerous cultural events and phenomena of that era, were signs that strongly presaged a rebellion like none seen before.

The Coming Out

Much of what was happening around the world remained unknown to most people. The vast majority either knew nothing of it or were unable to decode the signs of that revolution. In the metropolises the fuses had been lit, and we could smell it in the sparks coming from Vietnam, from the Prague Spring, from Bolivia, Chicago, and Woodstock. I could sense it, but no one person or thing had conveyed it to me clearly. You could feel it in the air, but it wasn't shared. What was known as "counter-information" traveled by way of odd channels that were not so easily found. Unlike today, there was no Google where you could type in "gay liberation" or "trans" and be able to find out everything there was to know. Even the term "homosexual" was not an everyday word. It was an "unspeakable practice," to cite the title of a booklet printed by FUORI!.[12] The first time I heard it spoken of publicly was in November 1975, in the aftermath of Pier Paolo Pasolini's murder. On television they made what were more veiled hints than out-and-out statements about his established or alleged homosexuality. It was actually during a school assembly organized because of Pasolini's murder that, with the support of other members of the student collective I belonged to, I first came out.

Usually almost all students took part in assemblies, with the exception of those few who weren't interested or the Fascist sympathizers, who were a scant minority. I remember that moment very well. I was extremely nervous because for me public speaking was an ordeal. Another member of my student collective, while introducing the topic into the agenda, said that the person who was going to talk about Pasolini's murder was someone who had personal experience of homosexuality. I don't recall his exact words, nor do I remember the arguments discussed by the speakers before me. I don't remember what I said, either, that's how stressed and nervous I was. I only remember that one of the Fascists, who had attended the assembly out of curiosity, said something like, "Now even the faggots have to have their say," after which he was encouraged to leave, and not very politely.

The practice of coming out did not exist yet or, if it did, I didn't know about it. In any event, it wasn't called that, wasn't a recognized political practice.

At my school we had the right to four hours of assembly per month, which we usually stretched into five or six. Those additional hours were requested or demanded to deal with what we considered urgent matters or emergencies, and the murder of Pasolini was seen as such. My speech was planned at a meeting of our student collective, which usually met in the afternoon at a time when, at our request, the school remained open to allow students more time for study. However, more than wanting to fill in gaps in our knowledge, we wanted to change the world, so we engaged in politics.

From the time I embarked on my new path, I no longer tried to hide my homosexuality. On the contrary, supported by my friends and fellow collective members, and strengthened by my new self-awareness, I was proud.

People talked about homosexuality only rarely, and to talk of one's own homosexuality was taboo. All around me, people were talking a lot about sexuality, or at least they were trying to. I believe that only in feminist circles was the topic explored a bit more deeply, possibly starting from oneself, in order to expand one's self-awareness. It was much easier for me to talk about my sexuality with the female members of my collective than with the male. With women there was less embarrassment and a sort of sympathetic, almost shared way of feeling, a deeper understanding of complex implications, a greater sensibility. The boys in my collective were much more curious. They would ask me endless questions intended more to reassure themselves, to guarantee their own integrity rather than do any soul searching. Once their own sexual integrity was verified and assured, once their gender normality had been acknowledged, then they could all indulge in degenerate acts. The beds I climbed into were many, and many the meadows in blossom, the haylofts, the basements, the attics, the shacks, and the river banks—in the sunshine and the moonlight, in the snow and in the rain, everywhere—but always in silence, in the shadows. I couldn't tell anyone, but I was involved in intrigues and amorous entanglements with everyone, all the while wondering if I were the exception, if mine were an isolated experience or one shared by others. All of this was fun, exciting, intriguing. It made me feel exactly how I wanted to feel—like a nonconformist, a rebel, a profaner.

(Translated by Danila Cannamela and Jennifer Delare)

Notes

1. The excerpts translated here are from the first chapter of Porpora Marcasciano, *AntoloGaia: Vivere sognando e non sognare di vivere; I miei anni settanta* (Rome: Alegre, 2016). iBooks. Originally published 2007.

2. In Italian, *pioniere* is the feminine form of "pioneers."

3. *Tra le rose e le viole* is a collection of stories of trans and gender-variant people, originally published in 2002.

4. The author uses this asterisk at the end of various adjectives at different points throughout the text to emphasize the fact she did not want to limit herself or anybody else to identifying uniquely as male or female in those instances. On the practice of using the asterisk, see the conclusion in this volume.

5. For more on Mieli's notion of "educastration," see his work, *Towards a Gay Communism: Elements of a Homosexual Critique*, originally published in Italian in 1977.

6. In Italian, the term *veterosessuale* uses the Latin verb *vetero* (to make old, to age) as a prefix to mean "old" or "old-fashioned," in regard to sexual norms.

7. To have a tail made of straw (*avere la coda di paglia*, as the Italian expression goes) is synonymous with having a guilty conscience. Its meaning purportedly stems from the fact that straw burns quickly, so, if someone with a guilty conscience thinks that others may have suspicions, they will get touchier about it (catch fire, in other words) more quickly.

8. Marcasciano is referring to the 1969 Stonewall riots. It is still debatable whether Rivera was the one who started the protest and it is not even clear if she was at the bar when the riot began. Rivera was undoubtedly an iconic figure in the 1970s trans movement in the US. For more on Rivera, see also the introduction and chapter 15 in this volume.

9. Marcasciano's story takes place in 1973. In April 1972, Mieli organized the first demonstration in support of homosexuality to take place in Italy, during a sexology conference in Sanremo.

10. For more on the story of Romina Cecconi, see chapter 9 in this volume.

11. Pier Luigi Vigna (1933–2012) was an Italian prosecutor, based in Florence. He became famous as an anti-mafia prosecutor as well as for his investigations of right-wing terrorism and of a serial killer known as the Monster of Florence.

12. FUORI!, or OUT! in English, was the first Italian association to create a gay liberation front. It was founded in Turin in 1971 by Mario Mieli and Angelo Pezzana, among others.

Chapter 2

From *L'aurora delle trans cattive*

Storie, sguardi e vissuti della mia generazione transgender
(*The Dawn of the Bad Trans Women: Stories, Fragments, and Lives of My Transgender Generation*)

PORPORA MARCASCIANO

L'aurora delle trans cattive might be considered the sequel to *AntoloGaia*. In this second book of Marcasciano's queer saga, the protagonist takes her first steps into the gender-variant community, creates strong bonds with trans women, and eventually turns into a leader of the trans movement.[1] Serena Bassi, who translated the excerpts included here, has observed that, in centering the voices and stories of a marginal subculture, Marcasciano's memoir connects the past to the present: "In an era of supposed transgender liberation through the attainment of legal rights and media visibility, the narrator addresses us directly, explicitly asking us to not forgo the legacy of the 'bad trans women' who have built the movement."[2] For Marcasciano, this rich legacy can be traced back to two serendipitous yet eye-opening encounters with the Neapolitan gender-variant community. The first took place in 1969, in an Upim department store in Naples, where for the first time she saw two trans women; the second occurred in 1977, when Marcasciano was introduced by her anthropology professor Pino Simonelli to the ancient rituals and traditions of the Neapolitan femminielli.

The Dawn of our "Wonderful Adventure"

The first time I saw a trans woman—two, actually—was toward the end of the 1960s. I remember when it was that I met these two strange characters because it was during a family trip to Naples, when my family were shopping for my older sister's wedding, which took place in 1969. In the old Upim department store in "via Duomo"—a top shopping and cruising destination—I met them for the first time. And it was from up close. I was standing in line at the checkout with my family when one of the heavy doors opened—suddenly and lightly—as if it weighed nothing at all. The door was being delicately and gently pushed open by two peculiar maidens, who greeted the shoppers and shrieked: "Good morning! Here we come, the variety show stars!" Slender, totally blonde, extra tight pants, heels so high they could reach the stars—the same stars they knew they were. Then my sister pulled me toward her and whispered in my ear, in a knowing tone, "They are men! They are men!" The girls heard and, as they passed us, they turned to my sister and said in Neapolitan dialect: "*Uè uè peccerè, que r'è . . . nun te fai capace!* ("Hey, little one . . . what's wrong? Are you not down with it?"). And it was hard to "be down with it" when we just had no tools to make sense of those two. According to common sense, they just didn't make any sense. They defied social logics entirely and did not fit within any given cultural model. . . .

Pino had been talking to me about the *femminielli* and their rituals for a while, but I was fairly indifferent to his stories. One night he came to pick me up, announcing that we had been invited to a wedding between *femminielli*. I was not there for the ceremony itself, but I did go to the flamboyant banquet that followed it, in an old tavern of the Spanish Quarter. The celebration was attended by about thirty people, many of whom were transvestites. Pino and I were some of the first people to get to the pizzeria, which meant I had the honor of being there for the entire ritual. Guests arrived, handed over their gifts, and profusely and theatrically greeted the bride, who was wearing a striking white dress. When we arrived, she greeted Pino loudly: "The Professor is here! Good evening, Professor. It is our pleasure!" Then she turned to me: "*Uè peccerè damme nu vaso. Madonne e quant'è bellella a peccerella, è proprio femmena, è femminella*" ("Little one, give me a kiss. Oh Virgin Mary! She is so beautiful this little one, she really is a woman, she is *femminella*!"). The only thing I remember about that night was how impatient I was. I wanted to run away from that strange scene, a hilarious yet foreign spectacle. Once again, the deeper meaning of what

I had witnessed was hard for me to capture and comprehend. Clearly, like in all beautiful tales, my relationship with the *femminielli* was only starting then. A few years after, my relationship with Valérie and Antonella—*'a Merdaiola*—gave me the instruments I needed to better understand something within me that I was struggling to bring into focus. The Merdaiola (I am using the nickname with which she was best known in the *femminielli* community because it is the one that suited her best and because it was the most beautiful) introduced me to the wonderful world of the *femminielli*, which had already started changing then.[3] It was transforming into something else. The little, contained, ancient world of the *femminielli* was already being replaced, slowly yet inexorably, by another world—an oversized and shapeless postmodern world. You could say that replacement was a move away from the *femminiella* to the category of the trans woman—but also, I guess, from the *femminiello* to the cis gay man.

I let that world seduce me. I immersed myself in it. I let myself travel toward that new world like Alice in my own Wonderland. Initially, I was afraid of upsetting an ancient balance of things, so I tiptoed my way into that world, holding a lantern and observing in silence. Just like all the other "worlds apart" (the worlds of those who were excluded from society and separated off from reality), it was not so much other people who pushed the *femminielli* out; it was they who consciously separated from the mainstream world. The reason for that is obvious, really: the walls and borders between our world and mainstream society were defensive; we raised those walls to protect our territory—the only place where we could survive and not break. I then started to get to know, respect, share the codes and rules of that world. I was starting to grasp its structure and interpret the gestures of its inhabitants. I slowly started to communicate with their language, a slang made out of words, sayings, gestures, rhymes that normal people would not understand. All the inhabitants of that fairyland had their own nicknames, which made them unique, and I could give lots of examples. Nonetheless, they'd all rather celebrate their name day than their birthday. On their name day, they would all celebrate the saint whose name was on their birth certificate and on their ID: Ciro, Gennaro, Antonio, Giuseppe, Raffaele. To this day, *femminielli* communities continue to keep their code unaltered, referring to themselves with male pronouns in certain situations and female pronouns in others.

I can still remember the day I was "baptized." It was a true initiation ritual, spontaneously put together and orchestrated by my new housemate, Merdaiola, who moved in with me and stayed for two years. Those two years turned out to be an essential school of life for me. About ten Neapolitan *femminielli* who lived in Rome were invited to our home for coffee, which in Naples is a symbol for friendship. The ceremony, which began in the early afternoon, went on until late at night and ended with an opulent ragout-based dinner. During the long, languid afternoon, spent drinking coffee, the baptism ceremony attendees talked about me as the new arrival—making comments and sharing impressions, advice, and recommendations as to what aesthetic and surgical transformations I may need. Throughout the afternoon, Sasà, also known as Messalina, slowly combed and styled my hair and then did my makeup. This routine took hours, as we kept drinking coffee—a lot of coffee—as if it was water. Every so often, Messalina would take a few steps back to take a good look at me. Really, she was looking at her work of art, as she was sipping coffee and smoking cigarettes. I must confess that the result was amazing, I hardly recognized myself in that fabulous reflection I saw in the mirror . . . *'O miracolo!* I was amused and fascinated as I looked at that new version of me, so much more similar to what I always was in my dreams. In those moments, I felt for the first time that my *trans/formation* was not just possible but, likely, doable. I moved, in a clumsily self-conscious way, among those ladies whose trans/formation was much farther along than mine. The attendees to my initiation ceremony were not sure about one thing: my name. *Nunn'era, nunn'era proprio* (It didn't work, it just didn't work), according to them. So they transformed it into more accessible versions: Porpa, Porpitiello, Polverina, or Spolverina. I was center stage, and on the sides they were all chatting and gossiping or, as we say in Naples, *inciuciavano*. We spent that afternoon talking about the trans women we knew at a point in time when we were setting out to conquer the world. At that point, our world was finally coming in from the cold and we were excited. That pushed us to think, speak and act, and it felt like time was never enough for all the ideas we had.

In that smoky room where the air was thick with hair spray and the scent of caffeine, we told each other stories, legends really, about the women in our community. There was that story about Saionara, who went to Florence to Dr. Luccioli to get a nose job, but it didn't turn out as well as Miss Seven Evenings's, because Saionara had had it done twenty times already, and at that point there was nothing left for the doctor to work with. Because Miss Seven Evenings was a lot younger, her face looked like Carrara marble yet to be sculpted, which was why we all looked up to her. Another one, Muscella, had had so much work done that it became a financial investment of sorts. She was much cleverer than all of us and went to London to the best gender-reassignment doctor in Europe, but she'd had to take out a loan from a loan shark. Another story was about La Scatulara, who, two months after her op in Casablanca, opened her window one morning and began shouting that she had finally reached an orgasm with her newly acquired vagina: "You can come with it! You can come with it! I came so hard, my cunt is the best!" She was so excited that her girlfriends thought she was going mad and, kindly and understandingly, called up an ambulance for her. Messalina, who had her op done in England, was far more composed and, with no yelling, showed her vagina by appointment to all her acquaintances. All she asked of her attentive observers was that they go and spread the gospel—that is, tell everyone how perfect her "cunt to die for" was. I remember very well when she came over to ours for a visit with her mum and her handsome brother. She was lying on my bed showing off a bloody shapeless mess of catheters and vaginal dilators, as she explained what it would all look like eventually, much to everyone's excitement. Messalina's mum was waxing lyrical about her daughter while frequently inviting her son, who was trying to feel us girls up, to leave the room because this was "a woman thing." La Pechinese had even organized a huge party that would culminate in a public viewing of her new vagina, with hundreds of invitees. Those were extravagant but ancient rituals that brought the community together and held our world together. Barbara—poor girl!—had no time to enjoy her new vagina, because soon after her op she was killed. Some say by a lover who went mad because of the huge physical transformation of his favorite girl. Others say it was a burglary.

In order to understand and interpret that fantastic world (its language, codes, and rituals) that ran parallel to that of normal people, you needed the right tools. I had found a secret passage in and I was delving deeper each day, learning new tricks with much joy and excitement. Gradually, I was learning the vocabulary, the turns of phrase, the gestures, the numeric codes, and all the other ways with which the *femminielli* endowed that fabulous parallel world with meaning. Twenty-one was what we called ourselves, because in the Neapolitan *tombola* it stands for "woman," while seventy-one, also known as *totore*, meant "man." In our jargon, butch lesbians were *a' totore*. People who were a bit slow and didn't quite get it were twenty-three. Forty-four was jail, and you could use it for people who were inside. Fourteen was the drunkard and sixteen was the ass (*'o vascio*), while twenty-nine stood for the phallus.

(Translated by Serena Bassi)

Notes

1. From Porpora Marcasciano, *L'aurora delle trans cattive: Storie, sguardi e vissuti della mia generazione transgender* (Rome: Alegre, 2018), iBooks. This text is based on the English translation originally published in *TSQ: Transgender Studies Quarterly* 6, no. 1 (2019): 124–31. We have slightly edited the translation to emphasize the regional features of the Italian text, in particular the use of dialect.

2. Serena Bassi, "Translator's Note," in "Excerpts from The Dawn of the Bad Trans Women: Stories, Fragments, and Lives of My Transgender Generation," *TSQ: Transgender Studies Quarterly* 6, no. 1 (2019): 125.

3. On the Merdaiola, see chapter 3 in this volume.

Chapter 3

From *Tra le rose e le viole*

La storia e le storie di transessuali e travestiti (Among Roses and Violets: The Story and the Stories of Transsexuals and Tranvestites)

Porpora Marcasciano

The story of Antonello is one of the many testimonies of gender diversity that Marcasciano has collected during her work as chronicler of her "trans generation."[1] In Marcasciano's 2018 memoir, Antonello makes another appearance as the protagonist of the chapter entitled "La Merdaiola," a reference to his playful nickname, which describes a shrewd and crafty person. Footage about La Merdaiola is featured in the documentary film *Porpora* (2021).

In this interview, Antonello shares his experience with transvestism and explains how his Neapolitan upbringing—he uses masculine forms to talk about himself—has shaped his gender identity. The style and linguistic texture of the piece help position Antonello outside mainstream culture. The language is modeled on the Neapolitan way of speaking: it resorts to regional constructions rather than standard Italian and is sprinkled with southern expressions and words in dialect. Marcasciano's writing mimics the informal tone of the conversation: brief, chopped-off sentences; abrupt changes of subject; the use of "you" as a generic subject pronoun; the use of slang. In the English translation, we have tried to maintain the colloquial and regional traits of the original text as much as possible. The excerpt given here includes Marcasciano's original introduction to the piece.

Antonello

Antonello, forty-two, lives in Bologna, but was born in Naples and has retained that city's sense of color, flavor, musicality, and performativity. He is not a trans woman, and it's rather difficult to define him.[2] To use one of his expressions, we could say that he is a *femminiello*,[3] an ancient word used in Naples to refer to gay men, transvestites, transsexuals, transgender people, and all those gender nuances located beyond the masculine. He is sturdily built, heavyset, actually. He has turned cross-dressing into an art and a lifestyle. His view of life is typically Neapolitan: He finds a way to scrape by! His colorful language conveys that ancient wisdom, typical of this underrepresented popular culture on the verge of extinction.

Antonello's story shines a light on an experience that might generally and very superficially be defined as transvestism, an experience that is fundamentally different from the transsexual path, in that our protagonist hasn't made any changes to his body. What is described here is the world of the Neapolitan *femminielli*—their history, their culture, their language—a world that has been disappearing under the endless battering of atrocious cultural globalization. Prostitution and the art of making do to get by, the rules and values of the street, a specific way of understanding sex and gender, superstition, tradition—this is a watercolor of Naples and its most colorful characters. I met Antonello in Naples in 1979, in the vicoli[4] that run down to the port, during an exciting "fox hunt."[5]

This interview was originally collected in Bologna, in the fall of 1999.

༄

My name is Antonello, and sometimes Luisa. I like to wear women's clothes; I enjoy it, it relaxes me, it allows me to escape, and it also earns me money. I'm from Naples, I'm forty-two years old, and I've been living in Bologna for about twenty years. I have moved a lot, actually: I lived in Rome for two years, in Milan for one, in Genoa on and off, and I worked for two years abroad—in Libya and Algeria, to be precise. Recently, due to various issues, I've stopped traveling and moving around, so I've been staying put in Bologna.

For us Neapolitans, getting by is an art, so I've always done whatever jobs I could find—as a cook for different Italian companies in Libya and Algeria, an electrician, a chef's assistant, a bellhop, a driver and, until very recently—to top up my wages and have some fun—I've always turned tricks.

I left Naples many years ago, around 1976 or '77, and what I left behind was a marvelous city that I never found again. My decision to leave was due largely to problems I felt I had—the presence of my family, for instance—which, generally speaking, can impact you a lot, especially at those times when you start discovering certain things about yourself that make you feel ill at ease. You try to hide them from the world, from others, and most of all from yourself—things that you've had inside forever, that you repress. Then all of a sudden you feel like you can't stand it anymore, that you need to bring them out into the light, otherwise you feel like Mount Vesuvius, which has to explode sooner or later. As is often the case in Naples, I had a big family: numerous siblings, aunts and uncles, cousins, and an authoritarian father. I thought that if I stayed there, sooner or later somebody would notice, and they might take it badly, there could be trouble. In short, I felt uneasy, and I worried about it so much that, in the end, I opted to leave home, to think of myself and make a life of my own. In truth, I believe that my family, for better or worse, always knew or at least sensed it, but they chose to pretend they didn't know. What you don't see can't hurt you!

I arrived in Rome in the mid-1970s. It was the closest city and also the most intriguing. It wasn't the one that offered the most job opportunities or quick and easy money, like Milan, but it was the most like Naples and, from that perspective, it was a place where you could make do to get by. Initially, I looked for an honest job—not that walking the streets is dishonest, but I preferred to have a real job at first, almost as if I needed to have a clean conscience. Then I started to rely on the street, too. When you are young, you like certain things and they put you on cloud nine, dazzle you, and make you lose sight of reality. You risk losing yourself. So, having a normal job was a check, something that made you keep your feet on the ground.

The truth is that, when you leave home, you have to get by somehow, so you go where you think you've got a chance of making it. I had already turned a few tricks, when the opportunity presented itself. These things happen at times and in places where you least expect them to—and so, if opportunity makes a thief, in this case opportunity makes a streetwalker. What should I have done? Let a guy who was going to pay me for a service get away—a guy that, all things considered, I kind of liked?

In Rome I already had a few gay friends who cross-dressed and also a few trans girlfriends; by following them and hanging out with them, I gained some experience. First off, they took me to their hotel, and so, one evening,

I started, almost as a game. The first thing I thought was, "If I have to do it, I'd better do it right." I put on a skirt, high heels, makeup, and out I went. I was nineteen. I had already cross-dressed a few times in Naples, but just for fun, with friends at parties, never for work. The first time I walked the street, I remember, I was really scared. I felt awkward and uncomfortable, but everything went smoothly. The second time, though, the problems started.

As soon as I got to the street, the other trans women came to chase me away, to threaten me. To find work, I was in fact going where there were other prostitutes, where the scene was—where I knew that, no matter what, someone was going to pick me up. Of course, those who were already there had something to say about that and got pissed. That's normal. It was the law of the street and it worked like this: everyone looked after their own area, their workplace. It's like, if I have a nice bowl of soup, and one person comes along and dips some bread in, and then another, and another—in the end, if you're not careful, you wind up with half a bowl, so everyone looks out for their own plate. In the beginning, I would run away, afraid, until one day I realized that I couldn't keep on running away and being scared because I wanted to keep on turning tricks. So, I decided to face the situation and show them what I was made of. It wasn't easy, because when ten transvestites are coming at you—who, at times such as those, forget to be women and act like men—it's absolutely terrifying.[6] I was ready for it, though. That's how it goes—you know you can take the slaps and the punches. If you really want to succeed, you can take them, once, twice—and, in the end, you get to stay. This is something that happens on streets everywhere—not only in Rome but in Bologna, Milan, and elsewhere. I fought with the others, violently, but in the end I was accepted and respected. That was the initiation ritual, the trial by fire, and, once I got through it, we became girlfriends. We went out together, we ate meals together. I had become one of them.

In those years, I became acquainted with police harassment—the stings, the holding cells, the insults when they were bringing us to the police station. They would do crazy things to us. They'd say, "You're disgusting, look at the state of you!" and then issue us citations and warnings. I've gotten warnings from Bologna and from Milan. In Milan, I even did fifteen days in jail because, when I was still inexperienced, I got into an argument with a customer. He didn't want to pay me, so I tore up his vehicle registration and insurance card, but then he flagged down a patrol car and said I wanted to rob him. Of course, the cops believed him, not me. I was put on trial and, besides charging me with a fine for cross-dressing, I was issued a warning to stay out of Milan. . . .

Now everything is more difficult. When you reach a certain age, you no longer have the opportunities and potentialities you had when you were young, either to find a normal job or to work on the street. I used to make a lot of money quite easily, through both of those methods, but now everything is harder and more complicated. The street—the more the years pass, the harder it gets. You tire easily, it's cold, and you're not as attractive as you were in your twenties. There's more competition now because there are many more trans people and women turning tricks. Back in the day, you got on the street and you couldn't rest for one second; you'd get out of one car and into another. At the same time, it's harder to find a regular job, not just because of unemployment but also because, after you hit forty, it's more difficult to find one. We could say that, between today and twenty years ago, there's an abyss. Everything seems more complicated and, although we go on about progress, people actually live worse.

I don't think in the long-term and my future is today. I can't say what I'll be doing in twenty years or even one year from now—but I do hope I can find some odd job that will let me turn a corner, guarantee me the bare minimum to survive, because you can't aspire to anything else. No one offers decent long-term contracts anymore. Right now I'm taking a training course at MIT [Trans Identity Movement][7] and I hope that, when it's over, there will be the possibility of a job. My problem is being able to pay the rent, which isn't cheap, and to eat—the certitude of food and shelter, in other words—but then, if I think that I might get a higher-than-normal bill or some emergency might happen, everything gets so much worse.

Lately, I try to turn tricks only when I need to. I would like to think of it as only a back-up job, not my main one. If one day I have some bills due, for instance, some extra expenses, and money's tight, I put on my wig and go down to the street, but only out of need, and certainly not to play at being a doll, not like I used to. I just can't do it anymore, not physically. I'm too old for it. So, if I find a job, I won't walk the streets anymore. Even going out in drag at night doesn't give me the pleasure or the satisfaction it once did; now it's only a necessity. As with anything, when you do it because you enjoy it, it's pleasant and easy. When it becomes an obligation, it feels burdensome and tedious. I gave this desire of mine free rein for years, in the full prime of my life, and now I'm a little tired. I'm not tired of cross-dressing, but I am tired of doing it so I can eat.

I've been cross-dressing for over twenty years now, ever since I had my first regular job. Back then I did it occasionally, when I had a chance. When I was working abroad, once every three months I came back to Italy, and my greatest joy was cross-dressing and getting crazy at clubs and at parties, and walking the street. On job sites in Libya and Algeria, I got up at five in the morning, and when evening came, I was exhausted. By nine I was already in bed. What's more, we were in the desert, so there was nothing to do. In our camp there were only men, so the situation was kind of oppressive, although I did have my flings with a few guys that I liked. There, though, I only thought about work, so as soon as I set foot back in Italy, I would explode. I'd spend fifteen days in a frenzy, day and night would run together, it was like being at Carnival in Rio.

I like to dress as a woman—a woman who's a little over the top, that's for sure—not like an ordinary woman or a housewife. Let's say, a woman who's a little more eccentric! Even though I cross-dress, I don't feel that I am a woman—but neither do I feel like a real man. I've never defined myself, there is no definition—I feel the way I am. It's a bit difficult to define oneself. I've always wondered about it, especially when I was younger. I'm definitely not a man, otherwise I'd have been with women and that would have been that. Maybe a transsexual, but I don't do hormones, so maybe . . . a transvestite, because I do cross-dress, but I don't do it just to go to work, but often also to go out and have fun at nightclubs—I dance better cross-dressed. I'm definitely not a trans person who's waiting for a sex change operation, because I'm not interested in that, but I like to dress as a woman, so it doesn't matter to me whether people refer to me as a man or as a woman. I haven't had hormone treatments or surgeries, but when I cross-dress, I make an impression—and a great impression, at that. The thing is, when I go to work the streets, I can't go in a regular [woman's] outfit. You have to wear really feminine, ultra-sexy clothing, otherwise you look like you're going to church or grocery shopping. Even then, though, there would always be someone who'd like you, even like that. There are plenty of strange people out there, much stranger than me!

Even as I am now, without makeup or anything over the top, when I go around during the day, many people say to me, "Good morning, ma'am!" They mistake me for a woman, but I don't care whether they address me as a man or as a woman. I am what I am, and I like being with men. For me, dressing like a woman is great fun. Sometimes it helps me to relax, to let off steam. I alternate, at times a bit masculine and at times a bit feminine; it depends on what side of the bed I get up on, on how my womb feels!

I look at myself in the mirror, and it's there, while I'm looking in the mirror, that everything happens. Imagine what a mess we'd all be in if mirrors didn't exist! The difference between Luisa and Antonello is only in that moment, when I'm getting ready—there, looking in the mirror, they meet each other and they swap places: Antonello goes to take a rest and Luisa wakes up; then, when I take off my makeup, it's Luisa who retires. However, these two parts often coexist, blend, get mixed up with each other, and sometimes they come into conflict. When I dress up and put on my makeup, I am a big girl, very much so, because I am rather large. I'm a Junoesque woman who radiates good health, that classic Bolognese *sciura* [ma'am] or the larger-than-life Neapolitan lady who sells contraband cigarettes at the Pignasecca market.[8] Something may change in the mirror, but inside I'm always the same, in the morning when I dress as a man and at night when I dress as a woman. I don't go around dressed as a woman during the day. These are things that are done in the evening, or better yet, at night, when the darkness gives you greater protection. Life is strange; many people see the dark and the night as dangerous, treacherous, while for people like me they are a protection—who knows which of us is right?!

Cross-dressing, for me, is something that is not always the same. It takes different forms, has different nuances; it depends on the situation. When I'm on the streets at night, I feel comfortable wearing revealing, sexy clothing, but when I go to a café or some other place, I don't want to be ridiculous, so I dress more modestly. Of course, if I had a different image, maybe if I were a trans woman or if I'd had a breast job, if I were aesthetically more feminine, I'd do it without any problem; obviously I wouldn't go out in a bodysuit and fishnet stockings, because I don't want to make people laugh—I'm the one who gets to decide when it's time for laughing. I like to use my sense of humor to make people laugh and have fun, but I hate to be made fun of. My age and my weight being what they are, well, I'm certainly no showgirl, but people often see you as a big doll—they laugh, they think you're funny, but they don't know what you have inside.

At other times I see myself and feel as if I'm an ordinary, simple woman, not in a nightgown or dressed for the theater—I do that somewhere else—but dressed like a housewife, a mother and wife; they're the women who work the hardest. Dressing as a housewife is something I do at home, when I'm hard at work in the kitchen, because I really love to cook. But in the evening the look has to be different, over the top, less kitchen and more bachelor pad—perhaps you could still wear an apron, but with fishnet stockings and no panties underneath, like the bunny girls in nightclubs.

At night I use wigs a lot, I have all kinds: golden brown, blonde, dark brunette. But I like myself best blonde. My tricks like all of them: blonde, brunette, green, or yellow. It's other things they're interested in. They cruise around and around and, in the end, they pick up whoever has stirred up something inside of them, aroused their fantasies. That's what customers are attracted to, even if on the streets there's always someone who's prettier or sexier; I'm certain of that. I'm convinced that, if you put a wig on a dog, they would stop to ask it, "How much?" Those people would even fuck a dog. That's true in the big cities of the north, the same as it is in the little towns in the south. The people who seek you out at night are all the same—whether you're here or anywhere else, in Bologna, in Milan, in the mountains, or on an island. The difference is that, in a small town in the south, if you go walking around the streets in drag, they'll come after you with a rifle and shoot you. There you need to adjust your attitude, but rest assured that, if you catch one of the local men alone in the woods at one in the morning, he'll bend to the wig! As they say in Naples, "Men like pussy, but everybody likes cock." . . .

For the time being, this is how I live, sort of day by day. I think I'm going to stay in Bologna, even though it's not the way it used to be, and I'll see what happens. I've gotten used to living here, I have my points of reference, my relationships, my friends. Bologna is an enormous village that, all things considered, has managed to preserve a certain humanity. My circle is made up almost exclusively of people who are trans, transvestites, or gay—mostly from the south. We do everything together: parties, dinners, vacations. The south is full of trans women, there are so many of them, more than in the north; the problem is that in the south there isn't any money, so we all move north. When I came out, Naples was already full of trans women, many had been taking hormones since they were girls, so they were fabulous. I recall a few who were just gorgeous, they looked like top models: I remember Chinese, Coca-Cola, Sayonara, Seven Nights—all of them fabulous.[9] Of course, where there is poverty, there are problems, so these trans women didn't have the ability or the chance to make names for themselves—as actually happened for some who became famous in the world of show business; those ones knew what to do, they used their brains as well as their bodies. Still, in Naples I saw some really beautiful ones, even though they all wound up destroying themselves with drugs!

If in Naples you could get 5,000 lire for a trick, in Milan or Bologna you could get 20,000 or 30,000.[10] But the boom came first in Naples, then it came here too, and I want to underline that—it arrived here after, not before. I recall, when I arrived here in Bologna, I was surprised that local people were so nice and friendly, so well-mannered and kind. At night you'd have a line of cars waiting for you along the sidewalk, and they gave you good money. You just had to say, "Darling, give me a gift and we'll stay a little longer, no rushing, let's take our time and have fun," and right away they'd give you a 50,000 lire bill, even if you kept on treating them the same as before. It was like they enjoyed being hustled! Most who worked in the Fiera and Via Stalingrado area were from the south, chiefly Neapolitans and Sicilians; very few were from Bologna.[11] I was the first to go down to Via Stalingrado, in 1977, when there weren't even sidewalks yet and everything around was countryside. I clearly remember the winter nights, with the fog and the damp that would get into your bones, or when there were three feet of snow on the ground, and me, the brave one, defying the elements. Not even an earthquake could stop me!

In my view, if a homosexual is born into a poor family, he immediately starts thinking about how to make money, and turning tricks is definitely a way to do that. So, since Naples is a city with very few wealthy people and a lot of poor ones, there are certainly more trans prostitutes, just like there are more delinquents, more thieves, and people that, one way or another, have to find a way to scrape by. It's not surprising then, that even here in Bologna, a group of southerners has formed. The bee goes where the honey is, and so we southerners moved to the north. We have our own way of doing things, our own attitudes, rules, and values, but I can't say whether we carried them with us, from before, or whether we created them here. Respect for friendship and for the family is sacred, even though many of us have been disowned and mistreated by our own family members. Some friends of mine haven't seen their families in years because they've transformed themselves with hormones and surgeries and they could face trouble in their home environments. Still, every month they send a lot of money back home, almost like they have to pay a fee for some sin they've committed. Many of them have burned all bridges with their families because their families are old-fashioned and a trans woman can cause a scandal—but when it comes to taking money, scandals and honor no longer exist.

Nevertheless, most love their families and, with time, relationships can be rebuilt. Even if we don't live in Naples, we have maintained certain traditions, even made them stronger. For me, Sunday lunch is a ritual. I start making the ragù sauce early in the morning; actually, I start it cooking the night before, when I get home from work, because the sauce has to simmer for a long time, and the longer it simmers, the more flavorful it becomes.

I invite the others and we sit around the table and chat. Talking is better at the dining table, and eating is better in company. At the table, we spin our schemes, we argue and make up. Do you know how people make up after a fight in Naples? Over a cup of coffee, because we say that coffee is friendship—and then you play those numbers in the lottery, where forty-two means coffee, and a table laid out for a meal is eighty-two. We do these lunches on Sundays but also on important occasions like Christmas, Easter, birthdays, and especially on our name days, which are very important to us, even if we do celebrate our male names.

One of our favorite pastimes after lunch—and also at night after work—is to play tombola, or *a tumbulella*, as we call it. It's more than a game, it's true entertainment, and some among us are quite the experts. The game of tombola has its own rules and traditions, you see. In Naples, only women and *femminielli* can play because "the pants"—men—bring bad luck. What's more, each number has its own meaning, and based on those we bicker back and forth as the numbers are pulled out of the basket. Starting with the tombola numbers, then adding words and phrases, we *femminielle* have built a language that only we can understand.[12] For example, forty-four means prison, seventy-two is astonishment, thirty-eight is a beating, then we add more words and phrases, like "A chi vò, a do và, chiò-chiò, bagdad, a man int'o sapone, inciuciare."[13]

We all know this dialect; when you learn it, you become a true *femminiella*. In the beginning, we used this language as a way not to be understood by others—especially the police—and to feel more united. Today, though, many of these terms have entered into common usage. It was also a secret language we used so as not to be understood by the boys. In the Naples of the past, years ago, it wasn't like it is now, with trans women, transvestites, gay people, and *femminielli* all hanging out together, all emancipated. Back in the day, a *femminiello* was a man who felt like a woman and fell in love with a man, with the kind of man who only had relations with women. So *femminielli* only hung out with each other and, amongst themselves, they spoke only this language so they could communicate better and the boys wouldn't understand. A Neapolitan *femminiello* feels like a woman in the most traditional sense of the word—not a modern and independent woman, who has a job and lives on her own, who doesn't have children but only a few lovers. No, absolutely not! A *femminiello* feels like a wife, a mother, a sister, a hard worker, a great cook, a good housewife, loyal, religious—everything he has never been able to be, everything he strives to do better and more, whatever the costs. Even though I don't go to church on Sundays, I'm very religious. In my house I keep little statues of the Madonna, Jesus, and all those saints who protect me.

The history of the trans world is a piece of the history of Naples, which is the only city where there have always been trans women . . . *since the times of Pappagone!*[14] The *femminielle* had their customs and traditions, their rites. I'm using the past tense now because that world has disappeared . . . and we have all become modern! I remember all those customs so well: the wedding and *figliata* [birthing ritual], the rites at the Montevergine sanctuary, at the Madonna of the Arch and the Madonna of Pompeii.[15] The wedding was a ceremony between two *femminielle*, one more masculine and the other more feminine. The ceremony was held in a church, with the help of some complicit sexton, then everyone would go to a restaurant, parading through the city center, and the people would be applauding and wishing the couple well. They would even distribute wedding favors and [the traditional] sugared almonds. The *figliata*, on the other hand, is something much more ancient, and I managed to see only one, when I was very young. It was the reenactment of a birthing. The woman giving birth was a *femminiella*, who was lying down in the center, screaming and writhing with the pain of her labor. Around her were all the others, including a few women who had taken on the roles of midwives and to help with her delivery. I never precisely understood the meaning of that whole enactment but, judging by the deep emotional engagement, it was clear to see that the birthing had great symbolic meaning for the oldest of the *femminielle* present.

I also remember pilgrimages to the sanctuaries, which people may still do today. We would rent a bus and go all together to visit the Madonna. During the trip, group prayers were interspersed with moments of hilarity and pandemonium. When we arrived at the sanctuary, we did penance rituals, we prayed and made generous offerings. Each of us was so immersed in our prayers and our suffering that at times it turned into a scene of collective hysteria. The most famous sanctuaries were those devoted to guardian Madonnas, miraculous Madonnas, among which the Madonna of the Arch is the most famous. On our way back, we were all better people, but as soon as the driver made a stop, we all went back to our hormonal frenzy.

I believe that Naples has much more heart. There are a lot of things that make it unlivable, but if you're not well, there are many people who'll help you out. Bologna, on the other hand, I find much more hypocritical—it's all smoke and mirrors, all window dressing. The only reason anyone does anything is for money. For that matter, though, it seems to me that, these days, all streets are alike, especially in terms of violence and crime, which there are a lot of everywhere. I have never experienced any actual violence, maybe because my physical appearance can be intimidating, but I have suffered a lot of psychological violence. The violence that words can contain often hurts more than a thrashing—the things they yell at you, not only at night, on the streets, but even in the daytime. It's not nice, and especially not on days when things aren't going your way. I've been mugged too, and with time I've learned that it's better not to fight back. Back in the day, when someone mugged you, the worst they'd do was throw a punch at you. Now it's different, more dangerous; you can get killed over nothing. They threaten you with a syringe and you freeze.

The streets at night have gotten more dangerous. Someone comes up who wants to have sex with you, and there's no way to know beforehand who he is or what his intentions are. As a rule, the surprises come from those from whom you'd least expect it. After all, the ones with bad intentions are the ones who put on a mask in the beginning, so to speak. It's not like they're going to say, "Hey, get into my car, I want to kill you." Many trans women and prostitutes have been killed, even people I knew well. I remember that a trans woman here in Bologna was thrown into a river, another was killed with a hammer. The most recent was Cora. She was killed two years ago by somebody who wanted to steal her purse—and her killer is already out. His defense was saying that she'd wanted to rape him.

I have a certain instinct that helps me. If I sense that something isn't right, if I feel unsure about something, even if it is just a feeling, I ask the person to stop the car and I get out—if I can! It did happen to me that a guy put his hands around my neck and wanted to strangle me, then there was another one who put his fist through the car window and injured me. With these things, I put my trust in luck and, like all good Neapolitans, I am a little superstitious. I think that some days are good and others not, and there are signs that you have to interpret, that can tell you things. I have customers who bring me good luck, for instance, while there are certain trans women who bring me rotten luck, and if I go down to work and I see one of those transvestites, I know I may as well go home because they've killed my night. By contrast, if I run into one of those customers I keep for good luck, then the night gets back on track. If, during the night, you come across a fifty-seven, a *scartellato*—a hunchback—the night of work is going to be fabulous. But if someone wishes you a good night of work, forget about it, you might as well stay home. Since I'm superstitious, I always play the lottery. It's a sacred thing for me—not a vice or a habit, but a ritual. I play the numbers that have meaning for me on a given day, like the numbers on a car license plate or of someone who's doing something strange, but I don't play numbers from dreams because those are rarely drawn. For instance, a nephew of mine recently got married to an Albanian girl, out of the blue, without saying anything to anybody. I said to myself, "He's crazy!" because we were all astonished. So, I played the Milan lottery—because that's where it happened: twenty-three, because he acted like a madman; seventy-two, because I was astonished; forty-four, which is the bride—and in the end I won, and I got a nice chunk of change.

It's not just violence that has left its mark on the life of the streets. When AIDS came, a lot of things changed. Paradoxically, some things have changed for the better, because now condoms are widely used, while in the past that wasn't very common. It was difficult to gradually make customers understand that we had to use "the glove," and there are still those who want to do it without, but they do it at their own risk. I've lost many friends to AIDS, men and women, and many from amongst the trans women who used heroin. Death, especially when it strikes so close to you, affects you, shakes you, makes you think, changes you, and you start to avoid doing a lot of things because you realize they can be dangerous.

Now, before making any decision, I think about all of my friends who have died. It feels strange, it makes me sad, because they are a lot of little pieces of me that are gone. Time goes by and you begin increasingly to live on memories, and the memories of those who have passed away are many, too many! These memories make me suffer, but they also bring me joy because they are good memories. Today, the things that bring me pain or joy depend very much on my health, on how I feel physically, because if I am in good health, it doesn't take much to make me feel good. The things that bring me pain are many, like problems in my family or some friend who isn't well. There are always so many problems—too many—but when you are in good health, the rest can be overcome.

(Translated by Danila Cannamela and Jennifer Delare)

Notes

1. This chapter was originally published in *Favolose narranti: Storie di transessuali* (Rome: ManifestoLibri, 2008) and then republished in an updated edition of *Tra le rose e le viole: La storia e le storie di transessuali e travestiti* (Rome: Alegre, 2020), iBooks.

2. The translation adopts the pronouns from the original Italian text, which alternates between the feminine (*lei*/she) and the masculine (*lui*/he) throughout.

3. For more on *femminielli*, see, in particular, part 2 of this volume.

4. *Vicoli* are narrow streets, typical of Naples's downtown.

5. Here Marcasciano is jokingly hinting at the cruising that occurred in the area of the port—one of the areas for prostitution in Naples.

6. The original Italian reads, "*la paura fa novanta!*" This expression derives from the game of tombola, a traditional Italian game, similar to bingo. Based on the *smorfia napoletana* (a Neapolitan traditional "dictionary" of sorts that equates numbers with dreams and life events), each number in the tombola has a meaning, and *novanta* (ninety) means *la paura* (fear).

7. For more on the MIT, or Movimento Identità Trans, see the timeline and introduction.

8. Pignasecca is a street market located in the Spanish Quarter area of downtown Naples.

9. These nicknames, all based on foreign identities, may sound disparaging to the contemporary Anglophone audience; however, in a 1970s Italy with very little ethnic diversity, coining names that sounded exotic was a playful way to create new identities, detached from the unpleasant reality.

10. To offer a rough estimate, 5,000 Italian lire is equal to about 2.5 euros, 20,000 lire to 10 euros, and 30,000 lire to 15 euros.

11. The Fiera and Via Stalingrado area was the prostitution district in Bologna.

12. On Marcasciano's use of the spelling "*femminielle*," see the introduction (note 64).

13. These are Neapolitan dialect words and words of a secret code that even native Italian speakers are not supposed to understand.

14. This Neapolitan expression could be translated as "for ages" or "for a long time." Pappagone is the name of a theatrical mask created by Neapolitan actor Peppino De Filippo, but in this case the name could refer to an imaginary character from the past or to an ancient noble family, the Pappacoda, who lived in Naples in the fifteenth century.

15. For more on these rituals and traditions, see chapter 5 and 6.

Chapter 4

From *Dolore minimo* (*Minimum Pain*) and *Dove non siamo stati* (*Where We Haven't Been*)

Giovanna Cristina Vivinetto

This selection of Vivinetto's poems comprises texts from two poetry books, *Dolore minimo* (*Minimum Pain*, 2018) and *Dove non siamo stati* (*Where We Haven't Been*, 2020). The first, Vivinetto's debut book, is the diary of a gender transition in which the poetic persona identifies with an atypical mother who gave birth to a renewed self.[1] The second is an exploration of people and places of the past, filtered through the deforming lens of a déjà vu, or of the ineffable feeling that we have somewhat already been where we haven't been yet. In different yet related ways, both collections highlight the central role that places—their traditions, shared rituals, and collective memories—play into the construction and reconstruction of one's identity. Many of Vivinetto's poems are rooted in Sicilian culture and feature Sicilian dialect.

From *Dolore Minimo* (*Minimum Pain*)[2]

The streets of the town
were dense squares of darkness
that met as on a chessboard.

The memory of a move
inherited equally
at each intersection.

On summer evenings,
Madonnas shouldered
from house to house
idly absolved
interchangeable sins.

The streets were full of faith,
brass eyelets,
and discreet windows ajar.

In the quiet of those streets,
the affliction arrived in August.
It toppled the Madonnas, ousted
the eyelets, ruptured the crossings,
gave no time
to shut the windows.

I nailed myself, faithless,
to the great chessboard.
Found myself unfit for the symmetry
of proportion—for the straight line
always faithful to itself.

And learned from the imperfection
of the trees to make myself a branch,
thin and sharp, to reach
sidelong
toward the truth of light.

∽

When I was born, my mother
gave me an ancient gift,
the gift of the seer Tiresias:
to change sex once in my life.

From my first cry, she knew
that my growth was resistance,
rebellion against the body,

sibling struggle between spirit
and skin. An annihilation.

So she gave me her clothes,
her shoes, her lipstick;
told me: "take these, my son,
become who you are
if what you are could not be."

I became a seer, another Tiresias.
I practiced the art of clairvoyance,
became sorceress, witch, woman,
and gave in to the murmur of my body
—yielded to her seduction.

It was then that my mother
remade herself in me, bore me again,
second-born daughter of my time,
in which you can live well provided
you wander in circles
—hiding, like Tiresias,
an unutterable question.

∽

The other birth delivered
the distance of the trees—
their trunks' green solitude.
It seemed—for so long—
that we could never touch, never reach
—however we strained—
one from the branches of the other,
unable to hurt with leaves
only ours—that the storm
did not drive us together.

It took nineteen years
to prepare for rebirth,
to transform the distance between us

into living space, the void in full,
pain in melancholy—there is no other
but imperfect love. We awaited
our bodies as one awaits spring:
sealed in cortical anxiety. We understood
that if the first birth had been all
chance, biology, uncertainty—this other
was chosen, was anticipated, was penance:
baring self to world to abolish it,
to patiently reinhabit it.

∽

There's a word in my part of the world
that's sharp as a spike,
a spell to ward off evil.

"*Scansatini*" is a prayer,
a high hymn of self-
preservation. "*Don't let it happen*,"
I often overheard,
"*Don't let it be so*," then
suddenly the lips would tighten,
the words become arcane,
sacred.

Yet the "*Scansatini, Signuri*"
drove in one by one: the evil
to avoid was everything conceived
in my womb—but there were no new
perjuries to concoct, no words
that could undo their words, no hands
to raise to heaven in surprise
to play the injured party.

All that was left was to set
the suffered years in order, to put
the words in their place, to clear
a space for that which I'd feared
with clasped hands. And that monster

I'd run from all those years
was so gentle when, unchained,
I finally took its hand.

~

Look at that mother: hers is
no common pain.
She remembers having a son,
and the train he boarded
in August to earn a future.
Years later, at Stazione Siracusa,
she saw her son return, but he was
no longer him. A girl, a young woman,
came to meet her. She looked
at her. *This isn't true*, she thought.
They look the same. What pain,
what strange pain, not to have
birthed you, my daughter,
when you needed me to.

Look at that father: his is
no common pain.
He remembers having a son,
brother to an identical twin,
born at the same time, both
healthy baby boys. How is it possible
to comprehend after nineteen years
that this son is not:
what mistake, what ancestral
punishment has struck him?
But the other brother didn't trick him.
What strange pain, he thought,
To begin again, at the first cry.
After twenty years,
to become a father again.

Look at that daughter: hers is
no common pain.
Take a good look at her: barely born

but made by no one.
No father wished for her.
No mother suffered her birth.
She came into the world with vivid certainty,
shining alone in her difference.
She does not ask, therefore, for common pain.
The wound that bore her stays open:
uncensored, she says, *Twenty years*
I've waited to step into the light. Look at her body:
lit with that curious pain.

⁕

What name do you choose, papa-judge?
What name do you give me? You've summoned
me to court to tell me you're almost
there—the time has nearly come.
Papa-judge, I feel your labor pains.
Your swollen hands on my documents,
head—such an ache—full of formulas,
articles, bylaws you've found
for me, prepared for my christening.
You know, papa-judge, I read a name
on your fingers. I feel your flesh
open to ease out my new beginning.
What name do you give me?

But that's not all, you tell me. You must
cancel your whole history.
These twenty years need correction.
Erase the "m"s on the forms
and round off the final vowels.
Papa-judge—thank goodness—you know
the remedy. I've been yours since the day
you decided to fix me.

I began existing in your courtroom.
No cradle, no cord to cut,
no staccato blow to the back

to start me breathing.
No cries, no anxious corridors,
no purple verbs, no
clenched hands, no *It's a boy!*
Only your voice, papa-judge,
saying my true name
for the first time—finally.

So I believe the elemental sound
of each birth is a voice that says
a name—its pronouncement
renders the living real.

Now what name have you chosen, Papa?

༄

The father had always sensed
something was off,
but he didn't seem preoccupied.
In the family history, after all,
there were similar cases.
Cousin Ciccio, despite
that little flaw, had grown
into a fine person. So he swore to us.
Early on, he loved without hesitation.
But the father never liked those
"half women," those transvestites
who were "neither fish nor fowl."
As a boy, he had seen one,
ridiculous, selling body
by night and bric-a-brac
by day in the market.
He laughed, recalling it.
Some time later, he understood.
His love only faltered a few days.
He took two years to learn
the new name. But beneath his gaze
remained a barely perceptible anguish.
A kind of soundless keening.

∾

The mother had always wanted
a daughter. At one time
she had fantasized about names.
Vittoria had been her favorite.
But when she had a boy, she didn't
hesitate to give him her father's name.
In some places, the memory
of a father is passed on in a name.
It relights the memory of a loved one
plunged into time too soon.
That name bears responsibility,
keeps custody of the past.
The mother could not have
imagined the name betrayed
just twenty years later. Then
the mother felt a double death.
The first, when she lost her father
at fourteen. The second when,
the age of her father at his death,
she was orphaned anew.

∾

My mother's mother was convinced
that my "disease" was treatable.
She didn't know what it was: for sixty years
she'd kept away from such troubles.
But come to think of it, in her village
there'd been a certain Pippo.
They'd labeled him effeminate.
To those who called him *queer,*
fag, ricchione, he flashed
his small breasts, budded
with hormones. But he was a man
in other ways—she didn't doubt it.
So when she heard, terror took hold
of her. She imagined her grandson
with those breasts, straw hair,

shame all over his face.
She thought it was her own fault:
this grandson didn't know how
to grow up. After a month
of anguish, she decided
to take it up with the priest, to disturb
even God. Though even merciful God
might be incapable of expressing himself
on a subject of such mystery. She brightened up.
In truth, it didn't take much to convince her
that this was no worse than a benign growth.
She gave her grandson a brief article
from a Catholic magazine, which spoke
of people like Pippo, like her grandson.
"You see, Nonna's darling, the Church
accepts you. They say here
that what you have is normal.
The Lord loves you, the Pope
recognizes all as God's children."
Since then my mother's mother
rests easy, now that she is sure
her grandson will have
a place in heaven, even if
it is the last and the narrowest.

    (Translated by Dora Malech and Gabriella Fee)

From *Dove non siamo stati* (*Where We Haven't Been*)[3]

At the town's entrance slept an ancient
house, reddish stones visible
under the crumbling plaster. No one knew
how long the door had been bricked up,
how long the windows. All that moved
within it went undisturbed.

But there was a law: whoever drove
past had to aim three blasts
at the house: *so the kids watch
out as they cross the street.*

When the house was demolished to make
a clearing, something emerged from the foundations:
some bones, some torn clothes, little else.
It is said that in the house at the entrance to town
lived three mad young sisters.
They were walled in there, alive, to ward off misfortune.

And so one greets the women with three
firm blasts of the horn—to show
we still remember them. Because
the spirits of the disowned dead are touchy
creatures—and some small balances
are better left alone.

∽

Briskly he covered the country roads,
torso pressed forward as if in a race.
He carried a bag of oranges for someone,
ill-concealed his urgency.
Those who saw him witnessed his ceaseless
dialog with himself—*'S'mine, mine.*

The children laughed at his difference.
They passed him on bicycles shouting:
Cammela's'mine, Cammela's'mine, mine!
This stirred a blind fury in him, jealousy's
violent pain. He threw the fruit in the air,
trampled on it in despair, ran here and there.

Finally, the urgency of his task calmed him.
He bent down, gathered the oranges, surprised
by those still whole as by an immense blessing
he risked losing *These're for Cammela*
whispered *these're for Cammela 'n' she's mine alone.*

∽

In Floridia there were days of great sleep.
Children went to bed and woke up

grown—ages advancing like weeds in vases—,
the elders closed their eyes and passages
creaked like closing doors. An air fell
dense with torpor over Floridia and all, all would have
slept. Rosanna at thirteen had nodded off
for a while. Just long enough to lift her drowsiness.
Waking, she resembled her mother's sadness.
Photos of those others—games left in a circle,
the baby clotted in the womb.
Carmelo at twenty-one slept on the terrace
in the February light, as Alessandro at eighteen
with a scarf around his neck descended the stairs.
Giuseppe at forty slept more than anyone else
and when his wife tried to wake him, she found
a syringe of sleep by his side and let him be.

But some happened never to fall asleep
—nor to understand the meaning of that rest
while everyone else dozed slowly off—
and so departed, staring into the low fog
and laughing as if they'd escaped a horror.

Then slowed, looked back: *what have you forgotten?
What have you left inside?*—*It's nothing. Let's go.*

※

It was said some girl had been offended
by Carmine the neighbor and his knotted hands.
In the fruit storehouse that evening, Carmine
had panted like a beast—like a beast crushed everything
his fingers touched, upended everything.
Some smashed cherries left large,
misshapen stains on her dress.

*What the fuck's going through your head when you do these things?
Is this the education we gave you?*

And when her father slapped her, her mother
squeezed her legs tightly and turned her eyes away

so that her body would not betray the offense
and spread it like an uncontrolled
germ through the air.

∽

Of the places she wanted to return, there was her body
at sixteen—when even death was a game
borne lightly as air between fingers.
Returning would have been confirmation, momentary
consolation, that nothing had been ruined.
To return to the Sicilia of their faraway play
and say in amazement: *Here I am,*
I am you! This is what you wanted for me,
to save me. It would have been a final cure
for the tremor she could not name.

But she had to know she could only return
as if to overturned ground, as if to a make-believe
place. With the distracted care of one
who stops by, well aware they cannot stay.

∽

The places existed because there were stories
and the stories had the faces of neighbors
—tapping their fingers at the glass
of the doors, voices rising from the walls,
mysteries contained in the eyes.

They existed because someone was always telling them
—to the children perched in doorways,
to the elders sunk into patio chairs. Telling
as if to say slowly that where we have not been,
in time past or to come—coiling,
we were in the stories of others.
The voice gathered around a lamp, the wonder
of knowing in time—of not being dead.

We understood we will never have existed
when these stories are no longer told.

(Translated by Dora Malech and Gabriella Fee)

Notes

1. On Vivinetto's poetics see Danila Cannamela, "'I Am an Atypical Mother': Motherhood and Maternal Language in Giovanna Cristina Vivinetto's Poetry," *Forum Italicum* 55, no. 1 (2021): 85–108; Vivinetto's *Dolore minimo* (Chicago: Saturnalia Books, 2022) was translated into English by Dora Malech and Gabriella Fee.
2. Giovanna Cristina Vivinetto, *Dolore minimo* (Novara: Interlinea, 2018).
3. Giovanna Cristina Vivinetto, *Dove non siamo stati* (Milan: Rizzoli, 2020).

PART 2

THE *FEMMINIELLI*: A GENDER-VARIANT COMMUNITY BETWEEN PAST AND PRESENT

PART 2

THE FEMMINIELLA: A GENDER-VARIANT COMMUNITY BETWEEN PAST AND PRESENT

Chapter 5

"*Et io ne viddi uno in Napoli.*" *I femminielli*

Ricognizione storica e mitografica; Spunti per una riflessione sull'identità di genere ("And I saw one of them in Naples." *Femminielli*: Historical and Mythographic Recognition; Starting Points for a Reflection on Gender Identity)

Eugenio Zito, Paolo Valerio, and Nicola Sisci

This chapter, from the edited collection *Femminielli: Corpo, genere, cultura*, investigates the figure of the *femminiello*.[1] Here the authors analyze the historical and mythological elements of this ancient gender-variant figure, which is part of the Neapolitan culture, and in particular of its underprivileged classes. The chapter begins by examining the first historical evidence that testifies to the presence of the *femminielli* in Naples at the end of the sixteenth century, exploring the possible reasons that have allowed for their social inclusion within the local *cultura popolare* (folk culture). The investigation proceeds with a focus on the unique performative languages and social roles that the *femminielli* have built over time and that contributed to making them an integral part of the Neapolitan *cultura del vicolo* (the culture of the narrow streets, the *vicoli*, typical of the Neapolitan Spanish Quarters and some other neighborhoods of the city). From the figure of the mythical androgyne and the myth of the Great Mother, the "divinity that participates in the feminine and the masculine," up to exploring the story of the goddess Cybele, the chapter traces a cultural genealogy of the *femminielli* in Naples. The text ends with a look at the present, discussing how the great transformations of the last few decades have threatened the very existence of this ancient figure.

Oh blessed of the Madonna!
O miraculous son!

—Curzio Malaparte, *La pelle*, 1949

Introduction

The possibility of a *beyond* in the biological subdivision of the sexes has inhabited, since the origins of humanity, the place of myth and representation. At the same time, different cultures have contemplated—and in some cases, still contemplate—the possibility of a failed correspondence between biological sex and the subjective experience of belonging to a given sexual gender, apart from any pathologizing category—from the Native American *Berdache*, to the *Hijra* still present today in the context of India, from the *Muxé* of Zapotec society in Mexico (Miano Borruso 2002, 2011) to the object of this research: the *femminielli*[2] of Naples (Zito and Valerio 2010). This last phenomenon is perhaps dying out under the pressures of postmodernity, running the risk of transforming itself into forms not immediately recognizable (Vitelli 2006).

Expressing it in present-day language, we could place the complex reality of the *femminielli* in the universe of *transgenderism*.[3]

The roots, origin, and evolution of this phenomenon particular to the city of Naples are, in reality, still historically obscure, in the sense that there is no continuous and documented thread extending to our time (Zito and Valerio 2010).

We would first like to highlight how only very few *femminielli*, often old, appear to survive today. The probable extinction, if use of that term is permissible, perhaps has among its causes, on the one hand, social evolution in terms of a multiplication of identified diversities and, on the other, a global push toward cultural homogenization. Even the metamorphosis of the urban fabric of the city of Naples, particularly its working-class[4] neighborhoods after the earthquake of 1980, probably could have contributed to the transformation and gradual disappearance of the phenomenon.[5]

Et io e ne viddi uno in Napoli
[And I saw one of them in Naples]

The first literary source useful in historical reconstruction of the phenomenon leads us to Giovanni Battista Della Porta, who writes, in *De Humana Physiognomonia* (1586):

> On the island of Sicily there are many effeminates, and I saw one of them in Naples with few beard hairs or almost none, small of mouth, with delicate and straight eyebrows and shameful eyes, like a woman's. The weak, thin voice could not withstand much effort. He had an unstable neck, was pale in color, would bite his lips, and in short, had a feminine body and gestures. He willingly stayed at home and always had a crinoline, like a woman, attending to the kitchen and distaff. He fled from men and would gladly converse with the women. And staying among them, he was more of a woman than the women themselves. He thought like a woman and always used the feminine form: "sad me, bitter me."[6]

We can perhaps detect in this fragment the first description of a Neapolitan *femminiello*. Until now, we have been unable to find any other text that might provide such detailed (if meager) details on a phenomenological level. The author dwells both on morphological aspects and on behavioral. It is on these latter that we intend to invest our attention. The figure described behaves as if they were a woman and reasons like a woman—in fact, "attending to the kitchen and the distaff," activities of consummate female expertise at that time. "He fled from the men, and gladly conversed with the women," thus assuming the typical relational mode of women of the time. No descriptions of discriminatory events surface in the work. What the author describes is what was present there, in that street in Naples that so strongly captured his attention and therefore probably falls within the "ecology" of that specific context. This may reflect the tolerance that the *femminiello* already enjoyed in those years. Gabriella D'Agostino (2000) writes:

> The people of the working-class neighborhoods in which they lived, generally scorned homosexuality, particularly in the form of pederasty, but recognized and respected the sex of the *femminielli*.

80 | Zito, Valerio, and Sisci

Their difference, which appeared in adolescence, was culturally accepted. In Naples, families did not consider this type of difference a disgrace and did not marginalize the person. They integrated him into the family circle and in the wider context of the lane, the street, the quarter. The *femminiello* helped with domestic chores, carried out errands for the neighbors and was entrusted by the women of the neighborhood with looking after the youngest children.

The Affeminati of Naples

In a bibliographical study carried out at the Biblioteca Nazionale of Naples,[7] the following reproduction came to light, published in the text *Il segno di Virgilio* (*The mark of Virgil*) (De Simone 1982) (see figure 5.1).

Figure 5.1. "Ballo di Tarantella del'Affeminati di Napoli" [Dance of the Tarantella by the Affeminati of Naples], unknown author, 1700s. Public domain.

In the text in question, the name of the work's creator is not specified, nor is any source, the collection to which it belongs, or even a specific date. However, the image carries a caption in which it is possible to read "Dance of the Tarantella by the *Affeminati* of Naples." Although it is a photographic reproduction in black and white and of suboptimal quality, an expert in modern art history[8] has hypothesized that it might be a watercolor or colored etching created in the last quarter of the 1700s: the century of the Encyclopedia, the Grand Tour, and the first travel guides and reports. Therefore, it is very probable that the work in question was included in a travel guide or report that we have not, however, succeeded in finding in the Neapolitan archives.

The watercolor shows two people wearing men's clothing, but unlike the other men depicted in the scene, they seem to be taking on feminine moves during the dance of the *tammurriata*,[9] surrounded by a dense crowd of musicians and spectators in celebration, all of them amused and participating in the event. In the upper right of the image, we can identify in the background a castle-like building on a mountain, presumably the outline of Mount Partenio with the abbey of Montevergine. The work confirms the climate of popular tolerance that previously emerged in the passage by Della Porta. However, it would be naive to assert that the watercolor in question depicts a scene captured from real life, like a photograph. Rather, it is most probably a case of a "compositional study" in which the artist, in his *atelier*, tries to condense, in a limited space, the elements of the subject he intends to exhibit. The watercolor would, however, give a measure of how much a phenomenon like that of the *femminielli*, through the mediation of tradition, may have a place in society, to the point of becoming iconographically representative of a culture and a particular social reality. What is the source of the possibility of integration that the *femminielli* enjoyed in working-class Neapolitan society?

Sanctioning Belonging

There is a widespread saying in Naples, *femminielli si nasce* [one is born a *femminiello*], as if, in the popular imagination, that of the *femminiello* was a kind of natural diversity. In reality, we can assume that traditional society had the necessity to "produce" the *femminiello*, as if to reassure itself that the ambiguity completely placed somewhere—that is, in the *femminiello*—was a type of suitable exception in reconfirming the dominant gender roles. But we will return to this sociological aspect below, preferring now to linger anthropologically on the active aspects of integration carried out by the *femminielli*. "The *femminielli* are protagonists of a whole series of acts intending to affirm, permanently display, and ritually sanction their gender belonging" (D'Agostino 2000). Among these, those of greatest relevance are the *figliata* or *partorenza*, the *spusarizio*, the *riffa*, and the pilgrimage to Montevergine.[10]

The Riffa [Raffle]

One aspect that probably facilitated integration into the social fabric resided in the popular belief that the *femminielli* brought good luck. For this reason, there was entrusted to them the organization of the "raffle," or rather the public bingo that was carried out in many zones of the historic center of Naples. According to D'Agostino (2000):

> These behaviors confirm the assimilation of the *femminielli* in an environment that goes beyond the forms commonly known as "homosexual transvestitism." By virtue of their ambiguity, there can be attributed to them powers of a magical-sacred nature, typical of beings associated with signs of an undefined nature, impossible to classify with certainty and, because of this, related to the supernatural order from which they draw their validation.

The Neapolitan *femminielli*, then, bring good luck in the popular imagination, just as in the Classical age it was believed that good luck was brought by the *agùrtes*, the priests of Cybele who ritually castrated themselves for the goddess, but we will return to this aspect later.

The Spusarizio [Wedding]

An early description of this rite is included by Abele De Blasio in *Usi e costumi dei camorristi* [*Habits and customs of the Camorrists*], published in Naples in 1897. The title of the chapter is "*'O spusarizio masculino*" ["*The masculine wedding*"]:

> At the first dawning of puberty, the fairies feel the need to be . . . enjoyed. And once they find *l'ommo 'e mmerda* [the active

pederast],[11] they love him, as Mantegazza expresses well, with a true, ardent passion that has all the demands, all the jealousies of a true love. The *vasetto* ["little vessel"], completely content with the acquisition made, covers the lover with caresses and then seeks to scrape together as much as is necessary to prepare the altar where he goes to offer himself in . . . sacrifice. The place of the sacrifice is almost always some lurid inn where, at an established day and time, he goes to find his lover, a few accordion and guitar players, and a host of fairies who encircle the timid . . . girl. After an erotic ballet, the most experienced in the . . . matter wish the happy couple a good night. But the little bride, before letting the guests depart, distributes the traditional *tarallucci* and wine to them. The following day, the old fairy, accompanied by a traveling coffee maker, brings the spouses two small cups of milk and coffee and then does a careful review in the bridal chamber to ascertain that the sacrifice was completed in full accordance with the rules. After a honeymoon that lasts no longer than 24 hours, and toward evening, the sacrificed individual begins to meander through the highest quarters of the city in order to obtain for himself, like the prostitutes do, someone they can lead to the inn of Don Luigi Caprinolo, known as *'o capo tammurro* ["the chief drum"], or if the person is clean (a gentleman), to the special house of Lady Benedetta, *'a turrese* ["the woman from Torre del Greco"]. Meanwhile, while the active individual wallows in that "*loco d'ogni luce muto*" ["place where all light is silent"],[12] another scoundrel, who was previously hidden under the bed, steals his clothes, wallet, and any other valuable. . . . By day, our *femminelle* see to domestic chores, just as women do, and then, at an established time, they go to the window and await their lovers. Many *vasetti*, in order to render themselves more attractive to their customers, make-up their eyes. Others have a beauty mark tattooed onto their face, and many, by means of padding, try to make their posterior parts more shapely and their chests more projecting. Some even feminize their names.

De Blasio, a physician and anthropologist who lived and worked in Naples in the late nineteenth and early twentieth centuries, speaks in this work from 1897 of so-called "passive pederasts by profession, distinguished in the underworld with nicknames of young women, fairies, or *vasetti* and called by Brouardel 'delinquents born semi-female.'"[13] He describes a "wedding" of one of them with an "active pederast" lover, refers to a honeymoon, and speaks of the allurement they perpetrate to the detriment of clients so that they can later steal from them.

In the first part of the excerpt, a clear split emerges between the *ommo 'e mmerda* (active pederast) and the *ricchione* ([fairy] passive)—the latter term referring, precisely, to the *femminiello*. In this conceptualization, a clear distinction is made between he who is identified as the "homosexual" in a narrow sense (i.e., the individual who assumes the "passive" role in the sexual relationship) and the individual who assumes the "active" role, who does not consider himself—nor is he considered by others—to be homosexual. After all, in societies of the past that were largely patriarchal, the concepts of gender identity and sexual orientation did not exist, or even the terms homosexuality and heterosexuality, but rather that of sodomy or relations between people of the same sex, and what was stigmatized was the feminization of the male, where the passive was the effeminate person or he who assumed such a despised role, while he who had an active role was normalized. Such a dynamic propels us to take into consideration the existence of a type of social defense mechanism, to be placed in relation to what today we define as homophobia. In fact, by equating sexual orientation and gender, the very concept of homosexuality—understood as relations between two people of the same sex—disappears.

It appears that for De Blasio, then, the *femminiello* of the late nineteenth century also personifies a type of homosexual that today we would define as effeminate, placed in the delinquent social context of the mob, in the environment of the crowd that moved about in the underworlds of the city of Naples. Interpreted according to the Lombrosian model of the time (Bastide 1975), which connected psychophysical anomalies with delinquent degeneracy, [the *femminiello*] is characterized as a sexual deviant largely inclined to commit a crime. It is evident that we are dealing with an attempt to give the phenomenon a scientific and nosographic framing that uses the terminology of a naturalist criminologist.

Furthermore, our author presents a significant case of suicide as a result of jealousy, which places into evidence the attachment of these figures to their own lovers, described as intense and genuine, from which it can be deduced that "mental sodomy is not a vice, but a passion." Defining the affection under discussion as mental captures some distinctive aspects of the human type under observation, like the assumption of feminine behaviors and traditional feminine roles, and even recognizing a certain genuineness in their emotional passion; in doing so, De Blasio moves into the realm of cultural anthropology with a watchful eye toward some socio-psychological implications. He indicates that the phenomenon of the *femminelle* is very complex and the subject he has before him presents a series of questions that cannot be addressed and resolved with the instruments and categories that the era's positivistic stance placed at his disposition. They could represent something more and different from what could be seen in the context of patriarchal society and the scientific stances of the time. Some interpretive embarrassment is visible even in the linguistic uncertainty manifested in assigning grammatical gender to the term *femminella*: the word is used in a neutral tone without an article, with the feminine article, and at times with the masculine article.

In Di Giacomo's *La prostituzione in Napoli nei secoli XV XVI e XVII* [*Prostitution in Naples in the fifteenth, sixteenth, and seventeenth centuries*] (1899), we read that in Naples, starting in 1530, among the places designated by the authorities for the exercise of female prostitution, also identified were those used specifically by transvestites. This consisted of an area, *L'Imbrecciata*, that extended from Porta Capuana to the adjacent Sant'Antonio Abate where, even until the end of the nineteenth century, there existed *Femminelle* Alley, frequented only by those who were defined, at the time, as transvestites. De Blasio himself also talks about this disreputable street at the end of the nineteenth century, connecting the activities carried out there with organized crime, which had controlled the entire quarter since the eighteenth century.

We find another description of the phenomenon of the *spusarizio* nearly a century later in an article by Carrano and Simonelli published in 1983 in issue 18 of the French journal *Masques: Revue des homosexualites*. The wedding begins with the dressing of the "bride" in the presence of the godmother or witness. After having taken photos for the album, the "bride" goes to the entrance of the church where the "groom" is waiting— usually another *femminiello* who, on this occasion, wears men's clothing. The *femminielli* do not enter the church, but remain in the church square, limiting themselves to descending the steps, surrounded by the joyful crowd of friends and relatives. The "newlyweds" then go together in a luxurious car, along with a large audience of friends and others, to a restaurant for a wedding banquet in which a great many invited guests take part, with popular singers performing. The party goes on until night. According to Carrano and Simonelli (1983), these rites only appear to be imitative, since the conditions and rules on the basis of which they are celebrated would indicate, more than a union of sexes, an abolition of sexual roles. In fact, during the ceremony, the "spouses" leave their position as *femminielli* to re-disguise themselves by taking on, this time, the typical roles of the two sexes, male and female, presented at the moment in which their greatest difference is displayed—that is, in the wedding. During the wedding, the *femminielli* would not limit themselves to depicting the roles they assigned to themselves, but they would interpret them within a complex game of ambiguity that is not only sexual but above all symbolic, probably beyond their own intentions. The wedding is clearly "fake," not only because it is not recognized by the state and the Church but because it does not provide for any social transformation of the *femminielli* and of the relationship that exists between the "newlyweds." With regard to this point, the anthropologist Corinne Fortier states, in the course of an interview in the documentary *La Candelora a Montevergine* [*Candlemas at Montevergine*] (Valerio and Sisci 2007), that the traditional *femminielli* would have considered such a wedding "against nature." Therefore, it is evident that it is not the wedding, understood as a rite of passage, that constitutes the ultimate goal of the staged affair, but a more complex meaning exists, one ignored by the *femminielli* themselves. Carrano and Simonelli (1983) assert that all of this takes place with the goal of celebrating the union of the sexes in a situation that could be defined as a "two-level ephemeral wedding." The existence of such rites would not, therefore, be justified by the need for normality and acceptance, which among other things already belong to the *femminielli*, thanks to the role they play within the fold of their social group.

Comparison between Della Porta and De Blasio

Comparing the characteristics placed in evidence by the two authors, there would seem to exist, even in the socio-historical difference of positions and terms, a continuity through the three centuries that separate Della Porta's *effeminati* from De Blasio's *femminelle* (Zito and Valerio 2010). Back in time, however, the thread of the *femminielli*'s history, winds itself again into a ball of many threads that is not easy to unravel because of the absence of certain documentation and the use of terminologies under which the old authors placed the different phenomena that, in order to avoid confusion, should have required distinct terms. There are, however, some traces and clues. There exist some reported rumors, but they remain in the field of legend, of "they say."

However, if the documents described earlier are better analyzed, useful clues can be gathered for a hypothesis for reconstructing, with respect to the *femminielli*, a path of collective reality that actually dates back, although in different forms and specific manifestations, to the very origins of the city of Naples or at least to the Mediterranean region more generally. Still, with respect to southern Italy, a very low physical population density, particularly between the sixth or seventh centuries and the ninth century CE (the period of the greatest demographic depression of the population, with effects that extended to the fifteenth century), could have caused interruptions in continuity with respect to the traditions, ethnic patrimony, and anthropological elements of southern Italian culture and civilization, creating difficulties in the historical reconstruction of many phenomena and events of a socio-anthropological nature (Galasso 2009).

However, it is admissible that the quoted authors, speaking of their own times, may have in some way directly or indirectly offered us elements that reached them from the past and from earlier traditions regarding the object toward which they turned their attention in that moment. This similarly applies to news gathered from crime reports or from iconographic documents.

Della Porta is a late Renaissance author. This could make one think that his *effeminati* may be linkable to the figure of the Renaissance sodomite, in the form that the latter emerges from literary sources of the period and from studies done on them (Ruggiero 1988; Tannahill 1994; Scholz 2000). In the Renaissance context, the figure of the sodomite is that of an adult who assumes an active role in sexual relations with adolescent males who are always passive, except those who later eventually become active as adults. The author does not mention this, and the *effeminato* whom he saw in Naples is linked to similar figures present in a relevant way in Sicily. This leads us to think, rather, that Della Porta may be following, as a reference, a geographic path tied to the Mediterranean region, where the diffusion has been established, especially in coastal regions, of a particular conception of the condition that, today, we would frame within the scope of homosexuality. Within that, those identified as sodomites, in particular, take on a passive role, capable of assuming feminine roles and attitudes. There was a clear distinction between someone who assumed a passive role in sexual relations and he who carried out an active role, which was not regarded different either conceptually or linguistically from the male whom today we consider heterosexual. There is reflected same valid frame of reference for heterosexuality in a social context with a patriarchal structure, just as it is presented today in many countries that front the Mediterranean and in many Middle Eastern countries. There was maintained then—and there is maintained even today, in many social and geographical contexts—the bipolar pattern of clear separation between someone who assumes the passive feminine role and someone who assumes the active male one, with the dichotomy male/female, active/passive. It was recognized that anyone who assumed an active role in a sexual relationship was, however, considered male, while someone taking on a passive role was feminized and stigmatized. The social system survived then and survives today because, although a male might have had sexual predilections for persons of his own sex, if he carried out a sexually active role, he preserved his social role and did not undergo any stigmatization.

It was necessary, therefore, to create a denotational system to indicate who lived a passive role—that is, a type of woman (*femmenella*)—thus producing a type of subculture in which a special jargon is used and group socialization among similar individuals is fostered. This is the path that may be able to connect the *femminiello* to the lifestyle of the Roman *mollis*[14] and the Greek[15] *kinaidos*.[16]

On the other hand, we must remember the episode of the fire that occurred in 1611 on premises placed in close proximity to the Sanctuary of Montevergine, where numerous bodies of male pilgrims were found wearing women's clothes.

This, together with the iconography of the dancing *effeminati* described earlier, brings us back to a type of religious transvestitism, itself widespread in the Mediterranean region, that is tied to the sacredness of motherhood and fertility, with locally variable forms, and that finds its most noted form in the cult of the goddess Cybele. We call this hypothesis "sacred."

In the end, De Blasio offers us two pathways: the linguistic one born of the term *ricchione* and the socio-anthropological one that connects the *femminielli* to the common people, considered the depository of the city's oldest traditions and customs, in a type of archaic subculture resistant to all forms of evident change but ready to absorb new aspects and forms that respond in some way to its need for survival.

Lexicon and Social Representations

Much has been opined about the origin of the dialectal term *ricchione*, which is certainly of southern Italian origin.[17] For Battaglia (1990) and Cortellazzo (1999), the word may be connected to the term *hirculone*, referring to the *hircus*, or the billy goat, and would have a negative connotation in the sense of being unclean in one's sexual habits. It would be born, therefore, from the idea that an excess of lust would necessarily be transformed into sodomy or relations between persons of the same sex.

Another hypothesis, perhaps more plausible, traces the term to a verb in Calabrian dialect, *arrichià*, derived from *ad-hircare*, or "go toward or desire the *irco*," that is, the billy goat. It was used to designate the female goat in heat that was seeking the billy goat. *Arrichione* was a man who desired another man, not an animal-like being. It is also a more plausible hypothesis than the one advanced by Ballone, who saw, as the origin of the term, the nickname *orejones*, attributed in the sixteenth century by the Spanish to notable Incas who displayed artificially enlarged ears and who they considered sodomites devoted to the unmentionable vice. This path, however, may be traced back to a topographic fact—that is, the Spanish Quarter[18] in Naples, where the *femminielli* had traditionally always been present.

This linguistic reference brings us back once again, however, to the Mediterranean region and the use of a term that serves to indicate, in zones within this area, the condition of a man who assumes female sexual roles and who behaves as a woman (Zito and Valerio 2010).

The socio-anthropologic evidence present in the work of De Blasio, then, is more mysterious and in a certain sense, takes in all the others. In fact, one could say that the *femminielli* must already have appeared to De Blasio as men who felt and lived as women and that their belonging to the underworld crowd did not just and only have a delinquent character but rather was born from a link with the "lower" common people that in some way connects them to most remote part of the city of Naples, dating, in fact, to its origins.

At this point, it becomes necessary to attempt to advance a lexical analysis of the term *femminiello*, in order to trace the representation it contributes to conveying. Our attempt does not presume to be exhaustive, given that the term does not seem to be recorded in the majority of etymological dictionaries and vocabularies of the Italian and/or Neapolitan languages. Further, we are aware that advancing a hypothesis on a linguistic and lexical level equates, unavoidably, to advancing an interpretive hypothesis of an anthropological-relational phenomenon.

The term *femminiello* consists of the root *femmin-*, the modifier *-ell-*, and the ending *-o*. The root *femmin-* would refer to a positioning/attribution relating to the female gender, which may connote a meaning that is largely of identity (feeling like a woman) or more simply of role (behaving like a woman). The orientation toward the gender role that seems to be justified by the socially shared representation of the *femminiello* may be deduced by the modifier and the ending. The modifier *-ell-* is a diminutive with an added value of endearment. The diminutive value would highlight both a "reductive" dimension of being (and, therefore, of not being) female, and an attitude of "benevolent subordination and covering" tinged with a perception of "small and incomplete." The added endearment value, on the one hand, would express an instance of consensus (with something sentimental, tender, and good natured implicit in the affective constellation of social representation). On the other, it would position the subject, who is the addressee, in a dimension of mocking and of light derision that probably refers to a necessity for distance from that which, being so different, elicits uneasiness. In essence, it is in the modifier *-ell-* that resides all the ambiguity implicit in the social representation of the *femminiello*. The ending *-o*, which in the Italian language expresses the masculine gender, would function as a counterpoint to the question posed by the root *femmin-*, mitigating the strength of the content it expresses, thus carrying, in such a denomination, the idea of a link to the principle of reality. Pushing further, we could presume that the root *femmin-* refers to "wanting to be," the ending *-o* to the "real being," and the *-ell-* to "all that could be"—the infinite intermediate emotional colorings tied to the representation of this "character" (Cuomo et al. 2009).

We hypothesize, then, that the *femminiello*'s anthropological and social function would reside, on the one hand, in creating an opportunity out of a collective defense mechanism rigidly structured in the patriarchal sense, through which the male subject who assumes a passive role in the environment of sexual relations is feminized or considered as a slightly "defective" woman, while he who assumes an active role is considered as a man in all effects. On the other hand, in the unconscious gratification in contact with the "feminine side," there is undifferentiated unity, the omnipotent fantasy of primary narcissism.

This "bi-logical" representation of the *femminiello*, articulated between fascination/attraction on one hand and distancing/isolation on the other, also seems to be confirmed in the socio-geographical contextualization of such a *character* within the Spanish Quarters, poor and working-class, close to Corso Vittorio Emanuele and Via Toledo, the "good" and middle-class streets of the city. In Naples, the principle structural elements that distinguish the figure of the *femminiello* are likely shared, and they constitute specific modalities of organizing, in terms of contents and familiar explanations, that which—conversely—is difficult for the consciousness to explain and comprehend.

From a Lacanian point of view (Lacan 1966), the *femminiello* may represent for others—men and women—a departure from the prohibited: the possibility, found in the similar, of being other than that which the symbolic codes prescribe with their transcendence onto the plane of the real.

On the other hand, still as a hypothesis, we could think that there functions a counterpart to fascination/attraction, the impulse to segregate, to hold enclosed within circumscribed spatial limits (the working-class quarters, *the belly of Naples*)[19] that which is most disturbing: the encounter with the realization of the original omnipotence-impotence and the relative anxieties described by Melanie Klein (1978).

It is this *belly*, a social fabric that is homogeneous yet loaded with heterogeneity, that becomes the only possible receptacle of the coexistence of feminine and masculine, of sacred and profane.

These "unions" or fusions of different elements also find a common root in the esoteric culture that, in Naples, dates back to the Middle Ages and even further, to the legends of the "Virgilio Mago" and in fact much earlier, to the Mysteries of Isis, tied to the culture of the Alexandrians, who made up a considerable colony in Naples. The figure of the god Nilo, dominating the small piazza of that name, is the evident symbol of that mixture of cultures and rites. The simultaneous presence of the sacred and profane is fused with *Neapolitanness* [*napoletanità*], understood here as the city's traditional and artistic manifestation. One need only think of the inclusion, in the Neapolitan crèche, of a figure so desecrating and profane as that of the *femminiello*, beside the figures of sacredness.

There the story must necessarily surrender the field to a mythography that must not be considered an eminent place of irrationality but a place that, upon inhabiting it, it is similarly possible to confront the uncertainty of the human adventure when it passes to the level of documentary checking of the certainty of sources.

The *Femminielli* between Myth, History, and Culture

In Greco-Roman antiquity, the androgyne, a human being seen in some ways as bi-gendered, was considered, in the acts and substance of daily life, evil even if numinous. For this reason, they were distanced from the city or actually eliminated. In some circumstances, the expulsion was accompanied by some rites like those described by Diodorus Siculus (frag. XXXII) and Titus Livius (XXVII, 36,7). Uprooted from reality, the androgyne played, as compensation, a considerable role in the field of the imagination. It was an archaic myth in the Mediterranean region, according to Eliade (1976), a *widespread universal archetype* of great socio-anthropological value that had taken on and summed up all of those sexual situations that were not neatly feminine or masculine but that participated in the nature of both. At the symbolic level, they were a symbolic myth, evoking the concept of the interlinked polarity of every form of duality, and they were the image of ambiguity.

Plato promoted this myth and originally set, in the existence of a third gender (specifically, the androgyne) the conceptual and metaphoric connection between the theme of love—which is central in the *Symposium* (Cerinotti 1989) and considered an expression of human nostalgia for a lost wholeness—and the theme of parity between man and woman, which Plato considers fundamental in the political thought expressed in the *Republic* (Lozza 2003).

Therefore, we may consider that in Plato's vision, there reemerges the ancient feminine soul of the Mediterranean, which constitutes another distinct and parallel expression of that original unity of the human psyche and its creative power, which is then manifested in the myths and rites descending from the distant tradition of the Primordial Mother. According to the contention of Neumann in *La grande madre* (1981, 1st ed. 1955), the myth of the Great Mother is a fundamental archetype, the synthesis of prolific fullness and the principle of transformation—that is, of a divinity that participates in the feminine and the masculine. It is a type of divine androgyne (Eliade 1976) that is a reflection and abstraction of the original unity of the human psyche considered in its dynamics between fusion and separation, between symbiosis and connection.

We are dealing with a complex of very ancient cultural traditions that also perpetuate themselves even through the memory of the first agricultural clans in human history, in which the woman-mother had part of her pre-eminence through her capacity to place into the world, and through her abilities in recognizing, preserving, and planting agricultural seeds. In this complex of cultural traditions, the female was often conceived as self-sufficient and therefore virginal. Descending from the Paleolithic, she was shown in the sculptures of the so-called prehistoric Venuses, and then found expression in, among others, the cult of the Great Mother. In the case of the self-sufficient female, within the Egyptian-Anatolic-Cretan zone during an age already historical (1500 BCE), there also recurred the iconography of the ornithomorphic sirens, virginal sirens that were half woman, half bird, like the original siren Parthenope from Campania (800 BCE).

We can hypothesize that the representation of the female in the "prehistoric Venuses," considered to be depictions of the Primordial Mother, may progressively pass, in iconographic form, through the *Venuses of Malta*, the *Matres Matutae* of Capua, and the *Magna Mater Cibele* of Frigia, arriving at the various images of the Madonna present in Christian culture. This testifies to—while taking on, in the course of millennia, different cultural values, more articulated and specific—the continuity of the primary and sacred value of femininity (Neumann 1981) in the Mediterranean region (Fernandez 1967) and more generally, in southern European-Asiatic territories.

This subject of the original female in the Mediterranean offers useful clues for tracing some of the anthropological and cultural roots peculiar to the phenomenon of the *femminielli* of the working-class quarters of the city of Naples. It is not by chance that the term *femminiello* has a strong allusive charge that is particularly meaningful. Grammatically, it is male in gender but, as previously noted, on the etymological and semantic level, it refers to the female universe (Zito and Valerio 2010).

In Naples, therefore, this type of transgenderism and transvestitism, specifically that of the *femminielli*, is differentiated from analogous phenomena of other large Western cities. And it is an urban transgenderism and therefore different from that which expresses tribal roles, as in the case of the *Berdache* among the Mohave of North America (D'Agostino 1998), or essentially religious roles present in some populations of the Far East (Herdt 1993). It is not a disguise of manhood. It is not simply tied to traditions of folk theatricality documented by works like the so-called *Ballo di Sfessania* or the *Canzone di Zeza*, which date, respectively, to the sixteenth and seventeenth centuries, in which often the *femminielli* were utilized in fundamental roles. In reality, it nearly presents the traits of a natural condition of diversity and of a sexual expression that has its own reality, broadly recognized and integrated within its social context, with aspects of ritual sacredness and an archaic flavor deeply stratified in the culture (Simonelli and Carrano 1987). And the two aspects of sacredness and social integration are correlated, because the current rituality presents itself particularly in the representation of fundamental ceremonies of social life, such as marriage, birth, and baptism, in the exercise of prophesy in various forms and in the recognized power to bring good fortune.

Naples is a city that carries, stratified within its distinctive culture, the ancient feminine soul of the Mediterranean. The anthropological literature highlights the feminine nature of the city, reviving the myth of the Great Mediterranean Mother, recalling the rites of Cybele and then of Venus, goddess of fertility, in the Platamonic grottoes of Chiatamone. Naples is still the menstruating city of San Gennaro and Santa Patrizia (Niola 1994). Its archaeology also alerts to us the existence of fertility rites in the grottoes of Piedigrotta and the ancient temple of Ceres in the area of Santa Patrizia (Arcidiacono 1999).

Naples, female city, therefore permits some men to present the feminine side of their nature even in a context that has always felt the effects of patriarchal order, dating back to the Greek colonization of the eighth and seventh centuries BCE and firmed up in the course of Western civilization's development, but joined with ancient matriarchal Italic cults and matri-centric familial structures (Belmonte 1997) that were active and dynamic in the configuration of the city's soul through transmission of a much displayed, almost theatrical, rituality such as in the "spusarizio" previously discussed. In fact, particularly striking in this latter case is the broad participation of the entire quarter, young people and old—men, women, and children whose presence highlights the reality that the *femminiello* does not represent a deviant (D'Agostino 1998), as much as an almost "magical" figure. In fact, through community participation in the rites at which the *femminielli* are the officiants, each person can cathartically achieve the sensation of obtaining temporary liberation from their own ills. This is analogous to what happened with the rites celebrated by the *Gallae*, the castrated and cross-dressed priests of the Great Mother Cybele, whose cult, coinciding and overlapping with the cult of the *Matres Matutae*, historically was widespread on Partenio (Montevergine) and in the entire area between the Phlegraean zone north of Naples and Capuan territory, starting from the second century CE.

The myth tied to Cybele holds particular importance both on the level of historical-cultural matrices of the *femminielli* phenomenon in Naples, through its ritual aspects, and for a possible interpretation of this phenomenon of transgenderism and its differences with respect to other forms of transsexuality, on a symbolic and analytical level through its substantive aspects. In the myth, Cybele produces a cycle of life and death centered on the emasculation of Attis, a divine figure whom she generates herself (through the fertile blood of her hermaphrodite son Agdistis and the nymph Nana), marries, and then indirectly kills in order to have him reborn. Through a process of mimesis, in the rituality derived from the myth, the priest-followers of Attis self-castrated themselves, cross-dressed, and carried out their duties as women.

The chronicles have passed down to us the existence, presumably situated directly in the zone of Montevergine in the province of Avellino, of a temple dedicated to the goddess *ctonia* of the grottoes and mountains closely related to the cult of Cybele. Giordano, the abbot of Montevergine and a historian, in *Croniche di Montevergine* (1649), asserts with regard to this that the local tradition cited by all the historians of Montevergine claimed that the mountain took the name Cybele from a temple located there. The hagiographer Bargellini, in *Mille santi del Giorno* (1977), speaking of the sanctuary of Montevergine's founding by Saint Guglielmo, also reports that it occurred on Partenio near the ruins of a temple dedicated to the pagan goddess Cybele. Finally, according to the tradition recorded by *Martirologio Gerominiano*, dating to the first half of the eighth century, also picked up and developed in the *Martirologio Beneventano di Santa Maria del Gualdo*, dating from the twelfth century, Saint Vitaliano, bishop of Capua in the seventh century, had withdrawn to Partenio (the current Montevergine) after having been involved in an obscure matter of transvestitism, and there he had constructed a chapel dedicated to the Madonna on the remains of a temple dedicated to Cybele (De Simone 1982).

The fundamental moments of the cult of Cybele were the ascent toward the sacred mountain, the adoration of a holy stone, and the presence of faithful males cross-dressed as women who displayed a frenetic and ecstatic devotion with unrestrained songs and dances to the sound of drums and cymbals. In the Christian era, this cult would have been progressively replaced, as happened in other pagan zones and sanctuaries, by the cult of the Madonna. However, some manifestations of this ancient rituality would be preserved, a specific dowry of transvestite and transsexual followers in Campania. Even today, the ascent to the sanctuary of Montevergine constitutes one of the fundamental and highly ritualized moments in the life of the *femminielli*. Every year, on the day of the Candelora, they climb the mountain bound for the sanctuary dedicated to the *Mamma Schiavona*, the Black Madonna. From the belly of Partenope to the peak of Partenio, the rite of the *femminielli*'s pilgrimage to the sanctuary is repeated: they are accompanied by people playing castanets, *tammorre*, and cymbals and dressed in a way that is decorously showy and neat, with particularly colorful garments. The first stop occurs near a grotto where a rough stone seat can be found, an ancient reminder of the sacred stone of the cult of Cybele. Then one leaves again in order to reach the holy staircase, a flight of twenty-three steps that one often climbs while kneeling, singing a verse on every step and, finally, presenting oneself before the Holy Mother. After the visit, in the areas facing the sacristy, they dance and sing with music and obsessive rhythms, with gestures that combine expressions of sincere devotion and movements of very ancient rituality that mimic the gestures of harvesting and gathering of fruit, not lacking in sexual allusions. It is meaningful that people are arranged all around in a circle: men, women, children, and old people watching admiringly, applauding, and often participating. Together in this event are elements of the present-day, of antiquity, and above all, expressions and demonstrations of great inclusion and integration (De Simone 1982).

If the myth of Cybele transferred its rituality into demonstrations of devotion to the Madonna on the part of the *femminielli*, thus offering proof of a continuity between the transvestitism of the *Gallae* priests and that of the present-day *femminielli*, in a symbolical and analytical respect, through the reading that Neumann (1981) gives it, it offers elements useful for framing the transsexual phenomenon. The transsexual would experience, in themselves, the myth of Attis, and as such, would tend to self-emasculate so that, through castration, they might become the Mother herself. We could therefore speak of a development of the mind through which the subject, not separating themselves from the primordial images, does not become autonomous in their own identity different from that of the procreational mother. The transsexual would not succeed either in ritualizing nor in living and overcoming on a symbolic level the urge to possess a vagina: they would live their own male body as an error of nature. In this respect, the symbiotic son described by Stoller (1968) may, in a certain way, be compared to Attis, the son-lover of the Great Mother. If not separated from one's real mother and from that archetype, he is deprived of the possibility of recognizing himself and identifying himself as male, different and separate from her. The solutions at this point may be of at least two types: that of either becoming a woman symbolically, keeping one's own male genitals intact, or the real one of castrating oneself by undergoing a surgical intervention of reconversion of sexual characteristics.

The two positions may be located along the chromatic system of gender described by Rothblatt (1995) at notably different points (Abbate et al. 2004).

We notice, however, in the case of the *femminiello*, a different situation in that he carries out the overcoming of his own masculinity on a more ritual and symbolic level. In other words, he perpetuates his symbiosis with his mother apart from achievement of a complete assimilation at the biological level.

We can assert that this may constitute the distinctive element of this transgenderism, married to an archaic, stratified origin in the particular cultural context in which it arose.

In conclusion, it would seem that the uniqueness of the *femminielli* of Naples, on the socio-anthropological level, is that of having perpetuated, with continual adjustment to historical and social changes, this archaic tradition of ritual and psychological identification with the original feminine and therefore with the Great Mother. That of the *femminielli* would therefore be configured as a third gender, with its own typical universe of meanings—that is, another identity, clearly distinct both from the female gender and the male without, however, crossing the border of the inferior, thanks to an accepting and tolerant society, the bearer of a culture that is so old, stratified, and in essence so evolved as to embody a type of *sui generis* post-modernity (Zito and Valerio 2010).

Concluding Reflections: Extinction or Transformation?

In conclusion, we would like to advance a series of reflections on the current state of the *femminielli* in the urban Neapolitan context.

The disappearance and/or profound transformation that it seems that the phenomenon of the *femminielli* is facing could also be thought of as a consequence of the profound changes at the urbanistic, architectonic, and cultural levels that Naples has undergone in passing into contemporaneity. The contemporary metropolis, an expression indivisible from the capitalistic mode of production, is born amid the overtaking of what were previously bound and limited urban organisms, including factors that could have led to drastic reorganizations. The metropolis is a more resistant organism because it feeds upon differences, producing new ones, beginning with diversified opportunities for investment and valuation of capital. The role and social function that the *femminielli* represented would seem, instead, to be tied to the idea of an "anti-capitalistic" closure of the street economy, to a type of self-management that, with the fraying of the urban fabric and the urgent pressure of globalizing impulses, has analogously let fray traditions, understood as "conservation and transmission of a culture," a way of "equipping oneself for life" that strongly connote belonging to this city. We are thinking of the disappearance of the street trades that are now iconographic in the sources in the historical archives. However, not wanting to reduce our analysis to just the urban context, we can assert that even the few *femminielli* who can be found in the countryside of the areas near

Vesuvius and Avellino move in a very narrow context and are included in a subculture of a rustic sort that, itself, seems to be on the way to extinction. This advancement of globalization has produced new social forms in which "diversity" can be set. We refer to these just as we do to societal forms, since we ask ourselves if the personal needs of those who request a change of sex, for example, might not respond, in a mirror-like way, to an offer coming from the society going in that direction (Cuomo et al. 2009). We then pose this question: Are those who, today, subject themselves to surgical experience for the reattribution of sex the ones who, in the past, negotiated their presence in society as "different," or rather are they to be considered of completely different subjective conditions, moved by different needs? In this regard, what Schinaia (2006) asserts seems interesting to us, in taking up the psychoanalytic thought of some Lacanian authors:

> We have passed from a culture founded on representation, based on the evocation of the desired object, to a culture of presentation that consists of automatically and immediately appropriating—unmediated—the object itself. In other words, we have passed from a culture based on the removal of desires, and therefore on neuroses, to another that recommends their free expression and satisfaction and, in that manner, promotes perversion.

According to this perspective, the *femminiello* would fall within the representative modality in which *being* female and *feeling* female were mediated by practices of transvestitism, playful vitality, and role, all within a lively frame of social relations (Zito and Valerio 2010). Conversely, transsexuality would suggest a passage to a reified desire that *presents* itself under the form of irreversible bodily *transformation*. All of this would also give the measure of a much more solipsistic process in which gender identity no longer seems to be an investigation of self in relation to the social other, but an abrupt process that manifests itself at the very moment in which the passage is concluded, first, to the *diagnostic-juridical* act and then to the *surgical*.

(Translated by Gianpiero W. Doebler)

Notes

1. The chapter is from the book, *Femminielli: Corpo, genere, cultura*, edited by Eugenio Zito and Paolo Valerio (Naples: Libreria Dante and Descartes, 2019), 37–68.

2. Translator's note (t/n): Pronounced fem-ee-NYELL-ee.

3. By transgenderism, we mean that reality of persons who, living a gender identity opposed to their own biological sex, do not desire to completely change their own body but want and ask to be able to express, in their behaviors and interpersonal relations, the feeling of themselves to be a man or woman, beyond their own anatomical structure and without having to be forced into homogenization of any sort. Further, the term also seems to have another, broader meaning, referring to a condition characterized by a gender identity in movement that does not identify steadily with the male or female gender.

4. Ed./n: The term "working class" does not exhaust the cultural and social nuances of the Neapolitan context examined in this chapter. The original Italian word, "*popolare*," with reference to the city of Naples, may include several social categories such as the underclass, lower classes, and/or underpriviledged communities that have changed over time. As Marzia Mauriello has observed: "If we are to speak of popular culture in Naples, it is necessary to add the adjectives 'urban and modern' to 'popular' (Signorelli, 2003: 21). This makes it even more complicated to establish 'objective' criteria—such as income (basically low), educational level (basically low), work (its lack or its tendency to be atypical, informal, and sometimes illicit)—as a means to identify the *popolino* or the lower classes in Naples." See Mauriello, *An Antropology of Gender Variance and Trans Experience in Naples: Beauty in Transit* (London: Palgrave Macmillan, 2021), 40, n. 4.

5. This probable phase of transition is very well explained in the documentary by the anthropologist Massimo Andrei, *Cerasella, ovvero l'estinzione della femminella* (*Cerasella, or the extinction of the* femminella), produced by the Università degli Studi di Napoli Federico II in 2007 and available in the archives of SOF-tel of that university.

6. T/n: The original Italian text employs the feminine form of the adjectives "sad" and "bitter."

7. We would like to thank Dr. Mauro Giancaspro for his kind availability shown during our research.

8. We would like to thank Dr. Luigi Corro for his guidance.

9. The *tammurriata*, or "dance or song with drum," is an ancient music-dance form still widespread in some areas of Campania, where it is practiced in many variants. It takes place principally in the environment of "festivals," seasonal celebrations of collective rituality associated with "working-class" religiosity and particularly with the devotional cult addressed to the different madonnas, venerated in these places. The *tammurriata* is a direct expression of rustic culture and is therefore connected to archaic beliefs and cults of very old pre-Christian origin.

10. With regard to the psychosocial and anthropological aspects of the pilgrimage, the reader is referred to viewing the documentary *La Candelora a Montevergine*, by Paolo Valerio and Nicola Sisci, produced by the Università degli Studi di Napoli Federico II in 2007 and available in the archives of SOF-tel at that university.

11. T/n: Literally, in Neapolitan dialect, "man of shit."

12. T/n: This is a well-known description in Dante's *Inferno* (5:28) of the second circle of hell, where the lustful are punished.

13. Abele De Blasio. *Usi e costumi dei camorristi 1897* (Naples: Torre, 1993), 99.

14. The expression literally means "effeminate" and is present in different Latin authors, including Petronius (*Satyricon* 23.3).

15. However, Salvian of Marseille, in the fifth century BCE, in *De gubernatione Dei*, stigmatized the fact that in Carthage there were men who dressed as women and were sexually passive.

16. The Greek term originally had the meaning of "dancer" and, subsequently, "effeminate young man" (Plato, *Gorgias* 494) and as such, it passed into the Latin language, becoming *cinaedus* (Catullus, *Carmina* 29).

17. T/n: A widely recognized pejorative epithet commonly translated as "fairy" or "fag."

18. Regarding this, in a note to his text, *Un paradiso abitato da diavoli* (*A paradise occupied by devils*), Benedetto Croce, citing Bouchard, reports rumors that circulated regarding the reasons why, during the sixteenth century, many Spaniards enlisted to go to Italy—among them, those homosexual tendencies—with the aim of fleeing persecution by the Inquisition, which was very active at the time in Spain. See Benedetto Croce, *Un paradiso abitato da diavoli*, ed. Giuseppe Galasso (Milan: Adelphi, 2006).

19. T/n: *The Belly of Naples* is a famous collection of articles in defense of the working-class neighborhoods of Naples by journalist and author Matilde Serao, first published in 1884.

References

Abbate, Luigi, et al. 2004. *Il Sesso*. Milan: Cortina.
Arcidiacono, Caterina. 1999. *Napoli diagnosi di una città*. Naples: Magma.
Ballone, Edoardo. 1978. *Uguali e diversi*. Milan: Mazzotta.
Bargellini, Piero. 1977. *Mille santi del giorno*. Florence: Vallecchi-Massimo.
Bastide, Roger. 1975. *Antropologia applicata*. Turin: Boringhieri.
Battaglia, Salvatore. 1990. *Grande Dizionario della Lingua Italiana*, v. 15. Turin: Utet.
Belmonte, Thomas. 1997. Originally published 1989. *La fontana rotta. Vite napoletane: 1974, 1983*. Rome: Meltemi.
Carrano, Gennaro, and Simonelli, Pino. 1983. "Un mariage dans la baie de Naples." *Masques. Revue des Homosexualities* 18, 105–15.
Cerinotti Angela, ed. 1999. *Platone: Simposio*. Milan: Giunti Demetra.
Cortellazzo, Manlio, and Paolo Zolli. 1999. *Dizionario Etimologico della Lingua Italiana (DELI)*. Bologna: Zanichelli.
Croce, Benedetto. 2006. *Un paradiso abitato da diavoli*, edited by Giuseppe Galasso. Milan: Adelphi.

Cuomo, Aurora, et al. 2009. "Los Femminielli napolitanos: Reflexiones preliminares." In *Salud y Sociedad: Perspectivas antropològicas*, edited by Florencia Pena Saint-Martin, 167–86. Mexico City: Istituto Nacional de Antropologìa e Historia.

D'Agostino, Gabriella. 1998. "Il sesso ambiguo: Pratiche e funzioni del travestitismo." *Archivio Antropologico Mediterraneo* 1 (no. 0): 93–112.

———. 2000. "Travestirsi: Appunti per una trasgressione del sesso." In *Sesso e Genere: L'identità maschile e femminile*, by Sherry B. Ortner and Harriet Whitehead, 11–51. Sellerio: Palermo.

De Blasio, Abele. 1993. *Usi e costumi dei camorristi*. Originally published 1897. Naples: Torre.

De Simone, Roberto. 1982. *Il segno di Virgilio*. Edited by Azienda Autonoma di Cura, Soggiorno e Turismo di Pozzuoli. Pozzuoli: Sezione Editoriale Puteoli.

Di Giacomo, Salvatore. 1968. *La prostituzione in Napoli nei secoli XV, XVI e XVII*. Naples: Edizioni del Delfino.

Eliade, Mircea. 1976. *Miti sogni misteri*. Milan: Rusconi.

Fernandez, Dominique. 1967. *Madre mediterranea*. Milan: Mondadori.

Galasso, Giuseppe. 2009. *L'altra Europa: Per un'antropologia storica del Mezzogiorno d'Italia*. Naples: Guida.

Herdt, Gilbert. 1993. *Third Sex, Third Gender: Beyond Sexual Dimorphism in Culture and History*. New York: Zone Books.

Klein, Melanie. 1978. *Scritti 1921–1958*. Turin: Bollati Boringhieri.

Lacan, Jacques. 1966. *Ecrits*. Paris: Editions du Seuil.

Lozza, Giuseppe, ed. 2003. *Platone: La Repubblica*. Milan: Mondadori.

Miano Borruso, Marinella. 2002. *Hombre, mujer y muxé en el Istmo de Tehuantepec*. Plaza e Vadès: INAH.

———. 2011. "Muxé et femminielli: Genre, sexe, sexualité et culture." *Journal des Anthropologues* 124–25, 179–98.

Neumann, Erich. 1981. *La Grande Madre*. Rome: Astrolabio-Ubaldini.

Niola, Marino. 1994. *Totem e Ragù*. Naples: Pironti.

Rothblatt, Martine Aliana. 1995. *The Apartheid of Sex: A Manifesto on the Freedom of Gender*. New York: Crown.

Ruggiero, Guido. 1988. *I confini dell'eros: Crimini sessuali e sessualità nella Venezia del Rinascimento*. Venice: Marsilio.

Schinaia, Cosimo. 2006. "Tra continuità e discontinuità: Intrecci del moderno e del postmoderno in psicoanalisi." *Psicoterapia e Scienze Umane* 40, 165–80.

Scholz, Piotr. 2000. *L'eros castrato: Storia culturale degli eunuchi*. Genoa: Edizioni Culturali Internazionali.

Simonelli, Pino, and Gennaro Carrano. 1987. "Mito e seduzione dell'immagine femminile a Napoli." In *Sessualità e sessuologia nel Sud: Atti del Convegno Società Italiana di Sessuologia Clinica*, edited by Rita Mattace Raso, 17–23. Naples: Società Editrice Napoletana.

Stoller, Robert J. 1968. *Sex and Gender: The Transsexual Experiment*. London: Hogart Press.
Tannahill, Reay. 1994. *Storia dei costumi sessuali*. Milan: Rizzoli, 1994.
Vitelli, Roberto, Mario Bottone, Nicola Sisci, and Paolo Valerio. 2006. "L'identità transessuale tra storia e clinica: Quale intervento per quale domanda." In *Gay e lesbiche in psicoterapia*, edited by Paolo Rigliano and Margherita Graglia, 281–322. Milan: Raffaello Cortina.
Zito, Eugenio, and Paolo Valerio. 2010. *Corpi sull'uscio, identità possibili: Il fenomeno dei femminielli a Napoli*. Naples: Filema.

Chapter 6

From *Altri transiti: Corpi, pratiche, rappresentazioni di femminielli e transessuali* (*Other Transitions: Bodies, Practices, Representations of Femminielli and Transsexuals*)

MARIA CAROLINA VESCE

This essay documents three specific performances of the Neapolitan *femminielli*: the game of *tombola*, the mock wedding, and the re-enactment of childbirth—the so-called *figliata*.[1] Anthropologist Carolina Vesce analyzes the processes that have turned *tombola* (a game similar to bingo) into an element of the Neapolitan cultural heritage. The essay emphasizes that the *femminielli*, who have historically been the main players of *tombola*, have contributed to the creation of shared cultural capital by shaping the game into a theatrical event. Vesce illustrates that nowadays the "*tombola* of the *femminielli*" is perceived by, and sold to, the general audience as an "authentic" Neapolitan tradition. She recounts here her fieldwork encounters with and participation in the games organized by local LGBTQ+ organizations, such as AFAN (Associazione Femmenell Antiche Napoletane). In the last part of this excerpt, Vesce explores how some of the *femminielli*'s performative practices, including mock weddings and *la figliata*, have contributed to the construction of their social identity, and in particular to the internalized and shared feeling of being (part of) the Neapolitan tradition.

Tombola: This Is Where We Get Crazy

In an article published in the magazine *Lares*, Alessandra Broccolini[2] recounts her experience of researching the game of *tombola*[3] in the city of Naples. At the height of the "Neapolitan Renaissance," when, under the leadership of Bassolino's city council and its "Department of Civic Identity," the city had been recolonized by tourists and enriched by cultural initiatives, Broccolini took an interest in the game of *tombola*, with an emphasis on its adaptability. Whether publicized for the media or the tourist trade or dramatized for theatrical effect, *tombola* lends itself to diverse spheres of communication, bringing in audiences of television viewers, tourists, lovers of folk culture, or, simply, members of the underprivileged classes, as in the case of the *tombola dei femminielli* organized by a well-known restaurant in Naples's historic downtown, to which Broccolini refers at the beginning of her article. However, the scope of Broccolini's field research does not extend to that version of the game, in which it has been transformed into a spectacle or public event. What interests the ethnographer, rather, is the type of bingo played behind closed doors, in *bassi*[4] in the Santa Lucia district, within the "private" sphere of the community of women who would come together every Wednesday, to paraphrase the title of Broccolini's article, for *pazzià a tumbulella*.[5]

Broccolini notes how we could speak of the "genderization" of recreational activities in Naples and underscores the redistributive function of the game of *tombola* within Neapolitan society. The clear distinction between the genders and the separation of male and female roles is one of the possible explanations for the fact that the game of *tombola* is typically associated with the feminine sphere, while card games, according to Broccolini, are viewed as masculine. Participants in the game adhere to a principle of gender that never makes provision for the presence of both sexes. As the author underscores:

> If a man wished to play with the women, he would run the risk of being ridiculed and called a *femminiello*[6] (meaning an effeminate homosexual, a transvestite), while a woman who played cards with the men would be a *masculone* (meaning a lesbian, a woman with masculine characteristics).[7]

Having analyzed the dynamics of the game as played in the *bassi*, Broccolini ponders the role of the *femminiello* within *tombola* games organized for recreational purposes in theaters and other venues, highlighting the air of folk theater the game assumed on these particular occasions.

> On these occasions, transformed into spectacle, with its vulgar and transgressive aspects emphasized, *tombola* is divorced from its working-class origins to be recontextualized in a socially protected context, as an important space for dialog between the social classes and for reshaping the local definition of Neapolitanness. This transforms the *femminielli* into true mediators, intermediaries in the dialog between the folk customs of an urban culture and the outside world, figures on the boundaries, whose task it is to amuse the customers by putting the linguistic conventions of Neapolitanness "on show," ushers in an extemporized folk theater.[8]

This patrimonialization of the game of *tombola*—which thus becomes emblematic of Neapolitanness and is offered up as an object to be sold in a cultural marketplace where traditions become typical products, no different from local produce—is particularly intriguing and merits examination, beginning with a few brief observations that I have had the opportunity to refine over the years.

Indeed, while conducting my field research, I have, on more than one occasion, had the opportunity to take part in *tombolelle*[9] "thrown," around Christmastime or on Candlemas, in certain venues in Naples and Avellino. All of the *tombola* games I have attended have been organized by associations or organizations working to promote recognition of the rights of LGBT people.

The *tombolelle* organized by the Montevergine Candlemas Network[10] have almost all been thrown by Gina. Every evening, at least three rounds of *tombola* were planned. Gina took great pains to avoid being repetitive, making sure that the stories she constructed around the numbers were always different. On a couple of occasions, Gina had a big basket full of fruits and vegetables of various sorts, which she gave out to those present, all while making wry allusions about their ambiguous meanings. Given that one of the goals of the *tombolelle* was to fund initiatives organized by the Network, the prizes to be won were obtained by the organizers in advance, through a network of friends, acquaintances, and backers, who put up knickknacks, beauty products, dinners, clothing, or foodstuffs. Each round included the traditional five prizes, awarded from two-in-a-row through bingo, and a round-trip plane ticket for a European capital was usually given out in the last round, paid for by the organizers, in the face of takings that were—it must be said—sometimes quite substantial. What's more, each prize was accompanied by a sex toy or lingerie item, which Gina would unabashedly brandish before her highly amused audience.

The use of lewd and suggestive language is, without a doubt, one of the defining characteristics of the *tombolella*, giving rise to situations of high hilarity, in which the audience gleefully participates. This interaction is, in fact, essential to a successful *tombola* game, which must, first and foremost, entertain. The characterization of *tombola* as a combination of theater and event is thus clear to see, even simply from this brief account of the scenarios I have observed.

In recent years, the AFAN[11] has also organized a *tombola* game, to which they have given the significant name *Sciò Sciò Ciucciuvè*.[12] Drawing heavily on the narrative thread of a video-chronicle of a wedding, which we will be examining below, the AFAN announced the event's 2012 edition: "The Grand Duchess Tore a Loff will receive, in her palace salon, as is the custom each year during this holiday time, her *femmenelle* friends from Naples and abroad, to play the grand *tombolata*."[13] As the press release put out by the Association states, the event schedule also includes a propitiatory rite and a performance by a musical ensemble:

> Gerardinella will consecrate the Grand Duchess's salon by performing the propitiatory rite (i.e. *sciò scio ciucciuvè*). A performance by the musical ensemble Gli Spaccapaese will follow; there will also be a special guest appearance by Peppino di Febbraio's historic *paranza*.[14]

Every *tombola* game I have witnessed or heard described ultimately falls within a context of rediscovery and renewed appreciation for the *femminella* and her culture. They are framed as events for gathering together, having fun, and learning about the historic "tradition" of the Neapolitan *femminelle*. Moreover, even when *tombola* games are organized by businesses for entirely pecuniary ends, the rhetoric they use is structured around terms like "tradition" and "authenticity."

An additional element that allows us to understand the ongoing process of patrimonialization is a peculiar product marketed by the brand *NapoliMania*. The product in question is *Nanassa, la tombola vaiassa*, an electronic *tombola* game in which "the real voice of a *femminiello*" reads out the meanings of the "true Neapolitan *Smorfia*."[15]

Having been introduced into popular culture thanks to televised *tombola* games, being staged as shows in theaters and leisure venues around Campania, and via a series of endlessly novel marketing formulas, the *tombola dei femminelli* may thus be considered a fully-fledged cultural product, which, together with pizza and the mandolin, is presented today as a symbol of Neapolitanness.

Wedding Pictures

During my research, I have come across a variety of conversations, documents, and images dealing with the practice of enacting or performing weddings between *femminielli*.

In the first half of the '80s, it was Pino Simonelli and Gennaro Carrano[16] who produced a number of meditations on the role of *femminielli* in the Neapolitan context, with the account of a wedding as their starting point. In the report they presented during the anthropological session of the Sexuality and Sexology in the South conference, Simonelli and Carrano provide a precise interpretation of the event, in which they argue the idea that, during the wedding, the *femminielli* are

> performers in a collective ritual—one in which theirs are the leading roles in a "union of the sexes par excellence," almost as if they wish to personify the "primordial couple," born specifically of their "sexual abstraction," which can be traced back to the "divine androgyny" mythos.[17]

It is interesting to note that, from the standpoints of several of the people with whom I spoke, the retelling of the wedding provided by the researchers takes on a role that is anything but secondary; rather, it is central.[18] Cascina, for instance, takes the same line of interpretation followed by the two anthropologists and, in his discourse, repeats some of the elements that Simonelli and Carrano identified as fundamental to understanding the social dynamics that cause the *femminielli* to be accepted within the milieu in which they live.[19]

Nonetheless, from the standpoints of the *femminelle*, the reason for the practice of staging a mock wedding is not some presumed social legitimacy but the opportunity—within a system of relationships in which the bonds of solidarity are very strong—to provide for the economic welfare of those *femminelle* who are no longer able to support themselves. We find, in Gianna's words, a clear reference to the redistributive role that rituals such as the wedding—described by my interviewee as pure spectacle, staged by the *femminelle* to help their eldest—play. Gina takes a similar stance when, as previously underscored, she clearly asserts that "all of these things were done for money."[20]

An intriguing video, produced by the AFAN and available online on the YouTube channel 15gigino, provides an account of the wedding of Rossella, a Neapolitan transvestite.[21] She is filmed showing the reporters an album containing photos from November of 2000, as evidenced by the date stamp on one of the pictures, taken in Piazza Municipio, in front of Castel dell'Ovo. Rossella is wearing a wedding dress and is posing for photos in the company of friends, acquaintances, and guests. In the interview, Rossella states that she and two other trans[22] women planned the wedding depicted in the photographs "for me, to have a memory, a memory of a wonderful day, just like a woman."[23]

In the opening credits, the AFAN offers us an advance idea of the meaning that Rossella herself attaches to her wedding: "This is the story of a white veil and a wedding dress. It is the story of Vincenzo, known as Rossella, who went to her wedding with a dream."[24]

The account describes how events unfolded, from choosing the traditional party favors given to guests at weddings to renting the dress, which she got from a church in Naples—where, in exchange for a donation, people can borrow wedding gowns provided by the local neighborhood community. Flipping through the photo album, Rossella recounts getting dressed for the wedding at the home of her friend Valentina; going out into the street, which had been festively decorated for the occasion; and the party that her friends and neighbors had planned for her. When asked by the interviewer, she states that they did not go to a church because "in church it's a sin!" but rather went directly to Piazza Municipio where, with her escort (whom Rosella explains was the boyfriend of a friend, "lent" to her for the occasion), she posed for photographs.

Rossella's wedding was a private affair. There was only a small number of guests, and the celebration did not include any banquets, performances, or events that would have required elaborate planning, as additional accounts confirm.

"There were about twenty of us," Rossella says, as she identifies the people in the pictures in the album, whose pages she turns with care. This is very different from that which was described, for example, by Patrizia.

In her interview, she tells how she *did* her wedding, and that as many as six or seven hundred people came.

In one of the interviews I collected early on in my research, Nina also describes a wedding she attended while living with Scappatella:

> This girl, she celebrated the wedding band and the engagement ring. When she celebrated the engagement ring, it was no big thing. Her family accepted it and all. But when it was time for the wedding band . . . oh, my goodness! It was beautiful! We were at Licola, by the sea, and all the relatives were there, friends and family, the whole nine yards.

It is interesting to note that describing her friend's wedding turned into an opportunity for Nina to ask me if I would be willing to photograph her in a bridal gown:

> This bridal gown thing . . . I want to wear one, too. Almost everyone has. What we could do is, sometime, you could come over to my house; I'll put on a white gown—you'll have your camera with you, in any event. I have to call a (friend) hairdresser of mine up from Naples; I have to get her to come here . . . because then you, of course, if you have to get touched up, too . . . a nice face wax, a nice make-up job—the right kind, nice and light.

In the words of Nina,[25] as in those of Rossella, the wedding ceremony becomes pure performance, the image of a happy day, to be shown and to be remembered. The white dress, the traditional gifts for the guests, the photographs: these are objects of a cherished desire, the desire for the social recognition generated by the memory and the telling of it.

Gerardina, too, during her interview, reminisces about the celebration organized on the occasion of her wedding, planned some years earlier:

> I did my wedding. I dressed as a bride in the year 2005. That was me, really me . . . the bride. We planned this wedding, right? And I really went all out, because I did it in Cetara, at a restaurant on the coast. . . . My friends got me a band for the music, a convertible car, a wedding gown, a concert at the restaurant, and the whole neighborhood was there. And the

> most wonderful thing was that one of the old *femminielli* from P***, who must be a good eighty years old by now, came to bring me this tray, this gift of flowers: a tray with flowers and candies on it, cash in coins—coins given in homage to the bride. He brought me this tray . . . so the oldest *femminiello* came to make this gesture, to honor the moment.[26]

The attendance of the oldest *femminella*[27] assumes a role of paramount importance within the tale and the recognition thus received is a source of pride for Gerardo. The performance takes on a public character, played out in a little town on the Amalfi Coast. In his account, Gerardo does not mention reappropriation of a religious rite; when prompted, he makes clear that the wedding consisted solely of the celebratory meal at the restaurant. It is furthermore important to underscore that no mention whatsoever is made of any videos or photographs being taken; what is instead important to Gerardo is to emphasize that he planned the wedding for the month of June and not during Carnival time, as was typical in the areas around A*** and P***.

A further reflection about the weddings of *femminielli* is inspired by certain documents available online.

On July 23, 2011, in Torre Annunziata in the province of Naples, the AFAN organized a one-of-a-kind staged production of a wedding of *femminielli*, recording an interesting video document that bears witness to the considerable level of public participation in this unusual "event." Unlike other initiatives presented by the association, this wedding of the *femminielli* was not promoted by the AFAN on social networks, nor was it announced on the blog '*O femmenell*, a fact that characterized the event as being very much a local affair. As can be clearly seen in the videos online, the residents of Torre Annunziata, a town at the foot of Mt. Vesuvius, gave a warm welcome to the procession, which, complete with horses and carriages, made its way through their streets that day. The images, put out by a small local web TV station, show the wedding cortège advancing amongst cars and motor scooters. There are at least four carriages, carrying about ten individuals dressed up for the ceremony in colorful clothes: men, women, trans people, no less than two brides, several coachmen, and bridesmaids, among whom we can recognize the actor Ciro Cascina, who was vice president of AFAN at the time.

In his brief remarks at the beginning of the video, the association's then-president explains to the cameraman what it is all about: "It's an ancient pagan rite. When the members of the priesthood, who were *femminielli*,[28] initiated the spouses-to-be into marriage."[29]

The definition "pagan rite," the reference to the "priesthood" of the *femminiello* (to whom, significantly, he refers using the masculine form when speaking to the cameraman and, through him, to the audience), and the idea of initiation, into which no further insight can be gleaned from the images: these are the elements he uses to provide a sparing description of the event, when obliged to communicate—in a few words and while surrounded by a jubilant crowd—its meaning.

In another video, also produced by the AFAN, the association adopts an entirely different rhetoric and, without providing any explanation about the wedding, enters directly into the scene of the "rite" during an interview with the "Duchess of Toraloff," the mother of the bride. The parodic dimension is evident from the first words spoken, and allows us to frame this "mise en scène" in a context that is completely different from those that we have seen thus far. In telling the story, the association chooses to pair the Duchess's tale with scenes of the procession, the bumper-to-bumper traffic, and the local people's participation in the festivities, combining "humor" with "folklore" and giving an almost hyperbolic interpretation of the wedding of the *femminielli* in Torre Annunziata. The construction of the story told through the video contextualizes it, in narrative terms, as somewhere between the serious and the absurd, with the marriage between the Duchess of Toraloff and Prince Romaloff becoming an expedient to breathe new life into the wedding of the *femminielli*. Meanwhile, the images also show enormous local attendance, with scenes of people in different neighborhoods warmly welcoming the procession, waving joyfully to those aboard the carriages, throwing rice, dancing, and toasting with the "guests." While the celebratory aspect is therefore perfectly conveyed, the video's construction seems intended to emphasize the point of view of a person who, through enacting the wedding, assumes a different identity.

This narrative structure hearkens back to an interpretation of the wedding of the *femminielli* offered by the anthropologists Simonelli and Carrano; the reference to the plurality of roles is effectively symbolized by the presence of two brides. All of this would appear to support the idea that, by depicting the event thus, the AFAN has chosen to rely on narrative structure in their attempt to convey the element of play-acting that the *femminelle* engage in on the occasion of these weddings. The lack of images recounting what happened during the reception means that we cannot know how the wedding unfolded. What is recorded is the procession and the celebrations in a number of cafés around the town. The Duchess of Toraloff's perspective, meanwhile, allows the AFAN to render the event theatrical, giving it a dimension of pageantry and one that is, ultimately, utopian.

Love Is Nigh, or "We Are Tradition!"

In Torre Annunziata, on April 9, 2012, exactly nine months after the wedding of the *femminielli* had been celebrated, the AFAN organized the spectacle of the *figliata*,[30] significantly entitled " 'Love is nigh,' or, when in April, for the blossoming peach tree, we wore white." It took place in the town, at the base of Mt. Vesuvius on Easter Monday, and was attended by about two hundred people, including some leading cultural figures and prominent members of LGBT associations from around the Campania region.

Fliers for the event promised attendees

> music, singing, dancing, wine, *casatielli*,[31] fava beans and artichokes, to reopen our arms to what we were before we became what we are.
>
> Yearly Easter Monday picnics in the working-class districts of Oplonti. This first edition will be hosted on Largo Fontana in the "Rione delle Carceri" neighborhood, on April 9, 2012, beginning at 4:30 p.m.

The event, in the words of the organizers, was part of the cycle begun nine months earlier with the wedding and which would come to a close in July with the celebration of an introduction to society (to take place at the same time as another marriage celebration, which never ended up being performed). It was, in essence, a neighborhood street festival, enlivened by performances of an artistic nature by trans people and *femminelle*, natives of Torre Annunziata and of the Campania region, whose numbers included Ciretta and Gerardina.

An examination of the rite, which calls for a much more detailed analysis than that which is possible here, nonetheless shone a light on the desire—expressed straightforwardly by Ciro during an informal interview that took place that evening—not to faithfully reproduce the dynamic of the rite as it was described by Curzio Malaparte and later by Liliana Cavani, but rather to offer the *inhabitants of the city's humblest streets* an opportunity for celebration while marking the arrival of spring.

The evening's climactic event was the birth of the "*criaturo niro niro*,"[32] a black-skinned doll birthed around 9 p.m., behind closed doors in a large garage located on Largo Fontana, while the folk music ensemble Gli Spaccapaese performed "Tammurriata nera."[33]

The majority of those gathered were women and girls. These were set to guard the entrance to the garage and were very lively in their interactions with the day's main protagonists, in particular with Ciretta and Gerardinella, but also with the numerous other *femminelle* and trans people present. The presence of Poppea, a Roman drag queen who, over the course of the evening, gave lip-synced performances of songs by Gabriella Ferri, was significant.

The indisputable star of the event, although she did not hold any official role within the festival's programming, was Ciretta Cascina, an adept crowd entertainer, capable of engaging women and children, young and old, "gypsies,"[34] and the town's native "torresi" alike, grabbing the onlookers' attention at intervals with her swoons, theatrically staged on the street, as though to underscore the power of the emotions generate by specific moments of the relational experience.

The spatial and temporal context of ritual tends to generate an ecstatic state in spectators. The organizers themselves took care to emphasize this, on the sidelines of the ritual performance, highlighting the fundamental importance of the event's social legitimation, whose aim would appear to be to render a precise subjectivity objective.

A short video available on YouTube, which was relatively widely disseminated on LGBT sites and social networks immediately following its release, offers further opportunity for reflection. It depicts a *figliata* enacted in 2014 at an art gallery in Naples. The protagonists of the performance are Gerardina—who, on this occasion, plays the role of the mother of the woman about to give birth—and certain of the young people who frequently attend initiatives organized by AFAN and performances by the folk music group Gli Spaccapaese.

The scene, off-limits to the public thanks to the interposition of a cloth tent, featured several *femminelle*(?),[35] who, on that occasion, took on the typical roles of a birthing scene: relatives, midwives, and friends, gathered to witness the infant's birth.

In my opinion, it is significant that, in order to quell the impatience of some of those who had come to see the spectacle, the performers spoke as one, reaffirming the need to remain silent and wait outside of the tent demarcating the ritual space. It was in just such a moment that one of them clearly said, "We are tradition," as though to reaffirm that the spectators were about to witness a scene that lay "beyond the boundaries of temporal conventions." I do not believe that this was a simple platitude. The desire to claim a place as part of a legitimate history, raising appreciation and awareness of a specific body of practical knowledge, is emblematic here of these subjects'/actors' distinctive desire. "We are tradition. We are part of a sphere forbidden to all but a few. We are different from others," the protagonists appear to be saying. From this perspective, it may make sense to speak of ritual as the space/time that demarcates a difference (to quote Pierre Bourdieu) in respect to which a distinction is drawn between those who can conceive of passing beyond those boundaries and those for whom, on the contrary, that possibility will always be out of reach.

(Translated by Jennifer Delare)

Notes

1. The excerpts in this chapter are from Maria Carolina Vesce's book *Altri transiti: Corpi, pratiche, rappresentazioni di femminielli e transessuali* (Sesto San Giovanni: Mimesis, 2017), 165–75.

2. See Alessandra Broccolini, "Vac' a pazzià a tumbulella: Etnografia di un gioco napoletano," *Lares* LXXI, no. 1 (Jan.–Apr. 2005): 7–40.

3. Translator's note (t/n): The Italian name for "bingo."

4. T/n: The small street-level apartments where, historically, Naples's poorest residents lived.

5. T/n: "To play *tombola*" in Neapolitan dialect.

6. Ed./n: The word "femminiello" has different spellings, which appear throughout this chapter; on this peculiar aspect, see the introduction and the work of Valerio, Zito, and Scisci, included in this volume (chapter 5).

7. Broccolini, "Vac' a pazzià a tumbulella."

8. Broccolini, "Vac' a pazzià a tumbulella."

9. T/n: Festive *tombola* gatherings.

10. T/n: Rete per la Candelora a Montevergine in Italian.

11. T/n: *Associazione Femmenell Antiche Napoletane*, or Historic Neapolitan *Femminielli* Association.

12. T/n: A traditional Neapolitan expression and ritual, used to chase away bad luck and the evil eye.

13. See http://www.femmenell.com/sciosciociucciuve/ (accessed March 22, 2016).

14. T/n: A band of Neapolitan folk musicians.

15. T/n: The *Smorfia* is a sort of code system or dictionary, in which people, things, places, actions, etc. are each assigned a number that appears in bingo, allowing the sequences of numbers to be transformed into elements of storylines during play; see http://guide.supereva.it/campania_i/interventi/2004/12/187870.shtml (accessed March 22, 2016).

16. See Pino Simonelli and Gennaro Carrano, "Mito e seduzione dell'immagine femminile a Napoli," in *Sessualità e sessuologia nel Sud: Atti del Convegno Società Italiana di Sessuologia Clinica*, ed. Rita Mattace Raso (Naples: Società Editrice Napoletana, 1987), 17–23.

17. Simonelli and Carrano, "Mito e seduzione," 20.

18. Ed./n: In May 2021, during the translation process, we asked the author to provide further details on this passage. Vesce explained that some *femminielli* consider the wedding a performance with a social function (first and foremost a way to redistribute resources within the community and support older community members who are no longer sex workers). However, other *femminielli*—usually those who are more educated and more active in cultural associations—have instead stressed the ritual function of the wedding and reclaimed the uniqueness of a Neapolitan figure that is intrinsic to the local landscape and cultural heritage.

19. On Cascina's perspective see also chapter 7 in this volume.

20. See chapter 4 [of Vesce's book], *Frammenti di un discorso etnografico*, section 4.3, *Gina*, 123–30.

21. In the video entitled "La margheritina bianca," Rossella defines herself as a transvestite. Upon being asked by the interviewer, "Are you a transsexual?" Rossella responds, "No, I'm a transvestite. This is how I am during the day, in the evening, in the morning . . . always!"

22. T/n: The word "trans" in Italian is often used in a much broader sense than it is in English, as a catch-all term to refer not only to transsexual people but also to transvestites. It often seems to mean different things to different people, both inside and outside of the Neapolitan community.

23. See the video "La margheritina bianca," available online on AFAN's YouTube channel, at http://www.youtube.com/user/15gigino (accessed March 22, 2016).

24. See http://www.youtube.com/watch?v=kXtLovf1jYk (accessed March 22, 2016).

25. Both of the accounts mentioned and quoted here are from the interview conducted in Avellino on April 20, 2007.

26. Gerardo Amarante, interviewed in Angri (Salerno) on December 29, 2010.

27. T/n: On the use of the different spellings *femminiello/femminella*, see note 6.

28. T/n: On the sacred role of the femminielli, see Valerio, Scisci, Zito (chapter 5).

29. See https://www.youtube.com/watch?v=UUN40142RnY (accessed March 22, 2016).

30. T/n: Birthing.

31. T/n: A local savory stuffed Easter bread.

32. T/n: "The black infant" in Neapolitan dialect.

33. T/n: A song written in 1944 about a Neapolitan woman who, following the Allied occupation, gives birth to the child of an African American soldier.

34. There was a large group of Roma at the festival. To refer to these people, the other attendees used the word *zingari* [t/n: the Italian equivalent of the English pejorative, "gypsies"]. However, their attendance did not seem to trouble those present, who interacted frequently with the [Roma] children and adults alike.

35. Given that I did not witness the performance I describe here or interview those who participated in it, I do not feel I have the right to identify the people in question as *femminelle*. I have therefore placed a question mark in parentheses, although I remain entirely convinced of the fact that, on that occasion, they would have chosen to take on the role of *femminelle*, as can moreover be inferred from certain lines spoken during the course of the ritual performance.

Chapter 7

Two Real-Life Perspectives on the *Femminielli*
A Conversation with Loredana Rossi and Ciro Cascina

Marzia Mauriello

This conversation took place during one of Summer Minerva's research trips to Naples for the making of their documentary *Summer Within*, a film inspired by their personal search for their own gender identity and Neapolitan cultural heritage. At the time, Summer was striving to define an "authentic *femminiello*" and make sense of an elusive figure that escapes precise definitions. The term *femminiello* is so nuanced that it might be considered a floating signifier;[1] Summer thus thought of asking their questions to some key personalities of the Neapolitan gender-variant/*femminelle*/trans community—first and foremost, Ciro Cascina and Loredana Rossi.[2] These two leading figures both identify as *femminielli* but have quite different views on what it means to embrace this gender and cultural identity in the present. While Loredana has recast her identity of *femmenella* into a form of activism, strictly related to her local culture, Ciro has taken an approach that is more artistic and rather theoretical. Both, though, share a deep sense of belonging to Neapolitan places, culture, and history.

Summer met them at Loredana's house on February 5, 2020, a few days after the celebration of the *Candelora* (Candlemas). The meeting originated from Summer's need to understand whether they could also self-identify as *femminiello*, but the conversation evolved into a broader discussion about the history of this peculiar figure across genders and the issues that the *femminielli* community is currently facing. The meeting begins with Ciro/Ciretta, who praises Loredana for being able to "reach everyone," thanks to her excellent communication skills. She responds by saying that the public speeches she has made in recent years have indeed helped many people to come out and gain greater self-awareness.

Loredana: I would give public speeches, of course, but then people would write to me privately to congratulate me and tell me their stories. Before I started my activity in Naples with ATN (Associazione Transessuale Napoli) nobody had voiced the social issues faced by the *femminielli,* ever! The issues discussed in public venues all revolved around gay people, and some *femminielli* complained that those who spoke [gay people] did not understand our problems—prostitution, for example! So, I thought I might help and give other people what I lost when my family kicked me out of the house. A place to stay, a job . . . I didn't have anything! I share this experience with other *femminielli* who, like me, in the 1970s and 1980s were thrown out of their houses and forced to walk the street and give blow jobs. This was a common experience, not only mine. However, I was the first to talk about certain things; although later other people pretended they began it all.

Ciretta: You are a great communicator, and you've used your skills to target important social issues. Of course, everyone has benefited from your work. Other people in our LGBT+ community, as far as I know, admire you because of this, and also because you do not self-pity. Rather, you give other people a chance to access the world of activism. I think that tragedy separates people, whereas positive empathy unites them, making it possible for others to understand and share one's thoughts.

Summer: What is a *femminiello*?

Loredana: The *femminiello* originated in Naples, and this happened roughly in the seventeenth century.[3] But in the 1950s, the *femminielli* were these here, in this picture.[4] And they looked like that because, at the time, there were no cosmetic surgery or hormonal treatments. Feminine-looking males . . . this is what they were, at least in the period around WWII. They would help women with chores during the war. Then the evolution began. Hormones became available, together with cosmetic surgery, and the *femmenelle* turned into—I don't like saying "turned into," because I'm still a *femmenella*[5]—but let's say it . . . the *femminiello* became transgender and transsexual. I don't know what label they will stick on us in the future, or what we will call ourselves. This is the story of the *femminiello*, as told to me by the older *femminielli*.

Ciretta: For me this figure is strictly related to this area [Naples and its hinterland]. However, let's be clear: the *femminielli* are not the protagonists, while the land serves as a background stage. Quite the opposite: it's the land that created the *femminielli*, and not vice versa. This is a particular geographical place that originated from the concerted action of a volcano, Vesuvius, and the Mediterranean Sea. These two agents have molded the *femminiello*. So, in my interpretation, the place is the actual protagonist! Parthenope [the mythical siren] emerged first [out of the Gulf of Naples], and then came the *femminiello*. . . . This is why in order to contend that the *femminiello* no longer exists, as some people like to say, you must first destroy Naples! The same applies to a spiritually iconic place like Montevergine. Before it was an abbey, Montevergine was a place in the hills where people went in search of spirituality. It was this rather enchanted environment that had already hosted pre-Christian temples that created the "terrain" for the abbey, because humans cannot wrap their minds around the abstract, and therefore they need to build material shapes.

Nowadays the *femminielli* exist in various forms, but they are the fruit of this land. In Oslo, in Bologna, or anywhere else, the *femminiello* doesn't exist. You only find them[6] here because this land has a peculiar way of understanding femininity and masculinity. Here any form of polarity is nuanced with its opposite, to the point of becoming an ambiguous duality that is singular and double, at the same time. All our mythology—starting with the twofold image of the siren—plays on this doubleness. In our area, the female genitalia is called *pucchiacca*, a term that derives from the ancient Greek *pyr*, which means "fiery," like vulcanic fire.[7] Hence, this ebullient femininity is perceived as the strongest sex. Even heterosexuality is double here. Think, for example, of our beautiful *femmene*,[8] who are the biggest gangsters in the world, just as the biggest men are all *femmenellone*.[9] Everything is twofold around here! And Naples is also where there is a vivid cult of motherhood, where the male figure gets closer to the mother figure and is deprived of his alleged power. Masculinity cannot help but soften, and become almost disempowered. For me it is this unique place—and the logic intrinsic to this place—that gives rise to the complexity of this whole Neapolitan "matter"—to a language, a cuisine, a culture—to a whole magical and colorful, yet also tragic land.

Summer: Why do you say that the LGBT+ community does not know this history?

Loredana: The LGBT+ community, or should I say the gay people, have tried to erase this history, our history. We came out of local folklore; this is what the *femminiello* is. And I speak of folklore not in a caricatural sense but in the sense of vibrant, joyful life. We, *femminielli*, are sunny figures, despite all the troubles we have been through. And I should add that those who come from the *paesi* [small towns] face even greater troubles than those of us here in Naples, which has always been more open-minded.

Ciretta: In part it is like this, yes, but moving from the small town to the city meant for us to become somewhat like tourists, and therefore we could enjoy more freedom. Coming to Naples from Torre Annunziata[10] was like entering a completely different world. There was a large community in Torre [Annunziata], but not as large as that of Naples.

Loredana: [Gender nonconforming] people used to come to Naples to join the *femminielli* of Naples.

Ciretta: We are talking about people who later became trans but also about those who died as *femminielli*, which means they never changed their appearance.

[Someone in the group talks about the significant community of femminielli in Torre del Greco and mentions the rite of *la figliata*, which in Curzio Malaparte's novel *La Pelle* (*The Skin*, 1949) is set in Torre del Greco.]

Loredana: Yes, *la figliata* comes from here, as does the *battesimo*,[11] and the *spusarizio* of the *femminielli*[12]—all these rituals came from Naples! I was still performing *lo spusarizio* in the eighties! These are all Neapolitan things, but we got rid of them twenty years ago. However, people in small towns have carried on the tradition and still keep it alive. It's great! The *Candelora*, too . . . we Neapolitans had almost lost that! I've organized *la figliata* here in Naples—I don't know if you saw it on Rai Tre[13]—and it was fabulous! I'm bringing things that had been forgotten for twenty years back to Naples, things that have survived in the countryside, and which we had gotten rid of. I have committed myself to retrieving the *femminielli*'s old traditions because I don't want the tradition, our tradition, to be canceled. Because once we've erased history, we'll have erased everything, and we'll no longer know where we're heading. These days the people who are erasing history are the gays . . . so I came forward, because I don't want this history to be erased. The *gaysmo* [gay movement, culture] that has become dominant is erasing us. It is changing history.

[Someone in the group argues that there are also many gays who support the trans community.]

Loredana: They are all gays without any associations, without any [political] interests. Otherwise, they cancel trans people from any communal project. There's an open war between trans associations and Arcigay in Italy. I can't stand them because they profit from the *femminielli*'s pain; if it were otherwise I wouldn't give them a second thought. That is why I decided to fight this dominant way of thinking, which is focused exclusively on gay priorities.

Summer: We are now part of an international LGBT+ community. What can we do to tell this story? What do you want to say to the international community?

Ciretta: The *femminiello* has no reason to knock on the door of power. People in power do not even know that the *femminiello* exists, because s/he is protected by and immersed in the culture and family networking that goes on in the alleys. From the point of view of modernity, the *femminiello* is undoubtedly a reactionary figure. The *cultura popolare* includes this figure within its structure and its rituals, and the *femminiello* does not even need to ask for inclusion. S/he is protected by the *tombola*, by the *figliata*, by *Mamma Schiavona*, and their millennial rituality.[14] However, when the *femminiello* evolves into a modern transsexual, that is when s/he has to claim a new sense of belonging to the community, and that is when the struggle begins. Or, to put it another way: when the *femminiello* evolves into the transgender, s/he embodies a new need to represent hirself in a single form rather than a double one, and here hir struggle begins.

Loredana: In the 1950s, in order to go to their pilgrimage to *Mamma Schiavona*, the *femminielli* left Naples all dressed up in cars filled with flowers. When they arrived at the sanctuary, they would kneel down and climb the stairs bent over, with their tongues touching the ground. That was their vow to the Black Madonna.

Summer: Is there any relationship between the *femminielli* and the *muxes*, or the two spirits?[15]

Ciretta: No, because the origin of the *femminielli* is tied to Naples and its hinterland. I'll give you a metaphor: if you plant a lemon tree in another place, the lemons will have a different flavor. In more theoretical language, I can only say that we are dealing with labyrinthine discourses: diversity is made up of diversity. People tend to unify, to say, for example, "I am a woman," or, "I am a girl." But that's a statement; it's purely language. In reality there's much greater complexity within each of us.

Loredana: As far as the relationship with other LGBT communities is concerned, for example with North American trans women, we share their resistance against the various forms of fascism. Just as you have been dealing with Trump,[16] we have been dealing with Salvini.[17] Twenty-two years ago, when Berlusconi emerged as a political actor, the fascist sentiment started to revive. Neo-fascist groups would go to places frequented by *femminielli*. They would beat them and then throw them into garbage cans. We would rescue the other *femminielli* and take them to the hospital. I was a victim of this violence too, and the next day I gathered all the *femminelle* of Naples and exhorted them: "*Femminè*, before they kill all of us . . . let's do something!"

[Another person in the group asks a question: For how long did the cultura popolare protect the femminielli?]

Loredana: The protection was out of interest: if you didn't give something back, you were immediately excluded. You reciprocated that social protection by doing things for people, for example taking care of the children or cleaning the house. There was always an exchange, but it was an exchange among peers, because we did it out of friendship.

Ciretta: It must be said that *femmenella* is an abstract term. If there was a *femmenella* who had a strong personality and knew how to behave in order to assert himself, s/he did not face any type of exploitation. But I should also add that, usually, those who asked for help at home—I mean the women of the neighborhood—were poor. It was poverty that made people equal, not gender.

Loredana: It is not true that in some neighborhoods the *femminielli* were accepted. I know that those who worked as prostitutes had to buy everything at higher prices. We cannot really talk of acceptance.

[At this point in the conversation, Luigi di Cristo, president of AFAN, explains how in low-income social contexts those with more are willing to share. S/he goes on to say that this kind of sharing is also typical of other places, for example Morocco.]

Luigi di Cristo: You must not take it as exploitation. If, during the war, the *femminielli* joined the women to fight fascism, they didn't do so because one day they were expecting a prize. It was not a matter of exploitation, but rather a thing that had to be done, according to that particular type of Neapolitan culture. This was also the case of people who were making money through illegal activities . . . even the *guappo*[18] tried to help out those in need. Whoever had more, gave more. This was the unspoken rule.

Loredana: I don't agree with you. If people did not exploit *the femminielli*, it was because the *femminiello*, at times, succeeded in not being exploited. In Naples, until thirty years ago, no one would rent places to the *femminielli*. I have a *basso*[19] here, and I was paying six hundred thousand lire a month when the regular market price was fifty thousand lire a month. I was a *femminiello*, and so I paid twenty thousand lire per day. I call this exploitation.

Luigi di Cristo: But maybe at that time you were making three hundred thousand lire a day . . .

Loredana: *Embè*. If I make three hundred, why should I give one hundred to you? Why? I am selling myself, my own body, why do I have to give what I make to you? People took advantage of things and abused the *femminielli*; this is the truth. We had to buy the friendship of the neighborhood, in order to be somewhat accepted. Otherwise we were isolated. Just as I'm saying that you had to buy friendship, I also say that if I happened to know that one of my neighbors was in trouble, I would bring them groceries. This is precisely what I call the soul of the *femminiello*. But, still, our solidarity was counterbalanced by a system of exploitation that ruled society.

Ciretta: In my opinion, experiences of diversity do exist and must be taken into consideration. Each story is a story in itself. And that is enrichment. If you go next door, people will tell you another story. You can't tell them everything, but eventually these stories come together and a common narrative unfolds . . . but still, it's something that has been manipulated to create a shared story.

(Translated by Marzia Mauriello)

Notes

1. On this, see Mauriello's "In *Nomine Femminielli*: Una ricerca etnografica sulla realtà gender variant nella Napoli contemporanea," in *Femminielli: Corpo, genere e cultura*, eds. Eugenio Zito and Paolo Valerio (Naples: Edizioni Dante and Descartes, 2019), 305–25.

2. The participants in the meeting were Summer Minerva, Ciro/Ciretta Cascina, Loredana Rossi, Luigi Di Cristo, Luigi Sconamiglio, Francesca Saturnino, and Summer's film crew, Adam Golub and Sylvaine Alfaro.

3. On the history of the *femminielli*, see Zito, Valerio, and Sisci's essay in chapter 5.

4. She shows a photo of a *femminiello* taken in the mid-twentieth century.

5. Loredana refers to her sense of belonging to the community of the *femmenelle* despite undergoing cosmetic surgery and hormonal treatments.

6. Ciro/Ciretta generally speaks in the masculine form when s/he talks about the figure of *femminiello*, making the agreement with the masculine form of the term. However, the word *femminiello* also has a feminine form, *femmenella/femminella*, which is mostly used by the *femminielli* when they are among themselves and talking to each other. We decided to use the neutral form used in English (s/he, hir) to express this gender fluidity from the masculine to feminine, although in Italian there is not a neuter form.

7. The term most likely derives from *pyr* ("fire") and *koilos* ("hollow"). There are other possible etymologies of this term, but we provide only that referred to by Cascina.

8. This is Neapolitan for *donne*, women.

9. "Super *femmenelle*."

10. A small town close to Naples.

11. *Il battesimo* (the baptism ceremony) refers to the visit that a newlywed couple of *femminielli* pays to another *femminielli* couple who had a baby (*la figliata*). This event symbolizes the entry of the newborn in the community. See D'Agostino, "I femminielli napoletani: Alcune riflessioni antropologiche," in *Femminielli*, 110.

12. See introduction and chapter 5.

13. One of the channels of Italian public television.

14. On this, see introduction and chapter 5.

15. Other gender-variant examples, which are present in Zapotecan Mexico and Native American cultures.

16. At the time of the interview, Donald Trump was still the US president.

17. Matteo Salvini is the current leader of the right-wing party Lega.

18. This is a historical Neapolitan figure tied to the lower classes and to criminality. His role also involved patrolling and protecting the alley's community.

19. A ground floor house, typical in lower-class neighborhoods.

References

D'Agostino, Gabriella. "I femminielli napoletani: Alcune riflessioni antropologiche." In *Femminielli: Corpo, genere e cultura*. Edited by Eugenio Zito and Paolo Valerio, 93–122. Naples: Edizioni Dante and Descartes, 2019.

Mauriello Marzia. "In *Nomine Femminielli*: Una ricerca etnografica sulla realtà *gender variant* nella Napoli contemporanea." In *Femminielli: Corpo, genere e cultura*. Edited by Eugenio Zito and Paolo Valerio, 305–25. Naples: Edizioni Dante and Descartes, 2019.

CENTER

PART 3
A FELLINIESQUE DOLCE VITA

Chapter 8

From *L'aurora delle trans cattive* (*The Dawn of the Bad Trans Women*)

Porpora Marcasciano

In this text, Marcasciano maps a Roman geography of sex work in the area spanning Piazza dei Cinquecento and via Quattro Cantoni.[1] Here, a peculiar urban *dolce vita* developed, stretching through a web of local trattorias, shady hotels, and rooms by the hour to encompass the cinema Volturno near the Termini railway station and, at times, the Regina Coeli prison—the final destination of the vice quad's stings. Her Roman setting parodies Federico Fellini's scenic shots of via Vittorio Veneto, the Trevi fountain, and luxurious houses. Marcasciano's vibrant narration turns the slow-motion Felliniesque ennui of an aimless bourgeois society into a series of picaresque blue-collar adventures, set in a "vast amusement park, an open-air bordello (brothel)." Populating these vibrant geographies were many trans sex workers, depicted by Marcasciano as divas, but also a host of "extras"—local residents who could not help but participate in the unfolding dramas. Her neorealist comedy focuses on invisible Roman lives, leading readers on a stroll through working-class neighborhoods that had not yet been gentrified, and through geographies of inclusion that were, surprisingly, based on a shared sense of belonging and class consciousness across genders.

Piazza dei Cinquecento

What was Piazza dei Cinquecento? What did that place, where I was stopped and later arrested, represent? A preliminary note is needed here, on the vocabulary and the terms, such as *shady, infamous, sordid, vice*, that I've used, and which might appear stigmatizing.

Everyday speech—used against us, to be clear—employed them regularly, as substitutes for our names and we, responding in kind, turned their meanings ironically and provocatively on their heads.

The Piazza faced the Termini train station. Like every area surrounding a station or a port, it was a place of transit and therefore of meetings and of looks exchanged, a place for cruising, for pick-ups, hook-ups, and for prostitution—a place anthropologically, architecturally, and aesthetically very different from how it looks today, without that awful fence that, since the horrendous restyling, has separated the archeological section from the area intended for strolling. It was poorly lit, and therefore full of areas of semi-darkness, suspicious from the outside but protective to those inside of them. The boundary was not clear or well-defined. It changed depending on the time of day, the temperature and the weather, on city events or the countless incursions of law enforcement, especially the infamous vice squad. That place worked non-stop, twenty-four hours a day. Each time of day had its particular category of female or male regulars that populated it. Visibility, like ostentation, was determined mainly by sunlight—modest in the daytime, more eye-catching in the evening, and definitely flashy by night. There was a time for quiet cruising for scouting purposes, for gathering information, for gossiping—amongst the regulars and between them and the various vendors, like the guy from the newsstand, the café attendant, the taxi driver and the guy who sold the contraband cigarettes. There was the time for the soldiers who, when on leave, would flow in from the many barracks still active around the capital to converge in the Piazza of adventure. It was practically adjacent to the Volturno, the famous cinema and cabaret theater that took its name from the street of the same name, which shares a corner with the square.

In Rome, the Volturno cinema was a true institution, one that everybody knew, not only for its shows but also because of the activities that went on inside of it—which were seen as shady and revolved around encounters, enjoyment, and socialization—making it a precursor to today's venues for *friendly* meet-ups. There wasn't a night it wasn't sold out. Performances and variety shows were staged and celebrated there until the end of the 1970s.

Even Giorgia O'Brien performed there several times. An actress, opera singer, and variety-act showgirl, she was one of the first of the famous transsexuals of the 1950s and '60s, renowned for her voice and her talent, who refused to be relegated to the usual "ghettos." The Volturno later became a porn cinema—not openly, but that's what it was—and it was still always completely sold out, thanks to its gay patrons. It was a grand bazaar of sex, carnality, and faggotry.

Throughout the surrounding streets, hundreds of trattorias, little hotels, and boarding houses sprang up, a vast array of "satellite activities" that were relatively accessible in terms of both cost and lack of inspections. There were the classic pay-by-the-hour hotels, where, with the complaisance of the doorman (whose tip was mandatory), one could get a room—brothels, really, with an unmistakable aroma of sex and the bed sheets still wet and spotted with the bodily fluids of the previous patrons. Piazza dei Cinquecento was a vast amusement park, an open-air bordello that put the city nearly on a par with the world's great capitals of vice and wordly pleasures—something which, historically speaking, Rome has always been. The male hustlers, seductive and alluring, would stand there in the classic waiting pose. The fairies, indifferent but attentive, would sit on benches reading the paper—the cheekier ones would wink. The pick-up would happen when these unmistakable little knots of people would form. They would have no discernable beginning or ending, and no one could even understand why they had come together. Usually they were mixed groups, including a couple of fairies, one or at the most two transvestites, one trans woman, and three or four if not ten male hustlers. The transvestites, vain and eager to climb the career ladder, would sashay across the Piazza like they were on a catwalk. The trans women would only appear after sunset, grabbing the spotlight, and, like guardians to whom one wisely gave due respect, they maintained their acknowledged control over Piazza attendance. Nothing got by them, and when they had blind spots, they had their various court informants and boot-lickers who would bring them the news of goings-on, of scams and deals, of dalliances and amorous intrigues, but especially of new arrivals. If the newbie was some young guy, everything would go smoothly, but when it was somebody even remotely interested in [MtF] transition, then tensions, arguments, and fights would kick off. Once all of that was over and the original guardian had cooled off, a spot was automatically created for the newbie, who had earned the right to become a part of the court of whichever lady had initially chased her off and then welcomed her. It was an ancient and predictable ritual, one that everybody knew and everybody hated but that everyone perpetuated. You just had to take into account the fact that taking the first steps as a "young lady" on the boulevards of any city, whether in the north or in the south, would involve a bloody initiation, one that the oldest inflicted on the youngsters. Bruised and contused, but finally "baptized," they could access green pastures, where they would run free until the time came for the encounter/confrontation with the next rash *mademoiselle* in need of baptism.

Piazza dei Cinquecento, being dimly lit, allowed people to conceal themselves better—which they had to do in order to spin those webs that today we call networks. These days we tend to categorize everything, are able to give a name to anything, even the most outlandish things. However, beneath the name, the essential part is missing, which is the thing itself: life, vibrant and pulsing.

Passing by the Piazza as a naive university student, I saw only strange activity. I didn't exactly realize what or how much of it there was inside, behind, above, below, and on the side. I'd understand it better only later on. There were the characters who were always standing around, almost like monuments. Some were integrated into the choreography, others were engaged in satellite activities, like the newsagent, the barman at the kiosk, and the souvenir seller, and all these acted as observers, inside men, middlemen, the madams of the open air and indoor brothels.

Of the classic figures whose presence informed the Piazza, I remember Marcellona well—this was before she had her surgery[2]—slim, tall with a Roman nose, sitting (or, better yet, hunched over) in her light-blue Fiat 500, the door open, one foot inside and the other out, always surrounded by strapping soldier boys. Like a spider, she pulled them into her web. The rumor was that she was a great charmer and an expert pick-up artist, which was why she was known in the milieu by the name of Audacity. She had been given that name by Jo Staiano, another famous denizen of the Roman night, who apparently would get Marcella to show up at parties and soirées precisely because of her talent for the chat up.

I often glimpsed Dario Bellezza,[3] who, in the true tradition of Pasolini, would be on the hunt for feigned or prospective rogues to whom to entrust his home, his poems and his treasures. Then, every time a romance ended, he would threaten to kill himself like Dido over Aeneas's departure.[4]

Pier Paolo, whose tragic story is emblematic of us all, had, in his turn, trod on that same ground, sexually and philosophically, until shortly before my arrival. It was there that he left the impressions of his last footprints before his encounter with tragedy, in the form of Pino Pelosi.[5] I came to know more about Pasolini through Anselmo, another district regular and procurer of encounters for Pier Paolo, a skill he also put to use later on, when he had the job of recruiting boys for closed-door encounters at the famous house of Sora Giulia on Via delle Vergini. Anselmo was another character who was well known in that milieu. From Sardinia but, oddly, blonde, his good looks and strapping figure allowed him to take on the role of the gigolo and roam freely through the Roman "Dolce Vita." We carried on a lovely affair during my frequent bohemian forays in the capital, when I was still eighteen and champing at the bit.

Amongst the people who passed through the Piazza, several were famous to varying extents, some more brazen, others more discreet. Of the many colorful performances one might easily enjoy, one of the most memorable remains that of Albertina, who showed up in the Piazza one night with a leopard on a leash, the incredulous throng parting to allow the passage of such an abundance, a superabundance, an overabundance! Always dressed in the most skin-tight clothes, so as to emphasize her extreme bustiness, she was the spitting image of Gina Lollobrigida. I believe she had taken the actress as a symbol to embody, given their close resemblance. Albertina was known for her flamboyant displays, like the leopard on a leash, her curves, her over-the-top figure, her long dark hair, her revealing clothes in eye-popping colors, and the fifteen-inch-long fake eyelashes that she would bat in quick time. She was known for having a life shrouded in mystery. She would appear and disappear suddenly, like Houdini, without a trace. No one knew where she lived or with whom. Nobody had ever seen her undressed, giving rise to the rumor that her curves were fake. It was said that her extremely generous breasts, along with her hips and buttocks, were made of foam rubber, skillfully sculpted and artfully sewn into her clothes—her figure was, indeed, too perfect to be real. The recurring rumor was that she was a "canary," meaning a police informer, so everybody kept her at a distance, but at the same they were careful not to make her into their enemy. The reason for her ill fame was tied to the fact that Albertina never got caught up in any sting, no one had ever seen her taken away by the vice squad, and when a sting did go down in a specific area, she always kept well away. Customarily outside of the internal rules of the trans world, she would walk the streets all across Rome, from the Flaminio neighborhood to Via XX Settembre, Via Veneto, and the EUR district, accountable to no one and drawing the ire of everyone who strictly followed the rule of the "*pizzo*," also called the "corner"—namely, that place, earned with sweat and tears, where each plied their trade, never invading the spot of another except to chat, laugh, or joke around. Still other rumors claimed she was the lover of some rich and influential character, who served as her guarantor in all of the city's milieus. It's fair to say that numerous fancies were spun around her person. What's certain, however, is that Albertina went away alone, along with her many innocent mysteries, towards the end of the 1980s. It was only quite a bit later that we learned about her death, which is why no one went to visit her in the hospital or attended her funeral.

This Rome, at once Felliniesque and Pasolinian, endured still, managing to generate a glamorous excitement that was untouched by the invasions of endless government drudges and hosts of pilgrims who, like locusts, would one day overwhelm and smother that enchantment.

Those who traversed that dark wood were quite likely to step off the so-called path that does not stray and find themselves, like Red Riding Hood, in a hidden recess, *pas seulement geografique mais*—and especially—*culturelle et sexuel*.[6]

The first time I passed through that place, accompanied by my hitchhiking buddy, it was the summer of 1974. After being ditched on the Great Ring Road, we had made it to Termini Station on the Metro B line and set out on foot for our beloved Piazza Navona. While crossing the wide open space in Piazza Esedra, we were picked up by Anselmo and Alberto, two charming young guys on the face of it, whom only our adolescent and provincial naivety could have made appear to be a couple of sexy career-driven heteros, but fell short of explaining why the two of them chauffeured us around Rome all night on board their loudly roaring Giulietta. That daring pair of fairies—whom, a few years later, I'd get to know better—seduced us not only with their good looks but also with their everyday knowledge of the capital, its places and its characters. They showed us a good time all over Rome, with stops in Trastevere and Campo de' Fiori, then all the way up to the Gianicolo hill where, at dawn, we gave our bodies and our sensuality free rein, above a Rome that was just awakening.

I would meet Anselmo again in 1985, when he was an integral figure in that circle of gay artists and intellectuals that included Massimo Consoli, Dario Bellezza, and Riccardo Peloso. He was living in the house of Sora Giulia [Sister Giulia], an elderly fairy who was the madam of the house on Via delle Vergini, a place that was quite famous in that milieu, as it was the sole well-known men-only brothel in the capital. The bordello was on the second story of a building that stood at the intersection of Via delle Vergini and Via delle Muratte. At the windows—which were always open—attractive and sensual young men sat in full view. Their actual intentions were not clear to my naive eyes; I assumed they were simply looking out of the window. I would eventually be informed of their "intended use" by Dario Bellezza and one of his most enchanting gigolos, with whom I was to share a love that would last twenty-two years.

(Translated by Danila Cannamela and Jennifer Delare)

Notes

1. Porpora Marcasciano, *L'aurora delle trans cattive*: *Storie, sguardi e vissuti della mia generazione transgender* (Rome: Alegre, 2018), iBooks.

2. Marcellona (big Marcella) was one of the nicknames of Marcella Di Folco. For more on this key figure in the Italian trans movement, see the introduction and part 6 of this volume (the interview with Simone Cangelosi in chap. 17 and the essay on Lina Pallotta's photography in chap. 18).

3. Dario Bellezza (1944–1996) was an Italian poet and playwright, whose literary work is deeply connected to his personal experience as a gay bourgeois man.

4. The Italian text consulted for this translation (the 2018 ebook edition of *L'aurora delle trans cattive*) has Ulysses in place of Aeneas. Not being able to compare this published version with any previous manuscript version, we are assuming that this is a slip, rather than an intentional joke. Therefore, in the translation, we preferred to use the name of Aeneas, who was Dido's lover in Virgil's *Aeneid*.

5. Here Marcasciano is referring to Pier Paolo Pasolini's murder, which occurred in 1975. Seventeen-year-old Pino Pelosi was convicted of the film director's killing, but the dynamics of the homicide still remain unclear.

6. [Not only geographic but also—and especially—cultural and sexual.] In the Italian text, the passage in Italics is in French, so we decided to keep the language as in the original but emended what is most likely a typo ["*sexsuel*"]. Marcasciano confirmed that the French phrase is not a quotation but a stylistic choice (private phone communication, June 21, 2021).

Chapter 9

From *Io, la "Romanina"*

Perché sono diventato donna (*I, "Romanina":* Why I Became a Woman)

ROMINA CECCONI

Romina Cecconi is one of the first Italian transsexual women who went through gender reassignment surgery. She is a pioneer of LGBTQ+ activism and fights for civil rights in Italy, and she is still regarded as an icon of the trans movement. In 1976, Cecconi published her autobiography, *Io, la "Romanina": Perché sono diventato donna*. The excerpts translated here provide detailed information about life as a gender-variant and low-income person before 1982, when the first Italian law regarding sex change (legge 164) was approved. Yet, they also shed light on how marginalized spaces can, in turn, create internal borders and margins, reaffirming sexist, racist, and classist logics. Unable to find a job in Florence—other than performing at a local circus, "il Gratta"—Cecconi migrated to Paris and then to Switzerland, where she joined two very different communities of migrants: a multicultural group of burlesque dancers and exiled Italian royalty. In Switzerland, Cecconi underwent gender reassignment surgery. As is typical of early transition memoirs, this pivotal moment is described as the correction of a mistake of nature. Back home, she was sentenced to *confino* ("confinement") in Volturino, a remote village in the south of Italy, where her presence created scandal and eventually reshaped the day-to-day life.

In Paris

My mother had found work in a trattoria in Santo Spirito.[1] Once a day, my brother and I would go eat at her place. We got half a portion each; if we had asked for more, my mother's salary would not have been enough to even pay for our meals. Turning up often at the restaurant was a very beautiful woman who made people stop when she passed through the neighborhood with her wide hips and clothes that clung to her rear, putting it on beautiful display. Her name was Anna. She knew how to make herself up; she knew how to move; she was my true ideal of femininity. I approached her once and timidly asked how she came to be so beautiful. She smiled at me and adjusted a white scarf I had placed around my neck. We became friends. She recommended perfumes, makeup, and clothes to me.

Anna was an institution in Santo Spirito. The bus drivers who passed through the quarter had developed the habit of honking when they would see her.

"What's happening?" people would ask themselves.

"They saw Anna," the more informed would respond.

Today, she's still an attractive woman, even if she shows the effects of her age. And not many months have passed since I went to see her to thank her for her recommendations.

"You've come a long way," she said to me. "I don't believe that it was all my doing."

It isn't, in fact, even if it is true that there were certain concrete examples, exactly like Anna was, who pushed me forward with courage in order to reach my goal.

It was a period of darkest poverty. Tickets for cross-dressing continued to arrive at my house, and by this time I was frequenting the Capannina delle Cascine every night. With Silvia and a few others, we spent long evenings waiting for our friends. They would arrive around midnight, after the movies, or after a game of cards. They were in groups of three or four, all of them squeezed into a Fiat 600. We would dance with them, joke, and then, if we liked someone, we would go off to the park. I never went too far; I was afraid of some assault, afraid that they would steal the little money I kept in my purse. The worst hostility we received came from a group of pederasts who for years had parked themselves on the benches of Piazza Vittorio Veneto. I remember they used nicknames ("Bianchino," "Processione")—all homosexuals by normal appearance, people of a certain age who would go off with the young boys under the arches of the Ponte della Vittoria, paying five hundred lire. Our arrival created problems for their activity.

We didn't offer money. We were, however, more attractive, and the boys preferred our company. There were also some prostitutes who couldn't stand us. I remember the "Venetian," an old woman who had worked in a brothel, who would stand behind the hedges until some client began to sing, "Venezia, la luna e tu."[2]

At that point, the poor woman would come out of the dark, a price would be agreed upon, and after having pocketed a few hundred lire, she would raise her skirts in the middle of the gravel, standing up, without even going up to a tree. Another famous prostitute was "Cheetah."[3] She was also old and had come to be called that for her great ugliness. Small cars overloaded with young boys would arrive, and you could hear them shout: "Cheetah . . . come out." The poor woman would begin to run after the car, throwing stones and everything at hand.

Beyond the bridge, on the pebbly bank of the Arno, was Fernanda. She was a tiny woman and spent the nights waiting for the sand diggers. A few grams of coffee were enough for her to make love, or she would get fifty lire from the young boys in exchange for a quick touch of her bust. Silvia, my friends, and I disturbed this entire world that had imposed its rules and prices in the park for years. Sometimes they would come looking for us, threatening us, but more often they limited themselves to badmouthing us with their clients, saying we were sick, that we had infected a bunch of people with venereal diseases.

I continued with the hormone treatments, ever more informed by the magazines that, by then, arrived regularly from Paris. I injected myself intramuscularly with folliculin and estrogens. My breasts were a beautiful reality by then. I could very well have been taken for a woman at that point: I didn't have any hair on my face or chest, my skin was smooth, and my hair was very light. One evening, I felt so secure of myself that I wanted to test whether I could truly pass as a woman. A group of soldiers came, and I went forward. I spoke with them in a low and pleasing, sensual voice. I saw that they were excited, that they were whispering among themselves, and in the end, one of them gathered the courage and asked me how much I wanted. It was clear that they thought I was a woman, because in those days, transvestites weren't known in Florence, let alone paid.

I threw out a number—three thousand, I think—and they accepted. I said that I was a beginner, however, and that on that particular evening, I was having my period, so they would have to be happy with other services.

They didn't ask for more, and that was how I earned my first money as a woman. But the more I earned, the more I got tickets. Twenty, thirty, sixty thousand lire at a time for an offence to public decency, cross-dressing, and all the usual terms of the vice squad.

There was a period in which I actually had to pay half a million, and I had to decide to work seriously—given what they were paying me—to cover all those tickets. All the more so since I was thinking ever more persistently about the operation. At that time, the only possible place was Casablanca. A million and a half for the surgery, the same for the trip and the stay—an astronomical figure that I could only put aside by prostituting myself. I would leave home with little black panties that hid the part in front, making it resemble a vagina with particularly developed lips. My testicles had never fallen, my scrotum was small, so that I didn't have too many things to hide.

I preferred to go by car, because in the confusion of a compact car (those who went with me were, for the most part, young men with little money available), I could easily fool the client. Some, however, knew who I was and came all the same. This was something extremely risky for those times, because a man who went with another man was considered homosexual himself.

There were always many people waiting for me, and I decided to raise the rate to five thousand lire. Business went really well, and I began to put aside the money for the operation, for the trip to Casablanca.

In that period, I met Very, a girl from Turin who had gone through my same routine and who had been operated on. She was generous with advice and regard toward me; a truly sincere friendship developed between us that continues even today. When I told her about the difficulties I was having in my family, Very advised me to go and live alone in a small pensione in Piazza Santo Stefano. In fact, it was called the Santo Stefano pensione and for the most part housed girls, dancers, and a few traveling musicians. It was an extremely family-like environment, and the owner was a very understanding woman, always willing to defend her clients. . . .

I left for Paris one morning in February with Silvia. A few friends came to accompany us to the station, asking us, if we got on well there, to let them know as soon as possible. It was not a trip; it was an exploration. Thinking back on it, I see myself very similar to the migrants who left the south of Italy to become metalworkers in Milan or Turin. We didn't have cardboard suitcases or black clothing—we took the express train with traveling outfits of real leather—but the spirit was that of any Gennaro Esposito leaving for Lambrate.[4]

Despite our repeated requests, Madame Arthur had not given us an actual contract, but just a generic letter that said we could perform for a few weeks at her place, under conditions to be defined.

"That's enough to start," we thought. She must have been thinking, "Once here, I'll take care of it."

The place was a small theater that was anything but clean. It was small and overflowing with smoke, frequented almost exclusively by homosexuals, a small hideout where, for at least three hours every day, transvestites of every part of the world would take turns. The first evening that Silvia and I presented ourselves at Madame Arthur's, full of energy and enthusiasm, we couldn't hide our disappointment.

"What do you know how to do?"

"We dance; we sing. If necessary, we can do a striptease."

"Come tomorrow afternoon to speak with the director. He will decide. I would recommend this hotel to you."

Money was not spoken of, and the hotel was an old building, all corners and lampshades attached to the ceiling, with no toilet in the room. We noted this to the doorman who accompanied us, and, shrugging his shoulders, he pointed out the bidet. The room, pompously called the "Provençal," had a curtain with a diamond pattern—Provençal, in fact—that matched the coverlet. A double bed and a wobbly nightstand completed the furnishings. By night, it was all opening and closing of the neighbors' doors, with people arguing and women who let everyone know, whether they were interested or not, that they were feeling pleasure.

We decided to take a walk around the most famous places in the city the next morning. "Paris awaits us!" we told ourselves without too much enthusiasm before turning out the light.

We saw the Eiffel Tower and Notre Dame, but in place of the romantic Paris we expected, there were dozens of skyscrapers. To reach the Seine, we had to spend half an hour in the subway. History and literature had given way to technology. We felt terribly provincial, and at the same time, so much richer than the people who were running around in front of us on the sidewalk.

The director was a short and thin little man. His head almost completely bald, he had a wisp of black hair on his forehead, as if he wanted to look like a scamp. He had been a dancer, he was a pederast, and now he taught the new arrivals how to execute a dance step. We perhaps knew more about it than he, but it was necessary to stand and watch and thank him for his advice. The most aberrant ideas came to him after long reconsideration—bad taste personified in the service of an audience that came, above all, in search of adventure.

I recalled my times at the circus. My performance at Gratta's had left the audience breathless, and not only because they liked my sexual teasing. In the dull faces of the Parisian customers, on the other hand, I managed to see only tension and dark desire. Never a smile, nor could a cheerful joke be heard.

They say that we Italians are loud because we shout and move our hands. But those people, all of them the same, those impenetrable faces capable of smiling only after having drunk half a bottle of cognac, made me long for the dear old Italians who laugh at so little and become drunk only by accident.

The evening of the opening, after the songs, the dance steps, the swings of the hip that at Circus Imperus had been accompanied by "Olé" shouted in unison, the audience applauded without warmth. I left the stage with a lump in my throat, and the director surprised me when, after forcing me to take a bow, he said into my ear, "Everything went very well."

No, Paris really wasn't what we had hoped for. No romanticism, no *bohème*—anything but. That illusion was still alive, but it had been made into an industry to extract money from the many provincials who arrived from throughout the world and particularly from that immense countryside that is France outside of Paris.

We had to fight hard to keep ourselves alive, to not be overwhelmed by the envy and nastiness of others. All of them wanted to be the most beautiful, the most admired. All asked for the closing numbers and strove to put the others in a bad light. There were Spanish girls, German, Finnish, American, even African. Inside, one could find drugs and pornography, but also knives, sulfuric acid, pistols. Every girl had her friends, her protectors, and every protector had his gang.

"Have you been operated on?"

"No, I'd like to do it as soon as possible."

"That guy doesn't deserve you. Hermaphrodites cost more. Let me see your breasts!"

Among ourselves, we learned to recognize one another in this way. Even before asking each other our names, we wanted to know at what point the development of breasts had reached. The few girls who were definitively women by then were snobs to the others. They spent hours talking about the details of the operation, defending the techniques used on their bodies. All modesty and all restraint collapsed in the face of the open competition that existed in that environment. You were appreciated for your own body, for your beauty, and for your level of femininity—a continuous challenge in which bluffing and bragging counted as much as real attributes. There were thirty of us, distributed among five suffocating dressing rooms. Thirty hysterical people who lived together for hours in a few square meters. Furious arguments drew in everyone: for a costume out of place, for a quip beyond those called for in the script, for applause stolen by someone coming afterwards. The recurring vengeance was to sprinkle a ground razor blade in the greasepaint. Many times, I ran the risk of cutting myself deeply, disfiguring myself, without having the strength to accuse them directly, even with certainty of the guilty party.

I was immediately disliked for my attractiveness, for the success that I achieved. Madame Arthur was happy with me, but the others were not. I would go out twice during the evening. The first was for an oriental dance, with a very small bra and panties from which were hanging colored scarves that I would let fall, one by one. The second time, I had to sing a medley of Italian songs, from Milva to Mina to Celentano, which ended (in exceptionally bad taste) with the Hymn of Mameli. At that point, I would take off the dress, which would be transformed, as if by magic, into the tricolor flag. I would go off that way, amid the applause of the people whom I absolutely could not see for the smoke that filled the room.

Madame Arthur paid us little. I remember that we barely managed to eat, and if we had not had a line of customers waiting for us at the exit, we would have been unable to survive.

In Paris, the transvestites were organized into very specific clans where, even then, exploitation flourished. There were the Corsicans, the Spanish, the Algerians, and naturally, the Italians. Each of these gangs struggled hard to secure the new arrivals, and from the first evening, I had offers to tie myself to one or the others. Madame Arthur didn't want anything to do with these matters.

"Outside of here, do what you want. Inside here, everything must go smoothly." . . .

I kept working at Madame Arthur's, and things went so well that I was offered to close the first part of the show with a type of patriotic striptease—that is, the Italian flag again, but instead of waving it at the end, I would enter from the beginning wrapped up in the tricolor and then play with the edges of the fabric until I was left completely nude. I didn't like the idea much, but at Madame Arthur's you either accepted the rules without a word or you were thrown out on the spot.

So I accepted without any objections, but Ursula, a German transvestite taller and more powerful than me, although getting on in years by then, was not at all enthusiastic that I swiped the spot from them. In fact, finishing an act meant leaving an excellent impression on the clients, and when, during the intermission, we would descend among the crowd, whoever had done the last number always found someone ready to offer them something to drink and perhaps set a date for outside.

Ursula began to boycott me in every way. I would find the clothing for the stage out of place or the wigs messed up, and the other girls didn't have any difficulty in telling me who it had been. One day, I decide to confront her with courage, threatening to tell Madame Arthur everything, and she, as her only answer, showed me a little bottle.

"It's sulfuric acid," she said, "and the Corsicans are my friends."

That was enough for me to accept everything, to the point that I asked the proprietress for my old post back.

"I'm not ambitious," I told her. "For me, where I was is fine."

In the meantime, things at the hotel didn't go better. The young Italian man procured many clients for me, but all of them were down at the heels. Algerians, emigrants, people who could spend little and expected a lot. Not to mention that they made me quite scared, with their shabby appearance and faces ready for anything.

The surprise came at the end of the first week. For the room, I should have had to spend fifty thousand lire a day, and I had thought of leaving a good tip for my friend, giving him fifty thousand lire altogether. But I was deceived. I was presented with a bill for 200,000 French francs, about 250,000 lire. I couldn't even find the strength to breathe. I said simply that I would be getting out of there immediately, since I hadn't even managed to earn that figure. But my friend had foreseen such a move.

"I wouldn't advise it. The French police don't like that you're here as a prostitute; if they come to learn it, you'll have to go back to Italy with a deportation order."

That's how I began to think seriously about returning. Florence has a thousand defects, but in the end, Romanina is everyone's friend, and robberies happen very rarely. In any event, it's possible to live in peace if you just manage to avoid certain circles. Silvia shared my opinion as well. That evening at Madame Arthur's, I did the worst number of that entire period. There was also some hissing, and once the show was over, I went to the proprietress and revealed that I wanted to leave. I asked her how much she owed me, but she laughed in my face.

"Dear," she said, "when one interrupts a work relationship so brusquely, one doesn't have a right to anything. In fact, one should pay a penalty."

I gathered my luggage, my clothes, and the few gifts I had received in that period, and I booked the train for the next morning. Someone advised me to try Soho in London, but I didn't feel like it. I was nostalgic for the streets along the Arno, for the Capannina, for my mother, for my little pensione in Piazza Santo Stefano, where the most that could happen was that someone might want to leap out to cause a little sensation.

In Switzerland

I decided to have the operation in Switzerland after obtaining, in Paris, the address of a clinic considered safe.[5] Although the expense was not specified, it was less than two million. I did my calculations. I had barely 600,000 lire in cash, and naturally, I couldn't ask anything from my family. I decided then to sell everything that I had and to leave before the sentence for confinement became enforceable.[6] I turned to a friend of mine and invited her to purchase my mink fur at a reasonable price. I had tried in various places and all of them, having to deal with a transvestite, tried to pay ludicrous amounts. Fortunately, my friend was willing to help me, and with that transaction, I succeeded in putting together something over a million. I knew it wasn't sufficient, but as a down payment, I thought, it could be enough. The rest I would have paid in any manner, even by promissory notes.

I left for Switzerland at the height of summer. I had a minimal wardrobe, the money in my handbag, and an address: that of the clinic, to be precise. It was the middle of July. A friend of mine from Messina who had been operated on in that clinic had assured me that in a few days I would have undergone the surgery.

My mother had accompanied me to the station. Not that we spoke much, but we understood each other perfectly. It was the crowning achievement of a childhood, an entire youth spent with the sole objective of being able to be a woman. My mother limited herself to kissing me and wishing me well. She didn't want to remind me of all the times she had surprised me dressed as a woman when she returned home, or of the arguments, the violent arguments on that subject that had divided us so many times. But it's clear that she thought of all that as she pointed out my compartment to the porter or as she waved a white handkerchief, like in old movies.

I was enthusiastic and exhausted at the same time. Scenes from my life came back to me—the first time that I had given myself to a man, the poor room in San Donnino, the death of [my stepfather] Cecconi, the expulsion from boarding school. All of it seemed to have the same denominator, a constant. I always saw myself as a woman, dressed as a woman, made myself up as a woman, or simply as a lover: sensual, attractive. My life had passed under that yoke, but now it was all about to end. I did not ask myself about my future; I was certain that as a first thing, I would begin the paperwork to have my new identity recognized, then I would decide what to do. A friend of mine had succeeded in getting married. Coccinelle had thrilled the world with her feats.[7] I could choose both an artistic career and a quiet, bourgeois, calm life with a man willing to accept me. Everything was possible, and everything was legal.

I arrived at Chiasso in the early afternoon. Once again, I had to endure the humiliation of a customs officer who scratched his head while reading my name on the identity card, who asked advice from his superiors. My compartment mates must have understood something, and from the border onward, a woman who had spoken kindly with me up to that point changed her compartment, red in the face, with a stubborn little boy pulled by the hand.

I knew that they were the final humiliations, and I accepted those as well. I will not give the name of the Swiss city in which I was operated on, nor the name of the clinic. Certain operations took place in complete secrecy, if not exactly illegally. The clinic was as I had imagined it, also because Switzerland, in its traditional cleanliness and beauty, risks in the long run even being dull.

It was a two-story building, set among greenery. Very beautiful cars in front of the entrance, an age-old park, English gardens. I sought out the doctor and learned that he had left for his vacation. His schedule was already full even for the next month. The operation could not take place before September—September 19, to be exact. I was told all this by a lovely nurse without being ruffled, without looking at me with that morbid curiosity I had always noticed toward me in jail as on the street, in boarding school as at customs. I felt like I was living in a different world—freer, more mine—despite the fact that I had known it for only a few hours. I was perfectly at ease, I no longer had anything to fear, and if I had to wait two months, I would spend them there, in Switzerland, getting by in some way.

The cost of the operation, now that I knew it with certainty, was 1,700,000 lire. I had just two-thirds of the amount, and I had to live for two months in that city, but I was not discouraged. I realized that there was no comparison to make with Paris, with Rome, with Florence itself. Everything seemed clean; people had no morbid curiosity. I could walk for hours downtown, stop at the windows, enter the cafés, the boutiques, and never notice the slightest wink of an eye, the slightest disrespectful gesture. Even our migrants [from Italy], whom I recognized by their height and by the color of their skin, stayed in their place and did not care about my presence. For the first time, I felt sure of myself.

A friend had given me the address of a private club where only figures of great prestige entered. It was an excellent opportunity to insert myself into good Swiss society, to get to know up-close a world that I knew only through glossy magazines. Further, thanks to the help of an unmistakably Italian barista, I was able to work with the wealthy merchants from all countries who found themselves in those parts.

Although the club was extremely restricted, once inside one ended up being part of a circle of friendships of the highest level. Marina Doria, for example. Vittorio Emanuele, Gunter Sachs,[8] Ira Fürstenberg, Victoria and Geraldine Chaplin.

I was immediately liked for my charm, my elegance, my unconventionality. Two, three times a week I would be invited to dinner by one of these figures, and once again, I was not the curious object to be presented to the guests, but a very normal table companion appreciated for who they were.

I never talked about my real situation, let alone that I was in Switzerland waiting for the operation. I limited myself only to spreading the rumor that I had to pursue some treatments at some clinic, and that I would probably stay for two or three months.

It was a wonderful summer. I was presented to Vittorio Emanuele as an Italian journalist, and immediately, that tall and blondish gentleman—who could have been such an important figure for Italy if only his grandfather had been more intelligent—complained to me about the Italian press, which in that very period had been speaking ironically about Beatrice and her Roman lovers.[9]

"You are merciless sometimes," he told me, offering me an aperitivo. "The Italians ridicule like few others."

"You are no longer Italian?"

"You are right; I often speak of Italy as if I no longer had anything to do with it. You understand, and it's normal after what happened."

I looked at that faded man, certainly lacking the impetuous personality I thought was the prerogative of royal families. I did not find him to be much sexually: he held his glass with delicacy, he moved it slowly between his fingers. He moved with naturalness among the guests of the villa in which we found ourselves. And yet, although he was a long way from that image of the Prince Charming that I had always unconsciously taken him to be, I realized that he possessed his own appeal, an aura of mystery, of impenetrability that attracted me, leaving me deeply curious.

I tried to act my part to the end. Vittorio Emanuele told me that he had suffered greatly in learning about the flood in Florence.

"It is a city that was always very dear to me. Did you suffer damage?"

"I have a villa near Piazzale Michelangelo," I responded. "I could see the water that flooded Santa Croce. I remember a tree that was stuck in front of the doors of the National Library for several days. There was no way to help anyone. The children, the young people of the whole world were very good on that occasion."[10]

He drank his martini as he drank my words. The villa near Piazzale Michelangelo had come to mind in order to respond with irony to a question that seemed ridiculous to me. Yet he took everything as true, he agreed with interest. No doubt even occurred to him that his way of speaking, his detachment, his official appearance in those very rooms where more than one lady was already showing her breasts and many guests had gone off behind the plants of the terrace, were absolutely ridiculous, and that they deserved a response similarly false and idiotic.

I don't think that the prince got along well with Marina Doria, his wife. It very often happened that I attended some parties where it was possible to meet one or the other, but unlikely together. These were decidedly animated parties. One well-known princess and sometime-actress princess carried on coarse scenes with her escorts. I saw her completely naked for an hour while all the others, that splendid international beautiful society, threw coins on her like a whore. And naturally, she accepted everything because that was precisely the intent of her exhibition.

Too high in the esteem of the poor folk, these people had no other choice but to humiliate themselves, being reduced to the most absolute pettiness when they were among themselves. Perhaps by doing so, they thought they were finding a balance, pursuing something that risked slipping from their hands.

The princess was the most unrestrained, but the most charming, the most sensitive, the loneliest, was Victoria Chaplin. Because of her reserved behavior she was considered lesbian, even if that, in that environment, could not have scandalized absolutely anyone. Victoria discovered, in my exuberance, a complement to her hesitations and her fears. That was how we became friends. We spent long evenings speaking of the affairs of the world; we walked for entire afternoons, hand in hand, going shopping. We had become inseparable, but ours was just a platonic love. . . .

I entered the clinic boldly. I had no fear and even fewer uncertainties. It was the crowning achievement of my life, and I was only worried about being as quick about it as possible.

The doctor was a gentleman in his forties, his temples slightly gray. He had a spotless lab coat and a professional air but for all that was no less humane and charming. He welcomed me into his office with a detached tone, and aiding himself with some photos and drawings, he explained to me the phases of the operation. He also explained what I could do, how I would have to behave when making love, the risks that I could run. He wasn't telling me anything new. For years, I had studied the subject, and I was able to understand everything.

I thought about how different the reality was with respect to how I had imagined it in other times. Even as a child, I had wanted to castrate myself, to cut off everything by myself. Now I had confirmation that an operation of that sort was not a castration, but a way of restoring to one's physique the female attributes that had remained in a potential state.

"You are from Florence," the doctor said to me, "and you know Michelangelo well. We don't do anything other than help your feminine forms emerge definitively from the indefinite, from the block."

I was not familiar with the statues he was referring to, but I understood what he meant. I anticipated the doctor's definitions; it seemed like repeating a lesson that I had always known, like writing a dictation that I knew by heart. I so identified with the part that it almost didn't seem that he was talking about me. The doctor managed to make everything perfectly normal; my knowledge of the subject did the rest.

I will not get into the details of the surgery. They are very painful for me and represent the divide between expectation and certainty, the boundary between discomfort and satisfaction. Specialized magazines and, recently, even weekly magazines for women have described the operation minutely with incredible casualness, masked only by a purported scientific nature. I will try, however, to give an idea of what it means, surgically, to become a woman.

In my case, the task was made easier by the fact that my testicles had never descended as normally happens with boys. I was practically half-woman already, and the surgeon could avoid the more complex and risky part of his work. My penis was also of very small dimensions. The amputation itself, a few millimeters from the base, could be made only after nerves and blood vessels had been gathered and made to pass elsewhere. The very small penis that remained would be needed for my physiological and erotic needs. The body was then cut between the penis and the anus to be able to insert the empty testicular sac which would then remain pulled in internally for about fifteen days, thanks to a special cylinder. At the sides of the opening, there would be constructed, via the methods of plastic surgery, two big labia.

I asked the surgeon only two questions. I wanted to know if I could receive a man normally in the vagina, and if I would feel pleasure. The response was what I expected. My new femininity had also been constructed with the help of the surgery. For example, the skin of the scrotum had had to be cut and then internally resewn at its apex. Therefore, after a certain period of time, a man could be received very well, but it was necessary to be careful that he wasn't too violent, because there had been confirmed cases in which the top of the cavity had broken, requiring a new, very painful operation. Furthermore, I could never feel pleasure other than a psychological one when receiving a man from the front, while my erogenous zone par excellence would be my clitoris, where the blood vessels and nerve centers of my organ had been built up. Finally, since my vagina would never be able to moisten on its own, I would have to use some lubricants to avoid excessive friction.

"But can the same thing be done with a normal man?" I asked the surgeon.

"Clearly not," was his response, "unless he wanted to risk losing his life with ninety percent chance."

It was the confirmation I had been lacking: the certainty that my nature had acted only halfway. At that point, I wanted only to get to the surgery as soon as possible. I asked the surgeon to speed up the stage of the diagnostic checks. I was brought into a very beautiful room where a bunch of flowers and a blonde nurse were waiting for me. For several days there were the usual examinations. Blood checks, continual visits in order to establish general conditions—all of it brightened by excellent food and an enormous television that had been placed at the foot of my bed.

On the day of the operation, the surgeon wanted to see me for the last time. "You know that tomorrow morning you will wake up as a woman?"

I was moved, but I couldn't find the strength to say anything. I asked only that they give me total anesthesia and whether, when I awoke, I would still feel a lot of pain.

"For several days it will be difficult," they replied, "but the joy of having put an end to your problems will surpass any pain."

"How many of these operations have you done?" I asked the surgeon.

"I couldn't say, but I can assure you that I have gained good experience. They arrive at my clinic from all parts of the world. By now we have made considerable steps; there is no longer any risk."

I didn't want to verify his ability. I was simply curious.

The nurses came to take me at ten in the morning. I looked out the window and saw that the sky was clouding over. Summer had ended a few days before; Switzerland was preparing itself for its very long winter. I thought of Victoria, and I asked for a moment of time to phone her. I don't know why, but I had the desire to tell her how happy I was at that moment. I would have given anything just to have her beside my bed when I woke up. I looked for her phone number, began to call, and I remembered suddenly that she didn't know anything about me and that I could not disappoint her.

I was alone once again, alone as always in my important choices, in my important battles. On the other hand, I always won, precisely because solitude did not allow me to lie back, to relax for just a moment. I tried to convince myself that reaching a goal of such vital importance on my own would give me more joy, more satisfaction.

I smiled at the nurse and told her I was ready. As I was lying on the gurney, I passed through very white corridors and felt my strength abandoning me—the anesthesia was beginning to have its effect. The nurse noticed and covered me even better with the sheet. I remember her voice, very distant as she entered the operating room, pushing the trolley. I remember passing a hand between my legs, in order to have felt a sensation that, through my free choice, I would never again feel for the rest of my life.

"God willing," I said, "tomorrow morning there will no longer be anything here."

I awoke euphoric. I was still under the effect of the anesthesia. I touched my abdomen and let out a cry of joy. I wasn't in the best condition. I had to remain with my legs spread, like a woman in labor, for the fifteen days with that cylinder in my vagina. Two tubes emerged from similar wounds, to let the urine and fluids escape. The surgery had lasted four and a half hours, but I still felt the strength to celebrate.

I immediately called Italy. I wanted to speak with my mother, with the landlady of the pensione, and with a friend. For all three it was a true joy, and they wanted to congratulate me. In the voice of my friend, I heard a veil of sadness, because she had also desired for a long time to undergo my same operation but didn't have the economic means.

But perhaps the most moving moment was the meeting with the surgeon. Forced into a position that was certainly not decent, I felt quite uncomfortable when I saw arrive that very distinguished gentleman who seemed incapable of feeling any emotion. He sat beside my bed to ask me, smiling, "Happy?"

"You can't know how much."

"I can imagine it, though. I know how much one waits and suffers before reaching this objective. See, today you are born for the second time. I didn't do anything other than correct a small error that nature had committed against you. I consider all this, even if the law does not know how to make any decision with regard to it, a specific professional duty of mine. You will not have any more complexes toward anyone. You always were psychologically a woman, but even on a sexual level, you already had many feminine attributes to begin with. Your abdomen, for example, is flat; your hips are wide. It seems that your entire body was formed for motherhood, but at the last minute that very small penis arrived to modify the rest of the work."

I began to cry. I realized that that man really believed in his work, aware as he was of creating happiness for so many people like me.

"Now, you have to know how to use this new and definitive femininity of yours with care. Don't risk, with violent intercourse, what we were able to do during the operation. Avoid an excessive number of contacts, and keep in mind that you will feel pleasure from the part of your member that I left you. I know through experience that no man will ever be able to notice that we had to modify your nature—the error of your nature—with an operation. My work can be recognized only by a scientist, and a man who is about to make love absolutely does not have the coolness necessary to conduct an analysis like a scholar. Therefore, give yourself with peace, with relaxedness, certain that your secret—if you want it to remain such—will never be discovered by anyone. I have clients who were able to get married normally in countries other than the ones they were from and who are happy with their men, who were not always informed about the operation. In a case of this sort, however, I would advise you to speak frankly to the man who might ask to become your husband. A surprise, a revelation, after a few years of marriage, could place everything into question again."

He was not only a surgeon, that man. He was also a psychologist, a friend, a true friend.

I was unable to stop crying, and he understood that I would have continued as long as he continued to speak to me in that way. He rose, he kissed my hand, and after several hours, I saw a very beautiful bunch of roses arrive in my room. There was written only: "To the beautiful Signora Cecconi," and in the signature, I recognized my surgeon's name.

My mother wanted to come to see me, although I had begged her to not leave Florence. Without realizing it, I must have told her on the phone that I was left nearly without money, and she hurried to bring it to me. Poor woman, she didn't know that with the circle of friendships I had created, it would not have been difficult for me, as soon as I left that clinic, to overcome the momentary difficulties.

I did not want tears for our meeting. I knew very well that if she found me emotional, my mother would have burst into tears of her own, so I appeared to be even happier than I was in reality.

As soon as she entered the room, I attacked her with: "Do you see that your Romanina managed to do it? What will they say now in Florence when I throw who I am in their faces? And the first who dares call me a transvestite, I'll send him to jail for defamation."

My mama smiled. She was accustomed to my moments of euphoria, but this was more intense, truer than all the others.

"Look, when you return to Florence, you need to leave for the compulsory residence: three years in the province of Foggia, as you feared and as they threatened."

Confinement

I had to change trains in Bologna and take the express that would discharge me at Foggia in the evening.[11] While I was waiting for the connection, with my suitcase at my feet, a voluminous purse in my arms, I recalled the gynecological appointment that I had had in Careggi. I tried to remember the expression of the doctors in order to understand if I had the least possibility of success. The lawyer to whom I had turned won a suit of that sort previously and gave me the greatest confidence. I decided, however, that I would not speak to anyone of the matter in progress, almost as if to ward off bad luck, as superstition. At the same time, I feared that the prosecutor in Florence could boycott me, once he learned of it.

The express ran along the sea, and I began to ask myself what was waiting for me. I couldn't imagine Volturino and, even less, the life of a compulsory resident. On the other hand, I had known how to survive jail, the very sad Parisian experience, the envy of Ursula, the nostalgia of the Swiss Christmas, and I felt capable of overcoming even that umpteenth sad experience—not without some fear, however.

I arrived in Foggia awhile after it had gotten dark. I presented myself to the carabinieri, as I had been ordered, saying simply, "I am Cecconi."

According to the written telephone message, they were waiting for "Cecconi, Romano." Raising his eyes from a pile of paperwork, the guard said: "Ah, the wife. And your husband, where is he?"

"I am the husband. The Cecconi you're waiting for is me," I responded, unperturbed.

The poor conscripted officer. He made a face of every color and assembled the colleagues and superiors he could find.

"You cannot go around dressed like that," I was told.

"I am a woman from the tips of my toes to the top of my head."

"Show us, then."

I had to undress. Then they called the boss. Even he did not want to accept what the operation had rendered evident even to a child.

"But how can it be, but how can it be?" he agonized as he scratched the back of his neck with a pen. "Our colleagues in Florence have played a good joke on us."

In the end, he asked me to take off my clothes, and for the second time, I slipped out of my dress. I hinted at two steps of a striptease. Before becoming completely nude, I let out a little shout—"Oplà!"—as I had done at Madame Arthur's when I would finish my strip.

If I had to undress myself, I preferred to do the catwalk rather than feel myself humiliated and pathologically observed. Naked, I began to show off my feminine attributes, calling on the corporals and sergeants to bear witness.

"She's really a piece of ass!" was their final comment—full of good taste, discretion, manners.

But with my extemporaneous exhibition, I at least obtained the ability to remain dressed as a woman. The leader decided I would spend that night in Foggia, I would be accompanied by a soldier in plain clothes to a hotel, and the next day, I would leave for Volturino, forty kilometers away, on a bus line.

It wasn't up to me to make decisions; therefore, I accepted without a word. This new adventure of mine, which was to last a good three years, had begun as I feared: coarseness, ignorance—and my sense of humor, which arrived to support me at the most difficult moments.

The next morning, the political commissioner came to my room to get me. The news had spread quickly. For a night, the policemen and carabinieri had sneered behind my back.

"But is it really true that you have to go to Volturino?" the commissioner began very shrilly.

"That's what they say," I responded, bored.

"You know, I'm from Volturino, and I know that your presence risks provoking revolution."

"Don't send me, then."

"Who knows what could happen!" was his final comment.

I had to spend the entire morning in the barracks. In Foggia, they didn't yet seem convinced of what I was, or perhaps the carabinieri on duty the evening before had promised their colleagues to show me naked one more time. I wanted to satisfy them, but I repeatedly expressed my disgust. Finally, after eating in the barracks with the soldiers, I left for my destination on a bus that must also have weathered the difficulties of the war. It was cold inside that motor vehicle that was older than I was. The wind came through all the windows, and I wrapped myself uselessly in my fur coat to protect myself. To travel the forty-five kilometers took at least two hours on uneven roads, with the asphalt having nearly disappeared. My traveling companions didn't take their eyes off me. Black—all unfailingly dressed in black—they would get off a couple of stops after having gotten on, and they would disappear into the fields of the Tavoliere plain. I asked the driver how many meters in elevation this Volturino was, and the response was not comforting. Nine hundred meters above sea level, harsh winters, frequent snow, and the risk of being isolated.

And finally, I got there. I arrived in a piazza that seemed deserted to me, but I didn't do it in time to look for anyone when suddenly two, three, ten people gathered around me from nowhere.

"A foreigner has arrived!" "A foreigner has arrived!" "Beautiful, this blonde woman." Of course, two very dark little men wanted to take my suitcases, and they asked me where I was going only after having gone twenty meters ahead without a specific direction. A young man better equipped than the others came toward me with the air of a Don Juan—"Do you speak German?"—and placed himself beside me to be my escort like the others. The line got bigger; the children ran behind shouting, "A German woman has arrived!" The more experienced commented: "It must be the sergeant's wife."

I felt like Lollobrigida in *Bread, Love and Dreams*. I began to move my hips; I felt the buzz behind me increase. Only then did I realize that among the many escorts there was not even one woman. And I would see very few of them around, even in the subsequent days.

I arrived at the barracks of the carabinieri, and I was finally able to take back possession of my baggage.

"You are Signora Cecconi?" a young sergeant with an accent from Veneto asked me.[12]

"No," I responded, annoyed, knowing by then what was going to happen. "I am Cecconi." And without giving him the time to comment, I removed my fur, slipped out of my dress, and began to undress completely.

The sergeant stopped me: "Wait, wait. What are you doing?"

"I am showing you who I am, even if my identity card gives me the name of a man."

The poor young man ran to call his superiors.

"Where do we put this one?" was their comment. "But are we sure it's a woman?"

The scene in Foggia was repeated, and I did the striptease this time as well, among the poor desks of that miserable barracks. No one dared make the decision to let me be dressed as a woman. They ran to call the mayor and a councilman. They arrived out of breath, their eyes out of their sockets, still in their work clothes.

"And you would be a man with a pussy?" the mayor said to me sternly, as if I had to apologize to him for something.

"I am simply a woman, and dressed as a man, I would really create a scandal."

I was forced to undress again. The sergeant from Veneto, in Volturino for three months and certainly with an insane desire to make love, went around the room as if driven mad, scrutinizing me from every side. There was a huddle among the notables. The marshal, mayor, and councilman were on the point of also calling the doctor and the parish priest but dropped it when someone mentioned that it was only a question of law. They came to agreement in admitting that, dressed as a man, I would create quite a few problems among the local population, which was accustomed to welcoming mafiosi and assassins but was in serious difficulty when faced with a very beautiful woman "like you see up north."

They decided that they would house me with a poor woman who rented rooms, and they advised me to not tell anyone of the reason for my stay. For the moment, they would indicate that I was the new gym teacher, both for my attractiveness and my height.

"Remain dressed as a woman and behave respectably. In this area, television has just arrived," advised the mayor. He ordered the town's police to escort me to my new landlady in the small patrol car.

I got into the Fiat 500 with difficulty. It was 1967.[13] I had a very short miniskirt, a red blouse, and boots higher than my knees, and my fur and hair pulled back on the nape of my neck made me appear even taller. The makeup did the rest. The Fiat stopped in front of a barber shop where a few young men were talking. I learned then that that was their meeting point, that the barber was the only place open until evening. There, the men conveyed their ideas to one another on the opposite sex, they discussed sexual encounters, they exchanged the latest pornographic magazines.

As soon as I got out of the car, my miniskirt rose even higher. There was a very long whistle and the comment that I expected: "What a smashing blonde!" "The blonde has arrived!" Ultimately, it pleased me.

Guided by the police, I entered the large entry door across from the barber, and I saw my new home. It was very cold, and it was dark. Finally, illuminated by a weak light, an elderly woman came to open up for us. She was dressed completely in black, just one tooth in her mouth, her face terribly wrinkled. The policeman explained who I was and asked if she could host me.

"My daughter," she said, looking me up and down with surprise, "if you are a good girl, I will be good with you. Be good, my daughter. This will be your room."

"I will be good," I said, just to say something, and I felt myself freeze upon seeing the room where I would have to live.

It was a very spacious room, furnished with a brass bed and a nightstand. It had a ceiling light and a gas stove in the middle, but the stove was not lit. The blankets wept with dampness. I immediately had to purchase a tank of gas to be able to light the heat.

Finally, I was left alone, and from the closed windows, I could hear in the street the comments of the men gathered at the barbershop.

"She's a wonderful woman!" "What I'd give to get her in bed!" "She's worth more than the prostitutes in Foggia." "There are only women like that up north, and that's why I want to migrate."

I was taken by an infinite sadness. I couldn't put up with staying three years under those conditions. I felt abandoned by everyone, even by my usual sense of humor. I saw perfectly the ridiculousness of the whole affair, but it was a tragic ridiculousness, and I absolutely couldn't manage to joke about it. I had given ten thousand lire to my landlady as a down-payment for a month's rent, and that banknote had had a miraculous effect. She seemed truly rejuvenated with that money in hand. Ten thousand lire still had a lot of value in those parts. They were poor, rough people, and precisely because of that, incapable of understanding anything that I might do. I was about to start crying—I absolutely could not manage to remain unmoved—when I heard a knock at the door.

"The sergeant is here," said the old woman. "Shall I let him in?"

I felt freed from distress. That sergeant from Veneto was the only kind person I had seen since I arrived in Volturino. Perhaps because he was also from somewhere else, he felt as out-of-place as me.

"Come in, come in," I said with enthusiasm, and let myself fall on the bed in a slightly sexy pose.

"You must excuse me," he began, "but I will have to come often to check if you are at home. You know well that at night, you cannot go out, and in particular, you must behave well, otherwise the penalties increase."

"Just come, you will always be very welcome."

He smiled, fortunately, and plucked up his courage.

"What beautiful legs you have, and what a beautiful bust. Do you know that for three months I have not seen a woman? And I'm hardly old; I'm thirty-three and my needs . . ."

I didn't even let him finish. Whether he was on duty or not, I didn't care. I wanted to make him my friend. I had too much need of one, and then, I seriously liked him. I didn't have time to undress. As soon as he entered me, he reached orgasm.

"I'm sorry," he remarked, "but I was wanting it too much."

"Don't worry, you can make up for it tomorrow."

"Thank you, *signorina*. Now I have to go, otherwise, the marshal will suspect."

"Stop. Tell me what there is to do in Volturino."

"Nothing, *signorina*, nothing. There's no movie theater; the men go to the barbershop and the women stay home. And as soon as it gets dark, there's no one about. The town has three thousand inhabitants, but half have migrated. There are only women and a few idlers. They work in the fields, they raise beets, and in the winter, they lock themselves up at home. There's nothing to do here, as I told you. It's been three months and already, I can't stand it anymore."

(Translated by Gianpiero W. Doebler)

Notes

1. Romina Cecconi, *Io, la "Romanina": Perché sono diventato donna* (Florence: Vallecchi, 1976). The excerpts from the chapter "A Parigi" are the following: 110–13, 122–27, 129–31.

2. A song from a popular comedy of the same name, first released in 1958.

3. "Cheetah" in the sense of Tarzan's simian companion, not the large cat.

4. Lambrate is a zone in northeastern Milan. In the postwar period, it was an industrial district and home to factories that attracted migrants to the north from southern Italy. Gennaro Esposito is a stereotypical southern Italian name.

5. Cecconi, *Io, la "Romanina,"* "In Svizzera: L'operazione," 158–63, 171–77.

6. A sentence for prostitution and curfew-related charges. This is discussed further later in these excerpts.

7. Coccinelle was the stage name of a famous French actress and singer. In 1958, she was one of the first celebrated Europeans to undergo gender reassignment surgery.

8. We corrected the original spelling Gunther with Gunter, as it is very likely that here Cecconi is referring to German photographer, author, and industrialist Gunter Sachs, who lived in Switzerland and received Swiss citizenship in 1976.

9. Vittorio Emanuele is the son of Italy's last king, Umberto II, who reigned for one month in 1946. His grandfather, Vittorio Emanuele III, had been king throughout the fascist period. Under the Republic of Italy's constitution, male heirs to the royal line were prohibited from entering Italy, a restriction that remained until 2002. Beatrice is Vittorio Emanuele's youngest sister.

10. A disastrous flood, the worst in centuries, hit Florence in November 1966, killing dozens and destroying countless artworks and books. Students were among those who helped carry items to safety.

11. Cecconi, *Io, la "Romanina,"* 182–89.

12. Veneto is the region in northeastern Italy that includes Venice, Padova, Verona, and Vicenza, among other cities.

13. This date is slightly different from what is indicated in the Timeline of Key Events. In a phone conversation with Cecconi (April 2023), she confirmed that her confinement was from January 1968 to May 1971. However, it is possible that she arrived in Puglia in late December 1967 and her confinement officially started in January.

PART 4
NARRATING TRANS HISTORY AS A MEANINGFUL EXPERIENCE

PART I

Chapter 10

From *Elementi di critica trans* (*Elements of Trans Critique*)

EDITED BY LAURELLA ARIETTI, CHRISTIAN BALLARIN, GIORGIO CUCCIO, AND PORPORA MARCASCIANO

The volume *Elementi di critica trans* is the conference proceeding of a seminar that took place in May 2008, in the Tuscan countryside.[1] However, the origin of this work dates back to 2006, when, following the proposal of ONIG (Osservatorio Nazionale Identità di Genere [The Italian National Observatory of Gender Identity]) to change the medical categorization of transsexualism from a gender identity disorder to a "rare condition," trans associations held several meetings to address the possible implications of this terminology. The goal of the 2008 retreat was precisely to host a conversation led by trans activists to critically examine the meaning of their embodied experiences and to create shared narratives. The discussion included a small group of people involved in LGBT+ issues, among them scholars Lorenzo Bernini and Nicoletta Poidimani, psychiatrist Paolo Valerio, and Pia Covre, leader of the committee for sex workers' civic rights.

The excerpt included here comes from the opening day, in which the participants debated a possible starting point for their trans narrative. The importance of finding words for self-determination becomes a central topic of discussion. In the translation, the speakers are identified by first name, as in the Italian original.

First Day

Our History from Denial to Visibility, from Oppression to Liberation

Porpora [Marcasciano]: My presentation is going to retrace the history of the trans movement, of the trans scene, in Italy, and for this reason, I am pleased to have next to me Roberta, one of the special witnesses to this journey. On different occasions, I have recounted her story, as it is one of those testimonies that can—and must—tell us something.

My speech won't be only historical, since, in covering our history, it will also touch upon cultural, political, and scientific matters. Therefore, I will offer a few reflections about our shared path that intertwine with issues that we are going to face in the next few days, by starting from ourselves— from our lives, memory, experience, and knowledge.

It is said that a trans phenomenon exists, but we may wonder if, besides the phenomenon, there is a trans movement or, to put it more simply, a trans experience. What path has led us here, today? And if a path exists, could we talk of a history?

To reconstruct a history, first of all, we should ask ourselves what could be considered "history." Reflecting and thinking about one's own path means reappropriating it. It means becoming writers of *our own* history and, by writing it, giving *our own* meaning to it—the point of view of those who made and underwent history, the perspective of the protagonists and not of some external observers who, being external, see things from a different angle.

[When I say "external observers"] I'm not talking about those who are close to us, but those who until now have observed us in the guise of researchers, experts, politicians, medical doctors, and maybe even in the guise of friends and allies. Very often our critiques and concerns focus on what I call proximity, or the people with whom, for better or worse, we debate. Let's pay attention not to confuse those who stand next to us and support us with those who annihilate us. I am saying this because, in a peculiar human inclination, we tend to see enemies in those who are close to us, because those who are closer are in a relationship with us and therefore can more easily make mistakes. My critique particularly targets a lack, within our groups, of self-reflection and debate, and, conversely, an excess of auto-celebration and attention-seeking behaviors—I include myself—which comes at the expense of an objectivity that overcomes personal accomplishments and can help us reconstruct our experience.

Sylvia Rivera used to say, in regard to the Stonewall riot, "I wasn't the first, but rather the second, to throw a bottle."[2] I invite you to think about this statement, because it means putting aside self-aggrandizement and putting oneself on an equal footing with a movement, with a collective experience.

To this premise, we should add an objectively vulnerable condition linked to our precarious, discriminated, marginalized path—something we have always denounced.

So, what is our history? If a history usually begins with the fateful "first time" that establishes a beginning, what was the "first time" of the trans experience? To what can we link it? To the first gender reassignment surgery?

From this point of view, the first Italian case was that of Romina Cecconi, in 1966: she had her surgery in Ginevra, but she is considered an Italian case.[3] But in 1952 in Denmark, Christine Jorgensen had already had her surgery.

By contrast, if "the first time" is linked to the discovery and development of hormonal therapies and the innovations of aesthetic surgery, this happens more or less at the beginning of the 1970s. But prior to these innovations, where and how was our experience manifesting itself? Or, if transsexuality originates with the coinage of its name and therefore more or less in 1952—but in Italy in the 1970s—before that, who were we? Or, finally, does our history begin with the struggle of trans people for their recognition?

If we think about it, there could be many different "first times"; it depends on which one we acknowledge as our beginning.

This question is for me an open issue: What is the "first time"?

Roberta F [Ferranti]: The first time you desired it.

Porpora: I mean the collective experience, not the individual one.

Roberta F: At that time there wasn't any collectivity. I didn't have any external recognition, but I was happy with some golden slippers. That must mean something: it was a desire that was coming to the surface, and I didn't even know what it was.

Porpora: That's it! Paradoxical as it might seem, our history—or our liberation path—could originate and intertwine with the rootedness and development of prejudice. The origin of prejudice is ancient, its presence can be retraced back to the origins of our culture, but its surge, its rootedness, seems to coincide with the beginning of modern and contemporary culture. Paradoxically, it is precisely the new order of scientific innovations, which gave a name to transsexualism, that created the conditions for prejudice.

Let me indulge in a brief historical excursus. The first stigma about transsexualism emerged in the nineteenth century with positivism, when

Western culture tends to create a so-called norm and imprison in labs all those who don't align: everything outside the norm was considered abnormal. Lombroso, scholar of the positivist epoch, would say that specific physical traits of people can denote or refer to a criminal personality, prone to crime. In the Lombrosian gallery of all "deformed people"—deformed in every way—were also included people of uncertain sex, people who didn't yet have a name that could define them. We were considered neither trans nor transvestites; we were of uncertain sex, hermaphrodites at most.

There is a photo from the time, which is a closeup of a person's genitals—I believe it was a case of an intersex person. Physical traits started to represent normality and abnormality, and the first traces of special units for transvestites and perverts in mental asylums date back to that time. The mental asylum of Aversa had a special unit for transvestites and perverts; the photographs that arrived to us testify to the presence of those who today we consider trans.

For brevity's sake, I'll get to the black hole of the twentieth century: the epoch of Fascism and Nazism. Historical records indicate that homosexual people were imprisoned in concentration camps and marked with a pink triangle. Transsexual people were not defined as such and therefore were gathered in the group of the pink triangle or with people suffering from mental illnesses. But their deportation to extermination camps happened and is now coming to light. We managed to track down and meet Lucy, an eighty-five-year-old transsexual person who was deported to Dachau.[4] While elsewhere there are records about the deportation of trans people as "pink triangles," in Italy we don't have those because even trans people are not aware of their past and their journey.

The subsequent decades of the twentieth century are a series of voids; the transsexual history must be traced; it's not linear.

Let's move to the 1960s, when small trans communities begin forming in big cities—metropolises. Although trans people are living at the margins, cities are the only place where they can survive. In this phase an important change occurs and the control on trans people shifts: until then, there was psychiatric control because transsexual people were isolated; they had not formed groups. In the 1960s, they began forming groups; they were no longer isolated madmen or madwomen. Social control shifts from the individual to the group, so it turns into another type of control and its strategies change: law enforcement, prison, confinement come into play—a whole series of strong and violent restrictions that mark our life experience.

I just traced a century very quickly, and there would be much more to say, but now I'd rather move to the second part of my presentation, namely to the proposal to envision and build a grassroots history, alternative to the official one, to the history of "normality."

The history, the one that they make us study, is the history of powerful people, of those who hold the means [of production] and information. We are not in that history: we are obscured or appear occasionally, torn into pieces, destroyed, twisted, because we are not in line with the flow of that story. We appear from time to time as degenerates, abnormal people to watch out for. Closed into cages, displayed in the centers of villages and cities, the criminal and the abnormal served as exempla of what one must avoid and beware of; it was a very targeted way of re-establishing normality.

But let's remember that history is made by people, and it's a story in which the sense of reality derives from the gendered dichotomy of male/female, which is disguised as natural. In that history we are at the margins, and yet we were subject to it, we paid the consequences. It's a history that made us disappear in mental asylums, prisons, in the "ships of fools."

Today a great accomplishment of many subcultures is to narrate their own history. Reading one's history by starting from oneself, or even the simple fact of becoming narrators, are ways that we can make grassroots history or counter-history, that we can create a new meaning that begins to enrich a desolate landscape made of war, famine, and desperation.

Now let's deal with the following matter: until now, we have located and represented ourselves—I'll use the gender-neutral form, with the asterisk *rappresentat**[5]—according to science and not according to history, on the basis of scientific discoveries and not on the basis of our screams when we first came into this world.

It's the scientist, in his laboratory, who said, "In the world there are transsexual people," but it wasn't trans people who said, "We exist, no matter what."

We have existed before, and the proof is that we have been locked up in mental asylums—photographs are records of this; we have been deported to extermination camps and Lucy's experience is the proof; we have been persecuted, sent to the stake; and if this is not true, history books must explain who those victims were. This is an epoch in which the tendency is to deny, and I believe that we have a huge responsibility to recast and reconstruct our history.

In the official history—the normal and normative one—there are good and bad people, just and unjust people, normal and abnormal people. I don't think I'm saying anything new by affirming that we are situated, or rather they have placed us, amid the abnormal ones, and everything we did or do is seen as abnormal. Our entire life is filtered through a sense of normativity, a sense that functions both from the outside, namely from the world of culture, and from the inside, or from us to the world. It's not only the world and others who see us, read us, label us as abnormal, but it's also we who read the world through the same lens. If it weren't like this, our path to liberation would be easy.

I'll provide you with an example: the never-ending diatribes that regularly erupt about the celebration of Pride, about how trans people participate and with what attire. The pulpit, meaning those who are in control of culture and the means of communication—and therefore are the directors of official history—issues a verdict: exhibitionism. We internalize the accusation, the guilt, and try to cancel the "abnormality" that resides among us and inside us by removing it. But after we do that, who among us is actually feeling "normal"? Always mistreated, we set ourselves up as judges of how to go to Pride, and we do it to align with something that resembles the so-called normal people. It's as if a dolphin used to swimming into marine water wanted at all costs to stay in a river and eventually goes aground.

I ask myself and all of you: Isn't it possible that this assimilated and internalized norm, which accompanies us in our finite or infinite transition, has turned us into judges of our own neighbors, our peers, our closest friends? What measure do we use when we confront prostitution, a reality that, like it or not, has allowed our survival—and therefore our visibility—in the 1960s, 1970s, 1980s? Can we think or imagine that among the many of us who turn tricks there are both those who don't have any other choice and those who choose it? Can we distance ourselves from the issue of prostitution by removing the synonym transsexuality equals prostitution—and therefore the stigma—without falling into self-censorship? Can we glimpse in this censorship the sense of norms that until now has crushed us?

It's easy, and certainly useful, to split ourselves between pro-prostitution and against-prostitution, between those who are in favor and those who are not. It makes me think of all us Italians as an example: the so-called people of saints and migrants who today don't recognize themselves and don't want to acknowledge another people's nomadism, when they actually experienced it first. Nomadism is also one of our traits, of us trans people, or people in transition: I believe we are nomads in transit across genders.

I'd like to quote from an article that I wrote and never published:

> Necessities, needs, and desires predispose the human being to travel, to move, to change. Our natural tendency is toward a never-ending search for better life conditions or, if we want, a profound and atavistic aspiration to happiness. At times this is a search for water and fertile soil to cultivate, and for a more favorable climate; at other times it is a desire for knowing, communicating, or socializing, but at the base there is always the will to improve one's existential condition, that well-known hunger that sharpens your wits, that moves and constantly relocates people and persons, in sync with the eternal and never-ending process of mutation underlying the whole universe. The search for better life conditions does not solely target the physical, social, and cultural environment, but also something much more intimate and personal; it could also apply to the body, made of the four elements, through which each individual can consider herself alive. We can intervene with our body, heal it, correct it, transform it, because it may be sick, ugly, disharmonious, because it feels estranged, or to put it very simply, because it doesn't belong to us. One is born a male and becomes a woman, or vice versa, is born a female and becomes a man: this is complex and creative movement that takes the name of transsexualism or transgenderism.

To conclude I am going to introduce a few matters concerning our history: the relationship with the LGBT movement and with feminism.

In relation to the latter, I'll read a passage—and I apologize for citing myself!—from *Altri femminismi* (*Other Feminisms*):

> To introduce this issue, I'll refer to a statement from my book *Tra le rose e le viole* (*Among the Roses and the Violets*) which in my opinion is evocative. Roberta, one of the protagonists of the Italian "trans debut," says: "Our high heels were very different from the zoccoli shoes of the feminist comrades: beautiful but uncomfortable the former, much more comfortable the latter. The transsexuals entered the stage on those very uncomfortable stilettos, wearing very short miniskirts and very heavy make-up—I'm using superlatives to describe those traits, exaggerated

markers, unmistakably of one's identity. In those fabulous '60s, trans women were constructing themselves, their experience, their history, and to do so, they were also using stilettos—an accessory and negative symbol for some women, e.g., for the feminists or for a part of the feminist movement; an element of fabulousness for others, e.g., for trans women."

The term fabulousness is used in the movie *Stonewall* by Miranda, who is meant to be Sylvia Rivera.[6]

After centuries of silence, denial, and violence, in the second half of the twentieth century, trans women began thinking about their life, about how they would have liked it. They were building their identity and were starting to do so from their body, corporeality, visibility, or like we say today, from their coming out. Mario Mieli in his *Elementi di critica omosessuale*, which we are referencing today, writes: "Even feminists often criticize us faggots—our fashion, our behavior, which in their opinion tend to replicate the stereotypical feminine fetish fought by women." We ought to deconstruct the male part and rebuild on its ruins not one's female identity, as many people thought, but one's trans identity. Two different experiences united by an intense femininity, somewhat opposed to masculinity, but with its own path and lived experience. With their stiletto heels and their over-emphasized femininity, trans women showed themselves to the world: "Right you are (if you think so)."[7] Had they appeared in tennis shoes, with large blouses, and the floral long skirts of the feminist comrades, nobody would have paid attention to them, not even the feminists. There was a need to be recognized in a world in which we were unknown, by reproducing traits that for others are considered caricatured. After a century-long denial, transsexuals came into the scene adorned with all those elements that characterized their own experience—traits excessively emphasized because they were linked to the birth of a new path. And, as it always happens, that birth becomes ceremony, ritual, celebration, and therefore an emphasized marker of one's identity. In those fabulous 1960s, we wanted to celebrate and we rocked it, with the best costumes and with the frenzy typical of celebration.[8]

Mine is an invitation to not mistake the liberation process for either the process of normalization or the process of transition, which lets us be ourselves, for a process that, conversely, gives us the illusion of being normal, of looking like—and I'm stressing *looking like*—the normative models: man–woman.

If we start from "a first time" that is the scientific one, meaning when hormonal therapies, surgery, etc., were developed, we are thinking of a path that, I believe, is normative, focused on a process of adaptation. On the other hand, if we think of a movement that starts from the fact that we exist—we feel ourselves, we perceive ourselves—then the view of the world and of our lives changes completely. In saying this, I don't want to exclude the scientific steps that helped us to be what we wanted, but I would like to include them in a broader perspective, because if we take into consideration only those, then we dramatically reduce the complexity of our experience.

As I was saying earlier, when did the trans experience begin? When the scientist coined the term or said that transsexual people existed, or when we were screaming and were being arrested? When I say "we" I'm obviously referring to an ancient "we," when we were imprisoned in concentration camps or we opened the first nightclubs in Berlin and Paris, and many years later, in Italy, too.

These are the questions that I am posing and that I'd like to discuss, but now I'm turning it over to Pia to hear about her perspective on transsexual prostitution.

Pia [Covre]: I used to be a prostitute in the '70s and '80s. While I was listening to Porpora, I immediately recalled the extraordinary effect that trans women had when they arrived on the street: it was really terrific! We lived in an epoch in which even female prostitution took an appearance that satisfied—the all-male, of course—imagery of the woman in high heels and her tits out. . . . In sum: we ought to dress in a certain way. Trans women entered forcefully in this role, with a bursting femininity, exuberant, even dominant. I think in particular of the big cities, where I've never worked but I visited and I can imagine.

Actually, I met many trans women through my political engagement: I had a chance to really get to know the first transsexuals who participated in radical groups and to see other aspects of their lives. But their impact on prostitution was world-shattering for female prostitutes, for men and, in turn, for the whole society, which was thrown off by this new thing. Ordinary people had heard of certain divas, of life in certain clubs in Paris or Berlin, but had never seen trans women closely. Men got crazy when they saw that these people existed and were so different, while respecting all the canons [they had in mind]: tricks would look for us [cis-women], troubled, and would ask, in fear, "But that one is a man or a woman?" And they were afraid of approaching trans women, of getting closer, but they were also terribly longing for that encounter. They would say, "That one is a man, but she is so beautiful, though, look what legs, what body!" I feel that it was actually a revolution.

Our society was quite shallow in relation to these things. . . . Homosexuals were already considered something strange, even though there were many of them. There was already a history, there was a homosexual path, they were somewhat accepted by their families. I remember that for a while I lived in the countryside and there was a man who was gay but didn't show it, but at home I heard family members whispering about this person who lived alone and wasn't married, in the same way as they were gossiping about the prostitute who lived in the village. In little villages you heard about these things at home.

Transsexual women were an extraordinary thing that threw off men and society both, as happened with feminism, too. The feminist was an unexpected subject—new, unknown—that triggered anxiety and fear; the transgender, the transsexual, the transvestite in the street created anxiety, perhaps even fear, but also a lot of curiosity, a lot of desire. They certainly opened a channel of male desire.

It is also interesting to examine the relationship between a female prostitute and a transsexual. The first transsexuals who arrived in the street were seen by women as rivals to chase away, but it wasn't possible. We immediately clashed. One day the little group [of prostitutes] in our village saw the arrival of a trans woman and the trans was a smash hit; she had the strength of a man. The methods we had used until then to protect our sidewalks, our areas, were not easily applicable to trans women.

One day with Carla Corso—who is not a small person—we went to work the street; so Carla comes across a trans woman who tells her: "You don't come to work here" and wanted to drag Carla out of her own car. But Carla stayed in the car and said: "Come in front and I'll plow you down." This was the first negative impact, we might say, because the trans prostitute was prettier than us. But we couldn't clear the field of trans women even if they came to muck us up.

Of course, a woman or a trans who had something more and was more beautiful than us was going to disturb the market. But, after a while, [women] prostitutes began getting curious, because if these trans or these new women or, at times the transvestites, were so interesting, then we needed to get to know them, to understand what was going on—and, eventually, discover that we were similar in our behaviors, in how we related to men.

I met many prostitutes that through their work developed their own emancipation from patriarchy: contrary to what's said, we are not victims at all, or at least not all of us are. After a while, women who practiced prostitution, if they had to support their husbands—a few of them had a pimp, but generally because they had chosen one; I'm speaking of the 1970s, it was a very different situation—developed a sense of superiority in relation to their partners, and men in general, but in particular in relation to their tricks. Speaking with trans women made us realize that we had this thing in common.

Roberta F: There is pleasure in being treated a certain way: not like a woman because you are not a woman, you are not a man either, you don't even want to think of yourself as gay, meaning, to have an equal relationship with another man; you feel more feminine and perhaps you want to express it with a behavior, with an outfit. Then little by little you look around and see what's there and your self-awareness gradually develops. Personally, this is what was happening to me until I met Coccinelle, when I finally said: "Here is the crux of the question!" Before that moment, I was just somebody who was following the direction of her desires, her diversities, and differences. I'm talking of the end of the 1950s: I talked about my golden slippers, but there was also a blouse that for me was to die for, but my mother would regularly take it out of my hands because it wasn't a decent way to dress. But it was still very powerful for me to be something different. The meeting with Coccinelle—it was like seeing the Madonna: the girl had drawn some leaves around her eyes with eyeliner—so refined!—her hairstyle was like Blue Bell of Paris. A little person, but so proud among people, so dignified; she wasn't hiding like a mouse. That's it! After my meeting with Coccinelle, everything was in motion—it was a new becoming.

Porpora: This was in Naples, wasn't it?

Roberta F: Yes, in Naples. Rome was tabula rasa.

Porpora: The "Coccinelle" Roberta referred to is the Neapolitan Coccinelle, a historical figure, considered the first trans in Naples and Italy. And, in a strange life coincidence, they both died in the span of a week, the French Coccinelle and the Neapolitan Coccinelle.

Roberta F: Now even a little girl, if she puts on the news, can see a trans woman, can understand that there is something else and can refer to it. But there are also those more prudish who discover that they are not who they thought they were and must invent everything about themselves or try to discover everything.

Pia: In the past where were trans people? The *femminielli* who, in Naples, represent a historical phenomenon, can we think of them as the first trace of transsexualism?

Roberta F: The trans phenomenon existed in Paris, in the clubs in Paris, it was considered a tradition of the city; there were places like the Carousel or Chez Madame Arthur.

Porpora: Those were two different paths. I believe that, paradoxically, the tradition of the Neapolitan *femminielli* started to come to an end when the transsexual path began, which is a liberation path where we began to reclaim that which is our experience. The *femminielli*'s experience gets lost in the midst of time; it's very ancient, dates back to ancient Rome, to ancient Greece, with a whole series of rituals that characterized that path. There was the *figliata* [birthing], the wedding ceremony, the pilgrimage to Montevergine.[9] All these things started to come to an end with the emergence of the new trans person: it's the modern that replaces the ancient.

There are similar examples in different parts of the world; in Italy and in Europe we find this phenomenon in Naples, and it is thought to be linked to the cult of the goddess Cybele.

Regina [Satariano]: I turned twenty-six without even realizing I was transsexual; I didn't have any point of reference. The references I had in Genoa, I couldn't acknowledge those—I saw them as shabby, because they lived in a ghetto, because they went out at night, transformed; they didn't seem real to me. That was my first impression, and I was living my life as gay, believing I was gay, and by chance I realized I wasn't. All of us eventually come to this realization and not necessarily when we are seven or eight. I felt there was something different in me compared to the other young gay people I knew and would hang out with. I had this certainty when I turned seventeen, but what I understood only later is that I was diverse within my diversity: for me, at that time, to be gay was already different. I lived in Genoa where I also had a "normal" life: I worked, studied, had friends—gay and heterosexual—the usual group of friends.

In the historic downtown there was criminality and transsexual prostitution—and after all, I wouldn't know if I can call it transsexual: it was much more transvestitism. Many guys I'd see during the day, who I knew, were gay but with some physical features modified with homemade silicon injections or hormones they'd got at the pharmacy—however, I couldn't recognize myself in that.

Then I discovered that in Tuscany there was another reality, far from my city and quite different from the one of Genoa's historical districts; 130

km away, in Viareggio: it was Frau Marlene, a historical club where gays and especially the transsexual community—both transsexuals and transvestites—hung out. There I could be myself. There for Carnival I cross-dressed and I started to look at those transsexual girls who came from Florence, who had a strong ego, what a beauty . . . I felt like the ugly duckling who was turning into a swan and I was looking at everything as if it was something incredible; I looked at these girls who for me were kind of goddesses on earth, with all their moves and poses. That was, of course, a type of posing; then outside the club they were who they were. But in that moment, they were crystal-clear images, Madonnas. It wasn't that I wanted to look like them, but I wanted to start to discover myself, to understand who I was.

And there I had the fortune to meet Anastasia, who told me, "Either you keep on doing the life of the frustrated gay and cross-dress, or you go through a transition journey." Engaging in a "journey" means to do hormonal therapy, electrocoagulation, and a whole series of things that I eventually achieved through prostitution, because at twenty-seven I couldn't live this thing with peace of mind and open up with my family. So I made my choice.

This is to say that each of us has an experience that in many ways is shared: we all went through suffering, lack of self-acknowledgment, lack of knowledge, perhaps even exaggeration. If I had to think how I used to dress at the time, in 1992 . . . I would go out from that house in Torre del Lago in such a way . . . but I was proud of what I was doing, of my transformation, and I'd do it again.

A center to help me with my transition did not exist, but the experience of other girlfriends helped me: a person who had already gone through the journey would say to me, "Buy Progynon, take Androcur." It worked like this: in those years, 1990–1992, it was a friend who would tell you, "Take this. No, take that." This has been my experience. Then in 1993 I did the surgery.

Later on, I realized that there was great ignorance in our world, meaning lack of knowledge; therefore it could be dangerous to do the transition as I did. I did silicone in Palma of Majorca because a girlfriend suggested that: "See, there they have a medical center, two people inject you with silicone and they do that in a medical center. It's not that the *bombadeira* comes to your house to inject you"—because that was happening too.[10]

What was passed down to me as transsexual culture taught me that, too: to have a big ass, hips, feminine shapes. . . . I was in a rush to modify my body as soon as possible instead of following a path and the time it requires. I strived to have everything immediately.

Then I acknowledged the many mistakes I made and I started to help, to advise other people. I started to collaborate with the movement, with MIT [Movimento Italiano Transessuale], in 1992.[11]

The only thing I ended up having pinned on me, after fifteen years, was this damn "Miss Italia Trans" pageant, which was born indeed to address the transsexual question, a topic that in 1992 was regarded very negatively. I thought it would have been a one-year experience, and today it has been an experience of almost sixteen years, and unfortunately, everybody remembers me in relation to this, while my fights for civil rights have been forgotten.

On the occasion of the beauty pageant, every year, we have faced a specific issue with MIT: for example, prostitution, or name change. . . . Very often the girls would show up to the conversation only because they had to, otherwise they wouldn't walk the runway and would be immediately expelled.

I am almost fifty, but my life experience extends beyond my age. Maybe my years were lived too much in a rush, but I learned very soon that we had to come out, speak up.

When I went back to Genoa, after two years of transformation, I realized that I had made a big mistake not to approach the people who lived in the ghetto. I got closer, I understood, I collected testimonies of people who really made history in Genoa too. The movement wasn't only in Naples! And many of the Genoese people were Neapolitans who had moved to Genoa. This has been my experience.

Massimo [D'Aquino]: In my opinion, the "first time," generally speaking, is a matter of coming out, because it's a sense of liberation, both collective and individual. The scientific discoveries, the fact that therapies could be available is undoubtedly important, but to come out of the closet is the trans "first time" even for what concerns us FtM [female to male].

Lorenzo [Bernini]: In Porpora's presentation it's important to see the distinction between the first time in which trans subjectivation emerged and the first time people were subjugated as "transsexual subjects," namely, when somebody else called them transsexuals.

In this respect, I wanted to highlight that tracing the history of subjection is easier: one just needs to study sexology manuals from the nineteenth century on. A curious thing that we should not forget is that the first definition of sexual inversion included both homosexuals and transsexuals. Therefore, a piece of this subjection history sees us united in the medical category of "sexual inversion." Karl Westphal, in 1860, was talking of "inverted sexual sensibility," a category comprising both transsexuals and homosexuals; this category of "inversion" produces some ripple effects on the process of subjectivation, which is in the appropriation of an identity.

I recall the wonderful novel *The Well of Loneliness* by Radclyffe Hall,[12] in which the protagonist, Stephen, discovers this term—"congenital invert"—because she reads it in a manual, *Psychopathia Sexualis*, by Krafft-Ebing and Havelock Ellis, so she lives her own life as a "congenital invert." Today we would probably call her transgender; from a medical point of view she would be a transsexual, a FtM transgender. Up to a certain point, the majority of the lesbian movement considered her a lesbian and criticized her for not embracing a process of lesbian subjectivation to instead adhere to a male model.

In this attempt to reconstruct a history of the transsexual movement, it is important to distinguish the many levels of this story. I'm saying this as a gay person, but I believe that it applies to transsexual people too: we must be very careful—in a moment in which we are emerging as stronger subjectivities than we were in the past: we have a movement, we have more of a voice—of assimilating under our categories, subjects who were probably something else.

A distinction must be made: those who considered themselves "congenital inverts" because they were taught to call themselves that were probably neither transsexuals nor homosexuals. The *femminiello* was not a transsexual, as you were saying. It's important not to turn transsexuality or transgenderism into a new identity that, within a certain environment, runs the risk of becoming an imperialist experience and swallowing up experiences that were something else, because they were undergoing other forms of conditioning and didn't have the support of a movement that, instead, exists today.

It seems to me that, in a complex way, the two levels, which I dubbed "subjection" and "subjectivation," add to each other, intersect, and even create different identities. It would be a mistake to assimilate them under a hegemonic label—the label of our current perspectives on historical processes.

Nicoletta [Poidimani]: I find Porpora's question about the first time interesting, but I think one should acknowledge the risk of giving a normative answer. Both in what Regina was saying and in Roberta's story, there is the feeling of being authorized by somebody else—not an authority, of course! Roberta sees Coccinelle and feels authorized by a person who mirrors the image of what she would like to be, the image that she desires for herself; I believe this is the experience of many trans people and many lesbian women too. For the gay world and the lesbian world, there was also literature, cinema, etc.; whereas the trans experience across centuries and cultures had moments of visibility, in which it was considered part of the social texture, and moments of concealment, of apparent disappearance, but then it came to light again. The *femminielli*, for example, are a phenomenon with a very long history.

Therefore, if Porpora's question is taken as a cue, it will allow subjective experiences and life events to emerge, rather than a normative discourse. But, in the end, who cares what medicine said: medicine is generally normative in relation to bodies, no matter if these bodies are transsexual or not. Instead, let's reappropriate the experience of each one of us: this seems to me the real political action that can give meaning to a seminar like this.

Christian B. [Ballarin]: I would like to draw on the experience of the *femminielli* and on what Porpora said, namely the fact that there is a before and an after. A history exists that has centuries-old origins, no longer traceable, where the story of the *femminielli* begins, but this history dies when transsexualism is defined. This leads to the discourse about language and definitions we will engage in tomorrow, but Porpora's statement is true if we see history as a sequence of events that has a beginning and an end, a before and an after. As a transsexual person, I find the idea of transformation more fascinating than the idea of the beginning or the end of something. Therefore, if we see history as the transformation of things, of events—if we see it in this way—then the history of those *femminielli* belongs to our history too.

Lorenzo is right when he says that we cannot appropriate or name something if we don't know what to call it: if I don't name a thing, that thing doesn't exist. We cannot engage in the violent action of naming something against its will or assuming what its will might be. But we can see this link, this leading thread that starts in the mists of time and then transforms itself, takes on different shapes, different names, and eventually arrives to us today.

I don't know if I'd search for the beginning of the trans experience; instead, I'd reclaim the very fact that the trans experience doesn't have a beginning, it has always existed, it has always been there. It had a beginning, perhaps, with a certain name, a certain path, a certain visibility, I agree with that, but I wouldn't want to pin it down temporally. I wouldn't do it especially because we are talking of an experience that has never wanted to be pinned down and has never placed those pins.

Giorgio [Cuccio]: There are some huge gaps in Porpora's reconstruction, namely, trans men. We have a controversy with lesbians and it's still not clear if some aspects of our experience are our stuff or their stuff. Aaron

Devor, a Canadian trans scholar, tried to retrace a few figures of trans men in history. On the occasion of a conference in Turin to which Christian invited him,[13] I told him that here we had this issue with *The Well of Loneliness*, as it wasn't clear if the protagonist was a he or a she. So, I asked him what the general opinion was in the United States and Canada. He answered that the same debate arose there, too, but unlike here, the majority of lesbians, once another subjectivity recognized itself in this character, renounced their claim on it; they said, if other identities can recognize themselves, this character no longer belongs to us, she is not so lesbian that we can claim her as ours.

Devor reconstructs the history of a series of characters; in his view, it's not so important to say who they belong to, who they were or what they were, but rather to say that another point of view exists in history, another perspective. When new subjectivities emerge in history, they can bring a new point of view and it's possible to read them from their own point of view; they can say things that don't correspond to truth, as they can say things that, in a historical reconstruction, are not so linear, but it's still a further point of view. Therefore, perhaps, the issue lies in reconstructing a history that has neither a beginning nor an end, because the trans experience is part of the human experience. For me, it can even start from Neanderthals. I don't have records about it, but I don't care; I know that it makes sense for me.

The issue of finding the beginning doesn't exist: the issue is to retrace signs that we can read in a certain way to say that those signs do exist, those stories do exist; then we can talk about them, but this is our core perspective.

We should open another conversation on corporeality in the nineteenth century.[14] The nineteenth century is the epoch in which, within the fixity of biology, gender also becomes fixed. The conception of the body is very static, and, within this idea, gender is fixed in terms of genitality; then these categories, for various reasons, have calcified. But before this moment, the history of the anatomic body had been much more fluid: it was much more fluid—in a certain sense, even much more interchangeable—the way in which the male or female body was perceived.

We are still from the nineteenth century in this respect, and it's difficult to think otherwise, but it, too, is a cultural moment. To read a body as feminine or masculine and petrify gender into genitalia marks a precise cultural moment and as such it can be changed: it's not a given.

One last thing: the first person to undergo gender reassignment surgery wasn't Jorgensen, but a trans guy.[15] This is little known, but I consider it a source of great pride, and every time I mention it, it's a great surprise for my audience. His name was Reed Erickson, and he underwent surgery two years before Jorgensen.[16] They were more or less contemporary, between 1950 and 1952.

The issue is that the history of male transsexualism, in the documents and reconstructions I read, is one of concealment rather than visibility. I am not talking of recent history, but of an older one, pre-Stonewall, prior to that coming-out in which there were also trans guys—and there are the names of these people: furthermore, one was Mario Rossi, he was an Italian American.[17]

Of course, I'm neither a historian nor particularly passionate about research, but to always be the big absence even when the closest people to me are telling the story—no, I cannot accept that!

It would be great if somebody said to me, "Now you tell the story." But I'd like to find a moment in which our stories could proceed together. Of course, we should distinguish them as they are very different indeed, but I'd like it if, in the storytelling, we were also included. Being a history of concealment, it's more difficult to retrace who these people were. The term "transvestite" is used also for trans men; these are stories of dodging, of people trying to disappear, to escape their families. I found out with great sadness that many of them enrolled as soldiers.

Nicoletta: Often one can get confused by stories of women who crossdressed to access opportunities that were denied to women at the time.

Giorgio: It's a different history of concealments, much more difficult to bring to the surface, but it's a history. There are those who are reconstructing it. I like to distinguish the paths, but let's also start to put them in conversation, even with their obvious distinctions.

Fabrizia [Di Stefano]: I'm fine with the main question Porpora posed, but I also agree with the correction Roberta made: in the beginning there isn't any story, there isn't any transsexual self-identification. . . . Roberta used a wonderful expression: there is a something made almost of nothing, it's a rather ineffable sensation in which you feel yourself and say: "But I'm not this!" And this is an open question, it takes time before you give yourself an answer, and that answer depends on the encounters you have: she recounted her encounter with Coccinelle very beautifully.

For me, the beginning was a magazine—not a porn magazine but an ordinary weekly magazine—that my brother bought. There was a very long article on the artists of Carrousel, featuring interviews with them. I must have been thirteen or fourteen and I got traumatized, but simultaneously sexually excited; I blushed by myself, only from reading that article.

I believe that, in this sense, the transsexual experience is very much related to our individual experience—not to a transsexual identity but to the singularity of each individual positioning.

I'd like to cast doubts on the idea of the transition path, which is the one generated by medical knowledge, by Benjamin—namely that there is a path of familiarization, an adaptive path. . . . Actually, a transsexual woman doesn't go along a path as it is generally understood: in contrast, she faces the issue of reaching herself. The essence of her "debut experience" is occupying a place where she hasn't arrived yet—in this gap that opens inside her, her experience is then situated. On the level of a more general history, in my opinion, transsexuality shouldn't be linked so much to modern knowledge, to medical knowledge, especially to that masterpiece that Benjamin's *The Transsexual Phenomenon* represents.[18] You can already retrace this discourse both in Ovid and Plato. When Jupiter, one day, was in a good mood and asked Juno, "But is it true that women enjoy more sexual pleasure than men?" "But what are you thinking?" Juno says, "You are always listening to rumors." There he understands that she is tricking him, and says: "I'm the father of all gods. I must know who enjoys more pleasure: it's useful to know." How does he solve the issue? He solves it by asking a transsexual woman, albeit an unwilling one: Tiresias had stepped on a couple of snakes that were copulating and immediately turned into a woman. And this immediacy for me matters; it's the immediacy of a self-identification made of nothing, accidental. Who starts from a concept? You don't engage in reasoning: you find yourself dislocated, thrown out from yourself, but you don't plan it with a rational method, with a deductive method. So, Tiresias was called in because he had been a woman for seven years, before he stepped on another couple of snakes and went back to his previous identity. Jupiter says, "Who can know it, better than her?!" When Tiresias arrives she feels embarrassed, Juno is gesturing to her to keep quiet, to say nothing. She feels nervous: to lie to the father of gods is too great an offense; the consequences, if he finds out, are severe—you know. Tiresias says, "Listen, I must tell you the truth—at first, she teases him a little—sexual pleasure is made of ten parts, nine are of women, one of men. For us women, in my opinion, it would have been better if the ratio was seven to three or six to four, because nine to one, it's a high price to pay."

Tiresias allows Jupiter and Juno to talk. It is as if the transsexual woman—and this is why I'm engaging in a discourse in which transsexuality is not solely understood as a sexual specificity—allowed men and women to talk again; she accounted both for the separation between women and men and for their encounter. In that story, she explains something fundamental.

So, what is a transsexual woman, or a transsexual man? A whole? A sex and its opposite? No, it's not like that, since transsxual men and women feel estranged from themselves—otherwise we wouldn't be here. But if we silence this great strength of ours, which explains the reason of that explosive eruption . . . [we cannot understand that] it's not only a matter of huge tits. . . . What troubles the mind is huge tits plus *that thing* underneath it: let's get to the core of the question! In my opinion transsexuality, in the dialogue among sexed beings, can allow for something more besides self-narration. Even in relation to feminism.

Paolo [Valerio]: I was struck by the last speaker, who went back to the discourse of subjectivity, of being a person. I believe that, actually, on the one side we need labels that can comfort us, on the other the most difficult thing is to think that each of us is an individual, has a history, and, on the basis of this history, develops a particular life journey. It shouldn't be taken for granted that there are similarities between gay people or between transsexual people; many times, there can be more distance between two homosexuals than between them and a heterosexual or transsexual person, and vice versa. The important part, if I understood Porpora correctly, is to contextualize everything. Does it make sense to talk about homosexuality in ancient Greece in relation to the way of being gay today? How could we "diagnose" today the Chevalier d'Éon—French ambassador at the court of England who was forced by Louis XIV to dress as a woman because it wasn't clear if she was male or female? Does it make sense to talk about pedophilia or pederasty if we refer to ancient Greece?

We should acknowledge in some ways that medical technology on the one side is oppressive but, on the other, offers answers to needs. In a good way or not, we cannot say. There are different answers: for some, medical technology is not useful at all, because it's enough to be recognized according to the sex recorded at birth and wear feminine clothes if one feels oneself to be a woman and masculine if one feels oneself to be a man. It's a different thing altogether to consider the needs of transsexual people, or the transgender dilemma.

(Translated by Danila Cannamela)

Notes

1. Translator's note (t/n): This excerpt, from the first chapter of the book *Elementi di critica trans* (Rome: ManifestoLibri, 2010), 17–41, is based on the first day of the seminar "Elementi di critica trans: Il transito secondo I transitanti" (Elements of Trans Critique: Transition according to Transitioning People), held in May 2008, in Terranova Bracciolini (Arezzo). The conversation was edited for space.

2. Sylvia Ray Rivera (New York; July 2, 1951–February 19, 2002) was an American trans activist. She became an icon of the transgender movement in the aftermath of the riots that erupted during the night of June 27–28, 1969, against the ongoing abuses perpetrated by the police at Stonewall Inn in New York—a club for gays, lesbians, and transvestites. Sylvia Rivera is remembered as the person who initiated the riot by launching the first bottle at the police. This event is considered the beginning of the LGBT liberation movement in the world. For this reason, June 28 was chosen as the LGBT Pride Day, often reductively called "Gay Pride."

3. T/n: In the mid-1960s, Cecconi began drawing attention as one of the first openly trans women in Italy. See Timeline of Key Events and chapter 9.

4. T/n: On the story of Lucy, see the conclusion. It is of note that Lucy, despite being a trans person, was deported to Dachau as a traitor and therefore was not grouped with the "pink triangles."

5. T/n: On the practice of using the asterisk, see the conclusion in this volume.

6. T/n: The original Italian reads *Star Well*; this is most likely a typo of the title *Stonewall* (1995), directed by Nigel Finch.

7. T/n: Here Marcasciano is jokingly referring to Luigi Pirandello's play *Così è se vi pare* (1917), translated into English as *Right you are (if you think so)*.

8. Marcasciano, "Trans, donne e femministe: Coscienze divergenti e/o coscienze sincroniche," in *Altri femminismi: Corpi, culture, lavoro*, eds. T. Bertilotti et al. (Rome: ManifestoLibri, 2006).

9. T/n: On the *femminielli*, see part 2 of this volume.

10. T/n: Typically, a *bombadeira* (literally, the "pumper") was a Brazilian migrant who had expertise in injecting silicone and would (illegally) perform injections within transgender circles. This figure is described by Don Kulick, in *Travesti: Sex, Gender, and Culture among Brazilian Transgendered Prostitutes* (Chicago: University of Chicago Press, 1998).

11. T/n: On MIT and the evolution of its acronym see the Timeline of Key Events in this volume.

12. T/n: The essay refers to the Italian edition of the book: Hall, *Il pozzo della solitudine* (Rome: Jouvence, 1997).

13. "Transgender nelle culture del mondo: Hijras, femminielli, berdache, muxes." Turin, November 11, 2006.

14. T/n: On this, see in particular Michel Foucault's masterpiece, *The History of Sexuality. Vol. 1: An Introduction* [French ed. 1976], trans. Robert Hurley (New York: Vintage Books, 1990).

15. T/n: This affirmation is not accurate; see timeline.

16. T/n: Most likely Giorgio Cuccio is referring to Reed Erickson; this is why we corrected the typo in the original Italian (Ericson), into Erickson. Erickson (1917–1992) was older than Jorgensen (1926–1989); however, as a patient of Harry Benjamin, Erickson began the process of masculinizing his body only in 1963. In 1964, he launched the Erickson Educational Foundation (EEF), a nonprofit philanthropic organization that invested in projects advocating on behalf of homosexuals, transgender (specifically, transsexual) people, and "those developing what might now be called the 'New Age' movement." A detailed account of Erickson's life and philanthropic activity can be found in Aaron H. Devor and Nicholas Matte's "ONE INC. and Reed Erickson: The Uneasy Collaboration of Gay and Trans Activism, 1964–2003," *GLQ* 10, no. 2 (2004): 179–209.

17. T/n: We were not able to find further information on Mario Rossi.

18. T/n: The essay refers to the Italian edition of the book: Benjamin, *Il fenomeno transessuale* (Rome: Astrolabio, 1968).

Chapter 11

Non siamo nat@ ieri
(We Weren't Born Yesterday)

Egon Botteghi

Egon Botteghi is a performer, educator, and trans activist based in Livorno. "Non siamo nat@ ieri" is the script of a performative workshop that Botteghi originally presented at Centro Donna in Livorno in 2019.[1] This theatrical work creatively elaborates on the biographies of two people who could be defined as "proto-trans"—Caterina (also spelled as Catterina) Vizzani, alias Giovanni Bordoni, and Eugenia Falleni, alias Harry Crawford. They lived in the seventeenth and eighteenth centuries, respectively, and their journeys toward gender self-determination are also stories of migration: Giovanni moved across central Italy, while Henry was an Italian migrant in New Zealand. The focus is on FtM (female to male) transitions, experiences that have typically stayed in the shadow but that, as the performance demonstrates, do not originate in the twentieth century with the introduction of surgical options, hormonal therapies, and new medical categories. "Non siamo nat@ ieri" aims to fight transphobic stigmas by placing trans identities into a broader historical context and by spotlighting experiences and embodied narratives that "were not born yesterday."

Part One: Giovanni Bordoni

(I enter singing, Ave Maris Stella)
 She looked almost like a saint. When he died, wounded by an "arquebus shell," "the body was promptly refitted with clothing," and his

head was adorned with flowers. As was the custom with those who "die as a maiden"—and thus, a virgin—he was displayed in the church of Santa Maria della Scala, in Siena. (Slide: image of the church)

And all the city rushed to see him, "all the more because some in a religious order professed that she, in preserving her chastity with regard to men with such perseverance, must have been a saint."

"But at the time, the condition of this supposed Giovanni was not yet known, nor was the reason known for his dressing as a man. And because of this, at the time, it was necessary to satisfy the people."

It is 1743, when Giovanni Bordoni died in Siena after several days of agony in the famous hospital of Santa Maria della Scala.

The Enlightenment was nearly at the door, and a famous medical pathologist, Giovanni Bianchi, professor of anatomy at the University of Siena, took an interest in the case and wrote a small book about it: *Brief history of the life of Catterina Vizzani, Roman woman, who for eight years wore a male servant's clothing, who after various vicissitudes was in the end killed and found to be a virgin during the autopsy of her cadaver.*

And so, through the doctor's investigations, it was learned that Catterina did not transform herself into Giovanni to avoid the attentions of men and to remain chaste in the eyes of God, as the prelates had believed and spread the rumor, but because she wanted to be a man and, in that way, love women.

What would have been discovered if a similar doctor had existed in the times of Saint Tecla, Saint Pelagia, Saint Giovanna, or Saint Eugenia?

Let's take this last one as an example: "Daughter of a noble Alexandrian prefect of Egypt, Saint Eugenia dressed as a man to escape from her father's house—along with her slaves Proto and Giacinto—and she converted to Christianity, having herself baptized by Eleno, bishop of Heliopolis. She withdrew into a male monastery and was elected abbot. She moved to Rome with all her family and converted many people to the Christian faith, particularly young women, before being decapitated on December 25, 258, under Emperor Publius Licinius Valerianus, along with Proto and Giacinto." (Slide of Saint Eugenia; Slide of the almanac)

Religious figures immediately constructed a noble genealogy for Giovanni as well, writing and publishing that she could have been the daughter of a Venetian gentleman.

I ask myself how many trans men could be hiding among the ranks of the Catholic saints?

But this did not happen with Giovanni. He was discovered by Doctor Bianchi, known as Janus Plancus (Slide of Dr. Bianchi). In fact, only through a series of extraordinary coincidences are we familiar with Giovanni's true story. We would know nothing about him if he hadn't been wounded near Siena; if he hadn't been brought to the hospital of Santa Maria della Sala; if he hadn't met the assistant of a professor of anatomy he had met two years earlier in a hotel in Florence; if he hadn't died; and if the autopsy hadn't been carried out by Giovanni Bianchi, a physician with an exceptional intellectual curiosity, a great passion for experimental research, an encyclopedic education, and a stubborn determination to fight for his ideas and for making the results of his investigations known.

The physician had met Giovanni in Florence a couple of years earlier, because they had found themselves in the same hotel, and Giovanni, in the service of the governor of Anghiari, had shared a room for a few nights with a servant of the physician, the same one that Giovanni encountered when he found himself dying at the hospital in Siena.

"That alleged Giovanni Romano who, dead, was found to be a woman and maiden in death, since they had dressed him as a woman, and at the time seemed to be such. But when he was alive—because he wore a black wig, because he had been greatly marked by smallpox, or because every other day shaved his face—since some type of hair grew on his upper lip, he seemed to be a man at the time. He was, however, short in height, and he made every possible effort to present himself truly as a man." (Slide: Giovanni Bordoni)

"He had made himself a type of red leather whatsit that he had filled with rags and always kept tied above his groin, and that he did not remove except a few hours before his death, perhaps because at the time it was bothering him." In this way, "he passed as a man who was well-equipped with the instrument of procreation." (Interactive workshop with the audience on the construction of a packer and illustration of the various types of packers that can be purchased)

Because of this description of a dildo, the good doctor had difficulty in having his booklet printed. But it finally was, in Florence, but stating a false location.

The book came out, as they would say, "stained," with false information: Venice, 1744, Simone Occhi, with the permission of authorities.

"Truly strange and exceedingly incredible are some of the human appetites regarding matters of love, for which reason no one should be surprised.

Thus I say that in Rome there was a young girl of low station, the daughter of a carpenter named Catterina Vizzani."

Caterina was born October 16, 1716, and was baptized in the basilica of San Lorenzo in Damaso.[2]

She lived in Piazza Farnese, in a dwelling with a workshop in Palazzo Mandosi, together with her father, the Milanese carpenter Pietro Vizzani; her mother, Margherita Petri of Orvieto; her sister Teresa; and her brother Michele.

"She, being fourteen years of age, never felt any other love ignited than for young girls—her peers, for which she fervently held that she loved them not as a girl, but as a man would have. More than any other girl, however, she took a fancy with someone named Margherita, and many times, at night, she went beneath the windows of her beloved, dressed as a man."

For two years they loved each other like that, until Margherita's father discovered it and threatened to denounce his daughter's lover in court.

So Caterina, wearing the man's clothing that she would never remove, fled to Viterbo, under false particulars. From then on, he would always be—to everyone—Giovanni Bordoni.

Giovanni remained in Viterbo until his money ran out. He then returned to Rome but did not go home. Rather, he began to wander about near the church of Santa Maria in Trastevere.

One evening, his suspicious and circumspect manner—like a fugitive—was noticed by the priest of the church, one Giuseppe Lancini, "who, seeing what he believed to be a young man wanting to modestly hide from sight, approached him."

And Giovanni told him that he had been hiding, in fear of being imprisoned for some foolishness that he had committed on account of a young lady.

The priest liked the young man's ways and invited him to his home, promising him that he would be safe from justice.

Also living in this house was a gentleman from Perugia who needed a servant, and so Giovanni was hired and left for Perugia. But upon leaving he told the priest whose son he was, "that is, a Milanese carpenter named Pietro Vizzani."

Giovanni, however, was not happy in Perugia, and so he wrote to his mother so that she would go to his good priestly benefactor and ask him to recommend Giovanni for a job as a servant in Arezzo.

His mother went to the priest and, "at the time remaining quiet that this son of hers was a woman, asked him for that which her daughter desired."

Giovanni was thus satisfied, and he went to Arezzo. But he stayed there a month without finding a job, and in the end was hired by Cavaliere Maria Pucci from Monte Pulciano, who was governor of Anghiari, which is why Giovanni went to Anghiari. (Slide of the governor's palazzo in Anghiari)

Giovanni was an exceptional servant, and the governor was very happy with him, "because he properly knew how to cook, shave, brush the wigs, pour the chocolate, read, and write. The governor, who was a very strict man, found fault with him for just one defect, that he was too fond of the ladies, since Giovanni, in order to be pleasing to women, had a completely masculine bearing and spoke freely."

When Giovanni was wounded in the neck by the hand of a jealous lover, his master, Cavaliere Pucci, was displeased about it to the point that he wrote to the priest of Santa Maria in Trastevere, who had recommended Giovanni to him, "strongly regretting that he had proposed such a rotten young man as a servant, who was so inclined toward women."

In turn, the priest, feeling betrayed in the trust he had accorded the young man, summoned Giovanni's father, "and strongly complained to him of his son's defect."

But, not seeming to be very disturbed, the father responded, "that his son had always been a ladies' man in that way."

The priest was furious: "I am surprised at you, since in some way it seems that you would like to excuse your son, who does you dishonor, along with me, who recommended him."

His father, seeing that the priest was upset, replied with a smile: "Sir, you must know that that son of mine is not male."

The priest was astonished and never revealed what he learned about Giovanni in that moment to anyone.

And so Giovanni, his secret protected by his parents and by the priest, was able to continue working for Cavaliere Pucci, who, "finding himself to be well-served by him in his house, continued to keep him in Anghiari for three or four years, sometimes even taking him to Monte Pulciano, where he was from."

And when the cavaliere was named governor of Ripafratta, he took Giovanni with him to that town near Pisa. (Slide: Ripafratta)

In Ripafratta, Giovanni enjoyed unexpected freedom because, his master often being away, he was left for days and days to act as custodian of the palazzo, and this great freedom seemed to be the basis for the tragic events that led the young man to his death.

In fact, Giovanni began to court the niece of the town's priest "and such was his longing that they ardently fell in love with each other."

The lovers planned to run away together to Rome, where they would be married.

For this reason, toward the middle of June of the year 1743, Giovanni prepared two horses with which they would leave early in the morning.

But the night before their escape, the beloved young woman related her entire plan to her younger sister who—wanting to flee the cloister in which her uncle, the priest, kept them—threatened to tell everything if they did not take her away with them to Rome.

And so, at dawn, at the appointed place for their getaway, Giovanni found his beloved accompanied by her sister, and "he who had never been discourteous to any young lady, at once responded that she could also come." He hoisted the two young ladies onto the horses he had prepared, and he followed them on foot toward Lucca (Slide: station of Lucca), being careful not to pass through the streets of Pisa, where the two young ladies were known.

Upon arriving in Lucca, Giovanni bought a carriage, within which he seated the two girls, while he arranged himself behind them.

"In this manner, all three headed to Siena. And with—as one might imagine—a pace that was not sluggish, they got underway." But upon arriving at a place called Poggetto, a shaft of the carriage broke, requiring them to stop, and Giovanni had to repair it before taking to the road again in great haste.

In the meantime, the uncle, upon waking in the morning, noticed his nieces' escape and sent another priest and two servants of Ripafratta's governor to catch them and punish Giovanni.

They caught up with the fugitives in Staggia, near Siena. "The priest began to yell at the servants for them to fire the arquebus upon Giovanni" who, having seen them from a distance, had gotten off the carriage.

Urged on by the priest's orders, the servants pointed the arquebus toward Giovanni's face, but with great cool-headedness, he pulled out the pistol that he kept at his side and pointed it at them.

Time stopped, "and for quite some time everyone remained still in that way."

Finally, as if reawakened, Giovanni quickly thought that if he declared himself to be a woman, justice would have little to demand from him for having abducted the two young women. So he gave himself up to the two servants whose master was his own and whom he knew well.

But the priest continued to urge that Giovanni be shot, and so Miniato, one of the two servants, pointed at the young man's leg, thinking to wound him without creating too much damage.

The shot went off and wounded Giovanni in his thigh. At the same time, that very shot killed a hound and wounded a small boy who happened to be there.

The story ends with the two young women locked up in a convent in Lucca and Giovanni brought to the hospital in Siena "on June 16 of the year 1743 and placed in bed number 70, and in the book of patients admitted to the hospital, a note was made with the name of Giovanni di Francesco Bordoni, free Roman, of the age of twenty-four."

Giovanni died there a few days later as a result of an infection from the wound to his leg, and his body was dissected by the physician Giovanni Bianchi, who had been seeking hymens to demonstrate that virgins could be recognized by the presence of that membrane.

And so, we know Giovanni's story thanks to "the very beautiful hymen that he had, intact."

Part Two: Harry Crawford

Two hundred years later: another physician, another criminal case, another book, and another story that reaches us.

In 1939, Dr. Herbert Michael Moran (Slide: Moran) published *Viewless Winds*, a book of memoirs of a middle-age surgeon; former captain of the Australian national rugby team; prominent figure in the medical community of his country; a man with a vigorous, curious, penetrating mind and some prejudices of his generation. The book was a mixture of life lived and clinical cases that Moran considered particularly interesting.

One of the stories discussed briefly was that of Harry Crawford, born Eugenia Falleni.

Here again: what would we know today of this obscure Italian emigrant, who arrived in New Zealand in 1877, if he had not been involved in news report; had not been convicted of homicide; had not had—through intercession of the very judge who condemned him—met a physician who, by chance, knew Italian; if this doctor had not found his story so special as to record it in his book of memoirs; and if this book of memoirs had not happened into the hands of a curious Australian journalist who re-wrote his story in the 1980s?

The book was translated into Italian last year, and now here we are, where everything began.

Harry Crawford was born at Ardenza, in the province of Livorno, on January 25, 1875. At birth, he was called Eugenia Falleni. (Slide: landscape painting of Ardenza)

On August 8, 1877, he landed in New Zealand with his parents: his father, Luigi Falleni, a carter, and his mother, Isola Gini, a seamstress.

Waiting for them in the port of Wellington was Eugene Falleni, a grandmother who had already arrived in New Zealand in 1875, with her second husband.

The first recorded emigration from Italy to New Zealand, in 1870, also left from Livorno. In fact, named as "Special Agent for Italy" by the New Zealand government was one John Glynn, an Englishman who lived in Livorno, where he had managed a restaurant and had been a theatrical agent, with the charge of recruiting workers willing to move overseas.

But the government was disappointed and dissatisfied by the migration from Italy: "From every point of view, very unsatisfactory, because the physical and moral character of the people introduced is completely unsuitable for the work of colonization."

The Immigration Act, which went into effect in 1901, limited admissions from southern Europe, reflecting the preference in Australia and New Zealand for white immigrants of British origin.

Southern Europeans had an inferior standard of living, they said, and would not be accepted favorably either in society or in the world of the Anglo-Saxons.

In particular, the Italians were described as "the Chinese of Europe."

Being Italian, Eugenia was therefore part of a gender minority within an ethnic minority and did not identify with either of the two.

When it came to choosing a name, Eugenia chose an Anglo-Saxon one: Harry Crawford.

According to police accounts, the Fallenis were good citizens, highly regarded and respectful of the law.

Eugenia seemed to be the only blemish in this story of successful immigration. She was restless, stubborn, and undisciplined. As soon as she could, she wore men's clothing and ran away from home. She had already been arrested for this at a very early age and brought home. Her nickname at the time was Tally-Ho.

In men's clothing, she got a job first in a brickyard and then in a laundry. Not yet twenty, again in men's clothing, Eugenia ran away from home forever and shipped off. (Slide: photo of Eugenia in an elegant portrait)

She reappeared on terra firma in Sidney, after passage as a cabin boy, with an infant girl in her arms.

According to Doctor Moran, she had given birth at sea after having been raped by the ship's captain.

Shortly after the birth of the child, writes Moran, Eugenia took the name Harry Crawford and began to work in a factory or as a handyman in the city's hotels.

Harry Crawford never remained long in the same place and wandered for ten years from one quarter of the city to another, living in boarding houses or in lodgings provided by the cafes in which he worked.

In 1910, Harry's destiny changed. He was hired by a respectable physician, for whom he was the dishwasher in the kitchen and a handyman. He lived above the stable. He cut the firewood and accompanied the doctor on his visits, driving the horse cart.

In that house he met Annie Birkett, the governess (Slide: Annie Birkett). Annie was thirty-five years old, a widow, and had a ten-year-old son.

After three years, an unaware Methodist minister married them.

With her savings, Annie had opened a candy store, and she moved with her son and her new husband to a house all their own.

Harry was forty years old but looked older (Slide). He was five feet, three inches tall and strong but with a slender frame. He had gray eyes, a hairless face, and dark chestnut hair combed back and usually covered by a gray felt hat. He dressed like most of the workers of the period with gray pants and a long coat to cover his buttocks.

He had a brusque and rapid stride and swung one arm when he walked.

Three years after his marriage, Harry Crawford was arrested, as one can read in the record: "Eugenia Falleni, alias Harry Crawford, forty-five years of age, handyman," was "accused of having killed with malice and premeditation Annie Birkett-Crawford on the first of October 1917 or around that date."

In fact, Annie had apparently disappeared without leaving a trace. During the same days of her disappearance, the burned body of a woman was found in a thicket. The discovery was recorded as the accidental death of an unknown woman.

But some time later, Annie's son went to the police, stating that the corpse could have been the body of his mother who had disappeared, and he accused Harry of the presumed homicide.

Investigations were opened.

Sergeant Stewart Robson, head of the investigations, went to the Empire Hotel, where Harry was working, on July 5, 1920:

"How long have you been working here?"
"A few weeks"
"Of what nationality are you?"
"Why do you want to know?"
"I think you are Italian."
"No, I'm Scottish. I am from Edinburgh."
"My real name is Harry Crawford and I am forty-five years old. I'm Scottish, born in Edinburgh on July 25, 1875."
"At eighteen months of age my parents brought me to New Zealand. At eighteen, I left home and boarded the steamship Australia. Working to pay for my passage, I landed in Sidney."
"I currently reside at number 47 Durham Street, with my wife, who was called Lizzie Allison when single. We were civilly married in September 1919. I had never been married before. Aside from my wife, I have not had any friends, male or female, since I arrived in Australia."

Harry Crawford was brought to headquarters and gave this statement. At the end, agent Robson stated he had some doubts as to the veracity of his declarations and had reason to believe he had previously been married to Annie Birkett.

Robson asked him if he had any particular markings that could prove his identity.

"Take your clothes off and let's see."
"No, I refuse."

Harry also refused to undress in front of a doctor.

"I suppose at this point you will send me to prison. What happens when someone arrives in prison?"
"I don't know, but I imagine they are made to take a good bath and are given clean clothes."
"Can I go to the women's unit?"
"Absolutely not!"
"Come with me, I must tell you something. You must know that I am a woman, not a man."
"This is not something for me to decide. You must have a medical exam."
"It's terrible. It's completely the life that I feared," commented Harry Crawford at the end of the exam.

The trial charging Harry Crawford began on Tuesday, October 5, 1920 (Slide), before judge Sir William Cullen and a jury of twelve people.

Charging him was prosecutor William T. Coyle, known as "Bulldog," and for the defense, a former farmer and now attorney, Andrew McDonnel, known as "Silent Mac."

A bulldog versus a silent lawyer, and in the middle, an illiterate Italian immigrant who had spent his life hiding his biological sex, feeling himself to be a man, and who had already built up a series of lies.

In the background, a woman dead of mysterious causes, first considered accidental and then, after three years, thought to be a probable homicide.

In the opening statement, Coyle said that Eugenia Falleni was known as "the man-woman" (Slide: newspapers), because he had worn men's clothes and carried out duties in a factory and elsewhere.

For William Coyle, the public prosecutor—expert, meticulous, theatrical, and who would become a judge a few years later—the only challenge represented by the case was the eccentricity of the accused.

"I find it difficult to refrain from using the male gender in speaking of the accused. Therefore, when I use it, I ask you to understand that I am referring to her."

There were frequent moments of confusion during the trial because some witnesses spoke of Eugenia as female, others as male, and in one case in a neuter way, using the neuter pronoun *it*.

Eugenia was sentenced to death and brought to the women's prison in Long Bay.

In 1920, the penalty was commuted to life in prison, and in 1931, conditional freedom was granted for humanitarian reasons, in consideration of age, health, and good conduct.

Doctor Herbert Moran visited Eugenia/Harry in prison twice, and twice after the release.

It was William Coyle himself, of the prosecution, who convinced the doctor to make these visits. He knew that Moran knew Italian and thought that Eugenia would like conversing in her language. (His language? Harry had arrived down under at the age of three, and he had pretended to be Anglo-Saxon for decades. What was his language? It seems, however, that he still spoke a Tuscan dialect, probably from Livorno.)

"She had darting and fearful eyes, a face of olive complexion, lined and hairless. Her head could have easily passed for the head of a man: short hair, combed back and graying, the nose large and straight. Her chest was flat, and her voice was hoarse and low in timbre (Slide). She seemed to deliberately emphasize a male stride."

"She was a semi-wild creature who felt different and marginalized. She felt persecuted; she was unaware of having done something truly wrong. It was the others who were wrong; it was they who did not understand."

Eugenia Falleni, alias Harry Crawford, died on June 5, 1937, hit by a car in a Sidney street. He had been calling himself Joan Ford and rented rooms.

He lost and regained nationality, in addition to gender. An Italian woman, then an Australian man. With his birth name, he returned to being a woman in prison, and in old age again assumed an Anglo-Saxon name, but a woman's.

Whether Eugenia/Harry was a killer is wholly open to discussion, but if I was looking for the victim of abuse, unjustly accused, I didn't find one. What I reconstructed was a sad and very complicated story.

(Translated by Gianpiero W. Doebler)

Notes

1. In this script, Botteghi has creatively elaborated on a number of publications, including Marzio Barbagli, *Storia di Caterina che per ott'anni vestì abiti da uomo* (Bologna: Il Mulino, 2014); Simona Baldelli, *La vita a rovescio* (Milan: Giunti 2016); Suzanne Falkiner, *Eugenia, storia di un uomo*, trans. Annamaria Biavasco and Valentina Guani (Genoa: Il canneto, 2019). For a study on Catterina Vizzani in English, see Clorinda Donato, *The Life and Legend of Catterina Vizzani: Sexual Identity, Science and Sensationalism in Eighteenth-Century Italy and England* (Oxford: Oxford University Press, 2020).

2. Two spellings of the name, Catterina and Caterina, are used in the text.

NORTH

PART 5

STORIES OF TRANS IDENTITY AND ACTIVISM

Chapter 12

From *AntoloGaia* (*AntholoGay*)

Porpora Marcasciano

In this passage, Marcasciano recounts a milestone episode that went down in LGBTQ+ history as "la presa del Cassero" (the storming of Cassero). The Bolognese Cassero represents the first case in Italy of a space obtained by a gay association, the Circolo 28 Giugno, from a municipal government. The storming of Cassero is a collective memory that is evoked and explored from different perspectives in this volume. What is particularly compelling in Marcasciano's account is, once again, her ability to tell a serious story about the recognition of civil rights and the struggle for liberation while maintaining a sense of levity, humor, irony, and self-irony. However, nostalgia for the past and criticism of the present emerge from her entertaining account: during the memorable parade that reached the Cassero, queer people were marching with pride, together; for Marcasciano, the movement must recover and fully appreciate the beautiful sense of unity, celebration, and political commitment manifested in the moment of that parade.

The Cassero

But let's go back to a few months earlier, to the historical victory of the storming of Cassero, which represents one of the most exciting pages of Italian gay history, and not only. That demonstration—colorful and politically happy, as you have never seen before—left from Piazza Neptune at around four in the afternoon. We were about six hundred, rowdy, joyful, few but determined. One of the first times we were parading proudly, fairies, proud of being gay, transvestite, transsexual; we were parading for the pride but mostly for a great victory. We were wearing the colors of war, yet ours wasn't a violent and bloody war but rather a celebration, the celebration they had always denied us. That wonderful chapter could be retraced, politically and symbolically, to the famous "laugher that would bury them."[1] That day in Bologna our pride was parading, far from all the issues that we are still stuck with today. The question of *how* one should participate in the Pride did not matter to us—all that polemical bitching, today, about the alleged kitschy circus acts, the exposed breasts, and all those vulgarities that, according to the right-thinking people, characterize our celebration. Neither did exist the great dilemma—all Italian—about the location of the Pride, simply because the movement was one and was marching united without divisions, except for purely aesthetic reasons. Like it or not, we were us and we were fine with that. There wasn't even an exact awareness of that experience, after all we were forging a path in progress. Nothing was taken for granted. Everything needed to be built. The only certainty was our self-awareness that was rebelling against two thousand years of repression, by taking back what we had always been denied.

Let's try to think before that date in Italy or before June 28, 1969, in the entire world. And let's try to think about the action that led the Bologna city council to grant [us] a place—not any place, but a gate [Porta Saragozza] dedicated to the Madonna. Do you think that today it would be possible? The Left that ruled the city and the region was still very strong, inasmuch as it won the negotiation with the Church and earned the victory. A great political gesture after which a low-balling began that would bring the LGBT movement to beg for shreds of rights that we still haven't achieved. That fabulous faggot parade, after traversing downtown Bologna, arrived at Porta Saragozza at around 7 p.m., creating a huge human chain that encircled Cassero and even blocked the traffic on the nearby boulevards for a few minutes. Those who cut the ribbon were Pugnales, Beppe, and Prussi, while Merdaiola[2] and Wonder unrolled the banner from the tower's battlements. We were all happy and content: that was a huge victory, a tangible sign of development and emancipation. We hugged each other dancing with the stars.

After a while we sat to rest at a table in a café of the piazza. I am reporting here the testimony of that moment that I gave in 2002, for the twentieth birthday of Cassero: that June 28, 1982, the Royal family had arranged a meeting in full force—empresses, czarinas, queens, princesses, and grand duchesses. As usual, we were camping in the residence of Josephine of the Kingdom of two Sicilies on via Clavature: a living room of roughly twenty meters, occupied by the occupiers of an occupied house. A year earlier, Aunt Anastasia Romanov, backed up by her mother, the empress Hilary, had kissed the communist Zangheri,[3] and for this, she was accused of opening the way for the Bolsheviks and therefore preparing the end of the empire—the things we had to do! This, and especially other matters, were at the center of our discussion in the occupied residence, for two days and two nights, with no sleep, and not only that. We sustained ourselves with stimulants and other helpers; we had to decide what to do after the storming of the Winter Palace! And the next day, after the queens, mistaken for courtesans, had placed the banners on the crenellated towers and could finally sit, exhausted but happy, to observe the new Porta Saragozza from far away, an old lady, astonished and amazed, whispered in a strong Bolognese accent: "I guess the men-women arrived here!"

(Translated by Danila Cannamela)

Notes

1. The sentence, originally attributed to the anarchic Michael Bakunin and later used by protest movements in the 1960s, became one of the slogans of Movimento del '77, a movement that, especially in Bologna, engaged with irony, creativity, and surrealist performances to offer forms of life alternative to the traditional sociopolitical environment. On this, see in particular Helena Velena's essay, in chapter 16.

2. Merdaiola is the nickname of Antonello, whose story is narrated in chapter 3.

3. Valérie Taccarelli kissed Renato Zangheri, who at the time was the mayor of Bologna.

Chapter 13

From *Favolose narranti*

Storie di transessuali *(Fabulous Narrators: Stories of Transsexuals)*

PORPORA MARCASCIANO

In this chapter, Lisa, a trans woman from Brazil, shares her story with Marcasciano, from her childhood in Rio de Janeiro to her struggle as an illegal immigrant in a beach town on the Riviera Romagnola.[1] In Lisa's account, a distinctively Brazilian view of gender variance and female beauty is interwoven with, and reshaped by, the experience of being an immigrant in Italy.

Marcasciano, in her two collections of interviews with people from the trans community—*Favolose narranti* and *Tra le rose e le viole*—abandons the humor that characterizes her memoirs and shows a strong commitment to remaining loyal to the words of her interviewees and the tone of their conversations. This chapter, with its plain and intimate style, conveys Lisa's vulnerability and her courage: she proudly affirms her identity, speaks out for her community, and boldly recounts everyday injustices, making no attempt to disguise her fear of being deported. We have included Marcasciano's original introduction to Lisa's account.

Lisa

I first met with Lisa in Lido di Classe, a little town on the Riviera Romagnola, where a small community of Brazilian transsexual women has settled.

The purpose of our meeting was to find a solution for the difficult situation they were facing as illegal immigrants. Lisa's kind and intelligent demeanor, her insight, and the interest she shares in the demands of her group have enabled her to be recognized as the spokesperson of her community. Her story begins in a neighborhood in Rio de Janeiro sandwiched between the touristy part of the city and the favelas. It was her passion for samba, Carnival, and dance choreographies, along with her search for prosperity, that led her to follow the route to Europe, exemplifying the dream and the reality of a Brazilian trans woman.

(This interview was collected in December 2007, in Lisa's house in Lido di Classe, in the Province of Ravenna.)

Lisa is the name I use to introduce myself today. I've put aside my original Christian name. I use it only when I need to and, if I could, I wouldn't use it anymore at all, because I am—and, most importantly, I feel I am—Lisa. I'm forty-three years old. I come from Rio de Janeiro, the most beautiful city in the world, where celebrations, the sun, the sea, and so much more are the ingredients that make up an incredibly magnetic mix, one that pulls in everything and attracts everyone. For about twenty years now I've been living in Italy, where, despite countless problems, I have settled in well.

I was born into a poor family, one of the many that populate my Brazilian metropolis. I recall my childhood with a mixture of joy and heartache. The joy comes from thinking about something that belongs to you—about that small world that, to the eyes of a child, appears vast and strange. But it is also a memory that is full of pain because the circumstances I lived in were not the best. My family lived in Vaz Lobo—I'm not sure whether I should define it as a neighborhood, a village, or both—just up against one of the biggest favelas in Rio, a place of transit, connecting the enchanted world of the tourists with the desperate world of the dispossessed.

My childhood I remember as being spent playing on the street with the other children, and I don't believe it was at all different from the childhood of any other kid in the world, let alone that of any other trans girl in the world. We all played with dolls, not guns, when we were little, whether we were here in Italy, in China, or in Brazil. Let's just say that I have seen a whole lot of guns—not toy guns, but real ones. Every once in a while, an alarm or a signal to take cover would go off in the narrow streets where I used to run around with the other kids. Mothers, sisters, aunts, and even friends and neighbors would start to shout, calling us all back inside houses or into one of the countless courtyards surrounding them. Although we were aware of the danger, we kids turned everything into a game, amusing ourselves by wondering what was going on. Everybody knew each other in that place; the social fabric, poverty-related problems notwithstanding, was cohesive enough to protect us. There was always somebody—usually a female somebody—keeping an eye on us. However, once I turned eight, despite the watchfulness of relatives and neighbors, I started slipping off to dance the samba. It was in my blood. I couldn't help myself. It pulled me in. That joyous, sparkling world enchanted me. All of that rhythm, the way those sinuous, sensual bodies moved, and above all the fabulousness of those costumes—it fired my imagination, budding young trans girl that I was. I would watch how the dancers dressed themselves up, did their hair, decked themselves out in bits and baubles, and I took note. I learned and internalized everything and, later on, that "apprenticeship" would come in handy on very different stages and dance floors!

I am the youngest of six children. One died. My father and my mother split up when I was still living with them. Their marriage wasn't working because, like so many other men, he was cruel and violent. Given that my mother had always been the one who worked hard to provide for the family, and seeing as she had always done it on her own, she figured she might as well keep on doing it without my father's mistreatment, so she left him. I must say, my father was always calm with me. He would tell me, over and over again, to be careful who I hung out with, who I went out with, because things could get dangerous. My mother, on the other hand, was much stricter, perhaps because she felt responsible for raising and educating us well. She would yell at me and dress me down every time I misbehaved. There was even the occasional resounding slap.

I have one indelible memory from that time in my life, which I'll always carry with me, a thing that shocked and terrified me—and that's the time someone burned down my house. My sister had gotten engaged to one of the bosses of the *favela*, a drug dealer and an ex-con, the kind who are always in and out of prison. Beautiful and damned—one of those guys who make you fall in love, not just thanks to their gangland bohemian allure, but also with the craziness of their lives, because, as we all know, the harder and more complicated things are, the more we like them. When my sister decided to leave him, because she couldn't stand that lifestyle anymore, the reprisals began, the most savage of which was setting our house on fire with all of us inside. We managed to escape, and we all survived. I didn't run to the front door like all the others, though, but towards the back. Once there, although I was protected by the ruins of the collapsed house, I was trapped because there was no way out. I watched, terrified, as my house went up in flames. To the eyes of a child, that fire was as big as a war. Everything was burning, outside and inside of me. They didn't just burn the house, either. They also fired multiple gunshots, and there was a gunfight with the police who showed up. We ended up moving to the home of my godmother, who took us in, and with the support of our neighbors we managed to survive, but things weren't easy, not as they should have been for a child. My mom just couldn't feed six children, so each of us had to do our part. When I was twelve, I officially started working, as a ticket seller on the bus, because on buses in Brazil there is a person who hands you a ticket—it's not automated the way it is here. The route was the one connecting Vaz Lobo to Copacabana. I started work at five in the morning, doing five or six round trips per day.

I shouldn't have been able to work at that age, but my mother took me to the judge who supervises cases concerning guardianship to get an authorization. So I had a work permit and a card that certified my eligibility to work. That wasn't the only place I worked, though. That was my main job, the steady one that provided a regular salary. I had another one, less official but definitely more fun. Together with some friends of mine—women and trans women—I performed at Carosel, a club in the port area frequented by sailors and drifters. We were a tight-knit group of friends, open to all sorts of adventures and to the opportunities that a place like that could offer. We did parodies of the big divas and lip-synched or sang karaoke-style. I had a lot of fun impersonating Tina Turner and Billie Holiday, both great African American performers to whom I am distantly related, because our heritage is the same; one way or the other, we can trace our roots back to the deportation of slaves. I worked at Carosel on weekends. I couldn't have done it any other way, actually, because I would get out of there and jump right onto the bus. It was absolutely exhausting, and I was only able to stick it out thanks to my youth and my intense desire to dance and enjoy myself. We Cariocas have dancing in our blood. Alongside the red and white blood cells and the platelets, we have rhythm—"*ritmo tropical*," as the song goes! My passion for samba couldn't help but lead me to the famous schools that parade along the *avenida* every year for Carnival. Rio lives for its Carnival. It spends the whole year getting ready. All year long, everything is just leading up to that week. It is celebration triumphant. There is nothing like it anywhere else in the world because the *Carnaval do Rio* is, itself, the very symbol of celebration—joyousness, frenzy, fantasies, sensuality, all those things that during the rest of the year we have to keep in the closet because we are accustomed to abstention and to our idea of sin. I was a member of the "Grande Rio" [Grand Rio] school, which numbered roughly 1,500 people. It wasn't the most important, but what matters most is not the size of the school but the spirit that animates it—a spirit of unity and rhythm, because everyone has to be in time with the rhythm. Schools prepare for that first night all year long and then, finally, the moment for the parade arrives. That is when the desire to have fun and the desire to win, combined with a respect for the rules and the rhythm—one grand rhythm—all blend and meld together. I say "respect for the rules" because there are actual regulations for participants in the parade. Those who don't follow them lose points. Each school has its day and time in the parade, and it cannot take longer than the time it is allotted. So, when the show starts and you enter the arena, or the "Passerella de Samba" ["Sidewalk of Samba"]—that's the name of the *avenida*—that's when the big competition begins. You have just one hour to parade—and to successfully allow all seven thousand people to parade through, with all of their costumes and adornments, and their floats, which have to be less than nine yards long, is no easy thing!

I used to reinvest a part of my earnings in costumes and accessories, some for me and some to resell. That has always been my greatest passion—making costumes for Carnival, for samba, and for every sort of exciting entertainment and celebration. I would buy all of the necessary materials: feathers, rhinestones, lace, and other baubles. I enjoyed seeking out the strangest and most unusual items. Then I'd retreat into my makeshift workshop and create true pieces of art. One of the most beautiful costumes I ever crafted took up a lot of space. Between the crown of feathers, the wings made of veils and ostrich plumes, and the twelve-inch heels—all entirely red—I definitely needed the right runway. That costume must still be around somewhere, maybe in a storage closet at one of the samba schools, ready to be used when needed. When I think about what I'd like to do with my life, the profession of costume designer is exactly what I think of. It's something I'd love to do—make costumes for parties, for Carnival, for the theater, and, using all of my imagination and creative flair, I think I'd make really beautiful ones.

I used to know all of the "Carnavaleschi"—that's what the people from the schools who would come to me to order costumes are called. Once they had decided what to wear in the parade, they would give me a paper pattern on which to model the costumes—which usually had to feature the two distinctive colors of the school. Mine had blue and white. The name of my school is Grande Rio, then there is Portela, Ilha do Governador, and the most important and famous, which is Beijaflor de Nilopulos.

There are a lot of trans women in the samba schools, but not only there. The whole of Rio, the whole of Brazil is full of trans people. I believe it's the most trans country in the world. When people think of Brazil, they think of its most famous products, which are soccer players, coffee, samba dancers . . . and trans women. Vice versa, when people think of trans women, Brazil comes to mind. It's a commonplace to associate trans women with Brazilian trans women, who commonly—and very vulgarly—are called *viados*, a derogative term deriving from *deviados* [deviants], which has become quite the buzzword here in Italy. Despite Brazil's very macho culture, trans women are pretty well-accepted there. Like in Italy, there are places where we are more accepted, like the big cities, and others where we are less accepted, like small villages. It's obvious that in cities such as Rio, São Paulo, and Porto Alegre there are many more trans women because they move there to have better lives. There are also a number of associations that defend the rights of trans women, but I don't know a lot about them because I have been living in Italy for a long time now, and when I go back to Brazil on vacation, I move in different circles.

I kept on working at Carosel until I decided to come to Europe. Among us trans women, there has always been an aspiration to move to Europe because it represents a goal, a wealthy land where you can live better, where human rights are better respected. America remains inaccessible because it's much harder to get into, except for tourism. What's more, in the US, prostitution—which is still the only way we can make a living—is forbidden on the streets, and I, personally, just can't live without the celebrated *catwalk*. I have to move, to walk up and down, exactly like in Rio. If I had to stay at home to wait for customers, I'd get bored—it would be so, so much more tiresome! In some European countries, the culture and attitude are similar to Brazil, so I feel less marginalized. Italy, like Spain, Portugal, and France, have many things in common [with Brazil]. These are countries where one can engage in prostitution on the street. I believe this is due mainly to the weather, as it would be impossible in the Nordic countries. I have some girlfriends who live in Berlin, a few in Hamburg, and they tell me that sex work there is completely different. They work in night clubs, but it's not like here. When you leave Brazil, you usually go to stay with a friend who left before you, so the choice of the place often depends on where your friend lives. It's a question of safety, of peace of mind—because arriving in a world that is not your own is no simple thing. You have a million fears and doubts, but what keeps you going is a strong desire to succeed. In Brazil, at Carosel, during breaks between our travels, we would always talk about the "famous" trip to Europe. It was almost an obligatory stop along our journeys. Many of us aspired to go to Paris or Barcelona, which are still the top destinations—especially lately, since Italy has become a bit closed-minded and not quite what it used to be.

My journey took me first to Barcelona, around the mid-1980s, then to Rome, where I stayed for two years. Rome was extremely chaotic, and violent, too—so, as soon as I was able, I moved and came here to Lido di Classe, a little beach town on the Riviera Romagnola. I was one of the first to arrive, when there wasn't yet any particular sign of the gay-trans hub it would later become. We chose to stay simply because it was a place where we could find places to rent, a thing that isn't easy for any of us. In Lido di Classe, as in all beach towns, the houses are vacant in winter and the owners want to make a profit, so they don't make too much of a fuss. Then, when summer comes, the owners get itchy, start to complain, get pissed off, and it becomes clear that, if we want to stay, we'll have to pay more. Usually, once they see the money, they stop their bellyaching. I'd say that we Brazilians have set in motion an economy that is not limited to rent payments but also impacts the shops where we buy our groceries, the clubs that we and our customers frequent, and everything else that goes on in this place—which, in winter, would otherwise be empty. In springtime every year, like clockwork, come the police inspections, the stings, and the deportation orders, not to mention the abuses of power we're subjected to and can't say a thing about because, as illegal immigrants, we are very easy to blackmail. I eventually succeeded in getting a residency permit, but they haven't wanted to renew it again since it expired a year ago. Other girlfriends of mine are in the same predicament. Under the current immigration law,[2] everything has become more complicated because we can no longer build lives here. We constantly have to deal with law enforcement, who usually see us as a danger to society. There are stings, checks, preventive detentions, and a whole string of nuisances that affect our well-being by making us feel like monsters. They've sewed a label onto us—the mark of danger—made us into the bogeyman. When you accept that way of thinking, it's easy to wind up playing that role, the only one you're allowed—since you don't have any other, anyway. We remain in this situation of uncertainty, and it deprives us of any desire or opportunity to think about the future. I, for instance, don't know whether my residency permit will get renewed or if, tonight when I go out dancing, since I don't have my documents in order, I'll be detained and sent back to Brazil—or, worse yet, to a CPT,[3] as has already happened to some of my friends. To get my residency permit, I had to find a job that could justify my stay here. I got a job as a waitress in a restaurant whose owner I knew, so he hired me, but it's no easy thing. There aren't many people willing to take responsibility for people like us, with the police running so many more checks on us than on other people and coming by often to ask the owner if we're working, what time we come in, what time we leave. Faced with those sorts of complications, even people who are generally favorably disposed towards us will back out. I can't plan a life for myself or think about the future under these circumstances. I get depressed, I lose my desire to do anything. You keep on going with the strength of desperation because you know that this is the way it is and you just hope that, one of these days, a miracle will occur and you'll be able to get your residency permit.

Here in Lido di Classe, we have formed a little trans community. Around fifty of us live here year-round. Within that, there's a group that's always been here because we've settled in and created a network of relationships—we could say that we've put down roots—while others come and go. The ones who wander around the most are always the youngest, who still have the energy and the desire to travel. They usually head for the big cities like Rome, Milan, or Paris, and then they come back here in search of some familiarity and a welcoming environment. They usually come here after they've had problems elsewhere and they stay until they get into trouble here, too, when the police start to target them or encourage them to leave.

The young ones are also the ones who cause the most problems, because their exuberance doesn't go unnoticed in a little town like this—especially not by the police, but they take it out on the older ones, meaning us. It's much easier for them to take it out on us because, since we have documents, we are real people against whom rules and laws can be enforced—or rather, repression applied. You see, if they stop a twenty-year-old, who will take care not to show her documents, they'll take her to the police station and ID her, but they can't send her home—because for her, unlike for us, there isn't any clear information. Here, we all know each other. Amongst ourselves we are friends with some, less so with others, and openly at war with a few. Envy and jealousies are deeply rooted in our community and, as this is a small community, it's easy to have arguments, to pull pranks on each other out of spite, which can lead to actual vendettas that sometimes culminate in scuffles.

In our milieu, nothing goes unnoticed. Usually, everybody knows everything about everybody else. We know the circles the others move in, their friends, their lovers, as well as their customers. Often it's the customers themselves who gossip and tittle-tattle. It's like some big embroidery piece that all of us cut and sew. I met all of the others here in Italy, because I've fallen out of touch with the girlfriends I was close to back in Brazil. At this point, they're scattered all over the world. For people like us, who have always moved around a lot, it's hard to stay in touch. You lose your cell phone or someone steals it and you end up losing all of your numbers, or you leave your house or find some other place to stay, and then your girlfriends no longer have your address, or you move to places where it's difficult to stay connected . . . in other words, we are susceptible to change—not just sex change, but life change in general. It can happen that you come across one of your old friends, and then you celebrate, but it hardly ever happens here. I'm much more likely to see someone again or hear news of them when I go back to Rio and visit the usual places where we used to hang out. Over the years, Lido di Classe and the whole surrounding area have become a popular gay tourism destination, so in summer there are parties and soirées where cross-dressing is pretty much de rigueur. What's a party without transvestites, after all? A lot of Italian trans women come, too, from Bologna, Milan, and the rest of Italy, but it's hard to build relationships with them. There's bad blood between us because Italian trans women see us as the ones who steal their business, so friendships with them are pretty rare. We observe each other, watch each other, criticize each other, but it ends there.

I have taken very few hormones because there were never any sure and safe therapies, but mostly because hormones have a big impact on sexuality, which is something I wouldn't ever want to give up. I have instead opted to embellish my body, make it more feminine by adding silicone, which doesn't affect the libido at all but has other side effects that people usually don't take into consideration. I started doing silicone injections at a very young age in Brazil. We Brazilians use it for every type of correction: to round out the ass and the hips, to lift the cheekbones, to enlarge the lips, or to smooth out sharpness in the face. We see it as a sort of magical substance we can always turn to, no matter what, and often we take it to extremes, with extreme consequences.

Many years ago, a friend of mine ended up in a coma for three weeks because she injected herself with silicone and, while doing so, she pierced a vein and a blood clot formed. She survived, but for many others that wasn't the case. Usually, silicone injections are performed by *bombardere*,[4] trained trans women who have worked as hospital nurses and therefore know how to do it, or who have learned in other ways, but anyhow they have a certain amount of experience. Usually they perform these services in private homes. You have to call in advance, make a reservation, and then go. While you're waiting your turn, you meet others and start to chitchat. You run into someone who advises you about what to do and where to do it or someone who shows you the successful results of silicone, lets you see the parts she's gotten fixed. With the passing of time, I've matured, gained a greater sense of responsibility and good judgment, and I've learned to stop at the right time. I've stopped overdoing it with the silicone, because I've realized that, if you don't, you can set yourself up for some big problems. For a trans woman, it's wonderful to look *fabulous* when you go out on the street. It makes you feel super, it gives you that charge that lets you overcome any problem, that energy that's essential for being "on stage" and making a lot of money. These are things you do for a while, when you're just starting out. You feel like the world is yours for the taking and you even dare to challenge it—but then you realize that there are other things, too, like your health, which should always be your first priority. I gained a better understanding of all of this when I started to have responsibilities—when I grew up, became more mature, and started thinking about my family. My relationship with my mother has always been central in my life. She is very important to me and, since she isn't rich, I've always cared for her, and especially now that she is old. Helping her with money makes me feel better. It's like repaying her, at least a little, for everything she did for me, all that love that only a mother can give. For a few years now, I've also been helping out my older sister, who's lost her job and is struggling with depression. I'm the only one who's there for her, because our other siblings have families of their own and couldn't care less. What's more, she was there for me during the tough times in my life. She was the one who understood me, the one I opened up to—a true port in a storm, because my mother, from that standpoint, was really harsh and strict. That was her way of raising her children, and it didn't leave any space for the affection I needed. There came a time when I decided to adopt a child, who is now fifteen, and I make sure he wants for nothing. He was the son of a family friend, and he'd been left all alone in the world after his mother died in an accident. My sister took him in, to save him from the awful fate of ending up on the streets, and, at that time, life was calling on me to take on some responsibilities. He thinks of me as his aunt. He knows everything about me and he loves me very much. I see him once a year when I go back to Rio. I have wanted to make sure he could study and build a future for himself that will allow him to escape from poverty, because, in Brazil, extreme poverty is still everyone's greatest fear. It's important for me to have these responsibilities, it helps to keep me on course, because I know that I'm useful, that I'm of service to somebody and to something. It gives me a feeling of loving and being loved, of having ties in a world where those things seem to have disappeared. It's certainly not a classic family in the traditional sense, but for me it's my family and it's the thing I care about most.

I recently attended a training course for street sex workers, a course created by the MIT [Trans Identity Movement][5] in Bologna, that should help us to lay out a plan for our work going forward and for our lives. I know there were issues with the police in the beginning, because to attend the course you had to be a legal immigrant and, since I'm waiting for my papers to be renewed, there were some problems. We're collaborating with the MIT on a few projects, the most ambitious of which is starting a samba school here in Classe. It would be a fabulous way to create jobs, allow us to socialize with the locals and wider community, and do something nice and fun that would let us build bridges, not fences. After all, we Brazilian women are masters—or rather, queens—when it comes to this, and it would give us a chance to give the best of ourselves. Imagine a Carnival here, where in winter everything is dead—just think how wild it would be, what fun! It would be enormously successful and have a great impact on the people and things here, one so huge that they shouldn't hesitate to fund it. In the meantime, though, we're working to build support services for the trans women who live here, to offer some kind of help and support for all the sorts of issues that a trans person might have, especially when she is undocumented and considered an illegal alien.

We could say that having MIT as a point of reference makes us feel safer. Although, here in Lido di Classe, we already have a group of social workers who have been driving around in a camper for years, with whom we have a great relationship. There's a center they let us use as a place to get together and hold meetings. Valentina, Andrea, Linda, Laura, who are the social workers at Lunatica—that's the name of the service—have become our friends and we are doing a lot of interesting things with them. They have become guarantors of a sort, for all of us, guardian angels who try to solve a variety of problems for us that we might not be able to deal with on our own.

I don't know if someday I'll go back to live in Brazil. I still have to figure that out. I miss Rio de Janeiro very much. I miss its warmth and its joyfulness, but I still don't know whether I'd rather visit there once in a while or go back to live there. I'm happy here in Lido di Classe. I've settled in here. I'd like to consider it my home, but I can't yet, not until I get my residency permit. I'd like to live in peace, like everyone else. After all, I've never done anything to harm anyone. In fact, when all is said and done, I do mostly good, and that should be enough.

(Translated by Danila Cannamela and Jennifer Delare)

Notes

1. The chapter "Lisa" was originally published in the book *Favolose narranti: Storie di transessuali* (Roma: ManifestoLibri, 2008).

2. Lisa is most likely referring to the Bossi-Fini Law (189/2002), which, in the midst of a heated debate on immigration, modified and further restricted the Turco-Napolitano Law, passed in 1998, which had provided a general method for systematizing and defining migratory flows entering Italy. The Bossi-Fini Law made it much more difficult for non-EU citizens to immigrate to Italy by shortening the renewal period for permits of stay from three to two years, and officially turning illegal immigration into a crime. The text of the law can be found here: https://www.normattiva.it/uri-res/N2Ls?urn:nir:stato:legge:2002;189.

3. CPT stands for Centro Permanenza Temporaneo (Center for Temporary Stays). CPT facilities, created in the late 1990s, were replaced in 2008 by CIE, or Centri Identificazione ed Espulsione (Centers for Identification and Expulsions), facilities where the Italian state detains illegal migrants who are expected to be repatriated but whose expulsions cannot be immediately processed.

4. For more on these individuals, see the introduction and chapter 3.

5. On the evolution of the MIT acronym, see the Timeline of Key Events in this volume.

Chapter 14

From *Camminavo rasente i muri*

Autobiografia tascabile di un transessuale
(*I Was Walking Along the Walls: Pocket Autobiography of a Transsexual Man*)

MASSIMO D'AQUINO

FtM trans experiences have generally drawn much less attention in the public opinion. D'Aquino intervenes in this "void" by recounting his experience.[1] This excerpt is from the first chapter of his autobiography—one of the first trans bildungsromans, which recounts the protagonist's journey from his childhood, in the island of Capri, to his adulthood in northern Italy. In this chapter, D'Aquino intercuts flashbacks and present time to piece together his hyphenated identity of trans man and migrant. The text tells a story of transformations and growing awareness by returning to fond and painful memories: a childhood in the south with a single mother; a tough adolescence in which, as a girl, he was victim of sexual assault; a troubled adulthood of difficult self-acceptance. The writing style, intimate at times to the point of brutal honesty, allows readers to enter into the author's "closet" and access uncomfortable feelings like shame and lack of agency that have accompanied him since his childhood and that he has gradually learned to challenge.

Massimo at age fifty-one:

Okay, this is it. No. I have to enlarge the font. Otherwise I can't read what I'm writing. And it's really important that this time I take it seriously. Write without lying, for the first time. Experience after experience. Taking my time.

It all started with the hair. When I got home, I decided to cut my hair, even though it was already really short. Because I don't have to work tomorrow, I wash myself more thoroughly than usual (which, sometimes, becomes: "Fuck it! I'll wash tomorrow!") and I cut my hair. An odd ritual? No, I think a lot of people do it. For me, though, it takes on a meaning that is absolutely and tritely symbolic: I remove, wash down the drain, toss into the trash everything that has stuck to me over the last few days.

We were talking about . . . the hair. My hands are under the hot water. I've shaved my hair off and thrown it away in the toilet, but congregations of tiny little hairs that no one could ever gather up completely remain, and so I rinse them down, one by one, or rather . . . one clump at a time; the water, flowing hot over my hands, engulfs them. What is it that bothers me so much about performing this delicate and obsessive sink-cleaning operation? I am still, motionless; my whole body is still, motionless. Only my hands move. They collect the water that runs hot from the tap and, section after section, direct the little hairs into the drain. Okay. The sink is almost completely clean.

However, there's something unsettling about this motionlessness.

I need a cigarette.

It's the water. It's not hot, but boiling, scalding! My hands burn and grow redder and redder, but they do not stop performing their duty: the sink MUST be pristine, everything in this bathroom MUST be neat and tidy tonight. Including me. That is the meaning of the ritual. Of my perhaps-not-so-trite-after-all ritual.

Meanwhile, I take another drag. Fuck! It's gone out!

The boiling hot water. I'm hunched, motionless, over the sink, my head down and my eyes fixed on the clumps of little hairs. For the first time, though, I shift my gaze further to the right, raise my head ever so slightly and see, on the edge of the sink, the clippers I've just finished using. On the edge of the sink, with the plug still in the socket.

The boiling hot water. I might scald myself, while I'm cleaning the sink. Scald myself and jump, bump the clippers, which would end up in the water that I'm letting run to wash away these goddamned little hairs. That's it! I'd be electrocuted. Maybe I wouldn't even be aware of dying. How should I know? Here's what frightens me: the idea that I can die.

How can that be? Isn't that just what I was trying so desperately to do until less than a month ago? Am I or am I not the person who, on January

25, 2012, bought a hose and a roll of tape so he could commit suicide in his Smart car? (Today is March 6, 2012.)

I have to write it down. I absolutely have to describe and write down these things I feel.

Right now would have been perfect—here, in the bathroom, having come in to take a shower bringing my iPhone with me, but I didn't, idiot that I am! Then, suddenly, the feeling of guilt vanishes. It's not like every writer always has something with them at all times in which to write, some way to record their impressions! Of course not.

They have the ability to recall every tiny detail of every impression, each feeling they've experienced. As they write, they relive the memory. But do I know how to do that?

Will I be able to convey to the reader the things that I wish to? Will the reader be able to laugh at me and with me? Be able to scream NO! along with me? I can only try.

But I have to hurry. Memories fade. There's the risk I won't remember anything anymore.

I've decided to take a quick shower to wash off all the little hairs. My shoulders are covered with them. Ah! If only I could walk out of the bathroom just as I am. But I can't. I live in a wonderful place, a beautiful house facing the sea. Enviable. However, it is also a B&B. I'm the owner, but I have another job, too, and today I'm not alone in the house. There's a man. Very distinguished, seventy-seven but looks at least fifteen years younger. I heard him go out about forty minutes ago. He could come back and catch me coming out of the bathroom half naked and, in any case, I have to leave the bathroom as clean as I found it, immaculate, each time I finish. It's a bed and breakfast.

Okay. Sink cleaned. I take off my underwear and get into the shower. I let the water get hot and step beneath it. Systematically, piece by piece, I rinse the little hairs off my body, then all the way down to the drain. Now I wash myself. I turn to pick up the shower gel and, in that instant, I remember that I used it up last time.

The guest! I'm saved! On the lowest shelf of the shower rack I see the guest's body wash. Damn it. It's shampoo, not shower gel, and I, too, have only shampoo and conditioner, but no body wash. I have to wash myself, though. What harm can there be in using shampoo as if it were soap? Why not? I wash only the "essential" bits.

Underarms . . . private parts . . . toes.

I have to hurry. I get out of the shower. I'm cold. I dry off. I put on clean underwear and "stuff" them. I adjust the sock. The stuffed sock.

After nearly twenty years of not doing it, now I'm back to using this time-honored system. It's so easy on the Internet these days. There are special sites where you can order your nice fake penis for casual strolls, but there's also the "combat" model, which is always ready to go.

I don't do this for me, mind you. I don't believe that I need it, but I have noticed, on more than one occasion, that it's always there that people's gazes wind up. It's not just women, either, but men, too; inevitably, sooner or later, they rest their gaze in between my legs or clap their hand over it—for no particular reason, just kidding around, just for a laugh, as they say. The environment I work in now is the sort with a lot of camaraderie.

I hear the street door open. The guest is back, and I've been in the bathroom since he went out; that must be an hour and a half ago, more or less.

Morning.

I'm woken by my neighbor in the room next door, the guest. It's early. I sit up on the edge of my bed, lift up my sleep mask. It's only eight o'clock.

I get back into bed. I want to go back to sleep, but I have to tell this story and I can only do that if I'm awake. I decide to go out.

Over the last year, I've revolutionized my life:

I've finally understood that not everything can or has to be planned out. A lot of the most exciting situations happen coincidentally, by chance or by luck.

I've learned to assert my rights. I, who used to walk pressed up close against walls, who was ashamed to exist.

So, I go out.

I've made up my mind to walk, goaded in part by prodding from the owner of the café, a truly distasteful person, both in looks and in manner. I had resolved not to go in there anymore, because he's a real asshole. But I wanted a croissant. Right away.

For the first time, I find him agreeable, in a good mood. Oddly enough, he greets me. He usually doesn't give anyone the time of day, not unless they're "Doctors/Lawyers/Engineers" or "hot babes," so he generally skips right over me, but not this morning. We even enter into a conversation. He's acting all pleasant.

But let's gets back to the penis. The fake penis. How many of those who are reading this know who an FtM (female-to-male) transsexual is? I didn't know, even though I was one. I consider myself a sort of pioneer, at least here, in Italy.

I'm one of the countless children of the south, who, in the late seventies, were thrust from a happy and oblivious childhood into an incomprehensible reality.

"WE DON'T RENT TO SOUTHERNERS!" *Southerners are dirty, they live a hundred to a room, you can't understand them when they talk, they'll do the most degrading and smelly jobs as long as it means getting hired, they take away "our" men because "their" women are hot-blooded and horny; they're criminals, they'll have an Alfa Romeo even if they can't put food on the table. Dirty southerners. Today we say those same things about migrants—even we, who read that sign in '68 that said, "WE DON'T RENT TO SOUTHERNERS."*

Massimo at age eight:

My mother is a maidservant. This means: she washes, irons, sweeps the floors, makes the beds, cooks—for me, for my brother, but mostly for my aunt Lia and my grandpa Armido, and she almost never rests. When she does rest, it's to go and take over from my aunt in the shop, from two in the afternoon until six or seven in the evening, more or less, and we go with her. I like sitting outside, on the stoop. A lot of famous people pass by. Capri is fashionable; it's high-end. People who come here on vacation have money. However, there's also a breathtakingly extraordinary Capri that makes you toil as you walk, as you scramble up into hidden places unknown to most, places where you truly feel like a microscopic dot upon a microscopic isle, azure and so beautiful that it moves you.

I've known for a while that I have something wrong with me. I like girls and I'm a boy—so far, so good. The fact is that I don't have a penis. Yeah, sure, from the outside I look like a girl, but in my head, inside, I'm not. I must have about thirty dolls; they're pretty, too, and I'm the dad to them all, but I prefer reading, writing, playing hide-and-seek down in the Certosa, and running barefoot in the street.

My father ran away with another woman, a lady from Naples, four years ago; Grandpa Armido had told my mama not to marry that scoundrel, and now she's a maidservant.

Today he, my father, called the house (actually he had my grandma, his mother, call first), and he wants all three of us to join him in Milan. So my brother and I have a dad and my mother's going to stop being a maidservant.

At age fifty-one:

What almost wound up being my last place in the world was that first little town, on the outskirts of Milan, that I was thrust into in '68. Marcallo con Casone. I couldn't run barefoot in the street anymore, there was no sea, and it was cold; the manholes steamed. People made fun of me for how I talked, and I didn't understand them either, sometimes.

Kids get used to things fast.

My mother didn't stop being a maidservant; she found my father in bed with his lover (the same one) and made the heroic gesture of throwing him out of the house. Now she had to do everything, not just be a maidservant. She had to pay the rent; she had to feed us. It took her a month to get her driver's license and then she went to work as a cleaning woman, dishwasher, cook, bartender, and hostess, all in the same disreputable pub. She spent nearly twenty-four hours a day there, but she managed to pay everything and everyone. She was a desirable, intelligent, generous, cheerful, and honest woman, strong as a bull, beautiful and young. Desperately searching for a father for her children.

Massimo at nine/ten years old:

I look at the pink bow on my black jumper, and already my mood sours . . .

Then I resign myself and put it on. A thousand thoughts are swirling around in my head.

I'm in a new elementary school, in a new town. Very far away from my own. Grade Three, Class B, girls only. I enter the classroom.

Everyone's already inside, the other girls and the teacher.

They fall silent and the teacher introduces me: "Girls, let me introduce your new classmate. Her name is Maria Giulia d'Aquino." The chatter resumes, but now I can feel the eyes of all those girls on me; my ears are burning, on fire. I walk to a seat, all the way down the third row on the left, beneath the window.

Chiara and I share a desk and, as the days go by, more and more often we meet at her house, in her garden. We wind our way through branches and bushes and race to see who can make it to the double swing first. We talk a lot, Chiara and I. I tell her about the sea, but I'd really like to talk to her about me. About what I feel inside every time I see her. About how quickly I eat so that I can run to be with her. My eyes are full of tears; summer has arrived and I'm going to leave for the holidays. I'll miss her. Our as yet unripe bodies embrace, then she looks at me, caresses my face gently, and says, "I can tell that you're not a girl, because you have a boy's eyes." I'm dumbfounded, for an instant; then I realize that this means I'm not crazy at all! And slowly my amazement transforms into joy. I sprint homeward; I'm late and my heart is beating like mad. Chiara cares for me! Cares in that way that people call love.

At age fifty-one:

I was nine years old and Chiara was my first sweetheart. Those were years ruled by melancholy; not a melancholy about living, but a sort of resignation, arising from the defeats my mind was subjected to on a daily basis by a body that every day became less and less my own. A peaceless resignation, an irrepressible desire to be a part of this world, but with someone else's body—even that of a cripple, an idiot—so long as it was male. This discrepancy was exhausting and increasingly difficult to mask. I began to daydream more and more. I imagined myself as an adult, with long hair, a beard, a mustache, tight-fitting bell-bottom jeans, and a "package" between my legs. It served my purpose to observe males so that I would be able to move like them, do the same things . . .

Massimo at age eleven:

I hate my brother! Yes, I hate him. I hate his nose. It looks like a pig's nose! He, himself, is like a pig. He's dirty, he doesn't often bathe, he's really fat, he stuffs his face when he eats, and he's mean. Ever since we moved, we've slept together in the same bed; there's not space for us each to have our own room or even two separate beds, so we sleep together. I'm four years older than him and, in theory, I'm the girl and he's the boy. Seen from the outside! Really, inside, I'm more of a boy than he is! At night he's constantly touching himself and I yell because I can't fall asleep. Either that or I start kicking him and then he pummels me. When we go down to play with the other kids is when I get back at him.

I go down, out onto the street; everyone's there. We have to pick teams for the game. We do it playing odds and evens, choosing a player on every turn.

The losers get picked last. I'm one of the top players. My brother is always the last to be chosen.

I've scored, we're winning. Droplets of sweat make my forehead and eyes burn. I'm running; a look is exchanged and the ball is coming my way; in my head it's already in the goal; I don't hear the others shout "Car!" I shoot: goal! It's the second. Damn it! I've fallen flat onto the asphalt; my left knee is bleeding.

I mustn't cry. Boys don't cry.

I've moved over to sit on the edge of the gully. Older kids drive by on souped-up mopeds. One, whom they call Reno, stops right behind me. I lift my eyes, shielding them from the sun with my arm to look up at him. He's the way I wish I could be, when I grow up.

No, I'm not crying and it doesn't even hurt anymore. Sure! Of course I'll come for a ride! I get onto the moped behind him. I like the wind. My legs are dangling down and on the curves I let my toes brush the asphalt. We're driving along a country road now, amidst fields of corn. We stop.

Be tough! That's a constant in my life.

"You know you're strange for a girl?
"Of course! I'm not a girl. I'm like you!"

Be tough! You can't enjoy this!

His tongue is moving feverishly between my legs, which clench. My whole body is clenched; they all blend together: fear, shame, guilt, humiliation, and . . . pleasure! How long will this go on? How much longer do I have to be tough? He licks me, sucks me, and meanwhile he's undoing his jeans. I'm about to faint; my muscles are shuddering. I bury my hands in his hair and try, try with all the strength I can muster, to push him away from me. He stops. He raises his eyes to mine; in mine is fear, in his, sweetness. He gets to his feet, and only now do I realize how much bigger he is than me. I can't hold that thing of his in my hand; my hand is too small. I try with two, so he won't get mad. He does get mad, though; worse luck for me. He turns me around, grabs my head with one hand and shoves me forward. With the other, he takes my wrists and pins my own hands behind my back. Wham! With a foot he spreads my legs. I feel an intense pain; it burns.

Be tough!

I can't. I scream in pain, cry, beg for forgiveness. I fall to my knees. He leaves.

I can't see the road because of my tears. I'm afraid I'll run into someone I know. Nobody can see me. Nobody can know.

I go into the bathroom, sit down on the toilet, and cry; these tears burn.

I reach around to touch myself, ever so gently. It hurts. I wash obsessively, until all the blood has vanished. I clean everywhere, checking tile by tile that everything is pristine. Lucky that no one is home. It hurts me even to walk.

I'm afraid. How do you get pregnant? I'll kill myself; if that happens, I'll kill myself. I have to pretend like nothing's wrong. No one can notice any changes.

It all has to go smoothly.

At age fifty-one:

I truly hated my brother. Up until a couple of years before he died, and this fact gives me no peace.

I have always denied, to anyone who's asked, having had relations—even consensual, sought out, clandestine ones—with men. Only a few know about the rape. I was ashamed. I feared they would think I was less of a man. However, those things that were done to me, those hands on my body, to me were no more than a source of information: I learned how boys behaved toward girls.

What I felt was also a yearning to experience pleasure, that pleasure. The ideal would have been to do it with a woman; that would have been the absolute best. Women weren't allowed to touch me, though. They couldn't know how I was made. I didn't give a fuck about what men thought of that; the important thing was that they kept their mouths shut. No one could know! And that suited everyone just fine. Some of them I've seen again. Years later, when I was finally myself on the outside, too. Some have recognized me and been afraid I would talk, right there, in front of their little families: "Hi! What luck to run into you! Is this your wife? You don't say! You're married? Oh, wow, don't tell me . . . is this your heir? Magnificent! Uh . . . I'm Massimo. It's a pleasure. Your husband and I have known each other for almost thirty years. We had a thing . . . uh . . . but not to worry, it was just sex!"

Even at the beginning of my longest relationship, I had a couple of flings with men. Like some Machiavellian Cyrano, I repeated the same acts, the same words with her, so that she wouldn't understand what actually lay beneath. I invented all kinds of things, ridiculous stories, chronic respiratory illnesses that could be triggered at any moment if she asked me to do more, ridiculous tall tales. Mariateresa believed everything I told her, beyond a shadow of a doubt. She wasn't and isn't stupid, not in the slightest; it's simply that she truly loved me. She may be the only one who ever has, up to now.

Massimo at age thirteen:

I observe the cars through the window. I see mama go down and I get back into bed. No man has ever come up to the apartment. Usually, as soon as she says that she has two kids, a nine-year-old boy and a thirteen-year-old girl, they run away.

Either they're young—too young to commit—or they're already committed elsewhere.

Not today; today he comes up with her. He's old; his face is lined, with two striking little blue eyes and funny ears that stick out. His name is Francesco and he delivers the bread to the restaurant every day. He wants me and my brother, too. On Sunday, he'll take us to the lake.

We'll eat out.

Scopa, Scopello, Stresa, Bognanco, Courmayeur, Gravellona Toce, Orta, Lovere—I've been to all these places and more, since my mom's been with Francesco. Each place has a restaurant he swears by, every Sunday, from that first one on. My brother eats like an ox and always makes me look bad in front of the girls I know. Often we set off happy and come back mad. Everyone: Francesco because of the traffic, my mother because she says we spent too much, my brother and I because we hate each other. Nonetheless, we're always blissfully happy when we're getting ready and heading off on Sunday mornings!

At age fifty-one:

Francesco managed to win my mother over, with his earnestness, with honesty.

He was a tireless worker. The kind who, if you knew how to act toward them, would give you their very soul. From '73 to '79 were years of contentment for my mother; we were finally a family. That was what was important to her. Our life took a dramatic turn for the better. We had our own bakery, a bigger home, a decidedly more comfortable life. One very sad parenthesis in all this was the death of my grandpa, Armido, in '74. I saw my mother at the pinnacle of her happiness, though, in '75, when she gave birth to my brother, who inevitably bears my grandfather's name.

Massimo at age thirteen:

In town they called me Crazy Horse, Woman-Man. Everyone knew me. Before heading to school, around 5 a.m. I'd set off with the first round of deliveries, to give Francesco a hand. He couldn't have done it alone; there were a ton of customers. I had an incredibly heavy, solidly built black bicycle with two enormous panniers, one on the front and another on the back. I would load them up with all of the bags of bread and off I'd go. Some customers had made their own cotton bags, with their names embroidered on them. I was incredibly fast; on that bicycle I flew, in winter or summer, riding into the dawn, singing at the top of my lungs, hands in the air. When the school year ended, I left for Capri. I came back in September. My mother and Francesco had pretty much stopped harping on about what I wore around town by then. Sure, every once in a while they'd make a little joke, chide me, but it would end there. Did they not know how to help me? Did they think I'd "get better?"

The year was 1974 . . .

I walk into the town barbershop. I don't know for what strange, inexplicable reason, but I have tacit permission to go get my hair (which I keep short, at the limit of what societal expectations will allow) cut at the barber's. It is a distinctive sort of shop, for men only.

Outside, it's winter. The manholes are steaming and they take me back to when, in amazement, I saw them steaming for the first time.

It's strange, the relationship that has developed between the barber and me. I know that he knows what I am. He touches my skin, lifts up the neckline of my sweater to tuck the towel in. What chance is there that he hasn't seen them?

Yeah, he knows. But he doesn't say a word. No one, in that oh-so-masculine shop, says a word.

At least, not from the moment I step through the door. Unusual, seeing as it's considered one of those prime places to share gossip.

So, in I go. I say hello and sit down in one of the quilted faux-leather and steel chairs. My knees are quaking. I throw a quick glance at the little table where the magazines are displayed. There's the sports daily *Corriere dello Sport*, the motorsports journal *AutoSprint*, a couple of adventure comics, *Diabolik* and *L'Intrepido*, and then some porn ones, *Il Tromba*, *Il Montatore*, and *Jacula*, and the inevitable tabloid, *Cronaca Vera*. If no one's watching, I flip through the latter choices, otherwise I go for *L'Intrepido*!

I pick up *Cronaca Vera*. After the first few pages of crimes of passion, sudden deaths shrouded in mystery and miracles free of charge, I turn the page and read:

"BORN A WOMAN, BECOMES A MAN."

Now my knees are quaking visibly, I'm sweating, my heart is pounding like crazy, and I can tell I've gone bright red. I fake a coughing fit, stand up, turn my back to the audience, and, at the same time, try to see whether anyone can see me through the window from outside. I cough louder and simultaneously tear the page out of the magazine and stuff it into the pocket of my jeans, pretending to look for a tissue. All of this happens in five seconds flat. I sit back down, reassure the onlookers with a wave, and bury *Cronaca Vera* underneath the stack of newspapers.

I'M NOT ALONE IN THE WORLD. There's somebody else like me!

(Translated by Jennifer Delare)

Note

1. Massimo D'Aquino, *Camminavo rasente i muri: Autobiografia tascabile di un transessuale* (Rome: Edizioni Croce, 2019), 11–25.

Chapter 15

Three Stories of Activism in Italy
Conversations with Christian Ballarin, Giorgio Cuccio, and Mazen Masoud

MARZIA MAURIELLO

In this text, Mauriello reports some of the central issues that emerged during our interviews with three representatives and activists of the trans FtM community in Italy.[1] The content of our conversations, which were based on similar questions, was later organized into a few major themes: (1) the discourse about identity, body, and recognition; (2) the experience of LGBTQ+ activism; (3) the struggle with translating the trans experience across languages and cultures. In the part entitled "Identity, Body, and Recognition," the interviewees share their perspectives on, and different paths towards, self-recognition. The section on activism features a broader reflection on the history of the Italian trans movement, while shining a light on the complex dynamics within LGBTQ+ groups and their relationships with feminist activists. The last section, "Lost in Translation," focuses on the terminologies in use to talk about gender diversity and on the difficulties that Christian, Giorgio, and Mazen have encountered in translating, linguistically and otherwise, their personal experience. They draw attention to the issues resulting from the global hegemony of the English language regarding LGBTQ+ categorizations, point out the difficulty in defining one's path through another language, and suggest possible ways to cope with the resistance that the Italian language poses in creating a vocabulary that is more inclusive for all.

Christian Ballarin

Identity, Body, and Recognition

I live in a small town that now has perhaps as many as one thousand people living in it, and until recently was even smaller. I have lived here since the age of five, and so I also experienced my transition in a very rural, very small, very agricultural context. When I turned five my parents took me to catechism to help me fit in this environment. Everyone spoke Piedmontese dialect. Sometimes we think of the "deep south"[2] in Italy, but here I was, in the "deep north," and I was a stranger. Since I was not born here, I have always been perceived as being different, and this difference only increased over time.

When I think of my transition, the translation of Judith Butler's book [*Undoing Gender*, 2004] into Italian, *Fare e disfare il genere* [*Doing and undoing gender*], immediately comes to mind. For me, more than doing and undoing gender, the matter was undoing *and (re)doing* gender. I don't feel very queer, and this is because I cannot live without such reference points. For me, the deconstruction [of gender] has required a reconstruction. During this process, I have never felt without identity. Actually, this "being without gender identity" bothers me a lot. But, at the same time, I realize that [deconstructing gender identities] has been very important for me and for my personal history of activism. I have to admit it: I belong to an older generation! Working as an advisor for LGBT people at a help desk, I talk to many of them, including many young people, and I realize that my view of identity is, perhaps, quite old-fashioned compared to theirs. As far as the "undoing" [of gender] is concerned, for me, the premise is surely the need to rebuild. My approach is probably linked to my age . . . people may say, "Yes, but what is more important is how I feel in the moment, what I am in a given moment." The truth is that until I saw the recognition of my identity reflected in the eyes of others, I couldn't feel good. My transition proceeded on two levels that have always been interrelated: one was how I wanted to feel, how I wanted to see myself in relation to my body; the other was how I wanted others to see me—because then I used to think everybody was a jerk for not seeing me as a man. The problem is that we have lenses for seeing reality and these lenses did not allow others to see that I was a man.

I don't even know if what I'm going to tell you can be of any use: when I was going through my transition path I basically wanted to gather information about surgery, and that kind of information was hard to find. At the time, the Internet was not this great resource [that it is now], so I thought of organizing a conference and calling all the European and American surgeons [specialists in gender transition surgery] I could find on the Internet—a conference where they would have a chance to present their operations, practices, results, and so on. Obviously, this event was never organized, but it gave me the idea of contacting Maurice,[3] a [LGBTQ+] center that gathered small groups for meetings, including trans people and a facilitator. I started attending this group regularly, on Monday evenings, and then the group grew bigger and became the Luna group. It was an identity group, to be precise. Maurice always had a characterization of *mixité*: that is, it has always truly been a broader LGBT association, whereas some associations in Italy define themselves as LGBT but in the end are basically gay. At Maurice, on the other hand, the first group was all gay men, but then they were joined by a few lesbian women who, in order to find a separatist space, created a new group that was and is still called *L'altra martedì* [The Other Tuesday]. Obviously, these smaller groups were separate, but the associative and democratic life was shared. The trans group—Gruppo Luna—formed at the end of the 1990s. We had a separate night for meetings, even if our group didn't have any separatist goal and we fully enjoyed the communal life of the center. Then I joined the board, for a short time I was president, and this is how and where my activism began. The people who come to us [at the Maurice] do so because they've decided to start a transition process and we help them. Others, those we call "questioning," don't know what they want to do but want to understand things better and meet someone who can answer their questions.

Activism

My activism has played out on three levels, which are also geographic levels: the first is my association, my local environment, we might say; the second is national; and the third is international. Thanks to my activism at Maurice, I began traveling around Italy and getting to know other associations and other situations. There has always been a need for networking among Italian trans associations, at various times and with more or less successful outcomes. For example, I was among those who joined the "Sylvia Rivera Steering Committee." This committee, which assembled trans people and associations across Italy, was named after the American trans activist Sylvia Rivera, who was invited to World Pride in Rome in 2000. I missed this big event because I had an endocrinological appointment that I absolutely couldn't miss, as it was the one that would authorize my hormonal therapy. Still, Sylvia has meant a lot to Italian activism and above all to Marcella [Di Folco], who at the time of the "Sylvia Rivera Steering Committee" was still alive. I think she was the one who proposed the creation of this group, or perhaps it was Porpora [Marcasciano], or all of MIT [Movimento Identità Trans]! However, when you mention Sylvia Rivera now, almost nobody knows who she is, even though movies have been made about her . . . and, already in the late 1990s, she was turning into a forgotten figure, a woman no one gave too much credit to. So, for us, naming our trans steering committee after her meant also acknowledging the importance she had, as well as the importance of all the trans people who contributed to the Stonewall uprising. From a more international point of view, this [act of recognition of Sylvia] had to be done! The committee brought together almost all the Italian trans associations of the time, and its activity went on for many years, until it vanished into thin air. This broader national dimension has been very important for me, because being in touch with other trans situations has always stimulated me, even if it is quite exhausting, in terms of effort and resources.

To be honest, I don't know how much I succeeded in engaging in activism on an international level. I don't remember what year it was, maybe 2005—at the time we were still the Luna group—anyway, I remember that we went to Vienna to the conference that led to the creation of TGEU,[4] and we were one of the founding members of this important European association. This broader engagement, despite being difficult at times, has been very enriching. I got to meet influential activists who had very different yet very significant approaches.

A nice thing that I remember with a smile is that, in 2012—I think— we went to the Pride in San Francisco. We'd expected to go to a Pride as we did in Italy and participate in the demonstration, and so we brought our Maurice flag and wanted to parade. But our American friend told us, "Look, participating costs money . . . I don't know, maybe two hundred or three hundred dollars per party." This meant that your group could have had four people or it could have had one hundred; it made no difference: you had to pay for one slot because it was your slot. So we said, "Wait, but we've never paid to participate in a Pride! We're not a business!" We soon discovered that a trans march was going to take place the day before the Pride, partly because these trans activists were a bit pissed off about the [secondary] role that the "trans issue" had within the Pride and partly because they shared our perspective and thought that the Pride had turned into a highly commercial thing that was all tied up in sponsorships. They thus wanted to host what I'd call a "people's" event, open to everybody. We went to this trans march where there were really weird characters, but also a really nice atmosphere. It was similar to how we imagine a demonstration to be. At the end, we arrived at a park where there was live music and stages for speeches: those kinds of things, basically. The next day we went to the actual Pride, the official one, and we were behind barriers: what we'd have [in Italy] for a march of the *Alpini* [the Italian Army's specialist mountain infantry]! This is how it worked: you watched the parade go by, they were throwing gadgets at you, and then Google was marching too, and airline companies—all this was inconceivable to us! And there were police patrolling the parade, on the side of the street. I remember that two girls who were a little drunk and also a little silly wanted to join the parade. They tried to climb over the barriers and the policemen took them and threw them out. They literally flew over us! My boyfriend, who is very *barricadero*—let's say that he has a strong revolutionary spirit—was getting pissed at the cops, and our American friend said, "No, you'd better not say anything." Overall, this San Francisco experience was quite peculiar and the Pride we experienced was very far from our idea of what a demonstration for civil rights should be, while the trans march we participated in was exactly what we'd had in mind.

I have always had this somewhat romanticized idea of being trans. I'm not religious—I have no mystical or spiritual convictions—but, still, I used to tell myself, maybe even just to make sense of a whole series of things, "Well, if all this stuff has happened to me, it must have a meaning, or in any case, I've got to find a meaning in it." And this idea of the revolutionary potential of the trans identity has fascinated me and has made me feel important, at least a little. It's given me something back in exchange for all the problems that my identity caused me. I must say that growing up, and maturing, I realized that the potential can remain as such, totally unexpressed. It doesn't necessarily have to produce results. On the other hand, my work in the associations has led me to reflect on the fact that one's personal experience probably becomes the sense of one's own activism. So far as trans activism is concerned, especially in Italy, I've realized that there is a tendency to remain self-centered, to navel-gaze, which is not leading us anywhere. It's like you can't get out of your personal perspective: "What happened to me must apply to everyone and what I feel, I perceive, must apply to everyone." For sure, everyone has their own experiences and knowledge! However, in my opinion those are often very unrelated experiences. It is not possible to systematize these experiences, and this is greatly impoverishing trans activism in Italy today. I would not even say the "trans movement." I don't see a movement, only a lot of stillness. It must be said, though, that we have this very human characteristic of rewriting the past in an emotional way so that whatever used to be is more attractive than what is happening today. I believe that we have made many strides and that this current revival of the right wing is partially due to the fact that we have moved forward, and that we are no longer a minority, hidden in a hotel room. We are people who can ask the authorities for a meeting room to hold our conference. That's why you find right-wing people who get mad. If you did it in the hotel and paid for it, they wouldn't give a damn. To give you a further example, I believe it was unthinkable until a few years ago that a TV series like *Pose* would go mainstream, reach so many homes, and have such high ratings. Of course, our enemies protest! In my opinion this is not a sign that we are going backwards but a sign that we have gone too far—in their opinion. And this comes with a price. It can also mean that you might run the risk of regressing, because certain political figures may gain support, and at times they do get into power, and this can have a detrimental effect. But still, it's a sign that things are moving.

Lost in Translation

I have been working in the city hall [of Turin] since 2018, in a service called "LGBT," and here we do a lot of training. When we do training sessions and explain certain terms, often people ask, "Why do you use so many English terms, for example gay, transgender, queer, and so on?" and we clarify that "unfortunately" the Anglo-Americans have a longer tradition regarding gender studies, and they have given names to many things and have certainly fostered a certain type of LGBTQ+ culture. On the other hand, it must be said that we have not been able to make the most of our Italian experiences, so maybe we could have coined terms, too. Earlier you were talking about the *femminielli*—another experience, another meaning, another story. But hypothetically, if instead of confining that reality to Neapolitan traditions there had been a study that had granted this experience a different place in our history, maybe today instead of saying "transgender" we would say *femminielli*. Who knows . . .

The use of language in some contexts makes me very uncomfortable. Speaking for myself, before my transition, I would try to use adjectives and nouns in a neutral way, when talking about myself. For example, I wouldn't say "*Sono* contento *o sono* contenta," but rather "*Sono felice.*"[5] So, when I spoke, I tried in every way to make sentences even more convoluted so as to maintain a sort of gender ambiguity. In the world of activism, you put the "at" sign [@], what in Italian we call the *chiocciola*, or you put the asterisk.[6] Moreover, when you write or when you speak, you try to cut off the final vowel or you use both male and female forms. But writing in a language, in our day-to-day lives, for example in a workplace, where one relates to people who have never thought particularly about gender, is definitely a challenge! So at times we try to use both the masculine and feminine forms of a noun or to choose words that do not reinforce binary constructs. This is what our language allows us to do. Or, even here in my office, we try to use expressions that are neutral. Instead of saying "all male and female workers," we say "all the people who are at work." It is a constant challenge, and sometimes a very hard one. In my office there are four of us, three women and me, and so I proposed that instead of using the male and female variations of the word *collega* [colleague], we could adopt the universal feminine. I represent a minority, I know, in the use of the feminine for a group of people, but I realize that you can do this in a context where there are many people and you can decide whether to favor one gender or the other. However, when you have a person before you and you don't know how that individual defines themselves with respect to gender or whether they want to define themselves at all, then it is a very tricky situation. I don't have a final answer for this. Something that I do, contrary to what happened with Porpora when you asked her what pronoun she preferred[7] . . . I never put this question to the people I work with and I've also taught other volunteers not to do it. But in this case too, I am approaching the matter from a personal perspective. In the sense that I imagine that if, back in the day, I had arrived at the *sportello* [help desk] of Maurice and people had asked me what my pronouns were, I wouldn't have thought, "Oh how nice, this *sportello* is so inclusive!" Rather, I would have immediately thought: "Here we go, so they don't read me as a man" and that would have created some distance. Ultimately, what I'm saying is that we can use neutral terms when we talk to people, and we don't necessarily have to define people with respect to gender. We should listen to how they talk about themselves and then we can adapt. For example, here [in my office] we ask people for their names: "What name should I use to fill out your registration form?" or "What name do you want us to register you with?" People have to tell us this, and we cannot know and cannot guess. And that's usually a good starting point.

Giorgio Cuccio

Identity, Body, and Recognition

Until some time ago, a fitting definition for the path I've taken was *trans man*. Today I would rather drop the word *man*; *trans* seems to me more than enough to bear on my shoulders, and *man*, all in all, is a burden that I happily leave to males. However, understanding and relating to others is, of course, not easy, so even if you say *trans*, people usually expect something different [from me]. I must say—and this might come as a surprise—trans masculinity does not reside in the collective imagination in any way, or so little as to be almost irrelevant. In fact, if you say *trans* the reference for other people is trans women, and if you talk about yourself as a male, they expect something else. Something that is not you. This might be trivial but it is one of those "trivial" things that I've constantly faced; therefore, if saying *man* is no longer necessary for me, it becomes necessary when I have to make myself understood. All this could be considered an old matter; however, it is not that old because it was never really addressed in the post-trans manifesto.[8] To date, trans people have not embraced their experiences independently from the terms *male* and *female*. I do not mean as a third gender but as an experience that does not necessarily have to be linked to an idea of beginning and end. The two acronyms FtM and MtF point precisely to an idea of "from-to"; I am stressing this because for me it is still a crucial issue. So, you have two uppercase letters—F and M—but the most important one, which is the "t," is lowercase, placed in the middle, and might even disappear between these two mastodons. In reality, though, the trans experience is right there, in the middle. However, reclaiming that little "t" is something that has gained ground because more and more trans people have legitimized their trans identity. They have conquered autonomy, in relation to their experience. They have no need to specify "from-to," or to say "I am trapped," and to resort to all those standardized discourses that have been crafted to deconstruct their transness. Those discourses were a way of explaining oneself to others and using the words of others. One ended being twisted around, trying to match those descriptions. Luckily, the narratives have diversified. We have moved on.

I think like this today, but I wouldn't have been able to do so many years ago or even more recently. For me, the use of the term *trans* as an umbrella term is a bit of a provocation and a stimulus to grasp *this* identity *and not* the two poles [male and female] that ultimately remain at the origin of all our frustrations. Language is not something created in a laboratory. It is something that goes through evolutions and involutions, something that has its own path and that can spur reflections, but which you do not rule by default. So let's have this trans experience fully, each of us in our own way, with our bodies, our words—each of us free to define ourselves. This experience [in itself], though, and not the final goal each of us might be striving to achieve. It is clear that what I strove to achieve was a male body. If today a person called me using the feminine—maybe Porpora is more open than me on this—I'd still leap out of the chair for a moment. That is, yes, [gender] fluid, but up to a certain extent. I should also add that using masculine or feminine pronouns is a personal choice, and it sounds like an imposition if somebody makes you gender fluid, ignoring your will. Still, what defines me today is not being a man but being trans. I don't know if I can explain myself well enough, and maybe this is a little contradictory, but I can't explain it in a better way. To put it slightly differently, what I would like to value is not the moustache I have today but the experience I went through. The physical appearance ultimately represents my body, my need, my satisfaction, my desire. But I want to emphasize this: let's take into consideration the path we have taken, not the moustache we might have today; the complexity of the experience, not the fact that today you can call me a man without difficulty. I understand, however, that this positioning does not fit everybody: if you drop the word *woman*, the word *man*—and I am referring especially to people who have a certain history [in the trans movement]—they might leap out of their chairs, and I can understand that very well. It's a matter of individual paths. Zero impositions . . . but when people make medicalized speeches . . . no, I cannot accept that! Of course, people have their own stories, they come from those stories, and we must respect those stories. If one made certain choices, one must have had good reasons. Are trans people totally free to choose? Are they implicitly forced? No human being knows exactly where their will begins and where social conditioning ends, where their own ambitions begin, and those of others end. Nobody knows where their Ego begins and the Other ends. Nobody. This also clearly applies to trans people because, as with any human experience, it has been influenced by the traditions of human culture. More to the point, on the twentieth anniversary of Law 164,[9] the debate between those [trans women] who had and had not undergone operations remains epic! The core of the issue was: "Those who have not had operations are not women." And that was the only issue—whether or not someone has had an operation. But that was part of a journey; you don't affect this [type of cultural transformation] in a lab. One starts long-term processes, brings some reasoning, tries to orient one's life according to what one thinks is right, or best, and to what one thinks makes people feel better. So I would never say to anyone, "You were wrong to say that you are a woman, and you must say you are trans." Never ever, because those are very personal choices and personal positionings. This is, for example, the case of the conversation we had in what became *Oltre le monoculture del genere* (*Beyond the Monocultures of Gender*, 2005). In that book I call myself straight. It is not a question of whom I like or dislike. Simply, at that point in my life, I needed to define myself through a heteronormative desire and my being a man depended on the fact that I liked women. Only later did I understand that using that word dragged up all sorts of bad consequences. Today I would never need to call myself straight, not because of what I like or dislike, but because my masculinity is no longer related to that, if it was ever related to anything at all. At the beginning we are all a bit fragile, and what I wish for trans people is that as soon as possible they may all gain the tools to be able to read their own experiences independently from the readings of others, from the needs of others, from the gazes of others. When you depend on those external things, you must always sound assertive, always be without doubts, always be linear in your narrations, always sound fully persuaded . . . I, too, have the right to have second thoughts, to have shadows, to live a life that is not all a positive or linear experience.

Our history is an orphan of tradition. We are still searching for trans history, trans biographies. We look for traces in history, at times applying criteria that are not always applicable to past experiences. However, forcing history is something that might always occur, anyway. It is true that the trans experience in Western cultures is a lab experience, and this unfortunately has generated a lab, or medicalized, tradition. There are reasons that explain why this path has become lost in the maze of history, and why diversity has been banned, but it is true that we have a memory contracted in medical labs. This is a serious shortcoming. People may call us medicalized, but as a matter of fact this is the origin of our experience in the Global North. We have given the keys of happiness to someone else and we continue to leave the keys to those gatekeepers. And by that I don't mean giving up the right to undergo [sex change] surgeries. I had some of them! So much so that eventually I had to tell myself, "Enough is enough." Even my body said, "Stop it, stop! I'm sick of it!" But at times there is nothing else, other than your body, to hold on to. The experience of the *femminielli* is the only thing in the West that leaves the memory of something that has endured; it is the only one, however. Maybe the sworn virgins in Albania. But these are experiences that in the end always remained quite localized. The Western trans model has really taken the lead in the world. Because, let's admit it, the lab has its own power, its own allure. The well-being it gives you is undeniable and it would be hypocritical to say that this is not the case. I recover pieces of history because I am truly a test-tube animal. But if there is no history, I have no history. This is a bad legacy to contend with. Indeed, we are now making our history . . . in roughly the last ten years we have been making a trans history. If trans people run after labels and cancel themselves behind *man* and *woman*, continuing to cancel the trans experience, then trans people will continue to have no history. I don't want to take away anyone's right to self-define, but there is one thing that should be done beyond hormones: in my opinion, today it would be important to create trans subjectivities regardless of the [medical] needs that this experience brings with it. Moreover, trans people are freeing themselves and the new generations are also freer from this point of view . . . perhaps they have more time to choose, they have more space to choose how to customize their paths. The technicalities excite me little. I am more passionate about the need to create trans subjectivities. I read a lot of interesting materials from the United States. For example, I recently followed a conference in trans philosophy, I have started to read up on transgender studies, and there is plenty of material by trans people who reflect on their own experience. So we're finally making history! This trend shouldn't be overlooked to focus on surgeries, hormones, and name changes . . . for me generating self-awareness is equally necessary. For the foreseeable future, other people might need to continue using the word *women* to self-define, but maybe in fifteen or twenty years, who knows, they might be more chill, more relaxed. You must have noticed this kind of approach in trans people of a certain age. At some point people definitely care less [about labels]! This carefreeness, this self-confidence, in my opinion, is important and creates spaces in which we can recover our trans experience, because if you are confident about yourself, about who you are, then other perspectives no longer threaten you.

Activism

I began attending trans community meetings when I moved from Palermo to Milan. At that time, I was at the very beginning of my transition. It was a moment of great vulnerability, and in Milan I found a self-help group that supported me. This [self-help group] got a little lost over time. For me, though, it was really fundamental that it was a group of peers . . . it made the difference! In the meantime, I was getting to know feminist activists. After the experience of self-help, I would have switched to a self-awareness group—which was, in a way, the next step—but I never had the chance. However, a nice thing, at the time, was that it was quite usual, almost automatic, for people to give back the help they had received [by volunteering in these types of groups], so I also eventually tried to figure out how I could contribute to my community. I should add that that was a period of great media visibility for trans people, at least in relation to our Italian situation. That visibility on screen, though, was the kind that I came to distrust . . . even my friends must have hated me at some point precisely because I've always said, "Girls, I don't do those things, I don't go there [on TV]." But, generally speaking, trans women used to think that that type of visibility was a declaration to the world—a bold "I exist." Still, it was also a way to be visible, without gaining any depth beyond visibility. They were on display to attract voyeuristic gazes or pitiful looks, since the discourse of legitimation was often articulated through a rhetoric of sufferance typical of Catholic cultures. For me, it was basically this: off screen—in real life—it was never trans people who got to say what we wanted to say. And even on screen, it was constantly a matter of having to explain ourselves to others and I was not interested in that. It was not what I wanted and it did not seem useful to me. The issues to discuss were always hormones, surgery, and name changes. For a variety of reasons, I said no and I'd say no again today. The trans experience remains perceived as a series of needs. But it cannot be that alone, because this is limiting and something limited to a certain phase of your life. After any transition, a person remains trans, whether that person wants to or not. You remain trans, with your new name, with all your hormones, and your surgical procedures. If people don't get this, they won't go much further.

The moment you feel cut off from a world you are desperately trying to fit into, another more comfortable world opens up, and curiosity eventually drives you to look for other things. My form of activism is currently this: finding ways to give trans people tools so that they can go through their experience in a positive way, be happy, be who they are—or, to sum up, see their trans experience as a blessing and not as bad luck.

As regards the open debate with feminist activists, in my opinion we are dealing with a sort of short circuit that I have seen many times, even within the trans community. People start to think, "An experience different from mine threatens mine . . . if you are not like me, then you deny my identity . . . you and I must be similar because otherwise . . . if you are not like me then you are threatening." This sort of circular reasoning was also created in the debate on the question of identity. However, going back to feminism, I believe that feminists should be much more aware than us trans; whereas at times it seems that they, or at least some of them, have shown some weakness or insecurity in their relation with trans people. The debate—if it can even be called a debate—has gone so far that the trans experience has been violently denied. You can't say that trans women are transvestite men! Some feminists, whose thought is rooted in biological essentialism, have spelled it out, without any possibility for appeal! This is an old positioning, paleolithic, I'd say, which has unfortunately been revived. Denying the lives of others . . . here we go beyond what can be considered a political debate. My existence, my difference threatens you because I'm not like you. That's all. This has happened in the trans and feminist world, as I said, and it's happening all over again with the new queer generations, in their approach to an old trans generation that was concerned with gaining the right to have gender reassignment surgery. We could sum up these new placements as non-medicalized. However, here too the conflict arises from people failing to listen to one another. On an individual level, you position yourself by gaining experience, gaining peace of mind, escaping from a series of discomforts also thanks to hormones, also thanks to having an appearance that suits you more. At that point you overcome a whole series of tensions and can look at yourself more serenely. You are no longer feeling that urgent need for acceptance and recognition—your own and that of others. You have been acknowledged now; then maybe you remain dissatisfied, but you have overcome that initial discomfort.

If I think of the positioning or statements that I might have had in the past, it is not that I disavow them; rather, it is necessary to understand why I did so. You take responsibility for what you said in the past because it is part of the limitations that you had in that moment. In fact, I consider it a good thing to have come out with bullshit in the past! It's great that I don't need to define myself in the way I used to. It means that I have solved many issues. I can look for my own words. Or, maybe, I will still look for the words of others but they will affect me in a different way, because I've moved on. I've taken steps forward on my own path.

Lost in Translation

I always talk about myself in the masculine. Always in the sense that, since I started the transition, I used masculine forms and pronouns. For me the issue was more about the time of transition, when I had to appear to the world differently. So I undertook the linguistic exercise to look for all the adjectives that sounded neutral, or I mumbled the final vowels. I already speak with my mouth half-closed; back then, I must have just whispered! When pronouncing the "o" vowel[10] no longer startled people, that "o" became fully mine. As for people who would like to get rid of the "a" and the "o," I must say that we have not seen a great use of plural pronouns—like *they*—in the Italian language. I cannot even wrap my head around how the use of plural [to define gender diversity] may sound in English . . . but, in Italian, I believe it would sound very odd. I remember when, roughly fifteen years ago, asterisks were starting to pop up in emails, and everyone said, "Sure, yes, beautiful in emails, but then in everyday conversation what do we do with the asterisks? How do we pronounce them?" There is only one answer: "I don't know!"

In Italy some people have started to use "they" as a more inclusive, gender-neutral pronoun, but always only in written language. I have never heard anyone speaking of hirself in the plural and I don't think it would solve the issue for us.[11] When people start their transition, well, not all of them are comfortable with using gendered language. I too, in addressing other people, if I see that the other person is not confident yet—maybe s/he doesn't like using certain words, maybe s/he likes it but s/he is still not at ease with the masculine or the feminine. In these cases, I'd rather mutter the final vowels, or carefully choose words. In sum, I do what I did for myself! I make the effort to choose words that are as gender-neutral as possible. Speaking of which, I remember watching a video—I was still in college. It was for my Anthropology of Art class and the professor showed us a video of this guy who did a bunch of things, and during all of it, he was deliberately speaking in an Italian that was not sexually connoted. In that case, the creator of the video must have sat down and chosen his words carefully, one by one. But he did it! He crafted an agendered and asexual discourse, and I'm talking of something from twenty years ago. I'm starting to be a bit *tranchant* [sharp] about linguistic choices, but, at the same time, I have some flexibility. Yes, it is good that people make an effort to understand you and your positioning, but you have to make an effort, too, to be accessible. Once again, it's a matter of meeting halfway.

Mazen Masoud

Identity, Body, and Recognition

My mother is Turkish, my grandmother is Jewish, my father is Berber. I feel like a citizen of the world, and I find it hard to identify myself. I was born in Libya, then I moved to Morocco, and I spent some time in Dublin after my parents' divorce. Now I'm thirty-one and, still, staying somewhere permanently is rather new to me. I have been in Italy for five years, but I will never belong to one single culture. In Libya, at a certain point, I was raised by a feminist sex worker who taught me Arabic and educated me about politics. Female and feminist figures have been a big part of my life. They were my point of reference and my starting point. Then there are the TERFs, but that's another matter.

Most trans people are proud of their identity; they don't want to "steal" the identity of a woman. I am proud of my body and of my femininity, which I manifest more than my masculine side. I do not belong to the toxic masculinity of the alpha male. Luckily, I was not born a cis alpha male. When I make comparisons with my brothers I find it hard to place myself in the male figure. I should add that the Berber culture is a matriarchal culture. Even today in many Berber or Tuareg families, in the south, the head of the family is the mother, the female figure. So, with this cultural and political background, I grew up a transfeminist.

I will always remember what those feminists who I like to call our godmothers did from the 1950s onwards. Now, yes, occasionally I do happen to come across feminists who do not accept me. Just to give you an example, I have been kicked out of a few parades. But I'm also involved in transfeminist activism. I am an activist of "*Non una di meno*," although now I'm taking a break.[12]

Sometimes it is important that I identify myself; however, it depends on the context, of course. Generally, I feel the need to self-identify in Italy more than in other contexts in which I have lived. Second-generation migrant refugees and LGBT (or not), trans, and intersex people: today they all have a great difficulty in being part of the collectives, of the movements that exist in Italy. I find it hard to belong to a group because society, including LGBTQ+ groups, has already identified me as a trans person. But I'm much more. I am intersex. I am a refugee. So here you have one more label that this society has put on me. I am Black and I am from Libya, so according to the dominant culture, I must speak Arabic and I must be Muslim. Italian society is very fond of putting labels on people. If you are an activist you have been pigeonholed, and nobody listens to you outside that box. After nineteen years of activism, I pulled out, even if, for me, activism is the air I breathe. Indeed, I breathe the desire to fight this violent heteropatriarchal system. I have never had gender dysphoria but I have a cultural, linguistic, and activist dysphoria. We, trans people, are often infantilized and we are the last wheel of the wagon in many movements. I am very lucky because there is MIT. I am very close to the activists of the past: what joins us is our shared fight against violence. I have been in prison and I was sexually abused many times. I'm not ashamed to say it, so I recognize myself in the past generation of trans activists who suffered so much violence.

Today there is still the fear of losing what is there, while activists like me are not afraid because we have nothing to lose. Violence, rape, killing oneself: they have done everything to us. We have nothing to lose.

Activism

I have been a transfeminist activist for nineteen years, since the age of twelve. I started for personal, family reasons, related to the separation of my parents, their divorce. My mom is a foreigner and doesn't have Libyan citizenship. I am a child of a mixed marriage and, at birth, I was recorded as female, despite being born intersex. Then my parents gave me the name of my grandmother. However, going back to my story, in Libya we have a law: when parents get divorced, male children have the maximum freedom to choose to stay with the father or go away with the mother. But if the mother is a foreigner, like mine, and, after going through a divorce no longer has a residence permit, after a certain amount of time she must leave the country. Since I was female at the time of my parents' divorce, according to the Libyan state, I didn't have the right to choose whom I wanted to stay with. In the end, I wasn't able to see my mother for four years due to Libyan laws, as my father prevented my mother from seeing me. So, I had no choice but to move to Morocco with my father because he was a pilot and, at the time, he worked there. I was ten years old. I dropped out of the international school I was attending. Then I started to walk more around the city. In the poor [Moroccan] neighborhood where I hung out, there were lively forms of grassroots activism, even though such political activism is forbidden there by law. Indeed, some of my comrades had been in prison for thirty years. I started attending the neighborhood meetings, and eventually I joined a mixed group. They raised me—feminists and communists—so my activism started from there, obviously with political knowledge, and starting from my personal experience, which was affected by patriarchy.

Lost in Translation

I have a rich experience with languages—Arabic, English, Italian, Berber, just to mention a few. For me, English is a limiting language, while Italian is richer, like Arabic. It gives me maximum freedom to express myself. But Italian presents the issue of a binary language, so we activists are using the "u" to escape from the a/o impasse.[13] The same thing applies to other languages. Conversely, Turkish is a nonbinary language, and neutral pronouns are used, and in Arabic too there are neutral pronouns. On the other hand, the Berber language is super feminine because it developed from a matriarchal culture. The feminine is used as a universal form rather than the masculine. As for the Arabic language—classical Arabic—I can also say that many poetic texts of this tradition testify to heterosexuality, of course, but also to female and male homosexuality. Homosexuality is something that is rooted in Arabic culture.

(Translated by Marzia Mauriello)

Notes

1. This text is based on a series of Skype conversations that we had with three trans activists—Christian Ballarin, Giorgio Cuccio, and Mazen Masoud—between January and February 2021.

2. Ballarin is hinting at the stereotype of the south as a culturally backward area of Italy.

3. Here Ballarin is referring to Maurice, an LGBTQ+ association founded in Turin in 1985.

4. Transgender Europe is an organization created in 2005, which counts 169 member organizations in 47 different countries; see https://tgeu.org/about-us/.

5. In Italian *contento* is an adjective of the first group (feminine -*a*; masculine -*o*), whereas *felice*, since it is an adjective of the second group (feminine/masculine sing. -*e*) allows some gender neutrality or ambiguity.

6. For the same reason, in order to allow gender neutrality when writing, in Italian the @ symbol, the shwa (ə), or the asterisk are used in place of the final vowels, which generally indicate, in the singular as well as in the plural form, the feminine or the masculine. For more on this, see the conclusion.

7. The interviewee refers to Danila Cannamela's dialogue with Porpora Marcasciano. During the interview, Danila mentioned that once she had asked Porpora what pronouns she preferred to use—she or they—and Porpora jokingly said: "You choose! Do whatever you prefer!"

8. He is referring to Sandy Stone's *The Empire Strikes Back: A Posttranssexual Manifesto*, published in 1987.

9. Law 164 of 1982 allowed sex changes in Italy.

10. In Italian, it is the final vowel that identifies the masculine.

11. We should mention that nouns and adjectives in the Italian language must agree in gender and number, so using the [they] form would not solve the binary issue of choosing a gender.

12. This is a feminist activist movement that fights femicide and patriarchal violence. It was established in Argentina in 2015.

13. In standard Italian language the final vowel "u" does not usually have a gender connotation; however, in some dialects from southern Italy (e.g., Sicilian) the "u" is used for the masculine singular.

PART 6
TESTIFYING TO VOICES AND IMAGES OF TRANSNESS

Chapter 16

Perverse Polymorphs Proto T* at the Dawn of 1980s Italian *Riflusso*

Helena Velena

Helena Velena is a singer, music producer, trans activist, and queer theorist. A key figure of Italian punk music, she is the founder of RAF Punk and of the label Attack Punk Records. As one of the protagonists of the Bolognese counterculture, Velena in this essay discusses how music generated practices of gender liberation in the 1970s and 1980s.[1] In offering a compelling historical and political testimony, her analysis highlights the role that underground music played in queering patriarchal binaries and how gender ambiguity turned into a pop culture phenomenon. While focusing on Bologna, Velena suggests cross-cultural parallels with American funk music.

Deliberately over-the-top, her writing is caustic, bitterly ironic, and thought-provoking. The essay reproduced here is an edited and shortened version of a text originally published in the volume *T** (2020). This version includes only Velena's historical reconstruction and her reflections on the music scene; the original, though, featured a fascinating selection of Giordano Bonora's photographs of Bolognese squats where trans activist Valéry Taccarelli—the Valéry of Alfredo Cohen's 1979 song—lived.

The Bologna of the 1980s, described as the "freest city in the world" (we made a record with this as a sarcastic title—"slaves in the freest city in the world"—and the slogan can now be seen on banners at punk, anarchist, & queer punk events) by its mayor Renato Zangheri, who did not hesitate to call in the tanks (Prague in our own backyard, one of the greatest suppressed memories of the Italian Left),[2] was indeed something special, and even succeeded in lifting from Pasolini's Rome the title of Queer City *par excellence* (and Pier Paolo Pasolini was an exile from Bologna, so . . .).

In reality it was in the year of (dis)grace, 1977—the year of the killing of Francesco Lorusso,[3] the event that sparked the revolt put down with armored vehicles, and then, in September, of the "Convention against Repression,"[4] which marked the death of the Movement itself[5]—that the ground was prepared for new forms of struggle: less "political" in the broad sense and more personal, these were linked to individual and specific paths and reflected the emergence of a need for real civil rights instead of theoretical demands. Not coincidentally, that year saw the birth in Bologna of the Collettivo Frocialista (Faggot Collective),[6] founded by Samuel Pinto, a Chilean exile who had made a daring escape from Pinochet's criminal fascist regime and who was better known as Lola Puñales, an apt description of the manifestly proto-transgender queer feeling of those times of subversion of identity.

Arcigay, the main Italian LGBT organization, is supposed to have been founded symbolically in Palermo in 1980, but it was not until 1985 that it began to operate officially, with its resurgence in Bologna once again. In 1977 the "gay" struggle was rightly still seen as an integral part of the whole Movement, although with fierce internal opposition stemming from the male chauvinist mindset of the majority Communist—when not declaredly Stalinist—component of the Movement itself. And it would be enough to take a look at the faces of the members of the Brigate Rosse (Red Brigades),[7] to find out what music they listened to, to remember the things they left unsaid, their omissions, their self-censorship, their ideological dependence on the fetish of the working class, a world to which, having got caught up in the fashionably youthful game of armed struggle, they no longer belonged. The logic was to "have the revolution first, and then think about the civil rights of women and homosexuals" but a look at how such rights had been "achieved" in the Soviet Union after its specious revolution/bloodbath that continued for over fifteen years, largely at the expense of the weakest segments of the population, certainly did not encourage blind faith.

In June of the previous year, in fact, at the Parco Lambro Festival in Milan, the Festival of the Youth Proletariat organized by the important underground magazine Re Nudo along with other groups, including anarchist ones, the stand of the FUORI (Fronte Unitario Omosessuale Rivoluzionario Italiano [United Italian Homosexual Revolutionary Front])[8] was attacked and destroyed by leftist *compagni* (comrades) already pissed at the faggots. This was partly, indeed largely, because of the speech made from the stage by Mario Mieli,[9] fiercely contested because objectively the bearer of a revolutionary message that went further, presenting the themes of sexual liberation as the premise for a total—political and economic—emancipation to a proletariat that was not ready for and decidedly hostile to such questions, and incapable even of handling its becoming a mass subject. Over one hundred thousand people took part in the festival, something unheard of in Italy at the time, and the whole thing ended up as a bit of a disaster, descending into unliberated chaos and scornful violence. It marked the beginning of the end for the Movement, whose funeral was held just over a year later in Bologna.

The FUORI had been founded by Mario Mieli & Angelo Pezzana[10] in January 1971 on the model of the French FHAR (Front Homosexuel d'Action Révolutionnaire).[11] In the Italian case, though, the name also involved a play on the word "fuori" that referred directly to the concept of coming out, *uscire fuori* in Italian. The FUORI was immediately joined by Mariasilvia Spolato with her FLO (Fronte di Liberazione Omosessuale [Homosexual Liberation Front]): although almost a one-woman group, it was, in fact, the first homosexual organization set up in Italy. Mariasilvia was the first Italian lesbian to come out, in Rome's Campo de' Fiori in 1972, at the first celebration of March 8 in Italy, where she turned up with a placard bearing the words "homosexual liberation." The photos were published in *Panorama*, a conservative weekly, and as a result of this and the articles she wrote, and despite being a gifted mathematician (her mathematical handbook for young people had been brought out by Zanichelli, an important Italian publisher), she was dismissed from the school in Frascati where she taught and was subjected to discrimination over a long period, ending up living on the street.

The FUORI immediately started to publish a journal with the same name that played a very important part in the Italian scene and for which Mariasilvia Spolato wrote from the very first issue. But the first official act of the Movement did not come until the following year, with its participation in dissident form in the First International Congress Of Sexology[12] organized by the CIS (Centro Italiano di Sessuologia [Italian Sexology Center]), a Catholic organization, on the subject of "deviant patterns of behavior in human sexuality," held at Sanremo Casino (in the city famous for its festival of pop music, which in the current era of homonormativity has become the main point of fusion between petit bourgeois Catholic morality and effeminate squeaks of gay ambitions imploring acceptance in nullified mediocrity—almost a Heideggerian "nullity that nullifies").

The conference had been organized to define a protocol with which to respond (positively) to a draft bill proposed by the PSDI (Partito Socialista Democratico Italiano [Italian Social Democratic Party]), a small and moderate socialist party leaning strongly toward the center, and the PSIUP (Partito Socialista Italiano di Unità Proletaria [Italian Socialist Party of Proletarian Unity]), a splinter group of the PSI (Partito Socialista Italiano [Italian Socialist Party]), which later allied itself with the PCI (Partito Comunista Italiano [Italian Communist Party]). This party positioned itself in a sort of median area between the other two and pursued a pro-Soviet policy (while receiving surreptitious funding from the Soviet Union) and, it should be said, was dissolved the same year. The PSDI and PSIUP proposed a toughening of the laws against homosexuality, and the Catholic world did not let the opportunity slip.

Such a request on the part of the two left-wing parties may cause surprise today, but it has to be remembered that at the time communists regarded homosexuality as a bourgeois vice and homosexuals as possible fascist infiltrators. Pier Paolo Pasolini, one of the greatest intellectuals in Italy, was expelled from the Communist Party precisely for this "bourgeois vice." Nor should it be forgotten that when Che Guevara was appointed director of Cuban prisons in 1959, his first act, as a medical graduate who had taken the Hippocratic oath,[13] was to arrest all the homosexuals and transvestites in Cuba, supposing—and never was a word better suited to the case—that reeducation in prison would "cure" them. Massimo Consoli,[14] anarchist and one of the founding fathers of the European homosexual movement, always fought great battles on this matter and made attempts to intercede with Castro, but his communist comrades justified themselves by arguing that those "were other times." A pity that, as Massimo Consoli has pointed out in several books, twenty years earlier Heinrich Himmler, head of the Nazi SS, after discovering the presence of a large number of homosexuals not only in the ranks of SA but also in his own SS, wrote a well-known letter in which he admitted that it would not be possible to cure them by imprisonment.

In any case, the Congress in Sanremo became, for all intents and purposes, the Italian Stonewall.[15] Around fifteen Italian homosexuals took part, along with delegations from several European countries, interrupting the conference. Françoise D'eaubonne[16] took the floor, leaflets were distributed, and the whole thing was fiercely contested. The resulting incredible exposure in the media made everyone realize that the road to go down was one of intense, direct, and head-on struggle.

This groundbreaking moment led to the rise of many other groups, some of which gained great visibility. For example, in Bologna, in 1978, after the "funeral of the Movement," the Collettivo Frocialista changed its name into the more formal and less provocative but still highly symbolic Circolo di Cultura Omosessuale 28 Giugno (Homosexual Cultural Circle June 28, date of the Stonewall uprising in America). In 1980, it embarked on lengthy negotiations with Renato Zangheri, still mayor of the city (who was also subjected to a gay kiss) to obtain a registered office for the club. This would culminate in 1982 in the Seizing of the Cassero,[17] long contested by the Diocesan administration as it was a key site on the annual procession in honor of the Virgin Mary. The battle for this space would last the whole year, with the laying of a plaque in honor of the Virgin Mary and the threat of a visit by the Pope, but all the countercultural forces (the Movement, as has already been pointed out, had died in 1977) and intellectuals of the city, including punks and women's associations, took the side of the queer world. A manifesto would be signed over by over ten thousand people and all possible means of struggle would be adopted, and even more. A national demonstration was organized too, and on June 26 a legendary proto-Pride March was held in the streets of Bologna, with the participation of several hundred marvelous happy faggots. Two days later, on June 28, the Cassero was seized, the symbolic Storming of the Bastille of the Italian queer scene. Captured and taken away from the reactionary Catholic world, it would become the first official seat of an Italian homosexual organization. The official opening would take place on December 19, with the ribbon cut by Valérie—the same Valérie who had begun to cross-dress at the age of just fifteen, firing the imagination of Alfredo Cohen, perhaps the first openly gay singer in Italy and one of the first activists of FUORI, to such an extent that he devoted a splendid song to her that describes her in depth, "Valérie." A song whose words were changed with his permission by Franco Battiato and given to Milva, who made it not only her most famous piece but also an international hit, under the title "Alexander Platz."

This phase of the rising Italian LGBT movement was still firmly embedded in a practice of revolution and struggle, influenced by Mario Mieli's graduate thesis *Elementi di critica omosessuale* (*Elements of a Homosexual Critique*),[18] brought out as a book in 1977 by Einaudi, an important publisher for the "traditional" Italian Left. Mieli's basic theory was that of transsexuality as the culmination of the process of homosexual liberation, in that it exploded the binary logic of male and female. On more than one occasion Mieli declared himself publicly to be a transsexual person, but in his situationist understanding of the term: it has nothing to do with the FtM or MtF transition but referred instead to a precise negation not just of a given identity but also of that obtained as a superhuman goal.

Mieli was severely critical of "transsexual" people in the proper and medical sense of the term, who at the time "went to Casablanca," that is, underwent sex reassignment surgery (legally and technically possible in Casablanca). This kind of operation was seen by Mieli as a process of "social normalization" that brought the deviant polymorphous pervert within the bourgeois family norm. Two faggots who from the bourgeois perspective were a cause of scandal for the family, for the neighborhood, for the whole world, were normalized if one of the pair "became a woman." In this way, a ritual of heterosexual reabsorption within the family was conducted to bring them back within the bosom of the Catholic Church. Once the documents had been changed following the operation, the Church even authorized their marriage (gay marriage magically transformed by surgery into a heterosexual one). Rebellious children disinherited by the family were reaccepted in their regained normality and could once again enjoy the privileges of the norm, that is, of the traditional bourgeois family, perhaps even getting their heritage back and being given an apartment to live in. All this, from the standpoint of the undermining of sexual morality and binary logic that the transgender (from here on I will use this term to render Mieli's concept of "transsexuality" in contrast to the "medical-legal" one peculiar to transition) hypothesis implied, was rightly considered a complete betrayal, or rather a form of proto-pinkwashing that would in fact lead to a process of homonormativization, reduced to begging for gay marriage, the adoption of children, and all the appalling rest of the swamp of normalization and counterrevolutionary defusing.

Mieli did not consider himself to be either a man or a woman and for this reason used to dress in public in the clothing of both genders, often stirring feelings of bewilderment, especially on the Milan subway or in front of the factory gates ("I'd like to meet you outside the gates of a factory," Alan Sorrenti[19] had sung a few years earlier), where he liked to put on a performance of his concept of the surmounting of gender as revolutionary praxis. With his shaved head, heavy makeup, exaggerated jewelry, and impossibly high heels, Mieli broke every mold, remapping his own body as a polysexual receiver transmitter. In fact he was an activist, an artist, a trickster shaman, perhaps a "holy fool."

In those years, even those who had not read Mieli had absorbed his ideas through their bones, for Mieli theorized on the basis of concrete experience. His was an anti-academic theorization of the street, which started from the asshole connected to the brain, and this was what he demanded, neither more nor less. Mieli was a great intellectual. He spoke several languages and read a great deal, traveled in France and England, and did his theorizing through an introjection and subsequent direct experimentation of the praxis that he proposed. Mieli was the street elevated to a university of sexually desiring life, and the body was the transubstantiation in which the physical/physiological/presymbolic struggle of transgender drive disidentification took place.

Ever since the time of Lola Puñales's Collettivo Frocialista, the dimension of homosexual revolt had had a clear and maturing role to play within the struggle of the Bolognese Autonomia Operaia[20] (autonomists who would later adopt the praxis of the Black Bloc from the German anarchists) and the Movement in general. And these struggles were supported (although not accepted by the more politicized communist fringes) by broad swathes of the student proletariat, as well as by the inhabitants of the working-class districts in the city center, who started to grow accustomed first to homosexual cruising and then to transsexual prostitution as modes of earning an autonomous income outside official circuits on the part of people unwillingly and de facto (self-)marginalized and prevented from gaining access to the labor market of the work by their aesthetic and identity choices—choices that were absolutely unacceptable for the dominant Catholic-communist mentality of the time, clearly demonstrated by the war waged by the clerical institutions of Bologna against the Cassero, which, however "veiled" in form, continues to this day.

It should be pointed out, however, that up until 1980, during the era of the Christian Democrat republic,[21] there was no law governing transsexualism in Italy, which meant that T* people enjoyed no legal recognition and could be fined in the act of "mascheramento," or disguise, as established by article 85 of the Law of Public Security, a hangover from the laws of the Fascist period, approved in 1931. In addition, repetition of the act of "transvestism or disguise" could lead to much serious penalties, starting with classification, on the basis of the same article, as a "socially dangerous person," an accusation that could lead to revocation of your driving license, loss of the right to vote, and even confinement, a typical sentence of the Fascist regime. But that was not all. A further repetition of "antisocial behavior" linked to dressing in a manner not keeping with your gender (at the time it was known as biological sex) could lead to imprisonment and even to being shut up in a mental home, a "total institution" that will be abolished in 1978 by the Legge Basaglia (Basaglia Law).[22]

In the years following 1980, all this was fortunately just a memory, even if a recent one, and my personal involvement in the punk and T* scene, which would have exposed me to similar risks, also allowed me a sort of "transitory transition." Dressed entirely in women's clothing, I carried out some social experiments, such as deliberately asking policemen for information or stopping to speak to them while cross-dressed, and was able to do it without being subjected to any kind of reaction or repression. So if living as a punk or transgender or transgender punk in 1980 was possible, even as an "illegal alien," the same could not be said for hormone therapy, to which there was no legal access. The only option was to get ahold of the hormones with great difficulty, from the black market, and inject them in do-it-yourself doses under objective conditions of risk to your health. Or nothing, especially if you wanted to keep your cock functioning.

LAW 184, passed in 1982 thanks to the political action of the Partito Radicale (Radical Party),[23] with which the FUORI had in the meantime merged (not without controversy and a rift between the grassroots activists, loath to come to terms with the State, and the component more interested in a strategy of compromise with a view to obtaining precise rights), and of the already formed MIT (Movimento Italiano Transessuale [Italian Transsexual Movement]),[24] changed all this. In fact the law, which was extremely simple and concise, permitted self-diagnosis (although later on, first in the Lazio region and then in other parts of Italy, a precise protocol of application was drawn up), and as a consequence hormonal treatment and sex reassignment surgery that would in turn permit a change of gender in your identity papers. It was one of the most libertarian and progressive laws in the world, as well as one of the earliest, but one that, in the Italian context today, has become a sort of dead weight, as it still does not allow a change in your identity papers without undergoing a surgical operation,[25] and thus the true recognition of the transgender condition rather than just that of the medically "transsexual" one. This is a problem and a grave limitation to which attempts are still being made today to find a solution through "indirect" sentences.

Broadly speaking, the 1970s and the early 1980s testify to a "transitory phase," especially from the point of view of individual processes of desire that transformed, albeit superficially, even Italian pop culture and music. We might think of a singer like Renato Zero,[26] whose character revolved on gender ambiguity. In 1980, Zero was already on the wane. His period of greatest success lasted more or less from 1973 to 1979, accompanying the rise and fall of Italian counterculture as a "mainstream outsider" but becoming a fixed point of queer culture, an icon of the transvestite faggot.

Zero had stolen first the camp choreographies of Alice Cooper and then the more refined ones of David Bowie's Ziggy Stardust, and had given a voice to all Italian faggots, especially the closet cases. He had celebrated in great un/ideological confusion the ass-peddlers of the housing projects and the pussies who would later become drag queens. But it was not the despairing rage of Pasolini's hustlers that he expressed in his music, but the pleasure-loving and uncommitted solipsistic indifference that was going to become the true essence of being gay and no longer queer.

In reality, Renato Zero's was a repressive desublimation of the faggots. And his recent Catholicistic, paternalistic, and revisionist, at times even markedly homophobic, change of tack is nothing but the squaring of a circle that was evident right from the start. And yet Renato Zero was a hero for many men and women and was enormously popular not just with faggots, not just with fag hags, but also with heterosexual girls looking for a less phallocratic model of masculinity. Even among female comrades, where the Marxist-Leninist males wanted the revolution to be confined to the bedroom and not extend to the kitchen, as Vi Subversa[27] of the Poison Girls, the first self-proclaimed anarchofeminist punk group, sang in that very year of 1982.

Renato Zero's world was that of disco music, fun-loving, frivolous, and unengaged. But it was the voice of the closet faggots, and those who were looking for a different way of expressing the fact of being a subject/object of sexual desire. And we can indeed connect his fancy-free sexuality on display, deprived of any political struggle, with the height of the "Riflusso"[28]—the withdrawal from political engagement that occurred in the 1980s, a concept perhaps very hard to understand outside Italy. The *riflusso* was the one that followed the "Convention against Repression," for whose manifesto, overflowing with red stars and hammers & sickles, the support of Deleuze & Guattari and various other great French thinkers was also asked for and given, although in reality they were already in a post-ideological and decidedly non–Marxist-Leninist phase.

Riflusso or withdrawal signified that "comrades" were suddenly no longer communists, that they cut their hair, shaved off their beards, threw away their parkas, and bought green loden coats,[29] donning Ray-Ban glasses to go to the discotheque to dance to disco music and try to pick up "pieces of ass that were hotter than their comrades" but maintaining the same phallocratic male chauvinist mindset as before. A generation above all (especially in Bologna) of students who were destined to assume the role of manager in the future and certainly not to go and work at the foundry or in the Yards of Italsider,[30] in support of whose workers they had gone on strike at high school and held assemblies at university.

A decade of struggle and awakening, from '68 to '77, was over and now, with a murder by the State Police and related chalk circles[31] behind them, and a subsequent revolt put down with tanks (whether you wanted to believe it or not), it was time for the students to repay the investment of their parents and become tomorrow's ruling class. This is how it was for many activists in the movement of 1968, and for some reason the movement of '77 too, but it wasn't like that for any of the punks, and this has to mean something.

The punks and queers were another matter. They had a battle to fight in which their skin was at stake. They had a great rejection to make.

When the Cassero opened, I was a punk. I was a cross-dresser, or rather I was a transvestite punk. Technically I was a heterosexual, I was going steady with the female drummer of the RAF Punk, my band, but in reality, we were already a queer couple.[32] Or rather, the punks were the queers of the countercultural scene. They were well aware of it at the Cassero. You needed a membership card to get in. This was mostly to keep out fascists, troublemakers, and curious heteros looking for dumb and gratuitous entertainment. We were punks and had no membership cards but got in without any problem, and at the Cassero we put on performances *en travesti*—as chance would have it—with Le Nuove Justine,[33] for instance.

One day I rang the doorbell, and right behind me appeared four "good boys dressed in loden" and conspicuously heterosexual. I was let in at once, without a card, while they were blocked because they didn't have one. It was implicit that they wouldn't be able to get one at the door, even though the Cassero handed out cards to all declared heterosexuals who wanted to dodge military service by pretending to be homosexual, precisely because of what I have always defined as dual militancy, in this case queer & antimilitarist. My first and only membership card for the Cassero was given to me in 2000-and-something, number 23,[34] my lucky number, but it could have also been 1.

The punks were the queers of the underground scene, but the queers were at our side in the protests, fleeing with us from the batons of the police, at the town hall meetings, at every moment in which we were struggling to obtain other rights or change the conservative mindset of a city enslaved by hyperconsumption in a pink communist key.

And yet, while our Marxist comrades with the *riflusso* started to go to the discotheque to dance to disco—the worst symbol of spectral nullification—and abandon all political struggle, punks & queers were already constructing the future (not only that of when many punks came out as queers, obviously!); that is, that of different kinds of struggle, not in the name of a political revolution that in the Soviet Union had culminated in the bloody massacre of the Red Terror and that no Trotskyism would ever salvage, but those on their own bodies, their own lives, their own gelling dis-identity.

And yet disco, viewed in the United States as the triumph of being gay (gay, not queer) in music, with the mythicizing of Studio 54 as the new Ideological Merchandise for the After Revolution Spectacle, in reality imposed very strict rules, from dress to the roles assigned to male and female. Curiously, although no one in Italy is aware of it, the period from '77 to '82 in the United States of the Afro-Americans saw the triumph of funk, not disco. To be sure, a funk sometimes no longer of brass but of keyboards, but still of bands of seven or eight musicians sexing it up on the stage, in contrast to the disco tracks laid down in the studio by a producer and a borrowed singer . . . Giorgio Moroder (an Italian besides) and Donna Summer, first a legendary gay icon and then turncoat, asking the Virgin Mary for forgiveness and repudiating the nancy boys that had earned her success and anticipating, in a completely unexpected way, the course taken by Renato Zero.

But funk was sequins and glitter, perhaps no longer the utopian transgender spatial imagery of P-Funk's Post Gender Black Liberation, and above all for the once again proto-transgender "males": the close-fitting jumpsuits, heavy makeup, absurdly high heels and wedges, thigh-high boots, colored braids, falsetto voices, explicit sex, and high camp of Parliament/Funkadelic,[35] George Clinton,[36] Bootsy Collins,[37] and company, invoking a free and pleasure-seeking world, as it happens, thanks to the future and to technology.

But that was instead Zapp,[38] the Gap Band,[39] Slave,[40] Crown Heights Affair,[41] Instant Funk,[42] Prince, or, who knows, even fucking Rick James,[43] where the talk was always of spangles and glitter, satin pants, men's makeup, and the musicians' flaunted camp, spontaneous and not deliberately concocted as it was for the still fundamental Village People. Funk had an edge over the rest, and for that reason did not even pass the test of the new "cultural hegemony of disengagement." It meant knowing how to play your instrument, and very well too, busting your ass, maybe even having something to say, knowing what's going on.

Disco was gay, funk was queer!

And it was out of sync, just as the four guys in the photo were out of step with their time, the proto-band from 1972 in 1982,[44] with long hair and the air of knowing a thing or two about their own needs, their own battles of a revolution that was not political but inner, their effort to attain a joy that only collective and inspired struggle—we'd call it sustainable—could give. If they had gone to the discotheque, they would certain have danced to "Super Freak,"[45] not to "Com'è bello far l'amore da Trieste in giù!"[46]

Because that staying anchored to a rebel aesthetic, one of challenge, instead of letting themselves be swallowed up by the new conformism of jackets & white pants and hair slicked down with brilliantine, showed them to be very young gender warriors projected into the future of the struggles for pleasure won and not granted on which we ought to be starting today, forty years later!

The future, the planet, rights, struggles are not just for human animals but pertain to all living creatures, plants and rocks (living too) included!

Notes

1. A longer and slightly different version of this essay was originally published in the volume *T**, edited by Ilaria Bombelli (Milan: Mousse Publishing, 2020). With the exceptions of notes 25 and 44, the notes featured here are from the original publication.

2. Editor's note (ed./n): The author makes reference to when, following the murder of Francesco Lorusso (see note 3), the then Home Minister, Francesco Cossiga, authorized the deployment of armored vehicles, which were widely perceived and described as "tanks," in the streets of the center of Bologna in response to the protests and major riots that had broken out in the city.

3. Francesco Lorusso (1952–1977) was a student at the faculty of medicine and a militant of "Lotta Continua" (one of the leading Italian extra-parliamentary left-wing groups of a revolutionary Communist and workerist orientation, active between 1969 and 1976). Lorusso was killed by a gunshot fired by a conscripted carabiniere during the riots ensuing from a student demonstration on March 11, 1977, in Bologna. The news of the death of a student from the Movement led thousands of sympathizers from the extra-parliamentary Left to make their way toward the university, thus forming a protest march, without forewarning the authorities, which was thus immediately dispersed with violent charges, leading to a day of urban warfare.

4. The "Convention against Repression" took place in Bologna from September 22 to 24, 1977, also organized in the wake of the appeal that had appeared on July 5 in the newspaper *Lotta Continua*, undersigned by a number of French intellectuals, including Sartre, Foucault, Deleuze, and Guattari.

5. Ed./n: The author refers to the Movimento del '77: a spontaneous extra-parliamentary movement founded in Italy in 1977 as the evolution and transformation

of the youth and workers' movements still to be found in the country post-1968. It was characterized by its outspoken contestation of the system of parties and trade unions, but also of political movements as they had been until then. In 1977, the creative and pacific wing of the Movement, along with Autonomia Operaia, which instead advocated armed clashes in the streets, marked a permanent break with the Italian Communist Party, fiercely contesting the policy of the "historical compromise" and the party's shift from class struggle to bourgeois power. One of the last events of the Movimento del '77 was the "Convention against Repression."

6. The Collettivo Frocialista is a politicized homosexual collective founded in Bologna in 1977 by the Chilean exile refugee Samuel Pinto, known in the environment as Lola Puñales, along with Beppe Ramina, Franco Grillini, and Valérie Taccarelli, and guided by Pinto himself. The name ironically draws on the venue where meetings were held, i.e., the headquarters of the Partito Socialista (Socialist Party). In 1979, the Collettivo Frocialista would change name to Circolo di Cultura Omosessuale 28 Giugno (Homosexual Cultural Circle June 28).

7. The Brigate Rosse (Red Brigades or BR) were a far-left subversive organization active in Italy from the early 1970s, the height of their activity dating between 1974 and 1980. In those years, the BR launched the so-called attack at the heart of the State with the killing, wounding, or kidnapping of politicians, magistrates, police officers, journalists, industrialists, factory bosses, and trade union representatives. Their most clamorous action was the 1978 kidnapping of Aldo Moro, leader and cofounder of the Democrazia Cristiana (Christian Democrats) party.

8. Initially Marxist in its approach, FUORI (or "FUORI!") was the first association of the Italian movement for homosexual liberation founded in 1971 in Turin by the bookseller Angelo Pezzana, along with other activists, operative until 1982.

9. Mario Mieli (1952–1983) was an Italian activist and writer, a theorist of gender studies, linked to heretical Freudo-Marxism of the Situationist kind. He is considered one of the founders of the Italian homosexual movement, as well as one of the greatest thinkers in Italian homosexual activism.

10. Angelo Pezzana (1940) is an Italian activist, politician, and journalist. In 1970, he was among the founders of FUORI. Of great media impact was his individual demonstration in Moscow in 1977 in support of the Soviet director Sergej Parajanov, imprisoned for his homosexuality,

11. The FHAR is an autonomous movement, founded in Paris in 1971 by lesbian feminists and gay activists including Guy Hocquenghem, Christine Delphy, and Françoise d'Eaubonne. The movement is known for having radically provided visibility for the gay and lesbian struggles of the 1970s, criticized for having left too little space for the emancipation of women and homosexuals. The group demanded the subversion of the bourgeois and hetero-patriarchal state, and of values deemed chauvinist and homophobic by the Left and Far Left.

12. The First International Congress of Sexology was held in Sanremo on April 5, 1972. The Congress included a section on the etiology of homosexuality

and one dedicated to types of therapy, especially of a psychological and psychiatric nature, to eradicate it.

13. The oath of Hippocrates is sworn by doctors, surgeons, and dentists before starting their profession.

14. Luciano Massimo Consoli (1945–2007) was an Italian writer, journalist, translator, essayist, and LGBT activist. He was among the founding fathers of the European homosexual movement.

15. The Stonewall riots were a series of violent clashes between the police and groups of homosexuals in New York. The first such clash took place on the night of June 28, 1969, when the police raided the Stonewall Inn, a bar in Greenwich Village, Manhattan. It is symbolically considered the moment in which the gay liberation movement was sparked throughout the world. For this reason, June 28 was chosen by the LGBT movement as the date of World LGBT Pride Day or Gay Pride. A symbol of the Stonewall riots is the trans activist Sylvia Rivera, who is said to have marked the start of the protest by hurling a high-heeled shoe at a police officer.

16. Françoise d'Eaubonne (1920–2005) was a French feminist and radical militant who introduced the term "ecofeminism" in 1974. In 1971, she was among the 343 signatories of the Manifesto 343 declaration in favor of abortion. Previously a member of the French Communist Party, in the same year, she helped to found the FHAR. In this role, d'Eaubonne was among those present at the contestation of the 1971 Festival di Sanremo, which marked the foundation of FUORI.

17. "Il Cassero" or Porta Saragozza is one of the gates along the third ring of walls surrounding the center of Bologna—in architecture, the "cassero" is the fortified zone of a castle (a sort of castle within a castle). Porta Saragozza gained particular importance when it was used as a starting point for the processions toward the sanctuary of the Madonna di San Luca. On June 26, 1982, the keep of Porta Saragozza was conceded by the municipality of Bologna, under the leadership of the mayor Renato Zangheri, to the Circolo di Cultura Omosessuale 28 Giugno (ex Collettivo Frocialista). From 1985 to 2002, the building served as the headquarters of the national association Arcigay.

18. *Elementi di critica omosessuale* is the first and most important writing by Mario Mieli, considered the scholarly underpinning of all the following gender studies in Italy. Originally a degree thesis in moral philosophy, it was published for the first time by Giulio Einaudi in 1977. It was published in English under the title *Homosexuality and Liberation: Elements of a Gay Critique* by the Gay Men's Press in 1980, and in Spanish as *Elementos de crítica homosexual* in 1979 by the publisher Anagrama.

19. "Vorrei incontrarti fuori i cancelli di una fabbrica" ("I would like to meet you outside the gates of a factory") is the first line of the song "Vorrei incontrarti," composed and interpreted by the Italian singer-songwriter Alan Sorrenti in 1972.

20. Autonomia Operaia was an extra-parliamentary left-wing movement active between 1973 and 1979, of which the ideological bases drew on workerist

thought, i.e., a contemporary reading of Marxist thought, insisting on the concept of the independence of the working class and on anti-authoritarianism. It was never a real party but an area in which a number of exponents of the movements of the extra-parliamentary (or revolutionary) Left converged, in opposition to the reformist Left.

21. The Democrazia Cristiana (Christian Democrats or DC) was an Italian political party of moderate, democratic, and Christian leanings, founded in 1943 and active for fifty-two years, up until 1994. The party played a key role in post–Second World War Italy and its process of European integration.

22. In Italy, the Basaglia Law refers to the law of May 13, 1978, no. 180, on the theme of "voluntary and compulsory health checks and treatment." The law, which was in force no more than a few months, up until the institution of the National Health Service (December 23, 1978), forced the closure of mental asylums and regulated the administration of mandatory health treatment, by creating public services of mental hygiene. Prior to the law's promulgation, psychiatric hospitals were often greatly connoted as places of social containment.

23. The Partito Radicale (Radical Party or PR) is an Italian political movement with a transnational vocation founded in 1955 as a split from the Partito Liberale (founded in Bologna in 1922), which promotes a liberal, leftist, and secular state framework. It was the first party to deal with civil rights in Italy, and it was the spearhead of various battles that led to the approval of innovative laws, such as the right to abortion, to divorce, and of course to undergo surgery for gender correction.

24. MIT (Movimento Italiano Transessuale), from 1979 to 1999; after 1999, MIT became Movimento Identità Transessuale, and then Movimento Identità Trans since 2017. MIT is an association that defends and supports the rights of transsexual, transvestite, and transgender persons. It was the first transsexual association to be founded in Italy, in 1979.

25. Ed./n: This law was changed in 2015 (see timeline). On the laws and policies regarding gender transition in Italy, see the conclusion.

26. Renato Zero, pseudonym of Renato Fiacchini (1950), is an Italian singer, showman, dancer, and record producer. He was one of the first Italian songwriters to write on themes that in the 1970s and 1980s were considered taboo, achieving great commercial success.

27. Frances Sokolov (1935–2016), better known by her stage name Vi Subversa, was the singer and guitarist of the British anarcho-punk group the Poison Girls, founded in Brighton in 1976. Their songs explored sexuality and gender roles, often from an anarchic perspective.

28. In Italy, the "riflusso" (reflux) was a period dated to around the turn of the 1980s (more precisely from 1978 to 1982) when the heavy ideological climate of the previous years began to lift (the period defined as the "leaden years" due to the extremization of the political debate, which led to street violence, armed strug-

gles, and terrorism), one which had led to a rapid escalation of social and political tension and brought the economy to the brink of collapse.

29. Ed./n: The author uses the "loden"—the typical coat in green wool—as a symbol of the new aspirations of the working class, who previously wore parkas—known as "eskimo" in Italian—to becoming the ruling class.

30. Italsider was one of the largest Italian steelworks.

31. Ed./n: By "chalk circles" (in Italian "cerchi di gesso") the author refers to the marks left by police around the holes left by bullets after a shootout. In specific terms, this is the mark left on the wall of Via Mascarella, in Bologna, from the bullets fired by police on the morning of March 11, 1977, which killed the student Francesco Lorusso. *Il cerchio di gesso* is also the name of a magazine founded in Bologna in June 1977, a few months after the killing of Lorusso, by a group of intellectuals who shared a critical attitude toward the policy of the "historic compromise" and national unity with the aim of understanding the reasons behind the Movimento del '77. The magazine closed in November 1979.

32. Ed./n: Gianpaolo Giorgetti (Jumpy and later Helena Velena) and Laura Carroli (then Laure de Lauris, the name of one of Sade's lovers) met in 1978 on the Treno di John Cage (the musical happening staged by the American artist from 26 to 28 June along a number of little-used railway lines in Emilia Romagna) and decided to put together a virtual group: the Rhutter Grøpp. The members of the band, the name of which would later be changed to RAF Punk, were Stefano "Steno" Cimato (bass), Carlo Chiapparini (guitar), Massimo "Mammo" Poggi (guitar), Laura (drums), and Jumpy (voice). In 1981, the band founded Attack Punk Records and issued the first single on the label, "Schiavi nella città più libera del mondo" ("Slaves in the Freest City in the World"). The band would break up in 1986.

33. Ed./n: Le Nuove Justine was a BDSM cabaret theater group founded by Laure de Lauris of RAF Punk, which Helena Velena was also a member of. Based on the figure of Sade, whose philosophy they would develop along libertarian, libertine, and post-feminist lines, they recounted the prim and proper ideas and adventures of four Justines who go through all the misadventures of virtue as an extremely corrosive form of satire, targeting political militancy and the Left. They produced a short feature movie and three video clips.

34. The enigma concerning the number 23 was noted for the first time by William Burroughs and was successively widely discussed by Robert Anton Wilson in his *Trilogy of the Illuminati*. Selective attention, focusing on anything, especially numbers, leads us to notice a series of occurrences and particular coincidences. This does not produce fear or superstition, but rather a positivist approach to our individual ability to transcend and therefore to overcome the meaning of such eventualities.

35. Funkadelic was an American funk and rock group originally from Plainfield, New Jersey, and active above all in the 1970s. Together with their parallel project Parliaments (a name later changed to just Parliament), also headed by George Clinton, the group gave rise to the culture of funk in that period.

36. George Clinton (1941) is a US musician, singer, and record producer, considered one of the forefathers and one of the leading names in the funk genre.

37. William "Bootsy" Collins (1951) is a US singer and bass player, known for his collaboration with James Brown and George Clinton and for his meaningful contributions to the evolution of the funk bass.

38. Zapp was a US funk group that formed in 1978, reaching the height of its fame in the early 1980s.

39. The Gap Band was a US R&B and funk group active throughout the 1970s and 1980s, made up of three brothers (Charlie, Ronnie, and Robert Wilson). They broke up in 2010, after forty-three years.

40. Slave was a US funk group founded in 1975 that met great success between the end of the 1970s and the early 1980s.

41. Crown Heights Affair was an R&B/funk/disco group founded in Brooklyn in 1967.

42. Instant Funk was a US funk/soul band from the 1970s and 1980s.

43. A pseudonym of James Ambrose Johnson Jr. (1948), Rick James was a US singer-songwriter, musician, and record producer. An exponent of funk and R&B music, he enjoyed great success in the United States in the 1970s and 1980s.

44. Ed./n: The author is referring to one of the photos of Bonora included in the original version of this essay. The photo, taken in Bologna, potrays a group of four young guys posing as a 1970s band.

45. "Super Freak" is a 1981 single by the US singer Rick James, written together with Alonzo Miller, that went on to become very popular. "Freak" is used in its slang acceptation here to refer to a decidedly promiscuous girl.

46. A citation from the ironic and light-hearted ritornello of "Tanti auguri," a piece sung by Raffaella Carrà (stage name of Raffaella Maria Roberta Pelloni [1943–2021]) issued in 1978 and that became an evergreen of Italian music. The lyrics describe the habits of a free and independent woman, stressing sex in all its manifestations.

Chapter 17

A Trans Revolution and Its Contradictions
An Interview with Simone Cangelosi

Danila Cannamela

Simone Cangelosi is a filmmaker and the director of the Bolognese audiovisual archive Out-Takes. In this interview with Danila Cannamela, Cangelosi draws connections between his first film, *Dalla testa ai piedi* (*From Head to Toes*, 2007), in which he documented his own gender transition, and his second cinematographic work, *Una nobile rivoluzione* (*A Noble Revolution*, 2014), which retraces the life of trans activist Marcella Di Folco. The conversation focuses on charting Marcella's personal journey from her Roman *dolce vita*, lived in a masculine body, to her Bolognese political commitment as a trans woman. Cangelosi's documentary films cast new light on public sites of generational culture, like Piper Club and the cinema sets of auteurs, where Marcella worked in Rome; the films also spotlight niche places, like MIT (the seat of the Italian trans movement in Bologna), that remain at the periphery of dominant culture.

The archival work that informed Cangelosi's reconstruction of Marcella's life has inspired a broader project of historical documentation: through the collection, restoration, and digitization of audiovisual materials, the Archivio Out-Takes has the goal of preserving and reviving the collective memory of civil rights and LGBT+ movements in the city of Bologna.

Danila Cannamela (DC): In 2014, you directed *Una nobile rivoluzione*, a documentary about Marcella Di Folco, one of the leading figures of the Italian trans movement. What inspired you to create the movie?[1]

Simone Cangelosi (SC): I thought of making this documentary for a simple reason: I was good friends with Marcella.[2] I had known her as a trans activist many years before her death [in 2010 at the age of sixty-seven]. I met her in the 1990s, when I came in contact with MIT (Movimento Identità Trans [Trans Identity Movement]) in Bologna. Initially, I went there for personal reasons, but then I got involved in its social action and commitment, becoming an activist alongside people like Marcella and Porpora [Marcasciano], among others. Since then, Marcella became a very significant presence in both in my personal and professional life. I should mention, though, that my first encounter with her was through cinema. Before transitioning, she worked as an actor with Federico Fellini. *Amarcord* (1973) was the first film I watched at the movie theater, when I was six years old, and there she was—Marcella—in the role of Prince Umberto of Savoy. Her cinematographic work—I could recall movies such as Fellini's *Satyricon* (1969) and *La città delle donne* (*The City of Women*, 1980), Mario Monicelli's *Un borghese piccolo piccolo* (*An Average Little Man*, 1977), and Elio Petri's *Todo Modo* (*One Way or Another*, 1976)—represents a further, or perhaps, the first point of connection in our lives.

When I started to work on *Una nobile rivoluzione*, in 2011, the first thing I did was to go back to the roughly one hundred hours of film I had recorded for *Dalla testa ai piedi*, a documentary short in which I retraced my own experience with gender transition over the course of eight years. Roberto Nisi, a writer who helped me with the script of *Una nobile rivoluzione*, suggested that I use the archive of footage I had collected for my first movie, which indeed included a lot of shooting with Marcella. Some of these materials came to be used in *Una nobile rivoluzione*; for example, a conversation that Marcella had with my mother and my sister, recorded at my house, became the opening of the documentary. Then, during the editing, we had to pick a closing scene for the movie, and we chose a shot of Marcella doing an impersonation of her idol, opera singer Maria Callas, singing the Habanera from *Carmen*. Originally, I had planned to use that footage for the ending of *Dalla testa ai piedi*. Ten years later, however, while working on my second documentary, I finally found the place for that shot. It was almost an epiphany! In addition, to strengthen the connection between the two movies, I inserted scenes from *Dalla testa ai piedi* into *Una nobile rivoluzione*: Marcella's speech at the 1995 Pride March in Bologna and the night drive with Porpora in the sex workers' district are both repurposed scenes.

Now, the deep connection between *Dalla testa ai piedi* and *Una nobile rivoluzione* is quite clear to me, but at the time it was still blurry. The first movie helped me process my journey with gender identity; the second served a similar function of self-reflection and re-elaboration, but in response to my grief for losing Marcella. When she passed away, it was vital for me to transform my mourning into an audiovisual creative project; it was my healing process. So, the documentary ended up being a portrait of Marcella that on the one hand contributed to keeping her memory alive, and on the other it was an homage, my way to thank her for everything I learned from her. My personal engagement, affective needs, and authorial purposes coalesce in this reconstruction. I aimed to do justice to Marcella and simultaneously commemorate what she had been—the meaning and worth of her life—even if I know that a process like this takes a much longer time.

DC: From an historical perspective, Marcella was one of the people who led the trans movement in Italy. She was among the founders of MIT, and her persona was definitely revolutionary for the time. Is this why you chose *Una nobile rivoluzione* as a title?

SC: Speaking of the title, I was interested in exploring two different, contradictory aspects of Marcella's life: her revolutionary impact and her noble lineage—she came from an aristocratic Roman family, later impoverished. As in *Dalla testa ai piedi*, my goal in *Una nobile rivoluzione* was to grasp the universal dimension of a personal story. In doing so, I intentionally situated the character of Marcella within the revolution of the LGBT+ movement, turning her experience into something much broader than an individual story—something inclusive and authentic, and in this sense, a noble revolution, a higher inspiration to collective social change. From this broader point of view, the context, or the geography we might say, in which Marcella acted becomes pivotal: for example, her presence gains visibility and greater meaning when, in Bologna, she is surrounded by other people. These collective shots made me think of the painting *Il quarto stato* (*The Fourth Estate*) by Pellizza da Volpedo from around 1901—the working-class crowd advancing together, trying to make progress, despite the potential problems or mistakes.

Still, it has been brought to my attention that the title of the movie sounds almost oxymoronic, even if for me it is not. In our culture, and especially in the culture of civil rights movements, the nobility and revolution are set in opposition: the French Revolution—to mention just one key historical event—was waged against the nobility, and the struggle against the upper class remains one of the main struggles of our times. I did not even realize it at first, but the inner tension between the nobility and revolution is revealing of Marcella's personality and runs throughout the movie's narrative in many ways. She taught me that a person can love you even when she is hurting you; ultimately, I had to accept her with all her contradictions. And even with those, what she could give as a friend far exceeded her shortcomings.

DC: Making Marcella's own contradictions visible without wanting to solve, judge, or explain them is one of the most fascinating aspects of your movie. One of the contradictions that was particularly striking to me, beyond the nobility/working-class dualism or, obviously, the masculinity/femininity binary, was her conflicted relationship with the Catholic Church.

SC: Absolutely! I didn't even think about it . . . at times when you investigate a character so deeply, you might even miss certain elements because the person encompasses them all. But, undeniably, this contradiction strongly emerges in the scene with the bishop who, despite acknowledging that Marcella never gave up her faith and was even participating in religious ceremonies, does not show any capacity for conciliation, for dialogue. Basically, the bishop was still declaring that not only transsexuality but even homosexuality is against nature.

DC: In narrating Marcella's complexity, your movie develops through the deployment of a dual, parallel structure: you are driving with her sister in Rome, talking about Marcella's past, roughly from her childhood to her thirties, and at the same time a second storyline unfolds, highlighting her more recent past, her life and activism in Bologna. Can you tell us more about the use of these two key locations—Rome and Bologna? How did Marcella change or redefine the private and public spaces she traversed in her life?

SC: In Marcella's life, two different dimensions are at play: one is public and cheerful, and the other is more personal and far more troubled, as I have attempted to show from a retrospective point of view. The narration of her life in Rome, which in the movie emerges through my conversation with her sister, highlights Marcella's public dimension prior to her gender transition. She was indeed public about her homosexuality: she never hid her sexuality when working in the film industry, and this definitely hindered her acting career in the 1970s. There is another important aspect in Marcella's Roman upbringing: as I've already mentioned, she comes from a noble lineage. In the movie, she jokingly says, "I was a Pariolina," to acknowledge that, until the age of sixteen or seventeen, she belonged to the privileged urban aristocracy of Rome's upper-class Parioli neighborhood. Then, after the death of her father, the family relocated to a working-class area on the outskirts of the city. A few years later, in the mid-1960s, she began working as a bouncer at Piper Club, a hip Roman disco that was a hub for the international jet set, a place where movie stars hung out regularly (Luchino Visconti, Michelangelo Antonioni, and Monica Vitti, among others) and top singers performed—Italian stars like Patty Pravo, Equipe 84, the Primitives,[3] Caterina Caselli, New Trolls, and also foreign musicians, including Procol Harum, Pink Floyd, Genesis, Duke Ellington, and Josephine Baker.[4] Marcella—as a staff member of the club who worked the door and had the privilege of keeping even celebrities out, and as a gay man cruising the city at night—got to know a chameleon-like city, the iconic Felliniesque Rome of *La Dolce Vita* (1961) where a cutting-edge yet rather commodified young culture was thriving, and a new, beat-generation Rome that was rapidly changing its habits and traditions.[5]

However, despite her high visibility, Marcella in the capital was just an extra among other extras. In Rome, she lived her bildungsroman in a male gender. Here in Bologna, she practiced her excellent personal and public-relations skills that she later honed as an activist. Once she arrived here, she took center stage and became a protagonist. Nevertheless, to go back to the overarching theme of contradictions and highs and lows, Marcella started her life in Bologna from scratch, by walking the street. In 1960s and '70s Rome, as a gay man, she had benefited from a sort of social protection that allowed her to lead a relatively open life, but in Bologna, in 1986, where she moved in her forties after gender reassignment surgery in Casablanca, she didn't have that advantage. However, it was precisely her experience as a trans sex worker and her closeness to other trans prostitutes that enabled her to achieve a stronger awareness of their shared condition, an awareness that soon evolved into activism. She started to contact local politicians to voice the needs of trans sex workers and put forward their requests into a coherent agenda. In 1988, just a few years after her arrival in Bologna, she founded MIT Emilia-Romagna, which, although it was just a regional section of the national association, acted as the de facto leading activist trans group in Italy. In that respect, another significant image from the movie might be a scene of Marcella that was shot in Pratello, a lively and rather bohemian district of Bologna. This footage shows that being in the street, being part of the crowd, was her gift, her affinity, something that she embodied and embraced—now almost a fifty-year-old-woman, far from her family, far from her Roman life. I would add that she really needed to break with her past, to get away from Rome, not only to fully experience her gender identity but also to unleash her charismatic personality.

Compared to Rome, Bologna is a small town, where Marcella began a new life within the trans community, and where building relationships with local authorities was easier. Despite the issues and arguments that arose, especially over the necessity of negotiating with political institutions, the LGBT+ Bolognese community was officially recognized by the city government and housed in the so-called Cassero, a building at Porta Saragozza, one of the city's ancient gates. To briefly recall what happened: in 1974, activists in Bologna had created the Collettivo Frocialista, that in 1978 formed the association Circolo 28 Giugno, the first such group to receive government funding—the group was the nucleus of Arcigay, Italy's first and largest national LGBT+ organization, founded in 1985. The Circolo 28 Giugno, or Cassero as we call it in Bologna, was the first LGBT+ center to obtain a space from a municipal government in Italy. In this encouraging environment, Marcella's contribution was crucial for the construction of new social and political synergies between trans people and the city of Bologna. In Bologna, she took the initiative on many fronts: creating spaces for discussion and debates with the local administration and representatives of the healthcare system, gaining access to negotiating tables, and becoming involved in the activities of Orlando, a center linked to feminist and women's movements. Nevertheless, she was not just an activist; in her spare time, she attended games of Bologna's basketball team and cheered them on together with other local supporters.

DC: Let's focus on Marcella's activism in Bologna. A passage in Porpora's memoirs describes the funny image of Marcella driving around the city on a little scooter that looked minuscule beneath her big frame. And yet, onboard that funny-looking scooter, Marcella was enacting a daily revolution by providing services and assistance to trans people, by reaching out to them. Like Porpora, you have shown that Marcella was indeed a leading figure who stood out, physically and symbolically—one who could lead, unite, and mobilize people. If you had to choose an image evocative of Marcella's political action in Bologna, which one would it be?

SC: For me, the most powerful image is Marcella participating in a meeting of Bologna's city council. Her political career testifies to the transformative impact she had on Italian society. As an LGBT+ activist and transgender person, she initially served in the early 1990s as a representative of the Saragozza district (a neighborhood in Bologna) and then, running with the Green Party, was elected to the city council in 1995—the first in Europe, or perhaps even in the world. This was huge! Another image, equally powerful, is a scene included in the movie, when she is shown marrying a couple in Bologna's town hall. Through her body and her voice, she represents the power and the potential of the transgender community; as Porpora maintains, Marcella not only gave a voice to the trans community, she was their embodiment.

DC: Through your work, you have continued to reconstruct and narrate the history of the trans community. In 2019, you made the video clips for Porpora's theatrical piece *Il sogno e l'utopia* (*The Dream and the Utopia*); this experience is directly related to your previous movie projects and your interest in archival work and audiovisual restoration.

SC: Porpora has had several books published, memoirs as well as anthologies of personal narratives, including *Tra le rose e le viole: La storia e le storie di transessuali e travestiti* (*Among Roses and Violets: The History and Stories of Transsexuals and Transvestites*, 2020),[6] *Favolose narranti: Storie di transessuali* (*Fabulous Narrators: Stories of Transsexuals*, 2008), and *L'aurora delle trans cattive* (*The Dawn of the Bad Trans Women*, 2018). While these works can be considered autobiographical accounts and collections of firsthand statements by other trans individuals, in my opinion they are primarily nonsystematic attempts to create a collective story of transsexualism and transgenderism in Italy by tying together different personal stories into a shared narrative authored by gender-variant people.

Some background in connection with *Il sogno e l'utopia*: in 2007 Porpora wrote *AntoloGaia* (*AntholoGay*, reprinted in 2016), a fascinating bildungsroman in which she recounted two decades of her life—from her teenage and college years in the late 1960s and 1970s to the early 1980s, when the AIDS crisis hit—and then adapted her memoir to create a show in which she featured some photographs of the time and original footage, and had been touring around Italy with this performance. Francesca Scarinci, who fell in love with the show, invited me and some other professionals to collaborate in revising this theater project. Porpora's text remained substantially the same, but I created some additional material by retrieving visual and audiovisual sources of those years (e.g., photos of private and public events, home movies, and clips from shows). Then we arranged all of them to form a coherent flow and made them part of the show. The goal was to create a visual element that would simultaneously document and converse with Porpora's script. Overall, the core of the work consisted of creating a background for her performance that would also enrich the show.

We started with Porpora's private archive of photographs. Selecting these materials led us to face a fundamental question that keeps coming back: history, biography, or autobiography? This is a relatively recent history, so activists—even when they are sociologists like Porpora, or contemporary historians—are still speaking in their own voice. They are part of the movement they are seeking to analyze and facing the issue of how to retrace their own experience, which is also a collective experience, then write it as history. So, we confronted the hard task of selecting materials that, hopefully, can serve as tools for future historical documentation and reconstruction.

We began with the materials that Porpora considered the most important: some photographs and, especially, the music score, which features a number of 1970s and 1980s hits, including Grace Slick's "El Diablo," David Bowie's "The Width of a Circle," and Patti Smith's "Frederick," as well as songs of Italian counterculture singers such as Banco del Mutuo Soccorso and Claudio Lolli. Then we tapped other sources: I conducted research in public and private archives. In the Cineteca of Bologna and other institutional archives, I found images that I wouldn't have expected to find. I also consulted the Alberto Grifi archive of audiovisual materials and visited a few theaters that had collected videos of performances from the 1970s. Once we agreed on the materials to include, I did technical editing work.

Besides this being a gratifying professional experience, it was a great opportunity for personal enrichment. In the end, our shared vision was not to overpower the written text but rather to produce a visual dialogue between Porpora performing on stage and the images projected behind her, and between the images on the screen and the images evoked by the text. The final result is very close to a documentary. In my opinion, Porpora—and I say Porpora because ultimately this is her work, even if I contributed to it—has constructed her own autobiography. The subtitle *Biografia di una generazione* (*Biography of a Generation*) was added after the title of the show to emphasize the aspect of the autobiographical narrative that also tells the story of a generation and its development.

DC: Speaking of the history of a generation . . . you are currently working on another important project, the Out-Takes Archive (http://www.out-takes.org/it_IT/) in Bologna. How can this new archive contribute to the retracing of memories that have traditionally been removed from established history and reweave them into the urban fabric?

SC: The first step in creating this archive was to obtain a location from the city and become a tangible presence. From a more theoretical perspective, I approached this audiovisual archive as a way to pass down stories—something I did in my first documentary and that became more urgent while filming *Una nobile rivoluzione*, which is when I realized that this work had to be done. My interest in preserving and narrating history is related to my personal training, having worked as a film restorer at the Cineteca di Bologna for many years. I am obsessed with images—with looking at them and connecting them—and I could spend my whole life immersed in images! Working on *Dalla testa ai piedi*, I began connecting with people who had private archives and gained access to audiovisual materials through personal connections—that is how it all started. Of course, in Bologna, there are other LGBT+ archives and documentation centers, such as Cassero. Historically, the more that people participated in LGBT+ associations, the more they began to produce and gather materials: handouts, fliers, photos, recordings, etc. Informal attempts to gather this documentation were already going on during the 1980s and 1990s. My vision for the Out-Takes Archive stands at the intersection of three different interests of mine: cinema, activism, and the latest technological developments in filming and recording devices, which have made filmmaking widely accessible. For example, think of the role that smartphones have had in documenting recent events! Media representation has great influence on us, so an audiovisual archive ultimately has the twofold goal of documenting LGBT+ communities while showing the social changes that are simultaneously represented by and, in turn, influenced by media representations. It is a complex notion to explain. What I can say is that the archive and the historicizing process that shapes its development are a means, not a goal in itself: they are tools of research and study of the role of audiovisual communication. The archive is like a prototype that allows me to reflect on how images and media representation inform self-awareness—and this inevitably brings me back to the beginning, to *Dalla testa ai piedi*.

DC: Of course, developing self-awareness depends on the possibility of making unspeakable realities speakable, visible, and shareable. Yet, creating a new narrative can present challenges. In Italy, the beginning of the trans movement history can be traced to the 1970s liberation movements, at a time when second-wave feminism and the Gay Liberation Front were voicing their gender and sexual revolution. As a scholar based in the United States, I know that the dialogue between feminism, on the one side, and trans studies and queer studies, on the other, has been difficult, especially if we think of the most radical feminist groups. We should remember, for example, that Sandy Stone's groundbreaking essay "The Empire Strikes Back: A Posttranssexual Manifesto" (1987) was a response to the bitter feminist criticism of Janice Raymond's *The Transsexual Empire: The Making of the She-Male* (1979). And the same still applies to Italian culture, when feminists accuse trans women of reproducing and re-enabling traditional stereotypes of femininity and appropriating the female body. I hope that the work you are conducting will spur new dialogue: in Italy, the very idea of creating a narrative, and therefore a history that starts from oneself rather than from the dominant patriarchal discourse, is a feminist notion that Porpora, among others, has beautifully reinterpreted in a trans perspective.

SC: Absolutely! The most precious feminist legacy is that they taught us to start from oneself, a practice that now goes almost unmentioned, insomuch that if one doesn't know that feminism developed this narrative mode, one might completely ignore this key historical connection between movements and practices. However, at times, it has happened that feminist productive discourses and strategies have been distorted to the point of becoming detrimental and divisive. Still, there are some fundamental tools that feminism invented—first and foremost the creation of archives, such as the Orlando archive in Bologna—and this legacy still has the potential to generate debate and action.

Personally, my interest in feminism dates back to my college years. In 1994, I did my dissertation on film theorist Laura Mulvey, and I became deeply engaged with feminist theory—perhaps fired up by juvenile enthusiasm—but what I learned, in the early 1990s, is that the most important thing that second-wave feminists achieved in the 1970s and passed to us was starting to collect materials and tell a story. We are undeniably in debt to their work; maybe to make peace with them once and for all would actually help. Honestly, it bothers me to think that we, LGBT+ activists, are a minority in the minority—"quattro gatti" [four cats], as we say in Italian—and we know quite well that some people would rather destroy us, so what's the point of fighting among ourselves? Why can't we build alliances instead?

DC: I'd like to close this conversation with a personal question that goes back to *Dalla testa ai piedi*, where everything started. Filming that movie must have been a very intense experience: you laid bare your life in front of the audience. So why did you engage with the genre of comedy to tell a story that for many people is anything but funny?

SC: Yes, the comedic tone of the movie is quite unexpected. Still, humor can help dig deeper into difficult topics, and so I was adamant about searching for humor in a dramatic story, and the humor you see in the movie didn't emerge immediately. But I believe that if you open a space for laughing, then the "other"—your audience, in this case—opens up in some way. If you succeed in entertaining your viewers, they feel more at ease, and you end up building a communicative bridge and an emotional transfer, in a way that is more effective than drama. This might just be me but I cannot stand dramatic movies! It's hard to make good drama, but it's even harder to make good comedy. Irony is the register that I'd like to adopt in my films, and it's a register that I believe I've successfully used to cope with dramatic moments in my life. It's a storytelling mode that gradually surfaced in my own story and that has enabled me to see myself as a narrator. Ever since I was a child, I understood that what was perceived as dramatic in the story of my family wasn't necessarily dramatic, and that by narrating it with a comedic tone, I could turn it into a story people could deal with, a story people could digest, if not enjoy. It's a deeply autobiographical choice: I want my audience to look at the screen and come closer, not turn away. Comedy is a rhetorical strategy that helps convey very dramatic and complex content. The more I avoid loading a story with drama, the more I'm able to convey its conflict-laden message. This is my "revolutionary" poetics—not an easy one, though.

Notes

1. This text is based on a video interview I did with Simone Cangelosi via Skype, recorded in August 2020. The interview was conducted in Italian; the translation of this text into English is by the author. I would like to thank Simone for his help during the final editing of this interview and Francesca Nardi for her help with transcribing the audio materials.

2. Cangelosi wrote a detailed article on Marcella's life and engagement with the trans movement; see Cangelosi, "Marcella Di Folco," 310–20. In 2019, journalist Bianca Berlinguer published Marcella's biography, *Storia di Marcella che fu Marcello* (Milan: La Nave di Teseo).

3. Mal Ryder is a British singer and frontman of Mal and the Primitives, a band that achieved popularity in Italy in the 1960s.

4. The club was such a trend-setting hub that one of the owners later became a discographic producer and used the Piper brand to launch not only Patty Pravo but also Mia Martini and the Primitives.

5. These details are highlighted and further explored in the documentary short *Felliniana* (2010), codirected by Luki Massa and Cangelosi. The movie features a long interview that Gian Luca Farinelli, the director of Cineteca di Bologna, conducted with Marcella.

6. Here I am referring to the new revised and expanded edition of this book; the first edition was published in 1999.

References

"Archivio Out-Takes LGBTQI Audio-visual archive." Accessed February 19, 2021. http://www.out-takes.org/it_IT/.

Berlinguer, Bianca. *Storia di Marcella che fu Marcello*. Milan: La nave di Teseo, 2019.

Cangelosi, Simone, director. *Dalla testa ai piedi*. Bologna: Vitagraph, 2007.

———. "Marcella Di Folco: Ritratto di signora." *AG About Gender: International Journal of Gender Studies* 4, no. 8 (2015): 310–20.

———. *Una nobile rivoluzione*. Bologna: Kiné, 2014.

Farinelli, Gian Luca. Interview with Marcello Di Folco. In *Felliniana*, directed by Simone Cangelosi and Luki Massa. Bologna: Out-Takes Production, 2010.

Fellini, Federico, director. *Fellini's Satyricon*. Rome: United Artists, 1969.

———. *La città delle donne*. Rome: Gaumont Italia, 1980.

———. *La dolce vita*. Rome: Riama, Pathé Consortium Cinéma, Grey Film, 1961.

Marcasciano, Porpora. *AntoloGaia: Vivere sognando e non sognando di vivere; I miei anni Settanta*. Rome: Alegre, 2016. iBook.

———. *Favolose narranti: Storie di transessuali*. Rome: ManifestoLibri, 2008.

———. *Il sogno e l'utopia: Biografia di una generazione*. Movimento Identità Trans Onlus (MIT) Bologna. Performed on November 9, 2019. Teatro Ferrara Off.

———. *L'aurora delle trans cattive: Storie, sguardi e vissuti della mia generazione transgender*. Rome: Alegre, 2018. iBook.

———. *Tra le rose e le viole: La storia e le storie di transessuali e travestiti*. Rome: Alegre, 2020. iBook.

Monicelli, Mario. *Un borghese piccolo piccolo*. Rome: Cineriz, 1977.

Petri, Elio. *Todo Modo*. Produzione Intercontinentale Cinematografica (PIC), 1976.

Raymond, Janice. *The Transsexual Empire: The Making of the She-Male*. Boston: Beacon Press, 1979.

Stone, Sandy. "The Empire Strikes Back: A Posttranssexual Manifesto," 1987. https://sandystone.com/empire-strikes-back.pdf. First presented at the conference "Other Voices, Other Worlds: Questioning Gender and Ethnicity" at the University of California at Santa Cruz, 1988; first published in *Body Guards: The Cultural Politics of Gender Ambiguity*, edited by Julia Epstein and Kristina Straub. New York: Routledge, 1991.

Chapter 18

Lina Pallotta's Portrait of Porpora
"Snapshots of a Moment" and Geographies of Friendship

Danila Cannamela and Stella Gonzalez

Photographer Lina Pallotta has documented Porpora Marcasciano's life experience and militancy in the trans movement since their college years, in the 1970s, when they were both students at the university of Naples.[1] Pallotta later moved to New York to study photography and is currently based in Rome. Through their long friendship, Lina and Porpora have shared countless memories—the tragic events of the so-called years of lead, their activism, their journeys across the world. As they jokingly confess in an interview included in the film *Porpora* (2021), their only regret is that they did not make the revolution. Still, Pallotta started a visual revolution through her ongoing photographic portrait of Porpora, which provides an intimate look at trans identities and questions the stereotypical LGBT+ imagery of exceptionalism and blatant transgression. This essay, which bridges the Italian and Italian American sections of the volume, analyzes a selection of Pallotta's photographs, taken in Rome, Modena, and New York, to discuss how her visual narrative of friendship provides a unique representation of gender diversity.

The art of capturing fleeting moments—cooking, stretching in bed, meeting family and friends, going for a walk, praying—these are the visual poetics that photographer Lina Pallotta has adopted in her ongoing portrait of human rights and trans activist Porpora Marcasciano from 1990 to the present. Porpora and Lina have been very close friends since the 1970s, when they met in the midst of student protests at the university of Naples. In 2018, Pallotta's exhibition *Porpora*, held at the Officine Fotografiche gallery in Rome, presented a series of intimate images that, in documenting Marcasciano's life, testified to a friendship that has resiliently traversed many years, places, and sociocultural changes.[2]

Pallotta has explained on her website (https://www.linapallotta.net) that the goal of the project was to create a cumulative portrait of Porpora by gathering snapshots of moments and that these photographs are fragments of life that refuse to provide an interpretation of reality—rather, they offer "iconographies of private moments" that have reason and value beyond any all-encompassing ideology.[3] Beyond the notion of shared moments that nevertheless remain almost inexplicable, her photos' reason and value might reside in their chronicling of friendship, which ties all the fragments together and creates new geographies of intimacy. The intimate experiences captured in these pictures impart an elevated immersive quality to the viewer's encounter with the images. Moreover, the spontaneity and simplicity of Pallotta's snapshots of such moments have the capacity to reorient the audience's gaze: her images of domestic settings and everyday rituals implicitly draw the viewer closer, and in doing so, they trace unexpected scenarios of proximity across (and beyond) gender identities. Creating spaces of closeness is indeed a key component of Pallotta's view of photography: "Photography for me is never about distance, but indeed is about being able to show, grab and feel more of what is out there. It is in the chaos of our emotions, in the ephemeral and imperfect disorder of life, that fleeting and ever-changing moments of truth take shape. It is among the crevices of the signs and simulacra of the contemporary that I hope to insinuate the joy of solidarity and a timid subversion."[4] Ultimately, one of the most fascinating aspects of Pallotta's photographs is that the visual representation of friendship becomes a universal language that allows the audience to intuitively grasp Porpora's gender-variant experience without fully understanding it. Being trans, very much like being friends, is a path "distinctively interstitial, unregulated, voluntary and driven by [desire]."[5] In Pallotta's pictures, friendship—a very common, quite ordinary, and yet difficult-to-define human experience—becomes a lens to visually access and connect with what might be termed the "ordinary uniqueness" of gender variance, which goes beyond conservative views of heteronormativity and at the same time dodges cries for radical queerization. By focusing on the imperfect intimacy that draws friends closer while allowing them to preserve their separate identities, Pallotta's photos engage viewers in the "intimate and complicit gesture of moving *athwart*"—in other words, obliquely, neither too close nor too far, neither for nor against.[6] Pallotta, in getting closer to Porpora—in the act of taking the picture—herself embodies a "desiring self inexorably drawn toward difference," who mediates an encounter for her audience and wishes that her audience, too, may experience proximity without necessarily achieving any final answer or interpretation.[7]

A small selection of Pallotta's photographs included here demonstrates how the artist, through her portrait of Porpora, has traced geographies of friendship, in which "the co-belonging of nonidentical singularities" has shaped paths of (imperfect) understanding, joy, and encounter.[8]

Pallotta's ability to portray intimacy stems from her fascination with the quiet moments in between events, the transitions from one action to another. This idiosyncratic quality of her work particularly emerges in a photograph, taken in Rome in 1990, in which Porpora can be seen lifting her hair up in a swift motion as she waits for a pot to fill up with water, most likely to make pasta (see figure 18.1). These random, simultaneous actions infuse a sense of everyday realism to the photograph. This is the snapshot of a radically ordinary moment—one that might never get men-

Figure 18.1. Porpora Marcasciano in Rome, 1990. Photo courtesy of Lina Pallotta.

tioned in conversation, that might remain out of focus or forgotten—and yet fleeting moments like this hold life together and enable us to move on and possibly change, as suggested by the image of Porpora's face captured in different positions just seconds apart.

Furthermore, because the kitchen is a universal space, Pallotta's decision to capture an image of Porpora in that room creates a relationship of immediate intimacy with the viewer. What's there is what all kitchens have: water, pots and pans, various implements, containers, and a source of heat for cooking. Seeing Porpora engaged in a daily practice typical of Italian kitchens—indeed, of almost any kitchen—becomes particularly significant for its ordinariness: viewers may not know Porpora, they may not understand her gender variance, but they can relate to her performing another action while waiting for the pot to fill with water. Capturing these otherwise invisible moments of everyday life creates a kind of familiarity that hinges on a sense of universal "muscle memory." This photograph conveys the spontaneity of a moment with the subject in visual flux and enacting a random yet characteristically Italian ritual. Here, Porpora's tending to her hair and filling the pot are acts of self-care and nourishment that transcend gendered constructs.

The visual poetics of Pallotta's work does not rely on specific gestures but rather on mundane situations that occur in nearly everyone's life. In the depiction of Porpora with both hands occupied, juggling the successive maneuvers necessary to cook a meal, there is a certain tension, a certain feeling of expectation built into the scene, but the stakes are extremely low. Such rituals, encompassing ordinary actions, periods of waiting, and feelings that wax and wane, are a shared experience of transition that Pallotta has been able to display effortlessly in this photograph, creating a closeness and a sense of intuitive understanding and co-belonging that does not necessarily entail full comprehension.

Co-belonging is a visual narrative that Pallotta further explored in this second picture: a snapshot of Porpora and her good friend and trans comrade Marcella Di Folco, taken at Festa dell'Unità (a Social-Democrat festival) in Modena, in the late 1990s.[9] In her memoir *L'aurora delle trans cattive* (*The Dawn of the Bad Trans Women*, 2018), Porpora commented on her stormy relationship with Marcella, affirming that they made a peculiar pair: "Some used to say we looked like female husband and male wife, others that we were Stan and Ollie, and still others that we were Scylla and Charybdis."[10] Here, Pallotta effectively exploits the camera angle, capturing something of the differences that both united and divided them in their shared trans activism and commitment to gender liberation: she shows Porpora with her head tilted up, looking away from the camera and toward something else, while Marcella looks slightly downward, her gaze fixed on a printed leaflet on the table (see figure 18.2). Pallotta's depiction of their comfortable inattention to one another, in a room where the summer heat they are enduring is palpable, conveys the regenerative, almost cathartic feeling that Porpora and Marcella both gained from their friendship. With her usual irony, Porpora recalls her many acrimonious arguments with Marcella, which all ended in a predictable way: "On time, perfectly on time, a phone call would arrive after each blowout. When I didn't answer, she remained on the line, full of trust, and insisted on waiting for an answer: 'Gersa! [Porpora's nickname], did you calm down? Why are you pissed off, it's not good for you! We have so many things to do! Arguing doesn't help.'"[11] They are two trans people—who indeed had "so many things to do!"—silently testifying to their own experiences, some in common, some unique to themselves. Over the years, both experienced feelings and emotions that cast them outside the normative: they both engaged in sex work; they both were leaders of the Bolognese trans movement. Yet they dealt in contrasting ways with their feelings and experiences of difference and marginalization. Marcella underwent gender reassignment surgery in order to be the woman she desired to be; "What made Marcellona [big Marcella] unique," according to Porpora,

Figure 18.2. Porpora Marcasciano and Marcella Di Folco in Modena, ca. 1999. Photo courtesy of Lina Pallotta.

"was her being a woman, and especially her will to declare it and establish it in a decisive and categorical manner";[12] while Porpora preferred to express her femininity through dress, behavior, and self-affirmation but always felt "beyond" any gender category. The photograph registers their contrasting personalities through their distinctive choices of clothing, summer fashion accessories—Marcella's fan, Porpora's sunglasses—and the dissimilar poses they have assumed in that moment. It is a testament to the multitude of effective strategies by which trans people express their own individual identity. It also makes clear that these two have chosen to engage with their shared experiences and feelings in ways that suit them best and to support each other en route.

This third photograph (figure 18.3), taken in Rome in 1990 at a birthday celebration for Porpora, could be compared to a triptych of the holy family: the first "panel" features two of Porpora's beloved friends and trans activists, Roberta (on the front of the "panel") and Lucrezia (on the back); in the middle "panel," there is a child—Zeno, the son of another friend—in the arms of a fatherly figure; and the third "panel," at the right, shows Porpora looking down, a cigarette in her hand. The photo, in emulating the traditional iconography of the Madonna with child as well as the

Figure 18.3. Roberta, Lucrezia, and Porpora in Rome, 1990. Photo courtesy of Lina Pallotta.

Western visual tropes of the "family portrait," offers an alternative to the heteronormative model of the nuclear family, understood as the foundational community; and Zeno is being held and cared for by a man, an image that challenges gendered standards of parenthood and childcare. Disrupting the idea of the conventional group portrait is the fact that no one is looking at the camera, yet the picture still achieves the primary purpose of showing everyone's presence individually and together as a collective, or as co-belonging singularities. Porpora's stance, clothes, and attitude give no indication that the gathering is a celebration, but her facial expression projects a serenity that suggests she is in a comfortable environment surrounded by people she knows well. Much like the previous photograph of Porpora and Marcella, the signs for friendship, closeness, and familial bonds are neither obvious nor prescriptive but remain as a visual subtext.

However, something seems "off" in this picture: the image of friends and family who have gathered together to celebrate is contradicted by the tank top Porpora is wearing, with its explicit message to "Piss Off"—a phrase that appears to be telling anyone who challenges the validity of this family that they should go away. Porpora's message inverts the dominant rhetoric of exclusion that often targets transgender people in familiar places and situations (such as their own homes and families) and in public contexts (public restrooms, places of work, sports events). Rather than expending so much effort on an acceptance and inclusion that might never come from one's biological family, or that could imply an assumption of transnormativity, the message conveyed by this portrait of Porpora suggests a redirection of labor to the construction of one's own inner circle, creating new opportunities for love and intimacy. This regenerative activism envisions an alternative that *pisses off* conservative heteronormative society precisely because it has the potential for establishing new practices of care and closeness across genders and identities—practices that disrupt the traditional normative/non-normative, cisgender/transgender, straight/queer binaries. The child's presence points to the possibility of new Italian generations who take for granted unconventional family structures as well as domestic responsibilities shared by partners of any gender. This photograph, with its simultaneous allusions to a trans-inclusive (yet not homogenizing) future and nonconforming present, asserts a particular sense of agency rooted in one's declared identity and the collective geographies that encompass it. Ultimately, Pallotta's choice to create an intergenerational family portrait supports the idea of a future that is not based on the (re)production of the same, but that actively explores new spaces for individual freedom, sociality, and mutual care in everyday venues, including a birthday party.

Out of all the photographs discussed thus far, this last (figure 18.4) one is the only one that shows the artist herself. The circumstances of how this photograph was taken are unclear: whether a mirror was involved, or another photographer used Pallotta's camera to capture this moment, is unknown. All that matters is that it records Lina and Porpora in this space and time together as two people who love one another. Connecting their bodies physically is the intimate gesture of a head on a shoulder, which is not as obvious or direct an expression of love compared to a hug, embrace, or kiss, yet it conveys a certain level of comfort and support. When Pallotta was studying photography in New York, Porpora visited her there several times, making the journey to bridge the distance between the two. The awe-inspiring backdrop of the cityscape of New York behind them alludes to the grandness, size, and expansiveness of the space they inhabit—two people alone with each other on a rooftop, among other buildings filled with thousands of people living their own lives. The strength of their connection trumps anything else going on in their surroundings; for once, New York stands still for these two friends. But no matter where they are, Porpora and Lina remain stable and grounded in their affection for each other; however, like the cityscape framing them here, which has dramatically changed in the aftermath of 9/11, their friendship has been shaped and reshaped by the life events they have faced.

Figure 18.4. Lina and Porpora in New York, 1996. Photo courtesy of Lina Pallotta.

One particularly unusual aspect of this image is that it is Porpora rather than Lina who holds the camera in her hands. In this instance, the photographer has become the photographed, reversing their established roles, but the inclusion of both of them here conflates the subject and object of the gaze. If documenting Porpora's life was Pallotta's way to show her love for her friend, this photograph shows Porpora reciprocating in kind, with Porpora stepping into Lina's world. She closes the distance between the two of them physically through her travels to New York and emotionally through her use of Pallotta's medium of choice. Moreover, they are gazing in the same direction rather than facing each other at either end of a camera, creating a commonality between them. Even if they see the world in different ways, they can still find common ground in what they see and what they feel. On the surface, this friendship differs from Porpora's connection to Marcella in that Pallotta is a cisgender woman and may never truly understand the experiences of a trans woman, but this photograph shows that those differences, albeit important, do not prevent the creation of strong bonds. Lina's and Porpora's concepts of femininity are (re)defined by their friendship, not by the external voices and forces of their separate backgrounds. Their relationship is a symbiotic one, one in which the artist cannot exist without her muse, and the woman cannot exist without the support of a friend who shares and complements her embodied experience of femininity.

This brief exploration of Pallotta's portrait of Porpora Marcasciano, though far from exhaustive, has traced some of the primary themes of Pallotta's photographic work—her goal of communicating and building closeness, her fascination with difference(s), and her interest in ordinary geographies. In memorializing fleeting moments in the life of a close friend who self-identifies as trans, Pallotta has recorded a rich reflection on friendship and drawn new potential landscapes of intimacy by portraying this ineffable relationship as "a process of coexistence through doing and thinking . . . a process of association that remains open as to what or whom may partake in it,"[13] a process that can foster the joy of solidarity through quiet everyday subversions.

Notes

1. This essay is a thoroughly revised and expanded version of a digital project that Stella Gonzalez completed in a class I taught in fall 2020 at Colby

College: "Geographies of R/existence: '70s Liberation Movements in Italy." Gonzalez, a double major in art history and American studies, and minor in Italian studies, graduated in 2022.

2. These reflections refer to Pallotta's description of her photographic work; see Pallotta, "Porpora," accessed May 10, 2021, https://www.linapallotta.net/porpora/.

3. Pallotta, "Porpora."

4. This is a text used for the panels of the exhibit *Porpora* and that Pallotta shared with us via email.

5. Sasha Roseneil, "Foregrounding Friendship: Feminist Pasts, Feminist Futures," in *Handbook of Gender and Women's Studies*, eds. Kathy Davis, Mary Evans, and Judith Lorber (London: Sage, 2006), 323.

6. Robyn Wiegman and Elizabeth A. Wilson, "Introduction: Antinormativity's Queer Conventions," *differences: A Journal of Feminist Cultural Studies* 26.1 (2015): 11.

7. Here we are drawing on Leela Gandhi's reflection on friendship in *Affective Communities: Anticolonial Thought, Fin-de-Siècle Radicalism, and the Politics of Friendship* (Durham, NC: Duke University Press, 2006), 17.

8. Gandhi, *Affective Communities*, 26.

9. We asked Pallotta about the exact date; she thinks the photo was probably taken in 1999 but is not completely sure (private conversation with the authors).

10. Porpora Marcasciano, *L'aurora delle trans cattive: Storie, sguardi e vissuti della mia generazione transgender* (Rome: Alegre, 2018), "Marcellona." When not otherwise indicated, translations from the original Italian are ours.

11. Marcasciano, *L'aurora delle trans cattive*, "Marcellona."

12. Marcasciano, "Marcellona."

13. Celine Condorelli, "Notes on Friendship," *Mousse* 32 (2012): 224.

References

Condorelli, Celine. "Notes on Friendship." *Mousse* 32 (2012): 222–27.
Gandhi, Leela. *Affective Communities: Anticolonial Thought, Fin-de-Siècle Radicalism, and the Politics of Friendship*. Durham, NC: Duke University Press, 2006.
Marcasciano, Porpora. *L'aurora delle trans cattive: Storie, sguardi e vissuti della mia generazione transgender*. Rome: Alegre, 2018. iBooks.
Pallotta, Lina. *Lina Pallotta*. https://www.linapallotta.net.
———. *Porpora*. Rome: Officine Fotografiche, 2019.
Roseneil, Sasha. "Foregrounding Friendship: Feminist Pasts, Feminist Futures." In *Handbook of Gender and Women's Studies*, edited by Kathy Davis, Mary Evans, and Judith Lorber, 322–41. London: Sage, 2006.
Wiegman, Robyn, and Elizabeth A. Wilson. "Introduction: Antinormativity's Queer Conventions." *differences: A Journal of Feminist Cultural Studies* 26.1 (2015): 1–25.

TRANSITIONS ACROSS THE OCEAN

PART 7

ITALIAN MIGRATION AND QUEER ROOTS

Chapter 19

Michela Griffo

"Io sono sangue": I Am Blood, or the Stonewall Story from the Perspective of an Italian American Lesbian

SUMMER MINERVA

In the context of our volume, Summer Minerva thought it was relevant, or rather necessary, to include Michela Griffo's story because it brings forward yet another site of Italian culture, but within a very unexpected place. Summer met Michela through their work with the Generations Project, an intergenerational storytelling organization, started in New York City. An artist, as well as a prominent figure in the fight for women's and gay civil rights, Michela has a commanding but warm presence and a sharp wit. Although Summer had heard this story before at an LGBTQ+ Italian American storytelling event that they produced, they contacted Michela again via phone, to have her tell it again so they could get any and all questions answered that still lingered. The following is a distilled third-person account of how Michela Griffo, a descendant of Italian immigrants, like the Italian mafia of her time, was able to advance the human rights struggle of her lesbian and gay community.

Michela Griffo grew up at a time in Italian American history where descendants of Italy in this country were considered low on the privilege totem. Her mother emigrated to the US at the age of twelve from Bergamo and went right to upstate New York—Buffalo. Michela grew up in Rochester, however. Michela recounts that as she was growing up, Rochester was a site of intense conflict between ethnic and racial groups, as well as home to the first so-called race riot in the United States, in 1964. Not only were Blacks being discriminated against, there was also antagonism between the Irish, Italians, and Polish, who all lived in clans around their Catholic churches (Italian services were usually held in the basements, with the Irish on top). Rochester, according to Michela, was a restricted town, and people were expected to live around *their kind*. The Italians were relegated to a part of town that was older, more decrepit. Michela had the privilege of being raised in a nicer part of town in spite of being Italian, a "WASP enclave," because her father was a well-known surgeon. The discrimination that Michela faced as an Italian American in schooling was very pronounced, though. The school was 99 percent Irish Catholic, and it was assumed by her teachers that all the Italian students were not as smart as the others, so, in spite of being "brilliant" as Michela put it, she was initially put on a non-college, secretarial track.

Michela's family had ties to the mafia. Her uncle was Joe Valenti, a famous mob boss, who upon arriving in the States looked for work in the construction business, which was predominantly owned by the Irish. According to Michela, the Irish at the time, looking down on the Italians, considering them "colored," refused to give them any work. So, according to Michela, Valenti took it upon himself to start his own construction business with some other Italian immigrants and also destroy all the Irish-owned current construction projects in process, to assert their dominance. "I knew about political power and anyone could be bought. The mafia knew how to buy people. And that's why they got away with a lot," Michela explained.

When Michela was a baby, famous mob boss Stefano Magaddino held her in his arms, to pose for a picture. Magaddino was considered the *capo di tutti capi* (head of all heads) and would run his illegal dealings with all of the crime families around the major cities in the United States. Even though there was tangential crime around Michela, her immediate, nuclear family was not involved. She was sixteen when she left Rochester to move to New York City's Greenwich Village, and her family ties to the mafia ended up influencing her prominent role in the struggle for LGBTQ+ rights.

"Once I found out that the gay bars were run by the mafia, I had no fear. I really was angry that it was *my* people that were running these bars that were so abusive." Michela Griffo didn't need to go to Kooky's more than a couple times before realizing that the way she and her other gay friends were being treated there was just not right. Kooky's was one of many New York City's Greenwich Village Stonewall-era bars catering to homosexuals that were owned and operated by the Italian mafia. "Kooky's was on Seventh Ave between Sixth and Seventh Streets, Sea Colony was on Eighth Avenue between Jane and West Fourth, and Gianni's was on Nineteenth Street between Sixth and Fifth Avenues," Michela recounted to me about the most prominent lesbian spaces at that time, traveling in her mind's eye to these long-lost spaces.

Going to Kooky's was somewhat of a degrading experience for the gay women who sought sanctuary there. At that time in New York City's history, gay bars were illegal. It was illegal for same-sex couples to dance with one another; it was illegal to wear the clothing that felt most in alignment with one's gender identity if their gender was outside the norm. Places like Kooky's attracted homosexuals because, even though the owner of the bar was not known for being particularly warm to her clientele, it was still a place where gay people could go to be together. "Kooky [the owner] was a real bitch," Michela remarked. "She would go around and stick her finger in everyone's drink and tell them the drink was too warm and that they needed to buy another. And those drinks were not cheap!" The resentment that Michela had for this maltreatment still lingered in her voice.

These bars would get raided by the police, often, and the clientele caught in the act of anything considered homosexual behavior or cross-dressing would be taken, often violently, to jail. The mafia would pay the police to leave the bar, and, after the police would leave, the bar would promptly reopen. But this was not the way Michela wanted to love her fellow women and socialize. Michela and the other members of the Gay Liberation Front (GLF) were fed up with this kind of treatment. They were determined to find a way for gay people to enjoy socializing with one another without putting more money into the mafia coin purse. They decided to make their own gatherings, dances, hosted by the GLF, with all of the money collected going back to the cause for gay civil rights. It was decided that because she and her friend Flavia Rando spoke Italian, they would be responsible for organizing and distributing leaflets at these mafia-owned spaces to promote their own dances.

Michela knew that she needed to be discreet in promoting GLF's events, as she would be directly responsible for siphoning clientele and profit away from the mafia. Having been exposed to the mafia at a young age, Michela knew what kind of violence she was putting herself at risk for. But, for her liberation, it was worth it. Michela knew that it was her Italianness that put her at an advantage in dealing with the mafiosi. Although Flavia was Sicilian and could speak in dialect, Michela's Italian was more typical of the north of Italy, where her mother was from. Michela would take one side of the block, and Flavia, the other. As partygoers descended upon Kooky's from the various subway stations, they would be intercepted by Michela and Flavia with fliers, promoting dances and gatherings in which gay attendees could have fun, without dealing with the homophobia and corruption rampant at pre-existing lesbian mainstays. They were promoting an environment that was truly for the gay and gender-variant community, and *by* the gay and gender-variant community.

Every now and then, gangsters patrolling their turf would spot Michela and Flavia handing out the fliers—their attempts at discretion were not always so successful. As soon as they were approached by a goon, they would make a run for it, screaming *"Non mi toccare! Io sono sangue!,"* meaning, "Don't touch me, I'm blood!" "They didn't expect us to be speaking in Italian," Michela recounted. "But when we did, they were surprised. They didn't know who we were. We could have been [mafia crime boss] Carlo Gambino's daughters for all they knew!"

As time went on, Michela and the GLF's attempts at growing their dances were becoming more and more successful. Most of the clientele who had been patrons at the mafia-owned bars were now attending the GLF functions instead. The mafia's counter-attempts at threatening and chasing Michela down the streets were no match for her sheer tenacity, will, and vision for a future in which LGBT+ would not need to be who they are in the shadows of illicit spaces. Somehow, though, the mafia found out about the GLF dances.

"They came up the stairs, we were having our [Gay Liberation Front] dance. By now, Kooky's down the street was empty on a Saturday night because all the girls got the fliers [and came to the GLF dance instead]. The mafia got a hold of the fliers as well, apparently." Michela took me to a horrifying reckoning with the mafia with her detailed account of what happened when the mafiosi appeared at one of the dances. "I'm standing at the top of this long staircase. The door would open up, I'd be there with the money box to greet everyone, get their two dollars or whatever, give them a ticket for a beer. I saw the door open and the flash of the silver gun. I didn't miss a beat. I slam the money box down and turn around—Donna Gottschalk was standing right behind me—I said, 'Shove [the money] in a garbage bag and run it down the back stairs as fast as you can!' And she began running down the stairs with that." Michela acted quickly and was as "cool as a cucumber" when the mafiosi made it up to the top of the stairs to retrieve the money they believed was rightfully theirs. "Can I help you, gentlemen?" Michela asked sweetly.

They responded with, "We want the money. Where's the money?!" and called her "every name: bitch, stugotz . . . cunt." Michela, in her sweet performative tone, responded with, "Well, I don't charge any money, these dances are free."

They responded angrily, "What about the liquor? Don't you charge for that?" "No, we don't have any liquor," Michela told them. With a chuckle, Michela explained, "I was lying through my teeth because we had been illegally selling beer. They started sauntering around the party with their guns. Suddenly they go up to Martha Shelley, and they say, 'Do you know who we are?' and so Martha—she's terrific—she says, no, and I don't *care* who you are. Do you know who *we* are? We're the Gay Liberation Front." According to Michela, that was all the mafiosi needed to hear. "They turned and just went down the stairs. I shouted down the stairs at them, 'Next time, bring your sister!' " The party that night raged on, and over the next few months, GLF dances started happening at more and more places around the Village. One by one, all of the illicit bars were closed down, and more and more safe spaces for the LGBT+ community were created.

Michela shared about how much more urgent it was for lesbians at that time to have safe spaces where they could go and meet one another, because the gay men were able to go to the pier and parks to hook up and have dates. "We couldn't just go and hook up with our girlfriends behind a bush, like the men could," Michela shared. The combination of the urgency of the situation and Michela's blend of Italianness, Americanness, womanhood, and lesbian identities is what positioned her to be the person to raise the flag of victory against the mafia in this case.

Chapter 20

What Does It Mean for the Italian American Community to be Trans?

Frances Rose Subbiondo, Erin Ferrentino,
Liz Mariani, Summer Minerva, and Liana Cusmano

This is the question that Summer Minerva asked to fellow Italian American and Italian Canadian LGBTQ+ activists and emerging artists in May 2021, inviting them to reflect on their shared cultural experiences. A selection of their answers was collected in this chapter. These texts voice the inner conflict and creative potential of second- and third-generation migrants who feel deeply tied to their Italian identity—its language, traditions, food, and family history—but do not fit, or openly challenge, the gendered stereotypes and heteronormative models associated with this heritage. Italian American and Italian Canadian queer people elaborate on how they have repurposed their memories and traumas into spaces for personal healing and community-building. Through different styles and genres, Frances Rose Subbiondo, Erin Ferrentino, Liz Mariani, Summer Minerva, and Liana Cusmano grapple with their Italianness, while raising compelling questions about the intersections of gender diversity and Italian American identity.

Arbors of Hanging Fruit

Frances Rose Subbiondo

My story begins well before i[1] was born, in a four-family duplex in the Flatlands—Brooklyn—on East Fifty-Third Street. Imagine an *earlier Brooklyn*—a time which saw only four houses standing, total, on the four blocks that contained my family's "tomato garden." In the 1920s, my Sicilian & Neapolitan forebears built an extended family house here, where an ever-shifting number of my ancestors & relations lived at any given moment (though somewhere around twenty-seven of them). With most of the square block undeveloped, its interior garden was fed a steady diet of steer manure & kitchen scraps, which in time grew grapes for the family wine, herbs for the family table, eggs, chickens, and so much more, in addition to the featured tomatoes that stayed so viscerally held in my grandmother's memory, more than eight decades later.

This humble place served as an incubator for my family's individual & collective American dreams. Here, my family with the four surnames—all stemming from the matriarch of the home, my Grandma's *Nonna* Rose—found & made a place where they could be together and support one another through hardship & sacrifice. There, they achieved a kind of success that had been systematically denied to them & their kin—first, through literally millennia of dynastic conquest, and then through the imperial machinations of the newly-formed Italian state. Two to three generations before my family emigrated, Neapolitans & Sicilians saw their societies conquered again, this time by northern Italians. Their kin were murdered and robbed of their wealth, their industry, their already-fractured sovereignty, access to education, and so much more—as Italy began its modern age of empire building at home.

New York City, *America*, represented a profound hope for my family & so many more—for themselves and for future generations. It not only offered a pathway out of abject poverty, it also allowed families to actually dream of success & greatness. The American dream was their reality. As they began to feel their slow, collective climb up from a place they knew to be some kind of bottom, the sparkly allure of the American dream only grew. Supporting this was a deep self-awareness of the true tenacity required, as a people facing brutal prejudice, to literally pave the streets of their new home, that they learned upon their arrival—so the adage at Ellis Island goes—were not actually paved with gold (as had been promised), nor paved at all, and indeed, they were the ones who were *expected* to pave them [deep breath].

The huge, shared basement kitchen of both my father's & my grandmother's youth featured a concrete dining table that sat thirty, cast in place by my grandmother's many uncles "in the trades." This was a place that I visited mostly just once a year, on Easter morning, on our way from New Jersey to my grandparents' apartment in the [Greenwich] Village. On these select visits of my youth to the basement kitchen on Fifty-Third Street, it felt clear to me that even when altogether, the family that did remain shared only whispers of the shouts that tales told once abounded in that space. For example, I tried to imagine the legendary Christmas parties that saw a hundred or more friends & relatives gathered in that very same kitchen. I tried unsuccessfully to fill in the gaps between the quiet, lonely life that i felt there in that basement, and the radiant hearth that, in a different age, baked & ate twenty-four loaves of bread, three times per week, for years upon years—led by a matriarch that saved & repurposed even the cloth of the sacks in which the flour arrived, for use by the family.

Contained in those many years in between were generations of striving within the dream—and then separation. By the time I was born in Bay Ridge, my relations in the house on Fifty-Third Street had mostly found at least some measures of success & self-sufficiency and journeyed down divergent paths, with smaller & smaller family constellations—most of them allying themselves with the standard geographies of the time & today still: Westchester, Long Island, Manhattan, New Jersey. Only a few stayed in Brooklyn.

Meanwhile, in the shadow of this family legacy of thinning connectivity, I grew to understand that the underpinnings of the American dream that my family held (and still holds) so dear grew from stolen land & multiple genocides. I also came to understand that wealth *collected* by folks at the top & in the middle effectively also means wealth *hoarded*—made possible only through land theft & resale, four hundred years of African enslavement (& its modern analogs), ruthless imperialism, and utterly pervasive, racist socioeconomic structures. Conveniently for those holding the wealth, these forces also excel at keeping social groups & peoples' movements divided—who might otherwise see fit to redistribute said wealth. Collectively, Italians & Sicilians, after a harsh welcome in the US, were eventually offered a trade, culturally—to occupy a mid-level caste within a brutal social hierarchy—in exchange for helping to hold up that very system. As my awareness grew, so too did my simmering discontent with the world, both as it is and as it continues to be presented and portrayed. The simmer became a boil, and, like a pasta pot with the lid on, I bubbled over & flowed out, unwilling to be restrained by the closed container that I was told was my (& the!) only choice. My queerness & transness have remained perhaps the most enduring forces in my life that seem to hold open portals of discovery & curiosity and drive the *interrogation of everything*.

Despite ubiquitous clues that the world is sick, and that a different approach to life on Earth is needed, my family of origin, largely, remains devoted to the myth of the American dream. They ignore the similarities between the forces of empire that drove our ancestors out of Sicily more than a century ago, to those that continue to outsource the costs of reckless profiteering from which they now benefit. They believe in the dream because, arguably, it did produce the relative comforts in which most of them live. They believe that through hard work anyone can be successful, and that the world could possibly be okay if we all kept on as is. Founded, though, as it was on murder, rape, pillage, and ecocide, the American dream, to me & so, so many more, has been an American nightmare from the start, rebranded. My adult life has been spent mostly trying to figure out how to live a whole life in protest—how to resist a system about which, seemingly, few in my family have been willing even to entertain critiques of—let alone join in challenging.

It was amongst queer & trans people that I found resonant & tonic affirmation of these feelings—amidst groups with collective identities that, at least in part, transcend religion, ethnicity, class, place, and time. I flower(ed) in queer community and indeed have been leveraging the tools, confidence, and stamina i glean(ed) wherein, to grow the cultural change work that now forms the fabric of much of my life. After many years, my family's insistence that there exists only the one "reality" was supplanted in my life by a conviction that there are more like *countless realities*, in the eyes & hearts of countless beholders, and, moreover, that any attempt to reduce them to one probably rises up from power & privilege. This belief unfurled over an at times slow & awkward coming-of-age spent quietly listening to and observing the world around me. With queer & trans people, i found kin who similarly had to break out of the many shells that were created to limit our expression since birth [deep breath].

Meanwhile, about ten years ago, i lost my dad—and then my grandma two weeks later. At the time, i lived with her, still five blocks from where she was born, doing my best to connect her with vital flows & younger people in the city. In the forested metaphor of my life, the falling of these giants cast both tumult & light upon the forest floor, where i grew in wait. With my grandmother's passing, so too passed my reason to live in New York City. With both this clarity and a sublimely-timed invitation to live with queer chosen faemily in Philadelphia, i left the city of my birth also, for a new, fully immersive queer life.

For clarity—and hints of the deeper journey—i'll share that New York City for me then was a *return*—and not a continual home. Along the way (after Jersey), i experienced my growth horizons expand—and my education round—as i lived & learned on the South Coast (Houston, Texas), and then the West (the Bay Area). Spiraling thereafter to Philadelphia, landing into *my first queer home*, i continued to cultivate a life *in service* and in protest of a system that recalcitrantly disregards life. Consistently choosing to live collectively, i found meaningful & joyful work in the realm of *community food*. Almost four years ago, my mate Acorn & i bought a house with an advance on an inheritance from my dad's passing. We sought to explore & practice together a realm that we had come to know so much more about through queer & trans communities. This *radical hospitality* represents a deep expansion of the concept of family as i knew it growing up and arises culturally from an abject need for home, from those too often denied it. *Whoever you are, whatever your expression, is welcome here.*

Our journeys on this path saw our awareness levels continue to grow as we felt surrounded by dedicated practitioners, all honing our individual & collective practices of *liberation*. We cultivated deeper & deeper relationships across lines of race, class, & culture. Naturally, there were (and continue to be) beautiful lessons—and hard lessons too, as our sociopolitical-economic analysis sharpened at its own uneven pace—in the context of the culturally & physically violent urban landscape [deep breath]. Ever keen to leverage our privilege to collective advantage, and to discern ways of being on Earth that both reflect our values, and meaningfully advance the cause of liberation, my mate, Acorn, & i hatched an intention—born of a vision, and birthed through loving friendships.

In short, we would offer our home in Philadelphia—a place in which we had invested great care, intention, and building for the future—to Black, Brown, and Indigenous beloveds. They would continue to make it the queer community hearth space that it remains destined to be, as we transplant ourselves to a spiritual home & a life on land, amongst an extended "family" community. *All parties involved* share dreams of home, of radically inclusive family, of gardens, of connection to land & place, and strong practices of love, magic, & justice.

My heart's longing trains toward *connection to place*, even as i feel in my own family's story, a lifting of our roots from the closest place we had to a homeland on this side of the ocean. Meanwhile, even if they hadn't left the city, the Brooklyn of today is a different place than the one that saw my family's coming of age in this country. For example, a beloved neighborhood grocer allowed my grandmother's grandmother to accrue years of debt to procure pantry staples through the Depression so that her large family could eat. I do not mean to insinuate that nice things no longer happen in Brooklyn. I do though mean that the identifying city of my family's US roots continues to be both a warning & a shining example of what can happen to a *place* under siege by rampant capitalism & the complex of forces that drive gentrification. Indeed these changes can occur in a "New York minute."

Flash forward to southwest Philadelphia—*Chingsessing, Lenapehoking*. To me, the place remains a sweet dream in my mind's eye & heart—a diverse, queer (!), human-scaled, bike-able, "more affordable" neighborhood with awesome overlapping networks of community and lots of tree-cover. All-told, this description is not dissimilar to the Brooklyn of my parents' youth. Acorn & i made the place our own and invested deeply our life-forces here. Meanwhile, many of the folks in our historically Black neighborhood—who actually carry the somatic & intergenerational memory, the physical meaning of living in the neighborhood for their whole lives—now struggle to remain in place. The struggle is real! The forces of gentrification are violent. I personally have been witness to gentrification-wrought *fatalities* in our neighborhood. It is with painful irony that i add that some of the forces driving hardest right now these trends in Philadelphia are New Yorkers—presumably endeavoring to escape the mean crucible of capitalism in one place, while literally driving it in another. So it goes [deep breath].

To me, it simply does not feel more important that *my* family be able to live & work here than it does for the folks whose families have been here for generations—and, importantly, who want to remain in place (unlike most of my family from Brooklyn, who chose to leave). So, we have entrusted the care of our extended-*faemily* home[2]—the one with the now-renovated community kitchen(!) (think the basement kitchen in Brooklyn with updated appliances & better light!), the good heat, and the soon-to-be solar-paneled rooftop (!)—into the loving hands of Black, Brown, and Indigenous community food workers, artists, and activists. And soon, we will sign over the deed of the home into a cooperative entity of their design & creation. Our intention is to remove the home, permanently, from the speculative housing market and to complete this magical working—at once a ritual and a material, social, political, and economic anti-gentrification direct action [deep breath].

With these actions, we consciously choose to carry with us—and continue to cultivate—my family's real legacies of love, care, food, devotion and more . . . while *co*-allocating the financial wealth they accumulated and the experience of a stable home place to families that have been systematically denied the accumulation of such wealth & stability. We do so as partners in this work—together determining how to move these resources and how to share this story. We acknowledge, and feel viscerally, the painful impacts of witnessing a neighborhood being stripped of its history through gentrification, as descendants of white families, whose wealth & access to privilege allowed them to escape to the suburbs decades ago, now come back en masse, with that same wealth grown [deep breath]. Dis*place*ment is violence—driving out the families who have been here all along, working hard—and together—since their own Great Migration—holding it down, through thick and, often, very thin.

Meanwhile, nine months ago, we welcomed home to us a bundle of light, love, and joy named Salvia Hope, or *Salviatore Spiranza*. Four months later, echoing some tangent of my own family's immigration pattern, i drove a truck of our family's distilled worldly possessions into *N'Dakinna* ("the Dawn Land"), also known as central Vermont. I delivered said belongings into the center of a web of landed communities that, in so many ways, already feels like family to us, and into a region that has felt like a spiritual home for some time. I offer the place name in the indigenous language of the *Abenaki* people to underscore that this place will never truly be ours either. This is part of a collective wound of a settler-colonial inheritance [deep breath].

I offer this prayer: may we live here respectfully and practice humbly at learning to live according to the natural instructions of this place, as the *Abenaki* have been doing in the region for over twelve thousand years—while helping to repair these ancient cultural wounds of separation and to help build Indigenous sovereignty [deep breath].

Through myriad senses of disconnection (from *place*, from Earth, from ancestors, from ourselves), i carry a bittersweet knowing that all people & life still need to be able to live *somewhere*. What then to do within the context of a common cultural truth that many of us can never go home again? Perhaps it is because *home,* as we or our families knew it—or perhaps never knew it—is not there anymore, or was simply figmented in the family imagination, or because the "old countries" are no longer old—or won't have us back, or because our connections to them feel more ancient than present, more lost than able to be found. Have any people on Earth *not* been adversely impacted by empire building? Most of Europe, for example, has been reeling from brutal conquest & domination since Ancient Greece, Rome, or well before. This trauma goes deep and routinely casts long, cold, retraumatizing shadows in the world today. And so, in response, we practice coming together for warmth and cultivating a belief in our eternal welcome, as *life on Earth.*

Our family carried with us to *N'Dakinna* a warm relic of cloth from the house on Fifty-Third Street—from the Old Country called *Brooklyn*—a soft piece of a wheat flour sack, the likes of which were always repurposed or upcycled after the family's bread was baked. Through its touch, we can offer our babe Salvia a physical connection to a land & time that feels almost otherworldly—when the value of a simple piece of fabric was known, felt, & cherished by their Great-Great-Great Grandma Rose, born *ni Sicilia*, in the late 1800s. Meanwhile, in *Lenapehoking*, we leave in our wake a *faemily*-kitchen, within a *faemily* house, for another, dear extended family—one not given nearly the number of opportunities that my still-hard-scrabbling Sicilian & southern Italian family had in this country, starting one hundred years ago.

I offer another prayer: may the aroma of bread baking for their extended families fill that kitchen as well—and may that nourishment fuel the bodies, minds, and spirits of those *doing the most* [deep breath].

What i feel most sure about is that, not unlike my forebears in Brooklyn, i'm in it for the arbors of hanging fruit, endless tomatoes, the connection to Earth for Salvia & our whole *faemily*, the woody plants, the herbs, and the chickens to whom we may offer the bread that falls to the ground—with the short-form prayer of *sacro pane* upon our lips. We know too that we carry with us now & always the wealth of our love, a child called Hope, and an apparently queer & trans Italo-Sicilian American dream of the better world our hearts know is possible.

Grazie. Grazie. Grazie.
Gloria. Gloria. Gloria [deep breath].

As a Kid I Saw my Father on Sundays

Erin Ferrentino

As a kid, I saw my father on Sundays. He would take my brother and I to our grandparent's house in Bloomfield, New Jersey. Nanny would be in the kitchen in her terrycloth slippers, browning *braciole* and pork bones, cigarette dangling out of her mouth and directly over the pot of red gravy. The men would stand around in the front yard in their too-white sneakers, shooting the shit. Jimmy Clementi, Joey Angello, and my father, Nicky Ferrentino. Gay men were faggots and fudgepackers. Trans people were sick puppies. People of color were "moolies," a derogatory term that loosely translates to "eggplant-colored" in Italian. One of them might be watering the driveway—a ritual I don't understand to this day. The others would posture themselves, legs at a wide stance, rubbing their thick, callused hands together, gold watches glinting in the early afternoon sun. Men were king. Women served. "Go tell your mother we're knocking boots tonight," my father would tell me when he came around on the odd holiday.

Female sexuality was invisible. Lesbianism simply did not exist. Transness was reserved for binary male-to-female women, but rest-assured they were just fairies in drag. I could not conceive of who I was because I was given no mirror with which to view myself. My desires swirled around foam-lipped eddies of some secret inner fantasy world going nowhere, endlessly spiraling downwards. I constantly observed the men and women around me for cues on how to hold myself, what to say, where to put my body when. In private, I mashed my barbies together, forcing them to have crude and violent sex. I stole my brother's clothing. I compulsively masturbated and it sickened me. I was sure my only salvation was to grow up, to find a man to love me and keep me.

Surprising to few, including myself I suppose, when it came time to find a man to love me and keep me, I balked. I jolted my fiancé a mere thirty days before we were to wed. Instead, I booked a one-way ticket to Naples. I found refuge in the city where decades prior my family fled to avoid starvation and disease. My heart swelled and ached at how familiar it all was—*la nonna* calling out "oof maddone" on the street corner, the kissing and face-slapping among men, the San Marzano tomatoes on every shelf. I hid away and tried to make sense of myself, my sexuality, what had transpired. The irony that I chose to do this in a largely homo- and transphobic city is not lost on me. Naples happened to be the last place I felt truly home, regardless of the conservative creed. It is also a city full of lust, desire, death, and raw human experience unabashedly on display. Sometimes you have to go all the way around the block to get back home.

I did eventually come out to my father, some two years after my time in Naples. "I've known for years," his wife reassured me. "You run through men like water," she said. "I don't care," my father responded too quickly. "You're gay. I'm gay. Your brother is gay." My brother and father are in fact not gay, which threw me off for a second. But maybe this was his way of telling me that we were family, that we all had secrets, and we were all a little freaky. I didn't skip a beat however, afraid of what would surface in the silence. "I know, I know," I said, "but it's still a scary thing to tell you, after twenty-eight years."

Here in America, I am often considered "the most Italian person" many people know. In Italy, I am strictly American. In my home, I am a nonbinary dyke. In the eyes of my family, I am a woman, a daughter, a "lesbian" at very best. The in-between is a warm, watery place. The transition can be confusing and painful. Other times it feels like floating, like opening your eyes underwater, unsure of which direction is up, unsure of where the light is streaming from.

Dove siamo? The Conversation with Death

Liz Mariani

day uno—I walk with my dead self—*Death*—next to me everywhere we go. We harmonize as the day breaks because the air is sweet.
day due—It feels like a meal to wake up again. Yet—still—like a consistent lover you bring me death on a plate in a cup to my hands. You tell me to drink. You demand I partake. I refuse and spill your metal water into the casual measurements of these living hips because we've made it this far. We have made it this far. Because we are alive.
    We don't sleep. We skip a day.
day tre never exists.
day quattro—She calls herself *Mortality* now but she's still not dead. I know she's the lover determined to suck me me dry—to trace the aura of my clit with her tongue. But these orgasms in your mouth are not yours to claim. I can do this on my own. I can do this on my own.
day cinque—The government is here again. They want me to sign papers declaring—*This is my old body. This is how you will remember me* but this is not who I am.
    *A duality surfaces: Into our wardrunk bleed, the rivers are filling with oil.
    The rivers are filling with oil.
    The rivers are filling with oil.
day sei—My lawyer says I don't have to sign your papers. I know who I am this century and the last and the one before that and the one before that and the one before that and the one one one *note: It's not my fault you don't know who you are.*

Don't project on us your murderous slow-moving maniacal bureaucracies. I know governments like I know cisgender men.
I know governments like I know white people.
I know fear and scrambling.

day cinque—*Ora*—You lean in. You tell me stories layered in small talk. I pretend to listen. You warn me about any sort of fortified inflection. You tell me it could kill my heart.

day sette—All I can hear are my great great grandmother's birthing songs 120 years away. Finally—I hear you ask—ripping the walls from our faces—I hear you ask, *Where are we? Dove siamo?*

I explain

When I can't find you, you're nowhere.
When you can't find me, you're everywhere.

You remind us in our dreams.
We pop up like prairie dogs at 3 a.m.
You tell us these are the things we could say when we feel death funneling in. *It pulls like a drain. It swims like the gurling pandemic like the sinking mare like the canyons Venice whistles about.*

day otto—You fold. You have become an outhouse of envy. A subterfuge of molded marble. Of gaslit granite. You're close.
You start to ask yourself questions.

Are we an army of empaths? A security force of punctured survivors? The loosened locks of people who learned not to hold to their tongues? The escaped spouses of palpable fahrenheits?

day zero—It's hot. You know there is no escape from America. You also know you've never left Italia but when you think of shame—in this country—it is delivered to your door minutes later.

day nove—All the frayed *speranza* is officially lost. This is a clear case of belonging to any family, any family, any family at all.
It calls for the reaching and asks—*Can you live? Will you live? Are you living?*
Yes—*I can live. Yes*—*I will live. Yes*—*I am living.*
Sono viva.

Pertenezza

Summer Minerva

Le Mani della Mia Nonna

Old country secrets are in my Nonna's hands[3]
Inscriptions on her palms are tickets to the motherland

Transportations to belonging on not stolen Earth
Her *pomodori*, basil and *melanzane* grew from more than just dirt.
The roots of my Nonna's garden go back to Naples
Her impoverished but happy family spending hours around a table
Belonging, the tribe, fiery hot emotion
Then suddenly serving capitalism across the vast blue ocean.
Goodfellas and Godfathers could never connect me to my roots
They lie, glorify men, and make a mockery to boot.
But, they taught you something, so you thought.
No sorry, that was just an American *paesan'* experience, packaged to be bought.
Bought and sold like the bodies of immigrants to start a new life
Though, we are all indigenous somewhere, right?
Bound to the factories and fields in this foreign land,
Still though, my belonging is contained in my Nonna's hand.
Hands holding howls of dogs, holding tears from falling down
I sogni della mia nonna were never allowed around
There was no room for this *donna emigrante* female
Brought here for her breasts and womb-damned to a jail
A familiar jail for women under masculine control
Her choices dictated by the fallacy of constructed gender roles.
She was misinformed, thinking she'd come to be free
But, like the house and car, was a piece of property.
She grew *un albero di fichi* in her tiny urban backyard
That she spoke to some nights under the stars
Not spoke, cried to "*portami a casa,* take me home"
Sobbing, weeping to the maiden, mother and crone.
The years of shattered dreams passed on and she proudly shepherded in 15 new lives
Still though, counts down the days that she will die
At 89 years old, my Nonna's hands
Are my only connection to our ancestor's land.

Summer Within

As a little faerie born into a working-class Italian American family on Staten Island, New York, I had this subliminal yet ever present sense that I did not quite fit in. I was immersed in a culture in which the more I could perform masculinity, the more successful I could be. I was not very good at this game, nor did I try very hard to be.

At family parties, the women would cook and clean while the men would play poker, boldly reminding each other of their superiority, based on the trophies they received decades ago as successful high school athletes. When I looked at my Italian American family, or to our few cultural references portrayed in the media like *The Sopranos*, I could not see how I, a bubbly intellectual girly boy, could be my full self and *also* be Italian American. My few glimpses into the mirror of my ancestral culture came from glorified crime families on television, and a blue-collar culture that seemed to value pragmatism and blood family above all. I was an enigma to myself. *I can't be gay*, I remember thinking as an adolescent. *I'm Italian*.

Not Italian like Nonna, though. Nonna was a *real* Italian—recipes, house dresses, rosary beads, and all. Not a caricature like one you might find on television or a cartoon on a pizza box. She was my maternal grandmother—my only living relative to be born in Italy. Nonna came over to Brooklyn in the 1950s as a twenty-something bride, recently married to my grandfather who was an American, living in Nonna's small town outside of Naples. She spoke *napolitan'* dialect mixed with English—she never wasted her time learning standard Italian.

I remember when I asked her opinion about what language I should study in school, Italian or Spanish, she said Spanish. "What you gonna learn Italian for?" she asked me in her familiar aggravated tone.

I took the cue and chose Spanish.

Her casting away of the closest thing to my ancestral language that I knew may have been my first cue that the whole world around me was open to explore, that I didn't need to pay any attention at all to the Italian part of my identity. I didn't see myself in Italian America. Home was not to be found in it. I set out to find a place in the world, or a culture, or perhaps a lover that could give me that feeling of home that I never could quite taste.

Leaving Staten Island totally on my own to go to college in Miami at the age of seventeen, without knowing another human, and adjusting relatively easefully to this new culture showed me that the world truly was my big proverbial queer oyster. There was a drop of fear in my heart as I left home for college, as no one else in my family had ever done it before. Even as a small child, though, my dream had always been to live in a dorm, study abroad, travel the world. This decision to study so far away from "home" was all I needed to break the travel seal. Over those next four years, I traveled to five continents, lived for months in various countries, and mastered Spanish as well as Portuguese. After college, because of a sizable amount of Catholic guilt that I accrued for having spent so much time traveling the world and away from "home" over my global wanderings, I decided to move back to New York and pursue a career in education, one of the few acceptable Italian American professions. This new, very structured, and difficult job as a special education teacher had its perks. Aside from creating a real positive impact on the students I served, teaching gave me the coin and time off I needed to continue to look for myself out in the world. I dove deeply into different Eastern spiritualities like Japanese Buddhism and became a certified yoga instructor. I fell in love with the dances of the African diaspora and began performing in a West African dance troupe. I went to Haiti to learn about the music and ritual of the Voudon tradition. My Italianness was a symbol for my relationship to my family, and since I was becoming more and more globally oriented, I prioritized little time to connect with my blood. Instead, I was on a journey of becoming nationless. I was a solo floating queer, and at every moment I could find, I traveled through the world looking for home—in the form of cultural identity, in the form of friendship, in the form of the kind of passionate, fleeting romantic love that can happen when we feel completely untethered to the world around us. I found that certain places that I had never been to before felt more like home than the home I grew up in. Each place showed me a new possibility for who I could be, who I could evolve into. As I explored other cultures, with my prominent nose, olive skin, wavy sun-kissed brown hair, and an Italian last name, I was often spoken to in Italian, before English or whatever native language was present. I couldn't deny my DNA's roots. And somehow, in spite of how I physically appeared, my Italianness had become a totally irrelevant part of my identity. It represented some small world in which my queer identity and gender fluidity had no place. A world of patriarchal values and limited imagination, an Italian American world where I just could not be me.

And, still, there was always a knocking at the door of my heart as I danced to those African drumbeats around campfires. The knocking begged me to come home to Italy. Eventually, in 2011, I opened the door.

∽

Setting foot in Napoli felt like a family reunion but with no one I actually knew. It was familiar, in the most literal sense, with all of the dynamic paradoxes that *familiar* might involve. It was an orderly chaos, a very closed openness. The men turned me on, but also intimidated me—not an unfamiliar experience for me. Every single older woman looked like my grandmother. Every middle-aged woman, my mother.

    I made the two-hour bus trip east of Napoli to Avellino, the biggest city near Nonna's town, where her nephew Augusto picked me up to bring me to Cesinali. I had only ever heard of Augusto from my parents, who last saw him in the 1970s when he came to visit New York. Augusto drove me through the Apennine mountains, on roads that my mother told me about when Nonna and Poppy saved all their money to make a family trip back here when they were all children. Roads that, at that time, were made of dirt and gravel, trodden by people on their way to and from their tiny mountaintop villages to bigger towns, cities, and American dreams. Now, the smooth pavement under the car made for a ride that featured this idyllic countryside in all directions: swirling clouds, snowcapped mountains, farmland, and olive trees as we wound around and around and around, to Cesinali, so that I could taste this site of profound ancestral history, to look into the eyes of my blood people, to meet my Nonna's only other living blood family, aside from us.

    When we arrived at the house, my two aunts, Zia Donina and Zia Gerarda, were sitting there together. With Gerarda's face shape, and hair texture, and deep blue eyes, she was an almost exact replica of Nonna. What was drastically different about her though was her aura, her energy level, her mood, which felt light and joyful, pure and unmarred, shining through her pronounced smile. She was so enthusiastic and brimming with love as she hugged me and looked into my overstimulated and emotional eyes. I soon understood that she wasn't totally sure which out of my Nonna's four daughters was my mother, or who I was exactly. It didn't seem to matter. She loved on me the same. Thankfully, a cousin appeared just in time to help with the translating—the Spanish and Portuguese that I had studied for years could get me only so far. I explained that Silvana was my mother. "Ah! Silvana!" she said smiling, and recounted a quick story that I understood because of her animated gesturing and facial expressions. This story was one that I heard the other side of, many times, the one of my mother visiting as a young girl and causing a stir in the town by sticking her tongue out to tease one of the boys.

    Before long, I was being taken by the hand and brought inside the house. I realized that Zia Gerarda was wearing the same style of house dress that Nonna, a seamstress, would make, cotton, flowing, and floral. Their palatial marble home was kept cool and dark, to prevent the sun's heat from penetrating. Mirrors and mementos were everywhere. I was brought into the kitchen, where the other family members were, all with sunshine pouring from their eyes and smiles on their faces. Plenty of wine was involved. And we were all excited! I was their *cugino* from *América*. The food started coming right as I sat down, so much food, so many courses, and we all found the joy in attempting to gather the drips of drabs of meaning from what the other one was saying.

Later that night, my cousin Annalisa, the one who translated for me, and Zia Gerarda guided me around this small town of a few hundred inhabitants, paraded me like a prized mozzarella, and attempted to teach me about the town's big feast that was in full swing, for their patron saint, San Rocco. It brought me back to the "Italian feasts" that I would go to in Brooklyn, as a child with my parents and later as a teenager with my older sister and her friends. This feast was much smaller than the ones we'd go to in Brooklyn but had similar lighting and food items. Popular Italian music pumped through the speakers in both places. People were here to celebrate and gather, like they did in Brooklyn. I felt myself on edge with the feeling that a homophobic or transphobic slur might be thrown at me, or someone might point and laugh at me, the way they did when I was a teenager, walking through these festivals with my sister who was being courted by guidos and thugs alike. That harassment never came though, just smiles and curiosity about my sojourn from *América* and relationship to this small town.

My cousins woke me up early the next day and drove us to a *funiculare*, which transported us past a layer of clouds to a colossal Roman cathedral. I was told that was Il Santuario di Montevergine, the site of annual on-foot pilgrimages of Nonna and her parents and siblings. They ushered me into a tiny chapel, on the side of the gigantic church, to a painting of Mary, holding Jesus. Mamma Schiavona was her name. I found out later, among many other things, that this name translates as Slave Mother. She was a Black Madonna. We stayed for a prayer and continued our final day together, as a sparkle of hope gleamed that I, myself, could be establishing my own relationship to this place, to my southern Italian blood.

When I got back to New York after this voyage, I found that the people in my family who didn't typically have any interest in hearing about my travels suddenly were drawn in and actually asked questions about what I saw and did. My aunts all wanted to know if I visited this part of the town or saw that person. My travel, for the first time, had meaning to them. This was a novel feeling that my soul, longing for home, cherished.

I continued to travel to distant places and dance ritualistically around a fire all night. I would hear the drums, and powerful energies would take over me. Movements that I learned in my various classes seemed to become relevant and manifest as sensual earthen worship. I was being asked to perform in New York at various venues. I danced at Carnival in Salvador, Brazil. I danced with a queer Voudon community in Jacmel, Haiti. My soul felt flashes of home in these places. But there was always a burning question of the equivalent of these folk dances from the land of my blood ancestors. Were there folk dances that honored Mother Earth in southern Italy? Did they still exist?

In 2016, while surfing the Internet, I happened upon a workshop being taught at the Italian American museum in Little Italy called Drums and Dances of Illumination. It was a Southern Italian folk dance and drumming workshop with Alessandra Belloni. I instantly reserved my spot. The workshop gave me hope that what I imagined I was looking for was *actually* to be found. The workshop gave me a basic introduction to some of the dances from Nonna's region. We learned a song in Neapolitan dialect to invoke the power of the sun. The call to Italy resounded again, five years after my initial stint, this time with Alessandra to various sacred sites of the Black Madonna around southern Italy. I offered the last couple thousand dollars that I had in my savings to this quest, and went.

One of the places that we visited was the Santuario di Montevergine, the same mountaintop sanctuary that my cousins took me to when I visited in 2011. I had heard that this Madonna was a Black Madonna, but I didn't really know what that meant or why she was considered *nera*. I learned that her grayish skin rendered her "black," and that the Black Madonnas are seen as the most compassionate and powerfully loving patronesses in matriarchal southern Italian Marian Catholicism. Mamma Schiavona is known to answer prayers quickly and to be a protector of those who have been cast out of society, particularly a group of people called the *femminielli*.

I didn't hear about *femminielli* for the first time at the sanctuary, though. It was on the street in Napoli by a deranged mendicant. Or maybe it was a street musician who finished his set and went around, collecting coins in his cap. I wrote the word in my list of Italian words to look up when I got back to the hotel. I discovered that, while places in Italy may use that word to degrade an effeminate or gay man, in Neapolitan culture, to be a *femminiello* signifies a sacred role within the devotional practices of Mamma Schiavona and other Madonnas in the region of Campania. A *femminiello* is a sacred third gender group, much like the Native American *two-spirit* or Indian *hijra*.

They hold stories, songs, dances, and traditional rituals that dance the line between the sacred and profane. They dress as brides and are married off to their town's most eligible bachelors, give birth to large brown phalluses, are considered lucky and call off the numbers in a Neapolitan version of bingo called *tombola*. They've always been there. Some say that their existence can be traced back to pre-Christian times, when worship of Cybele, a Phrygian earth goddess, was most popular. Cybele had a following of a third gender group called the Galli, who would castrate themselves in order to join Cybele's cult and become priestesses. It is said that today's Santuario di Montevergine sits where Cybele's temple used to be over a thousand years ago. The *femminielli* are the evidence of us: us trans people, us nonbinary people, us gay people, us faeries, us queer people, here since antiquity.

The more I learned about the *femminielli*, the more I could see myself reflected in my ancestry. At some point along the cultural migration from Naples to New York, the immigrants left the legacy of the *femminielli* behind. They were still around, though, in Napoli, continuing their magic.

I began to follow the tracks of the *femminielli*, looking for them everywhere. I knew their wisdom could hold the key to demystifying who I am—both queer and of Italian descent.

They reflected back the layers of my identity, introducing me as a *femminiello* born in America.

This journey of finding my people inside of my ancestral traditions was a search for belonging. I was looking for a place to belong, a way to know that I did belong. And, I was blessed enough to be able to not just find my people but integrate with them, build relationships with them, and make art with them. People often ask me about my thoughts on gender and identity now, after undergoing this rebirthing process, which has involved countless sleepless nights, financial instability, heartbreak, and tons of internal resistance. What I found is that the closer I look at myself through the lens of pre-existing notions of identity, the harder it becomes to really see myself. I needed to go to Italy to meet the *femminielli*, as a queer Italian American, of course, and yes, I found a rich music and dance and performance tradition, but the question looms. Will I ever actually be a *femminiello*, walking through the cobblestone streets of Napoli performing as *Commedia dell'arte* characters or singing classical Neapolitan songs? And would I need to be a *femminiello* in order to find that feeling of belonging? After excavating my depths through this process and examining my cultural context, I no longer feel that I need to surround myself only with people *like me* in some categorical way in order to find belonging. I feel that belonging is a gift that we give to each other and permission that we give to ourselves. If we zoom in enough, or zoom out enough, on any human, we will see that we are all related. As that young faerie on Staten Island, needing to find my tribe and community and finding it impossible to do so, I longed to hear that no matter my interests or behavior or feelings, I would be loved and a place would always be there for me. Now, as an adult, I can look at the little child within me, and lift her up, and remind her of her place in the world. I would tell her, "The home you are looking for is inside of you. Be free to meander across the globe, or through time and space, until you find it."

A Call from the Ancestors

Tammurriata, deep earth song
Nacchere in hand
Eyes on sparkling eyes
Bella figliola, bella figliola
Black beautiful and big
Daughter of the Earth
Si chiama Rosa
Rosa
On the land
On sacred sanctuary
The tambourine sounds
in loop
Bellowing ancient voice booms above as
Nonna's face emerges from our fire
Shadows dance on her hook nose
We circle around as we fly
Rotations, Chases
Locking hearts
Locking legs
Inseminating with the seed
Of love with every clack
Nacchere Nacchere
Locked eyes
Revolving in orbit

Blurred pairs of dancers
Switchboards of DNA alight
Memory in the bones
in the body
in the blood
in the wild spirit
La Tammurriata
Evviva La Tammurriata

Boyfriend

Liana Cusmano

My grandmother is tiny and old and Italian and she knows just enough English to ask me: "So, you have boyfriend?"[4] The Italian word for boyfriend is the same as the Italian word for fiancé. And so the best way for my grandmother to strike out in the dark, to sidestep linguistic landmines, is to use English words that are as unfamiliar to her as the concept of being with someone even when you have no intention of marrying them. Every time my grandmother and I have a conversation about a boyfriend I know that each of us will be reminded of just how many things we don't understand. We are as close as two people can be when they are part of one family that is split between two completely different worlds, like two different recipes of pasta sauce, like the arrabbiata of two different generations.

My grandmother doesn't understand why I can't just do things the way she did and the way her mother did and the way my mother did, as if we were all objects on an assembly line instead of items crafted by hand. When I tell my grandmother that I have something important to say to her, she asks me if I'm pregnant. When I tell her that I'm bisexual, when I tell her about men and women and people and about how much love I have to give, she says that she would have preferred it if I'd been pregnant.

My grandmother has always made me feel like I will always be more than enough. No small improvement stamped on a report card ever went unseen, no schoolyard grievance or petty workplace dispute was ever left unheard. But when I tell my grandmother that I am dating someone small, gorgeous, vegan, feminine, and Jewish, she groans like she can see the faraway specter of her healthy, bilingual great-grandchildren rapidly disappearing into nothingness. She doesn't see the simple elegance of my own devastation when she says, "Wouldn't it be better for each of you if you had a man, instead of one another? Wouldn't it be better for this girl if she had a man, instead of having you?"

When we broach the topic of the boyfriend, I start to believe that maybe there are exceptions, that the rules of my childhood no longer apply, that maybe not every feeling, big or small, is valid. It's only when we discuss the concept of the boyfriend that I understand that I will have to pick and choose which of my grandmother's words and thoughts and actions I will allow to affect me, because the alternative is to be fractured and splintered by her opinion on something she can't and doesn't and will never understand.

The words in my mouth are like stones in my pockets when I say, "Neither one of us wants a man right now, if we have chosen one another over every other man, woman, person, haven't we already proved that each of us is enough? Doesn't that prove that I am enough just as I am?"

My grandmother has told me that she loves me always, forever, without exception, with or without a boyfriend. I choose to believe her. That deadly distinction—between you are not enough and I love you anyway—is a twisted and double-edged reassurance that I would not accept from anybody else, but my grandmother is tiny and old and Italian and she loves me and she is mine. And this is all that matters, that love is what I pick and choose to remember when there is so much that still hurts and so much that I still don't understand. That love is all that matters, that love is a bridge that can be crossed even in translation.

Always.

My grandmother is tiny, and old, and Italian, and she barely speaks English. My grandmother chose to speak the standard language and drop her regional dialect when she emigrated from war-torn Seminara almost seventy years ago, because she didn't want anyone to think of her or her children as provincial, or uneducated, or uncultured. My grandmother doesn't know that this is code switching. She doesn't know that I perform my own version of this every time I visit her, and I pretend that I'm a woman.

My grandmother asks me why I have lost weight. She asks me how much money I earn. She asks me what directly translates to "Where are they? Where did you put them? Where do you keep them?" She looks at my flat chest in its new binder and men's clothes and I don't tell my grandmother that my breasts are right here, that I put them where no one can see them, that I keep them close to my chest. I never tell her the truth because to keep quiet is to preserve a relationship that we both treasure but that is subject to a generational gap where so many truths slip through our fingers and are lost. I don't tell my grandmother that eating is harder than it should ever have to be because even the food she cooks for me is no match for the mental illnesses I've inherited from her. I don't tell her that sometimes I perform poems about how much she loves me, and that sometimes the way she loves me makes it difficult for me to love myself. That because she loves me, she wants me to dress, speak, and behave according to rules that do not apply to me.

I don't get angry at her. I don't tell her that I like my breasts just fine. I don't tell her that, for reasons I can't always and shouldn't ever be compelled to explain, binding my breasts makes me feel more at home in my body than I do at my grandmother's house. And to tell her this when I know that she won't be able to code switch her way out of it, to wound her knowingly and on purpose, is not something I ever inherited from her.

My grandmother has taught me to do my best, always, to rinse out the sausage casing, always, to make time for myself, always—to add sugar to the tomato sauce, to try to remember everybody's birthday, to talk to your plants when you water them, to ask that kid alone at the park if his parents know where he is, to remember that my family loves me, always. It's because of my grandmother that I've been to the war-torn town she emigrated from almost seventy years ago and brought back my memories of her home, the place where she was born such a long time ago, before her eldest grandchild was ever even an idea. It's because of my grandmother that I am a person whose history spreads across space and time, that I can code switch my way out of a problem if I have to, that I learned what the rules were and decided I would not be bound by them. The type of binding I choose for myself is the only one that liberates me.

My grandmother asks me if I have a boyfriend. I wish I could tell her that sometimes, I am the boyfriend. I wish I could explain everything. I wish it could all be so easy as to choose rancour or rage. But this is not part of my inheritance. Even after everything, even after all this pain and all this hurt, each of us chooses love in our own way, every time, always.

Notes

1. Ed./n: The lowercase i and the ampersand (&), when used, are an intentional choice of the author.

2. Ed./n: The author uses the term *faemily* to designate her queer extended family.

3. Ed./n: *Pertenezza*: a word Minerva coined by combining two Italian terms, "pertinenza" (pertinence) and "appartenenza" (belonging). It evokes a meaningful sense of a belonging.

4. An earlier version of this text first appeared in *Transformations: The Italian Canadian Experience*, a project by the Toronto Catholic District School Board (TCDSB) and the National Congress of Italian Canadians (NCIC).

PART 8
NEW ITALIAN AMERICAN MIGRATIONS: BACK TO ITALY

Chapter 21

Summer Within

A Journey of Migration and Reconnection

DANILA CANNAMELA

This essay was inspired by the experience of witnessing the making of Summer Minerva's (her/their) debut film, *Summer Within*. The author watched some preliminary footage, the rough cut, and then different versions of the edited footage. Being involved in this creative process was her personal journey with a documentary film that, in recounting a milestone personal experience—Summer's encounter with the gender-variant community of the Neapolitan *femminielli* and her return to her Italian origins—is telling many other travel stories. Summer's journey is simultaneously the migration journey of their grandmother, the story of an Italian American community gathered in Staten Island, the identity struggle of a new generation of queer Italian Americans, and the love story born between fellow travelers. This essay explores the many narratives that emerge from Summer's counter-migration journey to Naples and discusses how the protagonist's investigation of their gender identity comes to trace a path toward self-narration, dialogue, and mutual understanding. Readers may gain more information about the film by visiting the film's official website, at www.summerwithinfilm.net.

The documentary film *Summer Within* (2023) is the story of Summer's migration journey from New York to Naples and then back to New York, in search of belonging. Their quest might be located at the missed intersection of cultures seemingly at odds: the rather conservative Italian American community of Staten Island, linked to Summer's Neapolitan heritage, and the progressive LGBTQ+ community that they eventually joined as a self-identified queer artist and performer. Between these clashing identities, the unexpected point of connection is the ancient gender-variant culture of the Neapolitan *femminielli*, who come to represent Summer's ancestors and a place for kinship in the present.

"What's this movie about?" we could not help but wonder after watching *Summer Within* many times—on our own, together, in its rough-cut versions, and then, finally, in its most recent edited cut.[1] The film, besides documenting a personal journey, raises broader questions on the possibility of pinpointing belonging as a specific place or as a final destination. The blurry situatedness of any sense of belonging is reminiscent of Lauren Berlant's observations on the ambiguous positionality of love and on its intrinsic potential to draw queer maps of desire: "The desire to become more than oneself, to become exchangeable, to become oriented toward a publicness that corresponds to an expanded interiority . . . so love queered marks an impossible desire for definition and for obfuscation, and a contradictory fear of the enigmatic and the clarified."[2] If belonging is ever found during Summer's quest, it is found within, in the borderless and constantly changing geographies of self-discovery that unfold from daring to reach oneself while mapping an "expanded interiority" that percolates into other territories. As typical of the documentary genre, the movie proceeds through a series of conversations—family members, strangers, lovers, and friends met on the road—that, in enabling Summer to better understand themself, also provide their interlocutors with the opportunity to confront the contradictions of their own paths. In its search for definitions that cannot help but remain precarious and enigmatic, the documentary succeeds in drawing people and stories that might seem distant, closer.

Interpreting *Summer Within* as a reflection on a collective and yet never-ending journey toward mutual listening, rather than as the retelling of a personal quest, is suggested by the visual motif of the sea that recurs throughout the movie, spanning the bay of Naples, the Atlantic Ocean, and the Long Island Sound. The marine scenes are often accompanied by soft and alluring background music, while Summer, dressed as a siren, is dancing on the seafront. This refrain is tied to the mythical story of the foundation of Naples: according to the legend, Megaride—the small island that constituted the first urban nucleus of the city—arose in the area where the body of the siren Parthenope dissolved into, and therefore shaped, the land.[3] The sirens were well known by southern Mediterranean people for their ability to bewitch sailors with their beautiful singing. Ulysses, on his journey back to Ithaca, was extremely curious to listen to the sirens' enchanting voices and, to avoid their curse, asked his travel companions to plug their ears with wax and tie him to the ship's mast.[4] Using this trick, he succeeded in appreciating the sirens' singing without jeopardizing his journey. Parthenope, extremely upset for failing to charm Ulysses, died of love, and her body still rests in the land of yearning and longing that bears her name.

What's this story about? Parthenope's story serves the purpose of a foundation myth, but at its core, it is a story of miscommunication. The legend is the retelling of a missed encounter and its aftermath. Parthenope and Ulysses's story hinges on a mutual curiosity and attraction that did not evolve into dialogue but only led to manipulative behaviors, deceit, and mourning. *Summer Within*, in returning to the myth of the siren and to her land, seems to envision alternative endings, where Ulysses, the traveler, dares to speak to the sirens, and the sirens dare to listen to the sailors, or where Ulysses defies the stereotypical imagery of the traveler and becomes a traveling siren. So, what's *this* story about? It is a story about challenging the ties that keep us fixed in our positions and moving together toward other possible narratives of belonging that are based on the liberating practices of giving voice and listening.

Summer Within is the story of a family of Italian American origins that, in different ways, is still struggling with figuring out what it means to embody a hyphenated identity and being part of a community without falling into cultural stereotypes. In the film, Summer's father, a man born in the US, who calls Staten Island home, recounts that he felt the need to alter his American accent to stress his Italian heritage. "I self-imposed my Italian accent," he admits, and he goes on to confess that he can barely speak any Italian, except for small talk—"Buongiorno," "che si dice?," "che fai?"—and a couple of swear words. To highlight the typical macho Italian-ness attached to that self-imposed accent, the conversation is filmed while the father is driving his van and conducting his business. As an Italian American man, he was expected to occupy the driver seat, lead his family, and be the breadwinner. The conversation leads Summer to a personal reflection about preset roles that their family imposed on them to keep their Italian traditions alive. Their given name, Anthony, is the name of their father, carried across time to foster the idea that "you are the copy of your father in the new generation." Thus, in order to remain tied to their family, Summer must remain Anthony, as the act of choosing a new name represents a rebellion against their parents' will, or more broadly, against a system that allows freedom only to those who observe its gendered rules and roles. Even if Summer's father explains that, in his view, belonging is the experience of living with those who we love, and enjoy life with them, he also implicitly affirms that being part of a community is not always a synonym of full acceptance: "I'm gonna still call you Anthony," he cuts it short. The name Anthony is a source of pain for Summer, but it is also what ties them to their heritage.

The question of the name returns in the conversation with their mother (Silvana). The setting—a neat kitchen, with audible background noises of a Netflix show that Summer's mom admits to having binge-watched—alludes to the place that a woman should occupy in a traditional Italian American household. The sequence begins with her helping Summer wear a dress: her bodily language immediately suggests closeness, hinting at her caring love and her capacity to understand, at least intuitively, her child's gender diversity. In some footage that was ultimately not included in the final version of the film, Silvana candidly stated that she had always known that Anthony was not going to self-identify as a (heteronormative) man. However, also her unconditional love struggles with letting go of Anthony and accepting what Summer wishes for: "I wanted to belong, but just as I am, as Summer." Their mother does not take any stance about the name change and purposefully avoids the topic, even when Summer teases her—"She calls me Summer, at times, when I remind her." Yet, belonging, for her child, might also mean hearing her voice uttering the name they chose.

This story of self-determination and unease resonates with the experiences of other authors gathered in this volume. In her poems, Giovanna Cristina Vivinetto put in verses her father's struggle with calling her with a feminine name. When she came out as trans, "his love wavered only for a few days / but it took two years / for him to learn the new name."[5] Her poetry grasps the ups and downs of a learning process that, as it happens with any new language, is never linear and inevitably exposes learners to hesitancy and vulnerability. Thus, even when, in public, Giovanna's father could finally say "my daughter," he was still not mastering many other new words, and occasionally, all his effort vanished when the wrong article, ending vowel, or noun slipped out of his mouth, making him blush: "In that moment, the father no longer / wished to be a father." Also Porpora Marcasciano, in a 2021 documentary about her life, *Porpora*, touches on the difficulty for her family members, especially her sister Filomena, to accept the change in language that accompanied her gender transition.[6] To allow viewers to experience the complexity of this struggle, the film features some 1990s footage from Porpora's private archive: Filomena is filming her children with Porpora, during the Christmas holidays. It is striking that, addressing her two children, Filomena insists on referring to Porpora in the masculine—as uncle Domenico—even though, at that time, Porpora was undergoing hormonal therapy and self-identified as a trans woman. In this scene, the use of masculine nouns and pronouns is particularly clashing, even though for Filomena, like for Giovanna's father and Summer's parents, those gendered words are perhaps only a way to hold on to something of their past that they fear might get lost for good. What is at stake, then, is a family history—a sense of belonging—that is forged by names.

If every family is rooted in shared origins and memories, *Summer Within* is in particular the story of *nonna*, Summer's grandmother, who can be considered a sort of co-protagonist. A fading and yet extremely vivid figure, she migrated from a little village near Naples in the Apennine Mountains called Cesinali to Brooklyn, in the 1950s. Nonna's fuzzy and spotted memories, altered by dementia, reconstruct an American dream that was animated by a search for freedom but eventually generated equally confining boundaries on the other side of the Atlantic. Her coercion into marriage with an American-born Italian "was [her] only way out," and she soon found herself trapped into the role of "Italian mother"—great caregiver, exceptional cook, good housewife—that she played within her conservative and Catholic Italian American community. Nonna's constant worry, throughout the movie, about feeding other people, about the empty fridge, or about Summer who is too thin—"you don't have breasts," she notices, pointing at Summer who is wearing a feminine outfit—are very indicative of a struggle for survival and belonging that her generation never overcame. "I don't come to America no more," she concludes, in her broken English. Turning this bitter statement into the testament of what their grandmother might still wish for them, Summer embraces her counter-migration journey to Italy as the possibility to be free. At a dancing class in New York, they come to learn about the Neapolitan *femminielli* and decide to explore if this gender-variant community might represent a link between gender diversity and their Italian heritage. In the movie, nonna is a maternal figure in which love, care, curiosity for a different world, and determination to find freedom coalesce. Likewise, for Summer, going back to the birthplace, to the "myth of origin" of her grandmother, entails searching for a sense of belonging that can be grounding and liberating at once.

It is no coincidence that in nonna's native place, Summer falls in love with Adam, the filmmaking companion who is sharing this self-discovery journey with them. Adam becomes a compassionate mirror, someone who observes Summer diving into their nonna's past to give meaning to their present. However, like Parthenope, Summer-the-siren is rejected by her beloved, yet unlike in the Neapolitan legend, they learn to cope with rejection through the healing process of crafting their own foundation story.

In the land of Parthenope, Summer's search for their origins intersects with her investigation of the city's history and culture of gender nonconformity. The Neapolitan *femminielli*, as the term literally indicates, are males at birth who behave as "women in training" and their centuries-long history is strictly interconnected to the syncretic culture that has shaped their land.[7] In exploring who the *femminielli* were and still are, Summer wonders if a traveler from the US can ever self-identify as a *femminiello*. In the context of Naples, the movie's visual refrain to the siren is enriched with other nuances of meaning. Besides being the protagonist of Naples's foundation myth, Parthenope is a hybrid creature that embodies the possibility to simultaneously belong to two worlds: the sea and the earth. In the Neapolitan gender-variant community, the image of the siren has been proudly recast into an identity symbol. This is due to the community's strong attachment to the city and its mythical origins but also to the fact that trans women feel an analogy between the siren's bodily appearance and their bodies. The body of the siren, at least in one of its best-known versions, is part woman and part "fish"; playing on the fact that the term "fish" in the Neapolitan dialect has also the meaning of "penis," trans women refer to themselves as sirens, since they are "half woman and half fish."[8]

Summer begins her search for the mythical sirens of their origin and their gender from the house of an old aunt, zia Gerarda, one of nonna's sisters. Despite being very welcoming, zia Gerarda feels quite uncomfortable when her American nephew self-identifies as a *femminiello*. When asked about who the *femminielli* are, she initially says, "*Chinni saccio*" (I don't know), and then awkwardly explains that they are men who live and act like women. The performative feminine role of the *femminielli* is an aspect that many of Summer's interviewees stress. Yet, a few of them—often artists—tend to idealize the role that these unique figures across genders have played in Neapolitan society. For example, an artisan of nativity scenes—we should briefly recall that Naples has a long-standing Christmas tradition of handmade nativities—remarks that nativity scenes have captured the city's multifaceted culture and the beauty of its diversity. Figurines of the *femminielli* find a place in Neapolitan nativities because diversity had a place in Neapolitan culture and society. The artist also adds that the *femminielli* were such an integral part of family life to be entrusted with the role of caregiver. Singer Marcello Colasurdo and then performer Ciro/Ciretta Cascina further expand on this narrative of belonging from a historical and mythological perspective. Through their testimonies, viewers learn that the *femminielli* are figures tied to ancient pastoral traditions that originated from the local cult of Cybele, an earth goddess who was worshipped in the area of Anatolia and then included in the Ancient Greek and Latin pantheon.[9] Through a process of religious syncretism, this Pagan deity came to overlap with the Christian figure of the Virgin Mary and became the *Madonna nera* (Black Madonna), or *Mamma Schiavona* (Mother Slave), venerated in the abbacy of Montevergine. As Colasurdo clarifies, this feminine divinity embodied the earth—female and mother—and the chants and dances that are still performed at the abbacy during the religious festivity of Candelora (Candlemas) derive from propitiatory rituals of fertility: "*State rint e vierno fora*" ("Summer come in, winter go out"), he sings to demonstrate his point. Yet, in these ancient cultures, invoking fertility was not necessarily related to the modern heteronormative order; as he concludes: "To be homosexual, lesbian, gay belongs to nature" and, in this collective celebration of nature that has conflated with a Christian celebration, people with different gender identities and sexual orientations are unified by their prayers to Mamma Schiavona.

Still today, the pilgrimage to Montevergine is a key moment of community building. The *femminielli*, or more broadly gender nonconforming people who identify with the *femminielli* identity, gather together for the annual visit to the Black Madonna, and the pilgrimage becomes the celebration of feeling at home by celebrating diversity. This narrative of inclusion and communal belonging develops through a scene in which Ciro/Ciretta is performing in front of an audience, at a local cultural center. Her dances at the rhythm of drums and her attire—heavy makeup, garish jewels, richly embroidered tunic, and colorful veils—evoke ancient rituals in honor of Cybele. Ciro/Ciretta is proudly embodying a past in which the *femminielli* were believed to be different for being closer to, or possessed by, the divine. As she emphatically puts it: "Cybele, who was Mother Earth had as her priests . . . guess who? The *femminielli*!" Here Ciro/Ciretta is referring to the fact that the *femminielli* might indeed be the heirs of the priests of Cybele, the Galli, who self-castrated during orgiastic rituals and dances.

Despite being fascinated by narratives of inclusion where past and present, archaic and modern, mythical tales and history intertwine, Summer-the-traveler is not easily enchanted by the songs of the sirens surrounding them. Their documentary strives to dig deeper than the performative facade of Neapolitan culture and engage in a more realistic investigation of what the day-to-day life of the *femminielli* might have been. A question, in particular, is driving Summer's inquiry: What did love mean for the *femminielli*? The conversation with Loredana Rossi, a Neapolitan trans activist who self-identifies as a *femmenella*, is a revelatory moment, in which the beauty of a mythical past that is still reenacted clashes with stories of social marginalization and harsh survival that had somewhat seeped out from the embarrassment of *zia* Gerarda. Loredana welcomes Summer in her house, a humble apartment in a working-class building of Naples downtown, where the movie *Ieri, oggi, domani* (*Yesterday, Today and Tomorrow*, 1963), starring Sofia Loren, was filmed. "Sofia Loren is the mother of all the *femminielli*," Loredana jokes, hinting at the fact that the hyperfeminine beauty of the actress has represented a model for the Neapolitan gender-variant community. The reference to Sofia Loren is visually emphasized by close-ups of Loredana's pictures, in which she poses as a pinup from the 1950s and 1960s. Yet, as she openly shares with Summer, her femininity came with a price. Up to the early 2000s, many *femminielli*, after being kicked out from their families, did not have any other option than resorting to prostitution. As the montage shows, this subaltern and scandalous role is documented in Curzio Malaparte's book *La pelle* (*The Skin*, 1949), and in the 1981 film based on the novel, which briefly touches upon the secret, corrupted life of American soldiers stationed in Naples, at the end of WWII.

Loredana is one of the few who stood up against a system of exploitation—she likes to call herself a *battagliera* (warrior)—and has turned her gender diversity into a place-specific form of activism. In representing a Neapolitan gender-variant community that has obviously evolved and changed, her association (ATN [Associazione Transessuale Napoli]) is also preserving the typical traditions of *femminielli* culture. Later in the documentary, we see Loredana leading a pilgrimage to Montevergine, during the Candelora. On the bus, she starts to sing a hymn for the Black Madonna and then announces that the *femminielli* are on their way to the sacred mountain: "*Ué, Maronna ne', stamme sagliendo . . . 'e femmenell*." ("Ehi, Black Madonna, we're heading up, the femminielli!"). In this shared attempt to keep traditions alive and (re)connecting social change with ancient rituals, we can perhaps find a unifying perspective in Loredana's fight for civil rights and Ciro's artistic embracement of the *femminielli* unique heritage.[10] In the movie, it is Ciro who offers a possible way to interpret the incoherencies of belonging and marginalization that are inherent to the *femminielli*'s history. As she affirms, they have always suffered for not being recognized as lovers, and only during their visit to Mamma Schiavona they were acknowledged as people worthy of love. Only in that context—in that particular spacetime of celebration—their diversity truly turned into community. For Cascina the vibrant community experienced at Montevergine can inform everyday life; as she concludes, living and joyfully expressing one's diversity is possible if life is allowed to flow freely and is not regulated by a pre-imposed system that deems some people as outsiders.

Experimenting with new possible ways of building a sense of belonging involves creating one's foundation myth, like Parthenope, and daring to travel and to return, like Ulysses. *Summer Within* is indeed the story of many returns: to Summer's Neapolitan origins and back home, in the US; to their grandmother's past and back to their fading memories; to their Italian American family and their American queer community. Ulysses was not immediately recognized upon his return, but coming home eventually led to a key moment of anagnorisis, or of deeper acknowledgment by his family members and allies. Also Summer's return marks a crucial moment of recognition. The final sequence features some footage from a family gathering—people dining and hanging out together, lots of children running around: while these shots might recall a stereotypical image of the Italian American culture, Summer's voice-over explains that their family is finally starting to call them by their (chosen) name and "this feels right." The montage emphasizes this rediscovered sense of belonging: they initially appear on the right corner of the frame, their gaze directed toward their parents and family; then, we see them taking center stage wearing a tea dress, laughing and dancing in circles while holding a younger relative. They are recognized and acknowledged.

In the subsequent scene, the circle expands, and Summer is teaching a traditional Neapolitan *tammurriata* to a group of queer friends. They go over the meaning of the lyrics—summer in, winter out—and learn the moves of this folkdance, at the beat of castanets. A typical American setting, a basketball court surrounded by city buildings, turns into a place where a traditional dance from Italy is forged into an Italian American *and* queer collective ritual, through which an emerging community is building new practices of self-recognition. The movie ends with one last return: Summer goes back to the house of her grandmother, after her death, to collect some personal affects. They switch off the light on their way out. The light abruptly comes back in the last scene of the movie, set outside, in the mountains near Montevergine. Looking at the horizon, Summer is thinking about her late grandmother—"I'll be listening for you, nonna"—

and suddenly runs away, out of the frame, in new directions of "extended interiority," of "Summer within," that will open the way to new encounters and narrations. As the open sky that closes the movie suggests, it is this welcoming openness, rather than a sense of tight enclosure, that creates and recreates a sense of belonging.

Notes

1. This question is also a reference to a previous version of the film, which opened with a tight close-up of Summer's face, asking, "What's this movie about?"

2. Lauren Berlant, "Love, a Queer Feeling," in *Psychoanalysis and Homosexuality*, eds. Tim Dean and Christopher Lane (Chicago: University of Chicago Press, 2001), 443.

3. The legend of Parthenope is narrated in different versions and by different sources, one of the oldest being Apollonius Rhodius's *Argonautica*; for more details see https://www.treccani.it/enciclopedia/partenope. The film creatively readapts some of the legends and local folklore related to the siren.

4. Ulysses's encounter with the sirens is narrated in the Odyssey, book 12.

5. Giovanna Cristina Vivinetto, *Dolore minimo* (Novara: Interlinea, 2018), 121.

6. The movie was directed by Roberto Cannavò and co-produced by Associazione Humareels, Maxman Coop, and Bo Film.

7. On the *femminielli*, see chapter 5 of this book.

8. Marzia Mauriello, "La medicalizzazione dell'esperienza trans nel percorso per la 'riassegnazione chirurgica del sesso.' Una ricerca etnografica nella città di Napoli," *AM: Rivista della Società di Antropologia Medica*, no. 35–36 (2013): 301.

9. On the history of the *femminielli*, see in particular the essay of Nicola Sisci, Paolo Valerio, and Eugenio Zito in chapter 5; see also Summer Minerva's piece "Summer Within," in chapter 20.

10. On these two different positions, see the interview with Ciro Cascina and Loredana Rossi in chapter 7.

References

Berlant, Lauren. "Love, a Queer Feeling." In *Psychoanalysis and Homosexuality*, edited by Tim Dean and Christopher Lane, 432–51. Chicago: University of Chicago Press, 2001.

Cannavò, Roberto, director. *Porpora*. Bologna: Humareels, 2021.

Cavani, Liliana, director. *La pelle* (*The Skin*). Neuilly-sur-Seine: Gaumount Italia, 1981.

De Sica, Vittorio, director. *Ieri, oggi, domani*. Interfilm General, 1963.

Malaparte, Curzio. *The Skin*. Translated by David Moore. Evanston, IL: Marlboro Press, 1988.

Mauriello, Marzia. "La medicalizzazione dell'esperienza trans nel percorso per la 'riassegnazione chirurgica del sesso.' Una ricerca etnografica nella città di Napoli." *AM: Rivista della Società di Antropologia Medica*, no. 35–36 (2013): 279–308.

Vivinetto, Giovanna Cristina. *Dolore minimo*. Novara: Interlinea, 2018.

Zito, Eugenio, and Paolo Valerio, eds. *Femminielli: Corpo, Genere, Cultura*. Naples: Biblioteca Dante and Descartes, 2019.

Chapter 22

A Queer 'Talian Pilgrimage

SUMMER MINERVA

In the winter of 2019, Summer Minerva organized a pilgrimage to Naples called the Sacred Gender Collaboration, for a small group of queer and trans Italian American people. The goal was to reconnect with their southern Italian roots and rediscover the unknown past of their gender nonconforming ancestors—the Neapolitan *femminielli*—while engaging in a multiday community building experience. The weeklong trip included a variety of events: meetings with local *femminielli*, a healing ceremony at the geothermal baths near the Venus Temple in Baia, a tour of the historical quarters of downtown Naples, a visit to the *Cimitero delle Fontanelle*, and a celebration of the release of Marco Bertuzzi's book, which involved a *tombola* game and *tammurriata* dancing.[1] During the event, the group met with Ciro/Ciretta Cascina and Luigi DiCristo, the leaders of AFAN (Associazione Femmenell Antiche Napoletane [Association of Ancient Neapolitan Femmenell]).[2] The pilgrimage ended on February 2 with the Candelora, the festival of the Black Madonna, Mamma Schiavona, at the abbacy of Montevergine. On the final day of their *'talian* journey, the American *femminielli*—as the group came to be nicknamed—joined the Neapolitan gender-variant community for a goodbye party, with plenty of good food, wine, and folk dances.

In March 2019, upon its return to the US, the group hosted a reunion in Philadelphia (where one of the participants, Frances Rose Subbiondo, lived and ran a community supported kitchen) to discuss their shared experience within a larger community.[3] The conversation came to revolve around two main points: the struggle with "translating" the archaic microcosms of the Neapolitan *femminielli* into contemporary American "language," and the surprising ease with which they all connected with people, places, and traditions radically different from their own. These conflicting perspectives are addressed in the question that a person in the audience named Adam asked during the presentation: "The *femminielli* are dying out, it's not really a tradition that young southern Italians are identifying with. . . . That's maybe inevitable, but how do you feel yourself, as trying to unearth or exhume something that may be sinking into the earth?" Ultimately, the challenge that the group faced was understanding whether reviving their remote Neapolitan past could offer new ways to re-engage with their Italian heritage—a heritage that is fading away and that, historically, has not provided positive representations of queerness.

The following text is a short, edited version of some salient points that emerged during this group discussion.[4]

Rio: I went to Naples to see the likely departure point of my great-great-grandfather, Saverio. So, the fact that my sexual identity was going to be central to my trip to Italy was something unexpected, because, in my mind, my Italian Americanness, or rather my Sicilian Americanness, was completely disparate from my queerness. I just never imagined those things coming together. Being in Italy, and being gifted a rock out of the Tyrrhenian sea, heated by Mt. Vesuvius—that's with me, right now, in my coat—is my touchstone for how I connect back to what that place represents. But it's still hard to put this experience into actual words.

Wim: I know what you mean, Rio. There is a certain alignment that happened, an integration, that started to make sense . . . I mean, our group of queer Italian Americans could have been anywhere. But the fact that we were in a place that was such a *part* of us made it so transformational, because from there we could see where we came from, and now we can go further down our path of self-discovery. It was like going backwards in time to be fully in the present—and this feels weird because, in your twenties, you want to go anywhere but backwards! My family, my mother in particular, came to the States when she was four and immediately started assimilating into the American middle-class way of working. She came from Cassino . . . their whole culture was "work and pray." And that's pretty much how her life continued when she moved to the States. Anyways, there wasn't much Italian culture that came my way, or not until I started stepping outside of my comfort zone and I found the faeries. That's where we [Summer and I] connected. And so, it's a very interwoven web, now: us and the *femminielli* . . . [laughs].

Christopher: I was very grateful to have met Summer, when I did. We're both from Staten Island, also known as "Staten Italy." Our culture is usually portrayed in negative or stereotypical ways, like the *Jersey Shore*, just to give an example. But in Naples I saw the positive aspects, like being a family sitting at a table, that are run of the mill for Italian America. That's a central part of our culture, of our tradition of conviviality! It was really valuable to my identity, and very powerful, because it felt almost like belonging. I had never been to a place where I felt I fit in like that.

Antonella: I went on this trip to reconnect with my heritage and finally reconnect with all those "things" I have always felt distanced from. I was on the outside of my own Italian culture, because of my queerness, my gender, the way I feel the world. And all of us, at a certain point, have intuited from the (dominant) world that we are not accepted. So, to go back to a place where *that is—we are—accepted*, was an experience of reconnection. I rediscovered a very ancient way of being that has been there forever. I found that those spaces do exist for us, and there can be unity between the people that we met there and us. Our last night there, that party we threw, was something truly amazing . . . to see that there is a family on both sides of the ocean, that there is just more there to explore, was really powerful.

Rose: I resonated with this notion of there being a separation between my queerness and my ancestry, and to go to this place where queerness was clearly embedded into the culture of my ancestry was a powerful moment, really powerful, for me too. Ciro, for example, looked like someone who could be in my family: here's this elder *femminiello* who is so fabulous and so comfortable, confident in themselves and their life, their culture. And their culture is so old! Ancient! It seems so radical to ask someone to think about a world in which people can create together such a rich culture infused with spiritual practices. But it's not! These practices are just so much older than Christianity. And, to be face to face with Mamma Schiavona—that portrait in the chapel, up on the top of the mountain of Montevergine—there, I was so very clearly looking into the eyes of a goddess figure older than Mary, and older than Christ. She took the form of Mary because that was how and what made this image of a mother goddess palatable to the Catholics and Christians in charge at the time . . . but I kind of like the punk aesthetic of snapping my fingers and saying, "This is way older," and dial back the time knob so much that all of a sudden, the church is like . . . what?

But there is another aspect I'd like to highlight, and it's about the different possibilities for expressing one's gender diversity that Neapolitan and American culture provide. In the States, there's so little in the way of tradition holding queerness to anything. It's rather like flying free. I don't feel particularly limited by my queer experience here in the States. I can make of it, and have been making of it, that which I find resonant and often reflected in my community, or not. But there, in Naples, the traditions run so hard and strong, and, yes, there is a word for this third gender—*femminielli*—but this word could not define the gender of my partner, Acorn, for example. It's way tighter. It allows for fewer possibilities, in a way. So, we have medicine for one another—this is the message that I found a lot of resonance with. We can create our worlds, our perspectives and paradigms together as we go, and engage in relationships that we create together in novel and beautiful ways, and not feel limited by it. And, we all do come from somewhere, and those traditions are real, and deep, and they do offer roots, a deep feeling of roots. Roots. To it all. Which feels like a union of opposing forces and magic in the alchemy of the cultural milieus meeting.

Acorn: Going back to your reflection about tight notions of gender identities, Rose . . . some young Neapolitans are gravitating more towards Westernized English identities of queerness, for a vast variety of reasons. Also, now there are medical transitions that were not available in the past. So eventually some people started to realize, "I don't have to be a *femminiello*, I can just transition and be a woman!" At this point in time, people have all different relationships to this ancient identity, and what it means to them, and who is still a *femminiello* . . . it's such a complex realm! We shouldn't romanticize the *femminielli* and the femininity they embody, but rather account for the (trans)misogyny they're dealing with, the discrimination that they're dealing with, and how they maybe have few paths open to them, so they end up being sex workers whether they like it or not. It's a survival path. It's acceptable to be their client, but not acceptable to be them. Or, it's acceptable to exploit them, but not to be fair with them: *we don't want them in our neighborhood, so we're going to charge more rent, if they want to live here!*—this is a popular way of thinking in Naples. I just wanted to bring in that contradiction that, I think, women all over the world also deal with, of being sacred and uplifted and essential, but also, kind of derided for their femininity, and this is kind of an element of the healing work that needs to happen, kind of everywhere.

Summer: This contradiction has really upset me. In this culture—think of the entire *tammurriata* tradition at the feasts of the Black Madonna—they worship Mary way more than they do Jesus. Mary is this compassionate intermediary between humans and the divine. However, southern Italian culture tends to be extremely patriarchal and misogynistic, and it was always really strange to me how there could be all this veneration of the mother figure, the Madonna, and yet, actual real-life human women and feminized identities are confined to a much lower status, to much lower paying jobs; they don't receive the same opportunities and are not able to access education in the same way men can. However, I'd like to touch upon some other fascinating contradictions we witnessed, the fact, for example, that Roman Catholicism is so intertwined with preexisting pagan cultures. That's part of what's so intriguing about the figure of the Black Madonna: that she is most likely the Christian version of Cybele, and Cybele's consorts and priestesses were castrated people called the Galli.

Rio: Who voluntarily did this . . .

Summer: Yes, they did it so they could join the mysteries of Cybele and would become her devotees. So, on March 24, the day of the blood, the Galli would go into the square and the new initiations would happen. That would entail public castration: there would be a whole ritual ecstatic practice of spilling blood everywhere and flagellating and biting and then ultimately slicing off the testicles and sometimes also the penis and then hurling them into neighboring windows. We know the modern LGBTQ+ rights movement as something that started at the Stonewall in the 1960s, but we've been here. Forever. So, this is kind of reclaiming the place of that past. And tracing it. So that it's not something that's just imagined or created from nowhere. But it's something that's experienced and embraced and known and seen and lived and evidenced.

Rio: But let's return to our conversation about gendered norms . . . as somebody from the US, I found that I had a lot more permission to disregard what the gender norms were, and had a lot more agency to self-define than I imagine a queer person from Naples had. It was striking for me seeing that there were so many people who would present as femme, but they would rather self-identify as "he." It seemed to me that there wasn't as much of an ability to take the identity farther—more into themselves. Of course, I'm talking about a small cross-section of people I met and I don't claim to know the truth. I cannot speak for the collective. Just to say, it's really easy to rag on the US, but one of the privileges we do have here is the liberty to decide for ourselves how we define and how we present. And I don't know if that's as true in Naples.

Summer: Yes. But we should also add that word *femminiello* is something that is becoming of the past. It refers to something that is provincial. It's not something global. It's not something that's glamorous, or fabulous . . . it's not that at all. The cultural perception of this identity is like your weird aunt. You know? She's loveable, we love her, but she's weird, and it's cool. *Femminielli* were not gay men, and they were not trans women, they were something that was very specific to Neapolitan culture. They were male-assigned at birth but accentuated their femininity by enacting stereotypical feminine gestures and wearing feminine clothing. So, with the advent of biotechnologies, like hormones and surgeries, now, young people—as Rose said—would rather just use the technologies that are available to pass as women, or, as gay men, and be a part of our global gay culture. And who are the deities of global gay culture? Not Cybele-Mary, of course! There are goddesses also with global gay culture, like pop stars, and most of this contemporary "pantheon" comes from America. You know RuPaul, Lady Gaga, Madonna, Beyoncé: these are some of the goddesses of the global LGBTQ+ movement. It's very appealing for young people, in Naples, to be a part of something that is outside of their *province,* and also outside of the limitations of their *province,* by embracing the fantasy that the global LGBTQ+ movement presents or shows. Some neighborhoods in Naples or the small villages surrounding the city are a place where, when you walk down the street, everyone is paying attention to you. This is not New York, where people don't notice you. Everyone sees you and everyone notices, and everyone is involved in everyone's business, so there's no escaping other people in southern Italy.

Antonella: The formations of our contemporary LGBTQ+ identities are very intellectual, rather than spiritual, and they offer countless designations. On the contrary, Italy, I believe, is very much in love with the binary. They love a binary. They love that they can pin you down, left or right, you know what I mean? They want to know *where* you are. And if you are in between, they don't know what to do with you. There is some sense of comfort in this binary practice. As you said, Summer, they see you every day, in the community, and this is how they can connect to you, by being able to define you as this or that, to include you in the group. And you want to be included so you would just choose this or that. But, we came with all of these different identities, and, personally, I love to play with words and gender, as many of us do here. I'm a *transfemme muppet* you know, that's my gender, *muppet*! I just sort of roll up and show up with that identity, and that presence is obviously not something Neapolitans know what to do with. Still, the *femminielli* created a diverse space in their own unique way, even though they are exclusively perceived as female. Whereas we, American queer people, have this intellectual multiplicitous idea of gender that literally could be anything you could write on a wall. Any word you want to pick out of a pile. That's your gender. And we brought that idea to this (Italian) party! I remember this moment that is quite telling of the anxiety related to daring to be in the middle: I had been doing my eyes for the past few days that I was there and I was doing Alessandro's eyes, and we were talking, and this little quiet one came over, with these big old eyes, and these lovely little lashes, and he was so quiet and with his white knit sweatshirt, you know, very timid, and then he was like, "You, can you do my eyes?" And I was like, "Oh! The quiet one talked!" And I was like, "We'll do your eyes, *girl.*"

Summer: I'll add that it is not solely a matter of binaries. Trans women, even when they embrace a feminine identity, are highly marginalized in southern Italian culture. It's really hard for them to find work, and there's a long list of murders and identity-based violence that have happened. So, in general, it's not that a feminine-looking trans person walking down the street gets any kind of respect. I lived in Naples for four months, and there'd be a lot of staring, a lot of sexualization. At nighttime, once it would get dark, the men would come out of the shadows and say the dirtiest things and try to lure me to some strange places, some of which I went to. But mostly not [laughs]. So, we're highly sexualized and violated. If you can think about both sacred and profane, dancing a dance, that's what we are.

Antonella: And just to wrap up by carrying further the idea of the globalness of queerness, and its place in society, beyond local characterization . . . our joy and experience in life, to skip on the sidewalk instead of walking, to enjoy life in a different way than most—think the *femminielli* dancing and playing *tombola*—can perhaps remind people that there are different avenues and paths to their own lives, and that's maybe a *place* for us, of all cultures, from gay Black and POC people to trans to genderqueer. We all remind people that there is a joy to life and that sometimes to find that joy you need to go outside of the avenues that you think are present to you. And sometimes it can be really profane. Sometimes it can be very sacred. But, we remind them that both can exist depending on what path you want to take.

Notes

1. Marco Bertuzzi, *I femminielli: Il labile confine fra il sacro e l'umano* (Florence: Multimage, 2018). On *tombola* and *tammurriata*, see Part 2.

2. *Femmenell* is one of the possible spellings and pronunciations of the term *femminielli*. On this, see chapter 5.

3. This is a list of the participants, including a brief description of how they chose to self-identify during the meeting: Summer: thirty-one, transfemme, wearing an old house dress that she got from her grandmother; Acorn: the moderator, late twenties, transboi, blonde, queer crew cut, wide-eyed, and light-filled; Rose: mid-late thirties, transfemme, solid earthen creature with water/earth essence; Rio: mid-forties, queer gay cismale, bald with a black hood on, fiery; Wim: early twenties, femme, model-ish, quiet; Antonella: early thirties, transfemme with facial hair, earthy, and quick witted; Christopher: mid-thirties, transmasculine, very butch.

4. The full transcript and audio of this meeting is available on Summer Minerva's website (https://www.summerminerva.com). The version provided here has been edited throughout, to avoid repetitions with previous chapters and make the content more easily accessible for a broader readership while maintaining its informal and colloquial tone.

Conclusion

Paths for Future Exploration: Language, Situatedness, and Glocal Movements

DANILA CANNAMELA AND MARZIA MAURIELLO

Pierpaolo Pasolini's documentary film *Comizi d'amore* (*Love Talks*, 1965)—his scandalous conversations about sex and gender in the Italy of the mid-1960s—has served, in this volume, as the starting point of a counter-mapping that retraces the voices and meaningful stories of trans people, both within the Italian peninsula and along the routes of the Italian American diaspora. Returning one last time to this movie can help recap our journey and suggest paths for future investigation.

As we pointed out in the introduction, while filming *Comizi d'amore*, Pasolini could not help but leave "deviant" geographies unexplored so that with very few exceptions his exploration reflected the traditionalist and patriarchal views that his interviewees were willing to share. But in the final sequence of the movie, which features footage from a wedding, Pasolini briefly alludes to what remains unsaid in his love talks. He touches upon the issue of "merciless forgetfulness" and warns the couple on screen and his viewers of a silence that ultimately is defined by guilt. His wish for Tonino and Graziella is that they not fuel, through their marriage, a scripted cycle of obliviousness—a history that is "neither happy nor innocent"—but rather nourish their relationship with mutual curiosity and "awareness of their love." More than forty years later, trans activist Porpora Marcasciano has similarly stressed Pasolini's point about the importance of cultivating (self-)

awareness in order to shift dominant narratives that have informed history. In her introduction to *Elementi di critica trans* (*Elements of Trans Critiques*, 2010) she states, "When the narration of oneself is missing, one loses the meaning of things and cannot build awareness."[1] Marcasciano further explains that, in the absence of audible self-narratives, other stories have become overpowering so that for centuries the apparatus of "veteran-patriarchy" has used religion, science, and politics to establish normative codes or, to paraphrase Pasolini, to manipulate a history that is "neither happy, nor innocent." This volume has sought to turn blind spots into meaningful sites of storytelling and convert forgetfulness into collective awareness, intellectual curiosity, and openness to listen to alternative narratives. Our anthology might be considered one of the first attempts to amend a past of obliviousness by bringing to a broader Anglophone audience a corpus that encompasses stories rooted in the cultural syncretism of Italy and the unfolding narratives of Italian, Italian American, and Italian Canadian trans people who are forging new ways to reconnect with their cultural heritage.[2]

But what other routes could be explored to build awareness of gender diversity and foster a culture of self-affirmation that creates geographies of encounter across genders and cultures? As editors, we have discussed this question together, "starting" from our different embodied experiences, backgrounds, research interests, and, of course, geographic locations. Ultimately, our conversation has revolved around three main topics: the potential and limitations offered by the Italian language, the situatedness of gender variance within Italian history, and the discrepancies between local experiences and global calls for diversity and inclusion.

Developing linguistic awareness of gender diversity is a challenge that we have faced particularly during the process of translating Italian into English, and it is also a concern that the LGBTQ+ activists interviewed in this volume have voiced from different perspectives. Language is a powerful instrument that shapes the way we think and perceive the world, but it is also a site for potential change, or, in feminist terms, it is what keeps us anchored to our origins and can set us free.[3] Marcasciano emphasized this crucial nexus between anchoring words and liberating practices when she reminded the trans community that it is fundamental to rethink the words that "name us and that we use to name ourselves."[4] Yet, from a linguistic perspective, we might wonder what terms have been coined in order to tell new stories.

Italian, a Romance language that requires agreement in gender and number, presents some obvious limitations to subjectivities that do not fit squarely into a feminine–masculine dichotomy. In recent years, sociolinguist Vera Gheno has become one of the spokespersons for the need to craft more inclusive language that might better express gender differences, including those of gender nonconforming identities.[5] One of the issues is the use, still prescribed by standard Italian, of the universal masculine to refer to broader groups. Her proposal of employing the character schwa (ə) as a nonbinary ending, rather than symbols like @ or *, has the advantage of offering an option that is not uniquely graphic but also phonetic (the schwa has a nuanced sound, similar to the muffled final "e" of Neapolitan dialect).[6] However, as Gheno has often pointed out, the schwa is first and foremost an open invitation to dare to experiment with alternative linguistic paths, namely to turn words and sounds into a creative toolkit at a time in which Italian speakers have not yet found a unifying way to talk about gender diversity.

In September 2021, the Accademia della Crusca, a society of scholars of Italian linguistics and philology that is considered the (rather conservative) authority for research on Italian language, intervened in the debate with the article "Un asterisco sul genere" ("An asterisk on gender"). Paolo D'Achille opens this piece by remarking that grammatical gender should not be equated to the gender with which people self-identify.[7] To make his point, he discusses a few cases that illustrate this missed correspondence: feminine nouns like *guida* (guide), *sentinella* (sentinel), or *spia* (spy) have been typically used to designate male identities; in Italian inanimate objects are assigned either a masculine or a feminine gender, and the feminine pronoun *lei* ("she," but also formal "you") is used as a polite form across genders. However, D'Achille goes on to note that the ongoing debate about genders and sexualities has already produced actual linguistic transformations, testified to by the inclusions of terms like *omoaffettivo* (attracted to the same sex) or *transizionare* (to transition) in Italian lexicography. Still, D'Achille cannot help but express reservations about the use of schwa and reminds his readers that even the dialects featuring this phoneme maintain the binary distinction of grammatical gender.[8] In sum, Crusca has explicitly praised Italian speakers for paying attention to word choices in order to avoid linguistic sexism but has also cautioned people from forcing change at all costs upon a language that is based on two grammatical genders.

Another approach to the linguistic practices regarding gender binaries recognizes that, despite complying with grammatical categories and rules of agreement, many Italophone speakers might have already reframed their understanding of femininity and masculinity, and as a result those two categories are still in place but have shifted their meanings and created new possible intersections. This view resonates with the experience of Louis Moffa, who was interviewed by Molly Lipson in a 2021 article published in the *New York Times*, "How Language Classes Are Moving Past the Gender Binary." A teaching fellow in the Department of Italian at Columbia University, Moffa self-identifies as nonbinary (their pronouns are "he" and "they"). In their interview, they have surprisingly highlighted the potential of a binary language like Italian in undoing stereotypical gendered approaches. They explain how learning and eventually teaching Italian has offered a liberating experience for them, as it has allowed them to critically examine how gender binaries appear in the language. Referring to the practice of assigning gender to inanimate objects, Moffa says, "Instead of calling it masculine and feminine, you can just pick other polarities: light and dark, full and empty, round and square. It doesn't even really matter what it is!"[9] Ultimately "being able to teach the gendered nature of Italian grammar has given [them] the opportunity to be more fully seen and understood by [their] students, because gender can never remain implicit or unquestioned in [the] classroom." We can add that the language classroom can mark a space of inquiry where genders are analyzed and questioned, but also (re)discovered as grammatical forms that have undergone centuries of transformations. Many feminine and masculine nouns derive from Latin neuter nouns that in the evolution from vulgar Latin into Italian turned into invisible, but still historically retraceable, forms. Thus, even if Italian appears as a binary gendered language, it retains within its linguistic history the memory of nonbinary forms and of the many influences—not only Latin but also ancient Greek, Arabic, or ancient French, to mention a few—that have come to inform the linguistic diversity and countless regional varieties of spoken Italian.

If we turn to consider language as a medium and vehicle of representation, it is important to note that in the last few years different attempts have been made to generate a broader discourse about trans identities in Italy, spanning academic research, creative work, and activism. From the perspective of scholarship in Italian and Italian American studies, a growing number of publications in the interdisciplinary field of queer studies—a field that might encompass but does not always overlap with trans studies—showcases the increase interest in exploring and understanding gender variance within Italian culture.[10] Yet scholarly discussions might have (even inadvertently) contributed to tensions, and in some cases they have reproduced binary logics and divides between the ivory tower of academia and the lived experience of activism.[11] Furthermore, the geographies of Italian LGBTQ+ associations are often characterized, in their turn, by hyper-segmentation and internal frictions: historically, gay associations took over the leadership of the LGBTQ+ movement by marginalizing trans voices, and a few lesbian associations have traditionally embraced exclusive approaches based on biological sex.[12] Finally, even groups like Non una di meno (Not One Less), which are based on an inclusive transfeminist fight against patriarchal violence, have struggled in creating a cohesive environment that could unify different subjectivities and identities under a shared agenda.

Identity is a rugged territory that simultaneously encompasses and exceeds questions of genders. In giving voice to trans people who self-identify with Italian or Italian American culture, the geographies mapped in this volume have stressed the situatedness of the trans experience and highlighted that identities should always be situated within precise space and time coordinates.[13] Contexts become fundamental elements in the process of identity construction, which is affected by cultural and social factors that are historical and place-specific. Therefore, if gender in its multifaceted forms and expressions comes to represent one of the constitutive elements of individual identities, together with geographic, historical, cultural, and social elements, then the way genders are constituted and represented is affected by these seemingly external factors. It is indeed this mutual and inextricable entanglement of inner and outer narratives that comes into play in the stories of people and places gathered in this book.

But since these stories center identities that have been typically displaced on the margins of history and memory, a thorough analysis of the politics, ideologies, and practices that have determined how gender-variant identities were experienced (from the inside) and read (from the outside) becomes crucial to fully reconstruct an Italian cultural history that remains rather unknown. In a 2016 article, historian Stefania Voli voiced this gap in the collective memory, maintaining that despite there being a significant amount of published biographical material about trans people, including various kinds of primary sources and works of historical scholarship, the trans movement's history in contemporary Italy has yet to be comprehensively reconstructed. She goes on to remark that the difficulty in historicizing the Italian trans experience most likely "is due to historians' general resistance to approaching themes that reveal, beneath the surface of seemingly straightforward political history, intense and intimate intersections of sexuality and power that complicate the conventional separation of public and private spheres."[14] Gabriella Romano, in her bibliography of Lucy Salani—a trans woman who fought in WWII and survived Dachau concentration camp—has shared a similar perspective, stressing the importance to look at the past and "listen to the grandparents" of the LGBTQ+ community.[15] While a more extensive and detailed Italian trans history is still in the making, this volume, in which personal memories, grassroots narratives, and theoretical perspectives enter into conversation, foregrounds the role that places have played in the historical process of (self-)recognition and representation of gender variance as individual and collective identities. What becomes evident in the narratives gathered here is that if each voice is a story in itself, all the stories are tied by a shared master narrative: they are all rooted in a common ground that is simultaneously local and global. These stories participate in the reconstruction of overlooked Italian sites of memory, yet they also express a joint vision based on the right to self-determination and validation of one's existence, experience, and reality. Indeed, trans history has been a story of struggle and defeats wherever it has taken place in Euro-American contexts, but it is also a story bursting with creativity and resilience.

From a broader anthropological perspective, trans history leads to reflections on key aspects that make up our human experience: body, community, representation, performativity, but also freedom, desire, and imaginativeness. It is a story that makes visible the frightening multiplicity that resides within each of us. Variance can burst boundaries and create spaces of freedom because it is capable, even within the normalizing logics that try to restrain it, of *subverting* the status quo, or—and this might be even more disquieting—of *participating* in the day-to-day norm without necessarily aligning with logics that set normativity and antinormativity in opposition. Rather, as Robyn Wiegman and Elizabeth Wilson have maintained in a thought-provoking piece entitled "Antinormativity's Queer Conventions," in the strict Foucauldian sense, "the norm, or normative space, knows no outside."[16] And yet, the normative can be generative of change if it is conceived of as a rich and vibrant relational space: "Antinormativity is antinormative, then, in a way that it presumably does not intend: it turns systemic play (differentiations, comparisons, valuations, attenuations, skirmishes) into unforgiving rules and regulations and so converts the complexity of moving athwart into the much more anodyne notion of moving against."[17] Unexpected relational geographies might emerge from a norm, or a "normal life," that might be less normative and far more unpredictable that what we might expect.

The issue with an anti-normative script that runs the risk of becoming too prescriptive can be addressed from another angle, if we consider the dominant role that Anglophone perspectives about gender play in North

American and European contexts. Over the decades, Anglo-American liberation discourses and scholarly approaches have undeniably provided important models—let's think for example of the global resonance of an event like Stonewall, or of the development of specific areas of inquiry like gender studies, queer studies, or trans studies in American academia. The Anglophone-rich discourse on sexual orientations and genders has fostered the recognition of the multiplicity of experiences and expressions of subjectivities that do not align with the heteronormative script.[18] But the cultural hegemony of this model has created a common language and forms of representation of gender and sexual nonconforming subjectivities worldwide, across contexts that are geographically and culturally very distant. In this sense, trans history is local and universal at the same time, geolocated and transnational—or glocal, in some way. Still, this glocal dimension is not devoid of contradictions: on one hand, it is inspired by globalized liberal views—calls for self-legitimization and the understanding of genders and sexualities as a wide spectrum with countless possibilities—yet on the other, this popularized LGBTQ+ narrative might be clashing against local realities, where individual subjectivities and groups are struggling with giving meaning to their existence in their own cultural terms. The latter issue vividly emerges in the testimonies of Italian American and Italian Canadian trans people included in this volume. They are striving to bring forward some concept of a cohesive LGBTQ+ identity that is simultaneously American and Italian. But their path is still dotted with uncertainties: What could be the future of queer Italian America? What cultural practices, shared interests, nuances, and languages are yet to be born of the strict identification with these particular categories? What new cultural memory is to be formed? What fascinating possibilities exist for a queer or trans Italian American future? These questions similarly apply to an Italian LGBTQ+ discourse that at present might lack of its own terminology and specific identity. During a presentation of her memoir, *L'aurora delle trans cattive* (*The Dawn of the Bad Trans Women*, 2018), Porpora Marcasciano pointed to the irony on the wide adoption of Anglicisms in Italian LGBT+ groups.[19] She shared a personal anecdote about a young Italian activist who overused the neologism *queerizzare* (to queer) to the extreme point of making their speech incomprehensible. "But what are we talking about?" Marcasciano asked her audience, stressing the fact that coining words, rather than simply borrowing terms and adjusting verb endings, has an important value.

From this brief overview of the tensions between global and local, two main issues emerge: the first one is the risk in labeling, or even worse, in essentializing subjectivities as LGBTQ+, thereby ignoring the situated nature of their identities. The second issue concerns the cultural context in which subjectivities move and change. In a global LGBTQ+ discourse that emphasizes differences but tends toward linguistic and cultural homogeneity, there remains a need to creatively express oneself. Yet this ongoing process of finding and (re)defining one's identity—or of becoming oneself—is counterbalanced by the need of creating a sense of belonging, of feeling rooted in a community. This is, particularly, the case of Italian youth of African descent who are fighting to affirm their rights as Italian citizens *and* queer people.[20]

The growing interest in alternative local experiences of gender should probably be read in this twofold perspective: global and anti-global at once. The recent attention to some site-specific Italian realities that represent a particular way of living and expressing gender nonconformity, and which might be regarded as "typical" if not stereotypical, is related to the great development at an international scale since the 2000s of research in gender diversity. However, this also implies recovering experiences of "variance within the variance" that have their cultural and contextual peculiarity, as we have seen with the Neapolitan *femminielli*, which are central figures of this book.[21] Thus, diversity intersects with global dynamics but is always connected to the territory and its sociocultural history, or to quote from the interview with performer Ciro Cascina included in chapter 7, "diversity is made up of diversity." The *femminielli,* for their long-time presence in the territory and elaboration of a specific gender-variant performativity and lifestyle, are regarded as one of the symbols of Naples: their niche culture and many contradictions are evocative of this southern Italian city—its history, its issues, and the rebellious search for legitimacy and autonomy.[22] Despite there not being a unified or precise connotation of these figures in the contemporary Neapolitan reality, the *femminielli* embody an ancient culture that continues to be generative of new meanings not only for the local trans community, but also for the broader population.

Tarantina, who is considered by many the oldest or even the last *femminiello napoletano*, was featured in the August 2021 issue of *Vogue* magazine and refashioned into a contemporary fashion icon. Recalling the baroque Mediterranean design of Dolce & Gabbana, Tarantina poses as a southern diva and matriarch. Sensual and austere, she reclines on a leopard-printed couch: a pensive gaze, blonde hair in a chignon, a long black dress, and a rosary as a necklace—the rosary might be even more provocative as it hints at Tarantina's sincere religious sentiment. It is interesting that in sketching the profile of this peculiar Neapolitan diva, the piece first contextualizes her life in the Roman Dolce Vita of the 1960s—Tarantina was well-known by directors like Fellini and Pasolini and beloved by writer Goffredo Parise—but then remarks how she felt at home only in Naples. "Naples understood me, helped me, and I returned the favor," she confesses.[23] Eventually, her life became embedded in that supportive Neapolitan environment, where Tarantina played a maternal role by welcoming and protecting other gender-diverse people. For them, she became "a *refugium peccatorum* (refuge of sinners), visceral like Naples, the menstruating city of Saint Gennaro."[24] Here, the reference to menstrual blood is crucial to emphasize a fundamental trait of Neapolitan culture: in its shared imagery, opposites like femininity and masculinity, or sacred and profane, blend together or at least come to juxtapose.[25]

In a similar way, a recent TV documentary on trans activist Loredana Rossi has turned the city of Naples into a co-protagonist and Tarantina into one of its many characters.[26] Produced by ARTE (Association Relative à la Télévision Européenne), a French–German public TV channel, *Schutzengel der Transfrauen Loredanas Aufstand gegen den Hass* (*Loredana's Fight against Transphobia*) adopts a dual lens by focusing on the struggle of the Neapolitan trans community during the COVID-19 global pandemic and on the lively cultural legacy of the *femminielli*. Loredana's many hats—*femmenella*, former prostitute, social worker, "guardian angel," and "*mamma*"—are always linked to her strong ties to the city, aspects of which are caught in almost every shot in the program: the *vicoli* (narrow streets) animated by theatricality, folklore, and idiosyncratic spirituality; the colorful clothes hung outside; tomato sauce slowly simmering on the stove; the cigarette smoked outside the window of her historical building. All these details become an integral part of Loredana's story, a story of a possible contemporary evolution of the old *femminielli* generation, embodied by eighty-five-year-old Tarantina, who shares memories of her life with Loredana while drinking the espresso that any meeting with friends calls for in Naples. The visual testimony of gender and social transitions narrated by filmmaker Giulia Ottaviano can only take place in this southern Mediterranean city, suffused by a resilient past that has shaped a changing present.

Both at national and international levels, the interest in the Neapolitan local dimension can be explained with the fascination for the distinctive aspects that the trans experience still represents in this area, in relation to the city's cultural history. Naples testifies to the crucial importance that finding one's own space and being recognized within the community play in the construction of individual and collective identities. Ultimately, what is gaining international visibility in the Neapolitan trans narrative is its unique relationship with a collective memory that assumes a central role in explaining and redefining the present. It is no coincidence that in this volume Naples and the *femminielli* serve as a trait d'union between different times and spaces: they serve as a possible origin for a specific Italian–Mediterranean discourse on trans identities and a bridge between stories of gender-variance in the Italian peninsula and stories of cultural reconnection of Italian American trans people. Naples metonymically stands for an *inclusive* past, being the site where an ancient gender nonconforming tradition and Italian ancestors coexisted. Exploring this place can give a sense of belonging to a broader Italian LGBTQ+ community on both sides of the Atlantic, as Summer Minerva's documentary *Summer Within* showcases.[27]

The trans geographies retraced in this book expand paths from the past and leave an unfinished map of the present, open to further explorations. We are unable to predict what new shapes will emerge from this mapping work in progress, but our wish for those who will venture in this exploration is that they draw new linguistic and relational geographies fueled by greater self-awareness and intellectual curiosity, nourished by the possibility to feel grounded and situated yet also free to express their gender identity, beyond LGBTQ+ places.

Notes

1. Marcasciano, "Introduzione," in *Elementi di critica trans*, eds. Laurella Arietti, Christian Ballarin, Giorgio Cuccio, and Porpora Marcasciano (Rome: ManifestoLibri, 2010), 11.

2. While this collection focuses on Italian Americans, Licia Canton, in her 2021 documentary *Creative Spaces: Queer and Italian Canadian* has interviewed queer Italian Canadians who share their view of Italianness.

3. Here we are hinting at the reflection on language articulated by Italian *femminismo della differenza* (feminism of sexual difference). For an interpretation of this feminist thought through a transfeminist lens, see Cannamela, "'I Am an Atypical Mother': Motherhood and Maternal Language in Giovanna Cristina Vivinetto's Poetry," *Forum Italicum* 55, no. 1 (2021): 85–108.

4. Marcasciano, "Introduzione," 12.

5. Among Gheno's publications regarding gender, see in particular, *Femminili singolari: Il femminismo è nelle parole* (Florence: Effequ, 2019).

6. For an overview of Gheno's perspective, see her interview with Cinzia Sciuto: "Lo schwa è un esperimento: E sperimentare con la lingua non è vietato,"

published online in *Micromega*, April 26, 2021, https://www.micromega.net/vera-gheno-intervista-schwa/.

7. Paolo D'Achille, "Un asterisco sul genere," *Accademia della Crusca*, September 24, 2021, https://accademiadellacrusca.it/it/consulenza/un-asterisco-sul-genere/4018.

8. One of the examples provided in the article is that the Neapolitan *buónə* is a masculine form for both the singular *buono* and the masculine *buoni* while the feminine *bònə* designates both the feminine singular and plural (in standard Italian the two forms would be *buona* and *buone*). This means that the use of schwa does not avoid gender rules.

9. Molly Lipson, "How Language Classes Are Moving Past the Gender Binary," *New York Times*, September 1, 2021, https://www.nytimes.com/2021/09/01/crosswords/gender-language-nonbinary.html.

10. Among recent interdisciplinary publications in queer studies, trans studies, and Italian and Italian American studies, see Bernini, *Queer Apocalypses* (2017) and *Queer Theories* (2020); Voli, "Broadening the Gender Polis"; Ross, Heim, and Smythe, "Queer Italian Studies: Critical Reflections from the Field"; and the special thematic section of *gender/sexuality/italy* 6, coedited by Ross, Heim, and Smythe in 2019. In Italian American studies, more specifically, we should mention Ryan, *When Brooklyn Was Queer: A History* (2019); the work of Mary Jo Bona, especially her essay "Queer Daughters and Their Mothers"; and recent edited collections, including Anatrone and Heim, eds., *Queering Italian Media* (2020); and Calabretta-Sajder and Gravano, eds., *Italian Americans on Screen: Challenging the Past, Re-Theorizing the Future* (2021).

11. This was a complaint voiced many times during our interviews: multiple Italian trans activists shared similar feelings of being disrespected by an academic world that either excluded them or that appropriated their work.

12. On this, see the introduction and chapters 15 and 16.

13. On the topic of identity, see in particular Fabietti, *L'identità etnica*; Hall, "Cultural Identity and Diaspora"; and Herdt, *Third Sex, Third Gender*.

14. Voli, "Broadening the Gender Polis," 236.

15. See Gabriella Romano, *Il mio nome è Lucy: L'Italia del XX secolo nei ricordi di una transessuale* (Rome: Donzelli, 2009), 93. Lucy was interned in Dachau as a defector, not as a "pink triangle" (the symbol used by Nazis to identify homosexuals). Romano also directed a documentary on Lucy, *Essere Lucy* (2011). Lucy's story has inspired another film, *C'è un soffio di vita soltanto* (2021), directed by Matteo Botrugno and Daniele Coluccini.

16. Robyn Wiegman and Elizabeth Wilson, "Introduction: Antinormativity's Queer Conventions," *differences: A Journal of Feminist Cultural Studies* 26, no. 1 (2015): 17.

17. Wiegman and Wilson, "Antinormativity's Queer Conventions," 18.

18. In the matter of public recognition at a juridical level, in Italy in 1982 Law 164 allowed sex change for trans people, and it is a type of treatment covered by the state (surgery on primary and secondary [breast] sexual organs). This law was

not clear enough about the name change on official documents without undergoing the three-year path to sex reassignment surgery, and almost all judges refused this change without the sanctioned path. In 2015, the Italian Court of Appeal and then also the Constitutional Court made it possible for trans people to change their names and other legal documentation without a requirement of genital surgical intervention.

19. We are referring to a video of the book presentation shared by Libreria delle donne di Padova (Women Bookstore in Padova), posted on YouTube, March 23, 2018, https://www.youtube.com/watch?v=bmHu5MWFbV4.

20. On this, see in particular the digital platform The Queer Black Italian Experience. A media project launched in 2020 by writer Jordan Anderson, it offers a virtual safe space of dialogue for Black queer people in Italy (the recording of a roundtable gathering seven Black queer Italians is available here https://www.instagram.com/p/CPYX7mhow8C/?utm_source=ig_embed&utm_campaign=loading).

21. On the *femminielli*, see part 2 of this volume.

22. On this, see Mauriello, "In nomine femminielli"; and Mauriello, *Anthropology of Gender Variance and Trans Experience in Naples*.

23. Marco Grieco, "C'è posto per tutti: La tradizione dei femminielli," *Vogue Italia*, August 10, 2021, 38. Our translation.

24. Grieco, "C'è posto per tutti," 38.

25. On the liquefaction of the dried blood of the city's patron saints, Saint Gennaro and Saint Patrizia, see the essay of Zito, Valerio, and Sisci, in chapter 5.

26. Giulia Ottaviano, dir., "Re: Schutzengel der Transfrauen: Loredanas Aufstand gegen den Hass," *ARTE Re:—Wie wir ticken. Reportagen aus Europa*, 33 min., September 2021, https://www.arte.tv/de/videos/100291-004-A/re-schutzengel-der-transfrauen/. The documentary was created for a specific format of Arte ("Arte Re:"), which covers European topics and is broadcast every evening.

27. On Minerva's documentary, see chapter 21.

References

Anatrone, Sole, and Julia Heim, eds. *Queering Italian Media*. Lanham, MD: Lexington Books, 2020.

Bernini, Lorenzo. *Queer Apocalypses: Elements of Antisocial Theory*. Translated by Julia Heim. London: Palgrave Macmillan, 2016.

———. *Queer Theories: An Introduction. From Mario Mieli to the Antisocial Turn*. Translated by Michela Baldo and Elena Basile. London: Routledge, 2020.

Bona, Mary Jo. "Queer Daughters and Their Mothers: Carole Maso, Mary Cappello and Alison Bechdel Write Their Way Home." In *La mamma: Interrogating a National Stereotype*, edited by Penelope Morris and Perry Willson, 185–214. London: Palgrave Macmillan, 2018.

Botrugno, Matteo, and Daniele Colucci, directors. *C'è un soffio di vita soltanto* (*A Breath of Life*). Kimerafilm, 2021.

Calabretta-Sajder, Ryan, and Alan J. Gravano, eds., *Italian Americans on Screen: Challenging the Past, Re-Theorizing the Future*. Lanham, MD: Lexington Books, 2021.

Cannamela, Danila. "'I Am an Atypical Mother': Motherhood and Maternal Language in Giovanna Cristina Vivinetto's Poetry." *Forum Italicum* 55, no. 1 (2021): 85–108.

Canton, Licia. *Creative Spaces: Queer and Italian Canadian*. Association of Italian Canadian Writers and Queer Studies in Quebec Research Group, 2021.

Fabietti, Ugo. *L'identità etnica*. Rome: Carocci, 1995.

Gheno, Vera. *Femminili singolari: Il femminismo è nelle parole*. Florence: Effequ, 2019.

Hall, Stuart. "Cultural Identity and Diaspora." In *Identity. Community, Culture, Difference*, edited by Jonathan Rutherford, 222–37. London: Lawrence and Wishart, 1990.

Heim, Julia, Charlotte Ross, and SA Smythe, eds. "Italian Queer Cultures." Special themed section, *Gender/sexuality/Italy* no. 6 (2019).

Herdt, Gilbert, ed. *Third Sex, Third Gender: Beyond Sexual Dimorphism in Culture and History*. New York: Zone Books, 1996.

"L'aurora delle trans cattive di Porpora Marcasciano." Video. From Marcasciano's book presentation at Libreria delle donne di Padova. March 23, 2018. https://www.youtube.com/watch?v=bmHu5MWFbV4.

Marcasciano, Porpora. Introduction to *Elementi di critica trans*. Edited by Laurella Arietti, Christian Ballarin, Giorgio Cuccio, and Porpora Marcasciano, 9–11. Rome: ManifestoLibri, 2010.

Mauriello, Marzia. *An Anthropology of Gender Variance and Trans Experience in Naples: Beauty in Transit*. London: Palgrave Macmillan, 2021.

———. "In nomine femminielli: Una ricerca etnografica sulla realtà transgender nella Napoli contemporanea." In *Femminielli: Corpo, genere e cultura*. Edited by Paolo Valerio and Eugenio Zito, 305–25. Naples: Libreria Dante and Descartes, 2019.

Ottaviano, Giulia. "Re: Schutzengel der Transfrauen: Loredanas Aufstand gegen den Hass," *ARTE Re:—Wie wir ticken. Reportagen aus Europa*. 33 min., September 2021.

Pasolini, Pierpaolo, director. *Comizi d'amore*. Film. Arco Film, 1965.

The Queer Black Italian Experience: MBQMBQ. https://www.mqbmbq.com/en/tqbie.

Ryan, Hugh. *When Brooklyn Was Queer: A History*. New York: St. Martin's Press, 2019.

Romano, Gabriella, director. *Essere Lucy*. 2011

———. *Il mio nome è Lucy*. Rome: Donzelli, 2009.

Ross, Charlotte, Julia Heim, and SA Smythe. "Queer Italian Studies: Critical Reflections from the Field." *Italian Studies* 74, no. 4 (2019): 397–412.

Voli, Stefania. "Broadening the Gender Polis: Italian Feminist and Transsexual Movements, 1979–1982." *TSQ: Transgender Studies Quarterly* 3, nos. 1–2 (2016): 235–45.

Wiegman, Robyn, and Elizabeth Wilson. "Introduction: Antinormativity's Queer Conventions." *differences: A Journal of Feminist Cultural Studies* 26, no. 1 (2015): 1–25.

Contributors

Christian Ballarin (he/him/his) lives and works in Turin. He is an activist of the trans movement and is responsible for SpoT, trans help desk of the Maurice GLBTQ association (https://mauriceglbt.org) in Turin. He coedited *Elementi di critica trans* (*Elements of Trans Critique*, 2010) and is the author of several contributions on the trans experience.

Egon Botteghi (he/him/his) holds a degree in philosophy from the University of Pisa and has worked for twenty years as an instructor of equestrian sports. In 2008, he decided to abandon this career and turned his equestrian center into a vegan sanctuary, "Fattoria della Pace Ippoasi" (Farm of Peace, Ippoasis). Botteghi is among the founders of the anarcho-queer-ecoveganfeminist collective Anguane and the collective Intersexioni; he is a member of the Rete Genitori Rainbow (Rainbow Parents Web), of the queer association Friend-li, and the research group Politesse (Università di Verona). Since 2015, Botteghi has embraced a theatrical career. His performances include the monologue "Mi chiamo Egon: Diario di un uomo transessuale" ("My name is Egon: Journal of a Transsexual Man," 2015) and "I love my sister" (2018). Botteghi currently collaborates with the City Hall of Livorno, his home town, as an educator on projects about diversity and inclusion. He also manages the Trans* help desk of L'Approdo, a LGBTQ+ counseling center in Livorno.

Danila Cannamela (she/her/hers) is an assistant professor of Italian studies in the Department of French and Italian at Colby College, where she teaches courses in Italian literature, culture, and gender studies. Through a grant of Colby Center for the Arts and Humanities, she designed the Humanities lab "Geography of R/existence," a new hands-on class focusing on Italian feminism, the gay liberation front, and the trans movement in the 1970s–1980s. Her first book, *The Quiet Avant-Garde* (2019), examines how Italian avant-garde poetics of the object repositioned the human and the nonhuman in an anti-hierarchical relation. This repositioning spurred a debate on women's self-representation as lovers and a broader re-envisioning of gender and sexuality constructs. Cannamela's articles have appeared in several peer-reviewed journals, including *Journal of Modern Italian Studies*, *Modernism/modernity*, *ISLE*, *Modern Language Notes*, *Quaderni d'Italianistica*, and *gender/sexuality/italy*. Currently, she is working on a research project that explores Sylvia Rivera's visit to Italy on the occasion of the 2000 World Pride.

Simone Cangelosi (he/him/his) holds a degree in film studies from the University of Bologna. From 1998 to 2010, he worked as a film restorer for the Cineteca of Bologna. In 2007, he filmed the short documentary *Dalla testa ai piedi* (*From Head to Toe*), a visual journal of his FtM transition. In 2010, he filmed *Felliniana* (codirected with Luki Massa), a long interview that Marcella Di Folco did with Gian Luca Farinelli, the director of Cineteca di Bologna, on her experience as an actress in the cinema of Federico Fellini. In 2014, Cangelosi directed *Una nobile rivoluzione* (*A Noble Revolution*) a documentary on Di Folco, and in 2019 he created the video clips for Porpora Marcasciano's theater piece *Il sogno e l'utopia* (*The Dream and Utopia*). Cangelosi is the project manager of Out-Takes, a historical archive in Bologna whose mission is the global and systematic collection, restoration, conservation, and digitization of the audiovisual memory of the movement for civil rights and of lesbians, gays, bisexuals, trans, and queer people.

Ciro Cascina (she/her/hers) is an actor, artist, and performer who has creatively intermixed Neapolitan culture, trans activism, and political commitment. A cult figure of the Neapolitan gender-variant community, Cascina began performing in the 1970s during LGBT events. Her most famous theatrical work is "La Madonna di Pompei." Cascina is a cofounder of AFAN (Associazione Femmenell Antiche Napoletane).

Romina Cecconi (she/her/hers) is one of the first Italian transsexual women. In 1976 she retold her experience with gender transition in the autobiography *Io, la "Romanina": Perchè sono diventato donna* (*I, "Romanina": Why I Became a Woman*). Since then, Cecconi has been one of the early icons of the Italian trans movement. Her story has generated great media attention and has inspired TV documentaries, theatrical works, a graphic novel, and a recent film, *La donna pipistrello* (*The BatWoman*, 2016).

Giorgio Cuccio (he/his/him) jokingly calls himself a "retired activist." Originally from Palermo, he was a member of many LGBT+ associations, communities, and steering committees. Among his fondest memories of activism are the panel "Un genere autonomo?" ("An autonomous gender?"), the book *Oltre le monocolture del genere* (*Beyond the Monocultures of Genre*, 2006) edited by Nicoletta Poidimani, the video "Crisalidi" ("Chrysalises") of Federico Tinelli (2005), the organization of the seminar "Elementi di critica trans" and the publication of the conference proceeding, and the volume *Esquimesi in Amazzonia* (*Eskimos in Amazonia*, 2013) edited by Christian Ballarin and Roberta Padovano. He currently lives in Tuscany, where he is working on an anthology of trans works (that hopefully will soon see the light) and studying classic guitar.

Liana Cusmano (they/them/iel/lu), aka Luca and BiCurious George, is a writer, poet, spoken word artist, and filmmaker. They are the 2018 and 2019 Montreal Slam Champion and runner-up in the 2019 Canadian Individual Poetry Slam Championship. A participant in the 2019 Spoken Word Residency Program at the Banff Centre for Arts and Creativity, Liana has presented their work in English, French, and Italian across North America, Europe, and Asia. They wrote and directed the film *Matters of Great Unimportance* (2019), screened at the Blue Metropolis Festival, and also wrote the film script for *La Femme Finale*, which screened at the Cannes Film Festival (2015). Their first novel, *Catch and Release* (2022), was published by Guernica Editions.

Massimo D'Aquino (he/his/him) is a trans activist in the association La Libellula and the author of *Camminavo rasente i muri* (*I Walked Close to the Walls*, 2019). His autobiography is one of the first books that raises awareness of the FtM trans experience in Italy.

Erin Elise Ferrentino is a trans Italian American from Bloomfield, New Jersey. They are a farmer, a community organizer, and all-around *scugnizzo* [street urchin] making magic wherever they can. Reach them at erin.elise.ferrentino@gmail.com.

Stella Gonzalez graduated in 2022 from Colby College with a double major in art history and American studies, and a minor in Italian studies. She is an aspiring curator interested in how resistive and revolutionary practice intersects with modern and contemporary art. Beyond her curatorial interests, Stella strives to make sure that the work she does utilizes art in a community engaged manner.

Michela Griffo is an artist and activist who came of age in New York City in the '60s. She was an early member of the Redstockings, a founding member of Radicalesbians and Lavender Menace, and an early member of the Gay Liberation Front. She was active in the anti-war, women's rights, and gay rights movements. The GLF, famous for its radicalism and intersectionality, worked closely with activists such as Yoruba Guzman and radical organizations such as the Young Lords, Black Panthers, and Salsa Soul Sisters. Michela risked her life with other gay and lesbian activists on the front lines of the gay rights movement standing up to police brutality and closing the mafia-run lesbian bars, which would pave the way for younger generations to come out and live safe and productive lives.

Porpora Marcasciano (she/her/hers) is a sociologist, public figure, and spokesperson of the Italian Transgender Movement. She is the former president of MIT (Movimento Identità Trans) and is currently the president of the Commissione Pari Opportunità del Comune di Bologna (Commission for Equal Opportunities of the City of Bologna). Marcasciano, besides publishing several books on the history of the Italian trans movement (including *AntoloGaia*, *Favolose narranti*, and *L'aurora delle trans cattive*), has also been featured in countless public events and lectures. She has recently staged a theatrical piece, *Il sogno e l'utopia* (2019), and is the protagonist of two documentary films directed by Roberto Cannavò, *Divieto di Transito* (*No Passing*, 2020) and *Porpora* (2021). She is also one of the protagonists of Roberta Torre's film, *Le Favolose* (2022), which tells the story of a group of trans women.

Liz Mariani (they/she/lei) is a poet, spoken word artist, teaching artist, painter, and photographer originally from Buffalo, New York, the ancestral lands and the traditional homelands of the Seneca Nation and the Haudenosaunee Confederacy. Liz is currently a candidate for an MFA in creative writing with an emphasis in poetry at Mills College. Their words have been published in several venues including *After The Pause*, *Two Serious Ladies*,

Advaitam Speaks Literary, the *Buffalo News*, *VTDigger*, *BlazeVOX*, *Medium*, *Poem Town Randolph*, and *the Brooklyner*. To know more about Liz's work, please visit linktr.ee/poetlizmariani / @liz_mariani_art.

Mazen Masoud (he/his/him) is a Libyan political refugee and transfeminist activist who has lived in Italy since 2016. Masoud was elected president of MIT (Movimento Identità Trans) in 2022 and he is the first trans man and intersex person to take the lead of the association. He worked as an anesthesiologist for the Libyan Red Crescent Society, before becoming a social worker and cultural mediator.

Marzia Mauriello (she/her/hers) is a research fellow at the University of Naples "L'Orientale" (Italy), where she teaches cultural anthropology. Her research areas cover gender, health and body issues, and food cultures. Based on over ten years of fieldwork in Naples, Marzia has published several articles in peer-reviewed journals and book chapters on the processes of medicalization of the trans experience, the dynamics of inclusion and exclusion of gender nonconforming people, and the intersections between food and gender. Her book, *An Anthropology of Gender Variance and Trans Experience in Naples: Beauty in Transit* was published by Palgrave Macmillan in 2021. She is currently working on street food culture in Naples, in relation to gender and migration. Marzia is an affiliate of the Gender History Research Center and the Centro Studi Cibo e Alimentazione, both based at the University of Naples L'Orientale, and of the Institute for Gender Studies at the University of Chester, UK.

Summer Minerva (they/them, she/her) is an independent researcher, performer, public speaker, filmmaker, and educator based in New York City. They hold a BA in international studies and journalism from the University of Miami and an MS in education from the City University of New York's City College. Over the past five years, Summer has retraced their Neapolitan lineage to the third gender group of Naples and documented the journey with a full-length documentary. *Summer Within* (2023). Their one-person play, *As Sylvia*, in which Summer portrays trans activist Sylvia Rivera, premiered at the FRIGID festival in New York in June 2022. Summer has presented their work at many institutions, including the New York Historical Society, the Center on Halstead in Chicago, Temple University, NYU, Columbia University, Sarah Lawrence College, William Patterson University, and Southern Methodist University.

Lina Pallotta (she/her/hers) is a documentary photographer. Pallotta received her diploma in photojournalism and documentary photography from the Center of Photography in New York. Her fierce motivation to make a difference drew her to the underground scene, to subcultures, to Mexican women, to underdogs, to tell stories that normally don't get told. Her most notable works include *Porpora e Valérie* (2013) and *BASTA: To Work and Die on the Mexican Border* (1999), on the lives of Mexican women who work in border factories. Her work has been shown in personal and collective exhibits in Europe and the United States and published in national and international magazines. Since the mid-2000s, she has regularly held seminars and conferences at the International Center of Photography and the Empire State College in New York, the Frontline Club in London, Spazio Labo' in Bologna, Limes in Cagliari, Minimum in Palermo, and F.project: School of Photography and Film in Bari.

Loredana Rossi (she/her/hers) is a Neapolitan trans activist based in Naples. She was one of the first trans activists in the city. In 2007 she founded the ATN (Associazione Transessuale Napoli [Neapolitan Transsexual Association]). She is a social worker and deals with trafficking, prostitution, and minors. Loredana has managed various projects providing services for the protection of the rights of trans people.

Frances Rose Subbiondo (fae/femm/faer) identifies as a queer and trans cultural worker, earth-mover, and community hearth-keeper and brings the lenses of magic, ecology, and justice to bear on faer paths of earth-healing and regenerative food system design. Fae can be reached at frances.subbiondo@gmail.com.

Paolo Valerio (he/his/him) is professor emeritus of clinical psychology at the Department of Neuroscience and Reproductive and Odontostomatological Sciences at the University of Naples Federico II, and director of the University Services Center for Active and Participated Inclusion of Students (SInAPSi), of which he is currently honorary president. He is president of the Gender Identity Culture Foundation and of the National Observatory on Gender Identity (ONIG). He has participated in numerous European projects, of which he was scientific director. He is the author of national and international publications on gender issues and psychological-clinical intervention.

Helena Velena (she/her/hers) is a cyberpunk artist and performer. One of the first to bring transgender theory in Italy, she is the author of numerous books, including *Dal cybersex al transgender: Tecnologie, identità e politiche di liberazione* (*From Cibersex to Transgender: Technologies, Identity, and Politics of Liberation*, 1998), and has collaborated on more than twenty books, writing about counterculture, extreme music, and alternative sexuality. She defines herself as anarcho-situationist and absolutely atheist and a fluid lesbian. She has a visceral love for black cats and frogs.

Maria Carolina Vesce (she/her/hers) holds a PhD in anthropology from the University of Messina. She has conducted on-field research in Naples and Samoa. Her research interests focus on body and gender, and in particular on nonheteronormative experiences of gender and on the impact that biomedical categories of gender have on local contexts. Her book, *Altri Transiti* (*Other Transitions*, 2017), is an ethnographic study of the *femminielli* community in southern Italy.

Giovanna Cristina Vivinetto (she/her/hers) holds an MA in Italian literature from the University of Rome, La Sapienza. She debuted as a poet with *Dolore minimo* (2018) and, in 2020, published her second book, *Dove non siamo stati*. Her poems have appeared in many poetry journals and websites, including *Atelier*, *Tigre di Carta*, *Nazione Indiana*, and the poetry blog of Rai.

Eugenio Zito (he/his/him) holds a PhD in gender studies, is a researcher in demo-ethno-anthropological disciplines, and teaches ethnology and anthropology of communication in the Department of Social Sciences and Medical Anthropology at the School of Medicine and Surgery of the University of Naples Federico II. Ordinary member of the Italian Society of Medical Anthropology, he is the author of several works on the topics of gender, corporeality, social vulnerability, and disease. He is the author of *Living (with) Diabetes: An Anthropological Look at the Body, Disease and Treatment Processes* (2016).

Index

Page numbers with an *f* refer to figures.

*. *See* asterisks (*)

Accademia della Crusca, 339
Acorn (Subbiondo's partner), 295, 296, 332, 336n3
activism: and academia, 340–341; Ballarin, Christian, 225–226, 227–228; Cuccio, Giorgio, 233–235; Di Folco, Marcella, 264, 265–267; *femminielli*, 115, 324; LGBTQ+, 6, 133; Marcasciano, Porpora, 2–3; Mieli, Mario, 8–9, 255n9; political, 238–239; Rossi, Loredana, 115; trans, 225–228, 233–235, 237
Aeneas, 128, 131n4
AFAN. *See* Associazione Femmenell Antiche Napoletane (AFAN)
Agdistis (hermaphrodite son of Cybele), 92
agùrtes (priests of Cybele), 80. See also *Gallae* (castrated / cross-dressed priests of Cybele)
AIDS, 30, 59, 267
Albertina, 129–130
Alexandrians, 89
Altri femminismi (Other Feminisms) (Marcasciano), 165–166

Altri transiti (Vesce): *femminielli*, survival of, 13; *figliata* (birthing ritual), 110–112; *tombola*, 101, 102–105; wedding, *femminielli*, 105–110
Amarcord (Fellini), 262
Among Roses and Violets (Marcasciano). *See* Marcasciano, Porpora (trans activist); *Tra le rose e le viole* (Marcasciano)
Anastasia, 171
Andrea (social worker at Lunatica), 209
androgyne (third gender), 75, 89–90, 105
Anna (from Santo Spirito), 134
Annalisa (Minerva's cousin), 306
A Noble Revolution (Cangelosi). *See* Cangelosi, Simone (filmmaker); *Una nobile rivoluzione (A Noble Revolution)* (Cangelosi)
Anselmo (from Rome), 129, 130
Anthony. *See* Minerva, Summer
anti-normative: movement, 5, 8, 12, 277–278, 279; script (gender play), 342–343

"Antinormativity's Queer Conventions" (Wiegman and Wilson), 342
AntoloGaia (Marcasciano): 1970s, 31–32, 34, 35–36; adaptation of, 267–268; Cassero, la presa del, 10, 195–197; on homosexuality, 34–35, 37–38; LGBTQ+ liberation, 9; memoir, 2; narrative voice, choice of, 29; Pasolini's murder, 37. *See also* Marcasciano, Porpora (trans activist)
Antonella (Sacred Gender Collaboration pilgrimage), 331, 334, 335, 336n3
Antonello *(femminiello)*: Cassero (Bologna), 196, 197n2; cross-dressing, 49–50, 51–54; early years (Naples), 48–49; *femminielli* traditions, 55–57; as *femminiello*, 48; religion, 57; street walking, 49–51; superstitions, 58–59; on turning tricks, 54–55; violence, street, 57–59. *See also* La Merdaiola
Arabic (language), 237, 239, 340
Aracne (friend of Marcasciano), 32
Archivio Out-Takes (Cangelosi), 261, 268–269
Arcigay (Italian LGBT organization), 118, 244, 256n17, 266
arrichione (man who desires another man), 87
Arthur, Madame. *See* Madam Arthur (Paris)
Associazione Femmenell Antiche Napoletane (AFAN): *figliata* (birthing ritual), 110–111; Sacred Gender Collaboration meeting with, 329; *Sciò Sciò Ciucciuvè (tombola)*, 104, 112n12; wedding, *femminielli*, 106, 108, 109–110
Associazione Transessuale Napoli (ATN), xvii–xviii, 116, 324
asterisks (*), 5, 19n24, 30, 163, 229, 236, 239n6, 339

ATN. *See* Associazione Transessuale Napoli (ATN)
@ symbols, 229, 239n6, 339
Attis (from Cybele myth), 92, 94
Augusto (family of Minerva), 305
Autonomia Operiaia (Bologna), 249, 255, 256n20
Autonomous Collective of Milan. *See* Collettivo Autonomo di Milano (Autonomous Collective of Milan)
Avellino: Cybele myth, 93; *femminielli*, presence of, 95–96; Minerva, visit to, 305; *tombola* games, 103

Ballarin, Christian (LGBTQ+ activist): activism (Maurice), 225–226, 227–228; gender identity, 224–225, 228–229; on language, 14, 174, 228–229; Pride (San Francisco), 226–227; Transgender Europe (TGEU), 226
Ballo di Sfessania, 91
"Ballo di Tarantella del'Affeminati di Napoli," 78–79, 78f
Ballone, Edoardo, 87
bard, Marcasciano as a, 3, 18n12
Bargellini, Piero, 93
bars. *See* gay bars
Basaglia Law. *See* Legge Basaglia
bassi, 102, 112n4
Bassi, Serena (translator), 41
Battaglia, Salvatore, 86–87
battesimo (*femminielli* baptism ceremony), 118, 122n11
Battiato, Franco, 247
beauty pageants. *See* "Miss Italia Trans" pageant
Bellezza, Dario (poet and writer), 35, 128, 130–131, 131n3
Belloni, Alessandra, 307
Benjamin, Harry (sexologist/endocrinologist), xv, 177, 180n16
Beppe, 196

Berber, 237, 239
Berdache (Mohave of North America), 76, 91
Berlant, Lauren, 318
Berlusconi, 119
Bernini, Lorenzo, 19n32, 159, 172–173
Beyond the Monocultures of Gender. See *Oltre le monocolture del genere*
Bianchi, Giovanni (anatomy professor), 182, 183–184, 187
bingo. See *tombola* (game)
biological sex. *See* sex
Birkett, Annie, 189, 190
birthing ritual. See *figliata* (birthing ritual)
Black Madonna. See *Mamma Schiavona* (Black Madonna/Mother Slave)
Bologna: Archivio Out-Takes (Cangelosi), 261, 268–269; Autonomia Operaia, 249, 255, 256n20; Cassero, xvi, 10, 195–197, 247, 252, 256n17; Collettivo Frocialista, xiv, 9, 10, 244, 247, 255n6; Convention against Repression, 244, 251, 254n4, 254n5; Di Folco, Marcella, xvi, 262, 263, 264, 265–267; "freest city in the world," 244–245; Lorusso, Francesco, murder of, 243–244, 254n2, 254n3, 258n31; MIT, 209, 262; Partito Liberale, 257n23; prostitution (turning tricks), 54–55, 60n11; trans movement, 10–11, 245, 247, 277; violence (street), 50, 57–58
bombadeira ("the pumper"), 21n66, 171, 179n10
bombaidera, 13, 21n66
bombardere, 13, 21n66, 207
Bonanno, Pina (transsexual woman), xvi

Bordoni, Giovanni (Vizzani, Caterina): autopsy of, 183; death of, 181–182, 186–187; escape with niece of priest, 186; FtM transition, 183, 184; history of, documented, 14; secret, protected by parents and priest, 185
Bossi-Fini Law, 210n2
Botteghi, Egon: on Bordoni, Giovanni, 181–187; on Crawford, Harry, 187–192; on identity, 4–5; "Non siamo nat@ ieri," 13–14, 181
Brigate Rosse (Red Brigades), 244, 255n7
Broccolini, Alessandra, 102–103
Busarello, Renato, 6–7

"A Call from the Ancestors" (Minerva), 309–310. *See also* Minerva, Summer
Camminavo rasente i muri (D'Aquino), 14, 211–221. *See also* D'Aquino, Massimo
Campania: Cybele, cult of, 93; *femminiello*, role of, 308–309; *figliata* (birthing ritual), 110–111; Parthenope, 90; *tammurriata* (dance or song with drum), 79, 97n9; *tombola* games, 105
Campo de' Fiori (Rome), 130, 245
canary (police informer), 129
Candelora (Candlemas), 15, 93–94, 103, 118, 323, 324, 329
Candlemas. *See* Candelora (Candlemas)
Cangelosi, Simone (filmmaker): *Dalla testa ai piedi*, 261, 262–263, 269, 270–271; on Di Folco, Marcella, 14–15, 261–264; on Marcasciano, Porpora, 267–268; Out-Takes Archive, 268–269; trans movement, 269–270
Canzone di Zeza, 91
Carcere della Dozza, 11
Carousel (Paris club), 170, 176–177

Carrano, Gennaro, 83–84, 105, 109
Casablanca: gender reassignment surgery, 45, 136, 248, 265
Cascina, Ciro / Ciretta (activist, actor): on *femminielli* history, 117, 323, 324–325; *femminiello*, evolution of, 119; *figliata* (birthing ritual), 110–111; identity, 13; on poverty, 120; on Rossi's communication skills, 116; wedding, *femminielli,* 105, 108
Cassero (Bologna): as archive and documentation center (LGBTQ+), 269; Circolo di Cultura Omosessuale 28 Giugno (first LGBTQ+ center), xvi, 10, 266; la presa del (the storming of), 10, 14, 195–197, 247; membership cards, 252; Porta Saragozza, xvi, 10, 196, 197, 256n17, 266
castration, 80, 92, 94, 145, 308, 323, 333
Catholicism, 234, 245–246, 247–249, 286, 331, 333
Cauldwell, David Oliver (sexologist), xv
Cavani, Liliana, 110
Cecconi, Romina (Romanina): Circus Imperus, 138; confinement *(confino)* (1969–71), xv, 8, 36, 133, 149–155; gender reassignment surgery (1968), xv, 8, 133, 145–148, 161, 179n3; hormone treatments, 135; *Io, la "Romanina"* (autobiography), 8; in Paris, 136–141; Santo Spirito, 134–136; Switzerland, 141–144; tickets, offences, 134, 136
Centro documentazione Sylvia Rivera, 11
Centro Italiano di Sessuologia (CIS), 245
Centro Permanenza Temporaneo (Center for Temporary Stays) (CPT), 205, 210n3

Chaplin, Victoria, 143, 145, 147
Cheetah (from Santo Spirito), 135
Chevalier d'Éon, 178
Chez Madame Arthur, 170. *See also* Madam Arthur (Paris)
Christian Democrats. *See* Democrazia Cristiana (DC)
Christopher (Sacred Gender Collaboration pilgrimage), 331, 336n3
chromatic system of gender (Rothblatt), 94
Chu, Andrea Long, 12
Circolo Mario Mieli (was Collettivo Narciso), 9
Circolo 28 Giugno (LGBTQ+ association), xvi, 10, 247, 255n6, 256n17, 266. *See also* Cassero (Bologna)
Circus Imperus, 133, 138
Ciretta. *See* Cascina, Ciro / Ciretta (Neapolitan activist, actor)
Ciro. *See* Cascina, Ciro / Ciretta (Neapolitan activist, actor)
Coccinelle, 142, 155n7, 169, 173, 176
coffee (symbol of friendship), 44, 56
Cohen, Alfredo, 9, 36, 247
Colasurdo, Marcello, 323
Collettivo Autonomo di Milano (Autonomous Collective of Milan), 9
Collettivo Frocialista (Faggot Collective) (Bologna), xvi, 9, 10, 244, 247, 249, 255n6, 266
Collettivo Narciso (Rome), 9–10
coming out, 4, 12, 29, 37–38, 166, 172, 245
Comizi d'amore (Love Talks) (Pasolini), 1–2, 16, 337. *See also* Pasolini, Pier Paolo (director)
Commissione Pari Opportunità del Comune di Bologna, xix

Commission for Equal Opportunities of the City of Bologna, xix
communism, 9, 197, 238, 244, 246
concentration camps, 162, 163, 341–342
condoms, 59
confinement *(confino)*: of Cecconi, Romina, xv, 8, 36, 133, 149–155
confino. *See* Cecconi, Romina (Romanina); confinement *(confino)*
congenital invert, 173
Congresso internazionale di sessuologia su comportamenti devianti della sessualità umana, 9
Consoli, Massimo, 130, 246, 256n14
Conundrum (Morris), 7
Convention against Repression (Bologna), 244, 251, 254n4, 254n5
Coodinamento Trans Sylvia Rivera: foundation of (2006), xvii
Cora (trans woman, Bologna), 58
Corso, Carla, 168
Cortellazzo, Manlio, 86–87
Covre, Pia, 159, 167–169
Coyle, William T. (prosecutor), 191
CPT. *See* Centro Permanenza Temporaneo (Center for Temporary Stays) (CPT)
Crawford, Harry: birth of daughter, 189; Botteghi on, 14, 181; marriage, 189; medical exam, 190; murder investigation, 189–191; New Zealand, emigration to, 187–188; prison, 191–192; trial, 190–191. *See also* Falleni, Eugenia
Croniche di Montevergine (Giordano), 93
cross-dressing: Antonello, 48, 49–50, 51–54; a crime, 8, 50–51, 134, 136, 249–250, 287; Marcasciano, Porpora, 36; Mieli, Mario, 9; popularity of, 207; priests of Cybele, 86, 92, 93. *See also* transvestitism

Cuccio, Giorgio (LGBTQ+ activist): activism, 233–235; pronouns, 236; on trans history, 174–176; trans identity, 230–233
Cullen, William (judge), 190–191
Cusmano, Liana, 310–312
Cybele: *agùrtes* (priests of), 80; cult of, 93–94, 170, 308, 323, 333; myth of, 92, 94, 323; Naples and, 91–92, 170; religious transvestitism (cross-dressing), 86, 92, 93. *See also* Great Mother

Dachau (extermination camp), 162, 341–342
D'Achille, Paolo, 339
D'Agostino, Gabriella, 77–78, 80
Dalla testa ai piedi (From Head to Toes) (Cangelosi), 261, 262–263, 269, 270–271. *See also* Cangelosi, Simone (filmmaker)
"Dance of the Tarantella by the Affeminati of Naples," 78–79, 78f
D'Aquino, Massimo: bathroom routine, 213–214; Chiara, 216; childhood, 214–215, 217, 219; on coming out, 172; Francesco (stepfather), 219–220; FtM transsexual, 214, 216, 221; hair, cutting of, 212, 221; Libellula Italia, 14; mother, 215, 216, 219–220; penis, fake, 214–215; rape, 218; suicide ideation, 212–213
The Dawn of the Bad Trans Women (Marcasciano). *See L'aurora delle trans cattive*; Marcasciano, Porpora (trans activist)
D'eaubonne, Françoise, 246, 256n16
De Blasio, Abele, 80–83, 84, 86, 87
De Humana Physiognomonia (Della Porta), 77

Della Porta, Giovanni Battista, 77, 79, 84–86
Democrazia Cristiana (DC), 249, 257n21
deviants, sexual, 2, 82, 92, 204, 248, 337
Devor, Aaron, 174–175
di Cristo, Luigi (AFAN president), 120–121
Dido (Aeneas's lover), 128, 131n4
Di Folco, Marcella (Marcellona): Bologna, 265–267; Cangelosi, Simone, impact on, 14–15, 263–264; city councilor (Bologna), election of (1995), xvi, 266–267; death of (2010), xviii; and Marcasciano, Porpora, 276–278, 276f; MIT, xvi, 265; photo of, 276f; Piazza dei Cinquecento (Rome), 128, 131n2; Sylvia Rivera Steering Committee, 226; *Una nobile rivoluzione* (Cangelosi), 261–264
Di Giacomo, Salvatore, 83
Disclosure: Trans Lives on Screen (Netflix), 16
disco, 251, 252–254, 265, 271n4
Di Stefano, Fabrizia, 176–178
Divergent. See Divergenti (international festival of trans cinema)
Divergenti (international festival of trans cinema), xviii, 11
Dolore minimo (Minimum Pain) (Vivinetto), 61–69. See also Vivinetto, Giovanna Cristina
Donina (Minerva's aunt), 305
Doria, Marina, 143, 144
Dove non siamo stati (Where We Haven't Been) (Vivinetto), 69–72. See also Vivinetto, Giovanna
The Dream and the Utopia. See *Il sogno e l'utopia* (Porpora)
Duchess of Toraloff, 104, 109, 110

ə. *See* schwa (ə)
"educastration" (Mieli), 31
effeminates, 77, 82, 98n14, 102, 307
effeminati, 84, 85, 86
Elbe, Lili (first transsexual woman of history), 16n2
Elementi di critica omosessuale (Mieli), 8–9, 13, 166, 247–248, 256n18. *See also* Mieli, Mario
"Elementi di critica trans" (seminar), xviii, 159, 179n1
Elements of Trans Critique (Marcasciano). See *Elimenti di critica trans* (Marcasciano); Marcasciano, Porpora (trans activist)
"Elements of Trans Critique" (seminar). *See* "Elementi di critica trans" (seminar)
Elimenti di critica trans (Marcasciano): Busarello, Renato, 6–7; self-awareness (cultivating), 2, 337–338; trans experience, 4, 13
Ellis, Havelock, 173
Emanuele, Vittorio, 143–144, 155n9
emasculation, 92, 94
Emilia-Romagna region, xvi, 11, 14, 265
"The Empire Strikes Back: A Posttransexual Manifesto" (Stone), 230, 240n8, 269
English (language), 239, 342–343
Erickson Educational Foundation (EEF), 180n16
Erikson, Reed (trans male), 176, 180n16
"esperienza umana significativa" ("meaningful experiences") (Marcasciano), 16, 22n68
Eugenia, Saint, 182
Euro Pride, xviii
experience, subjective, 76, 96, 174
extermination camps, 162, 163, 341–342

Fabulous Narrators. See *Favolose narranti* (Marcasciano)
fabulousness, 36, 166, 201
Faggot Collective. *See* Collettivo Frocialista (Bologna)
fairies, 6, 31–32, 35, 80–82, 127, 130, 299
Falleni, Eugene, 188
Falleni, Eugenia, 14, 181, 191. *See also* Crawford, Harry
fascism, 34, 37, 119–120, 155n9, 162, 246, 249
Favolose narranti (Marcasciano), 199–210. *See also* Marcasciano, Porpora (trans activist)
Feinberg, Leslie (transgender activist/writer), xvii, 6
Fellini, Federico, 262
females: feeling like, 96, 97n3; "inverts," 2, 17n4; pronouns, 43; prostitution, 167–168; role of, 77, 84, 86, 87–88, 102; as self-sufficient, 90–91
female-to-male. *See* FtM (female-to-male)
feminism: and trans people, 165–166, 235, 269–270
femmene, 117
femmenella, 86, 115, 116, 120, 121n6, 324
femmenellone, 117
Femminelle Alley (Naples), 83
femminielli: battesimo (baptism ceremony), 118, 122n11; Candelora, 15, 93–94; customs/traditions, 45, 57; as deviant, sexual, 82, 92; evolution of, 13, 95–96, 170, 344; exploitation of, 120–121; extinction of, 76, 95–96; *figliata* (birthing ritual), 57, 110–112; gender reassignment surgery stories, 44–45; history of, 77–79, 78*f*, 84–85, 116–117, 174, 307–308; homosexuality, compared to, 77–78, 82; language spoken by, 45, 56; LGBTQ+ community, relationship with, 117–118, 119–120; luck, as bringers of, 56, 80, 307–308; Marcasciano's introduction to, 42–43; name day celebrations, 43; numbers (symbolism of), 45, 56, 59, 60n6; *ricchione* (fairy/passive pederast), 82, 86, 98n17; Sacred Gender Collaboration (pilgrimage to Naples), 329–330, 331, 332, 333–334; Spanish Quarter (Naples), 87, 88, 89, 98n18, 98n19; *spusarizio* (wedding), 80–81, 83–84, 105–110, 113n18; term (analysis of), 87–89; as third gender, 89–90, 95, 173; *tombola*, 12, 102–105; and transgenderism, 76; two spirits *(muxes)*, compared to, 119; violence against, 119–120. See also *femmene; femmenella; femmenellone; femminiello*
Femminielli: Corpo, genere, cultura, 75
femminiello: evolution of, 119; explained, 48, 56, 77–78, 82, 96; exploitation of, 120–121; history of, 116–117; as magical creatures, 92; *spusarizio* (wedding), 83, 108, 109; term, analysis of, 87–89, 91; term, use of, 115, 121n6; *tombola* games, role of in, 102–103, 104. See also *femminielli*
Fernanda (from Santo Spirito), 135
Ferranti, Roberta: Coccinelle, meeting with, 169, 173, 176; on history of trans people, 161
Ferrentino, Erin, 298–300
fertility rites, 92
FHAR. *See* Front Homosexuel d'Action Révolutionnaire (FHAR)
Fiacchini, Renato. *See* Zero, Renato

fifty-seven (*scartellato* / hunchback), 58
figliata (birthing ritual), 57, 110–112, 118
"first time" discussion, 161–162, 167, 169, 172, 173–174
Florence: flood (1966), 144, 155n10
Foggia: confinement in Volturino, 150–155
Ford, Joan, 192. *See also* Crawford, Harry
Fortier, Corinne, 84
forty-four (prison), 45, 56, 59
fourteen (drunkard), 45
Francesco, 219–220
Frau Marlene (club), 171
Freud, Sigmund, 17n4
friendship: coffee as symbol of, 44, 56; geographies of, 275–280
From Head to Toes (Cangelosi). *See Dalla testa ai piedi (From Head to Toes)* (Cangelosi)
Fronte di Liberazione Omosessuale (FLO), 245
Fronte Unitario Omosessuale Rivoluzionario Italiano (FUORI!): attack of stand, 244–245; banning of booklets, 37; foundation of (1971), 9, 39n12, 255n8; and Partito Radicale, 250, 257n23
Front Homosexuel d'Action Révolutionnaire (FHAR), 245, 255n11
FtM (female-to-male): D'Aquino, Massimo, 214, 216, 221; transitions, 172, 173, 181, 211, 230, 248
funk, 243, 253, 258n35, 259n36–43
FUORI!. *See* Fronte Unitario Omosessuale Rivoluzionario Italiano (FUORI!)

Gallae (castrated / cross-dressed priests of Cybele), 92, 94, 308, 333. See also *agùrtes* (priests of Cybele)
Galli. See *Gallae* (priests of Cybele)
gay bars: mafia, 15, 286–287; role of, 6, 11
"gay ghettos," 5
Gay Liberation Front (GLF), 9, 39n12, 269, 287–289. *See also* Fronte Unitario Omosessuale Rivoluzionario Italiano (FUORI!)
gaysmo (gay movement, culture), 118
gender: chromatic system of (Rothblatt), 94; as fixed, 175; roles, 82–83, 87–88, 102; sexual, 76; subjective experience, 76; and terminology, 223, 228–229; third (androgyne), 89–90, 95
gendered norms, 332, 333
gender fluidity, 8, 175
gender identity: in past patriarchal societies, 82; and sense of place, 5
genderqueer, 8
gender reassignment surgery: Cecconi, Romina, xv, 8, 133, 145–148, 179n3; Coccinelle, 155n7; Di Folco, Marcella, 265, 277–278; *femminielli* experiences, 44–45; first (1931), 16n2, 175–176; Jorgensen, Christine, xv, 16n2; as lifelong destination, 4, 7, 8; Mieli's thoughts on, 248; name change without, xviii, 347n18; and trans history, 161, 235. *See also* gender transition
gender transition, 8, 62–69, 264, 320–321. *See also* gender reassignment surgery
Genoa: transsexual culture, 170–171, 172
geographies: definition used in this book, 5–6, 18n21
Gerarda (Minerva's aunt), 305–306, 322. See also *Summer Within* (Minerva)
Gerardina (Gerardo), 107–108, 110, 111

Gheno, Vera (sociolinguist), 339
Giacinto, 182
Gianna, 106
Gina (Gianna), 103–104, 106
Ginevra (Switzerland), 161
Giordano (abbot of Montevergine), 93
Giulia, Sora, 129, 130
GLF. *See* Gay Liberation Front (GLF)
Graziella, 337
Great Mother: as divine androgyne, 90, 105; early representations of, 91. *See also* Cybele
Greenwich Village (NY): Kooky's (gay bar), 286–287, 288; police raid on Stonewall Inn (1969), xv, 6, 256n15
Griffo, Michela, 15, 285–289
Gruppo Luna (trans group at Maurice), 225
guappo, 120, 122n18
Guevara, Che, 246
gypsies. *See* Roma

Habits and customs of the Camorrists (De Blasio). See *Usi e costumi dei camorristi*
Hall, Radclyffe, 173
harassment: of street walkers, 50–51
Harry Benjamin International Gender Dysphoria Association (HBIGDA), xvi, xvii
HBIGDA. *See* Harry Benjamin International Gender Dysphoria Association (HBIGDA)
hermaphrodites, 92, 138, 162
Hijra, 76
Himmler, Heinrich, 246
Hippocratic oath, 246, 256n13
hirculone/hircus (billy goat), 86–87
Hirschfeld, Magnus (neurologist/modern sexology pioneer), 16n2
history: importance of documenting, 30; medicalization of, 160, 172–173, 177, 178, 232–233; reappropriation of, 160–166; of subjection, 172–173; trans, 173, 232, 341–342. *See also specific histories* (e.g., *femminielli*, Naples)
homophobia, 8, 34–35, 82, 251, 255n11, 288
Homosexual Cultural Circle June 28. *See* Circolo XXVIII Giugno (LGBTQ+ association)
homosexuality: *AntoloGaia*, 34–35, 37–38; and communism, 246; *femminielli*, compared to, 77–78, 82, 85–86, 102; history, 9, 17n4, 162, 168, 172–173, 178, 255n6–256n15; as illness, 36, 39n9, 246; pink triangles, 162, 179n4, 347n15; rights bill, 7. *See also* pederasts
Homosexual Liberation Front. *See* Fronte di Liberazione Omosessuale (FLO)
hormone treatments, 116, 135, 161, 207, 234, 250, 334
"How Language Classes Are Moving Past the Gender Binary" (Lipson), 340
humor, as a storytelling device, 3, 18n11, 195

I, "Romanina." See *Io, la "Romanina"* (Cecconi)
"I Am Blood" (Griffo). *See* "Io sono sangue" ("I Am Blood") (Griffo)
identities: appropriation of (subjectivation), 172–173, 178; challenges with, 237–238; gender, 224–225, 228–229, 334–335; limitations of, 4–5; trans, 230–233, 341
Il risveglio dei faraoni (Mieli), 8
Il segno di Virgilio (The Mark of Virgil) (De Simone), 78, 78*f*
Il sogno e l'utopia (Marcasciano), 267

immigrant experience: Brazilian Italians, 199, 200, 205–206, 209–210; Italian Americans, 285–286, 295–296
immigration laws, 205, 210n2
initiation ritual, street walking, 50, 127–128
injections, silicone, 171, 179n10, 207–208
International Congress of Sexology, protest of (1972), xv–xvi, 9, 245–246, 255n12
International Day Against Homophobia, Transphobia, and Biphobia, xvii
intersex, 4, 5, 162, 237, 238
inversion, sexual, 17n4, 172–173
invertite, 2
invertiti, 1–2
inverts, 1–2, 17n4, 173
Io, la "Romanina" (Cecconi), 8
"Io sono sangue" ("I Am Blood") (Griffo), 15, 288. See also Griffo, Michela
Irish Americans, 285–286
Isis, 89
Italian (language): as binary gendered language, 88, 121n6, 228–229, 239, 239n5–240n13, 340; and gender diversity, 236, 338–339; LGBTQ+ terminology, anglicized, 343
Italian Americans: gender diversity and identity, 294, 298–300, 307–309, 310–312, 319; immigrant experience, 285–286, 295–296; mafia, 286–287, 288–289
Italian Communist Party. See Partito Comunista Italiano (PCI)
Italian Sexology Centre. See Centro Italiano di Sessuologia (CIS)
Italian Social Democratic Party. See Partito Socialista Democratico Italiano (PSDI)
Italian Socialist Party of Proletarian Unity. See Partito Socialista Italiano di Unità Proletaria
Italian Transsexual Movement (Movimento Italiano Transessuale). See MIT
Italy. See Italian (language); *specific people* (e.g., Di Marco, Marcella); *specific places* (e.g. Bologna, Naples)
I Was Walking Close to the Walls (D'Aquino). See *Camminavo rasente i muri* (D'Aquino)

Jagger, Mick, 31
Johnson, Marsha P. (trans movement Black icon), 6
Jorgensen, Christine (trans woman), xv, 16n2, 161, 175–176
Juno, 177–178
Jupiter, 177–178

kinaidos, 86, 98n16
koilos (hollow), 122n7
Kooky's (gay bar, Greenwich Village), 286–287, 288
Krafft-Ebing, Richard von, 173

La Candelora a Montevergine (Candlemas at Montevergine), 84, 97n10
Lady Gaga, xviii, 334
La grande madre (Neumann), 90
Lancini, Giuseppe (priest), 184, 185
languages: challenges with, 329–330, 338; and gender, 228–229, 236, 239, 239n6, 338; terminology (gender diversity), 223, 228–229. See also pronouns; *specific languages* (e.g., Italian, English)
La prostituzione in Napoli (Di Giacomo), 83
La Scatulara, 45
Laura (social worker at Lunatica), 209

L'aurora delle trans cattive (Marcasciano), 2; baptism ceremony *femminielli*, 43–44; *femminielli world*, 42–43, 44–45; as sequel to *AntoloGaia*, 41; sex work, 125–131
Law 164 (sex changes), xvi, 10, 133, 231, 347n18
Law 184 (self-diagnosis), 250
Legge Basaglia, 249, 257n22
Legge Zan (Zan Law): approval of by the Camera (2020), xviii, 6; rejection of by Senate (2021), xviii, 19n29
Le Mani della Mia Nonna (Minerva), 301–302
leopard, 129
lesbians: experiences of, 173, 174–175, 299; safe spaces, creation of, 225, 287–289; words to describe, 45, 102, 173
LGBTQ+: Bologna, 269; history, lack of knowledge of, 117–118; language, homogeneity of, 343–344; liberation movement, xv, 9–10; marginalization of, 5; safe spaces, creation of, 287–289; and trans community, 118–119, 165–166, 226–227, 340–341
Libellula Italia (trans association), xvii, 14
liberation process, 166–167, 170
Libya, 237–238
Licinius Valerianus, Emperor Publius, 182
Lido di Classe (Province of Ravenna), 200, 205–207, 209–210
Linda (social worker at Lunatica), 209
Lipson, Molly, 340
Lisa (trans woman, Brazil): appearance, 207–208; Carnival (Rio), 202–203; Carosel (club in Rio), 202; childhood (Rio de Janeiro), 200–202; family, importance of, 208–209; Grande Rio (school), 203; Lido di Classe (Italy), 205–207; MIT training course, 209

Livorno, 181
loden (coat), 251, 258n29
Lombrosian model of time, 82
Lombroso, 162
l'ommo 'e mmerda (pederast), 77, 80–81, 82, 97n11, 134, 137
Loren, Sofia, 324
Lorusso, Francesco, 244, 254n2, 254n3, 258n31
"lo sportello Cgil." *See* Sportello Trans CGIL (job help desk for trans people)
Louis XIV, 178
Love Talks (Pasolini). *See Comizi d'amore (Love Talks)* (Pasolini)
luck: *femminielli*, as bringers of, 56, 80, 307–308
Lucrezia, 278–279, 278f
Lucy. *See* Salani, Lucy
Luisa, 53. *See also* Antonello (femminiello); La Merdaiola
Luna group. *See* Gruppo Luna (trans group at Maurice)
Lunatica (social worker service), 209
Luxuria, Vladimir (trans activist), xvii

Madam Arthur (Paris), 137, 139–141, 170
Madonna nera (Black Madonna), 323. *See also Mamma Schiavona* (Black Madonna/Mother Slave)
Madonnas, 57, 62, 91, 93–94
mafia: gay bars, 286–287; Gay Liberation Front (GLF), 287–289
Magaddino, Stefano, 286
Malaparte, Curzio, 110
male-to-female. *See* MtF (male-to-female)
Mamma Schiavona (Black Madonna/Mother Slave): Candelora ritual to, 323, 329, 331, 332–333; *femminielli* pilgrimage to, 119, 307, 324–325; sanctuary dedicated to, 93, 306

Marcasciano, Porpora (trans activist): baptism ceremony *(femminielli)*, 43–44; Cassero, la presa del, 195–197; childhood, 32–33; city counselor (Bologna) (2021), xvii; coming out, 37–38; as contemporary bard, 3, 18n12; cross-dressing, 36; and Di Folco, Marcella, 276–278, 276*f*; *femminielli*, 42–43, 44–45; "first time," 161–162, 167, 169, 172, 173–174; history of trans people, 161–166; homosexuality, 34–35; *Il sogno e l'utopia*, 267–268; memoirs, 2, 12; name, 33, 44, 320–321; narrating voice, choice of, 29, 39n4; photos of, 275*f*, 276*f*, 278*f*, 280*f*; Piazza dei Cinquecento, 126–131; president of Commissione Pari Opportunità (2021), xix; pronouns, 229, 240n7; self-awareness (cultivating), 337–338; storytelling as instrument of transformation, 2–3, 30; terminology, Italian LGBTQ+, 343; trans woman, first time seeing a, 42. See also *AntoloGaia* (Marcasciano); *Elementi di critica trans* (Marcasciano); *Favolose narranti* (Marcasciano); *L'aurora delle trans cattive* (Marcasciano); *Tra le rose e le viole* (Marcasciano)

Marcella. *See* Di Folco, Marcella (Marcellona)

Marcellona. *See* Di Folco, Marcella (Marcellona)

Mariani, Liz, 300–301

The Mark of Virgil (Il segno di Virgilio) (De Simone), 78, 78*f*

marriage. *See spusarizio* (wedding)

Martini, Mia, 31

masculone (lesbian), 102

Masoud, Mazen (LGBTQ+ activist, Libyan refugee), 14, 237–239

Mastrantoni, Pietro: Law 164 signing (1988), xvi

Maurice (LGBTQ+ association), 225, 226–227, 229, 239n3

McDonnel, Andrew (defense attorney), 191

"meaningful experiences" (Marcasciano). *See* "esperienza umana significativa"

medicalization and trans history, 160, 172–173, 177, 178, 232–233

Mediterranean region: female, early representations of, 90–91; *femminielli*, presence of, 117; Naples as female soul of, 91–92

La Merdaiola, 43, 44, 47, 196, 197n2. *See also* Antonello (femminiello)

Messalina (Sasà), 44, 45

Mieli, Mario: about, 255n9; on "educastration," 31; *Elementi di critica omosessuale*, 8–9, 13, 166, 247–248, 256n18; FUORI! foundation, 245; *Il risveglio dei faraoni*, 8; protest of International Congress of Sexology (1972), xv–xvi, 9, 29, 36; on transsexuality, 8, 247–249

Milan: industrial district, 136, 155n4; Parco Lambro Festival, 244; police harassment, 50–51; prostitution (turning tricks), 50, 54; self-help group, 233–234; trans protest in public swimming pool, xvi, 10

Mille santi del Giorno (Bargellini), 93

mimesis, 92

Minerva, Summer: Adam, 321–322; A Call from the Ancestors, 309–301; family, 301–302, 303, 304–306, 319–320, 321–322; *femminielli*, 307–309, 322–323; given name, 319–320; interview of Ciretta and Loredana, 116–121; Italian

American identity, 303–304, 308; Italy, visits to, 305–306, 307; Le Mani della Mia Nonna, 301–302; personal journey, 115–116; Sacred Gender Collaboration (pilgrimage to Naples), 329, 330–331, 333–334, 335. See also *Summer Within* (Minerva)

Minimum Pain. See *Dolore minimo (Minimum Pain)* (Vivinetto)

"Minuetto" ("Minuet") (Martini), 31

"Miss Italia Trans" pageant, 172

Miss Seven Evenings, 44

MIT: community-based and cultural events, xviii, 11; courses (training), 51, 209; Emilia-Romagna (regional section of MIT), xvi, 11, 265; health centre *(consultorio)*, xvi, 11; name changes, xvii, xviii, 10–11, 257n24; official foundation of (1981), xvi, 10; steering committee of TGEU (2016), xviii

Moffa, Louis, 340

mollis, 86, 98n14

Montevergine: abbey (sanctuary), 57, 78f, 79, 117, 307, 331; Candelora, 15, 93–94, 329; Cybele cult, 92–93, 308; fire (1611), 86; pilgrimage to, 80, 170, 306, 323, 324

Montevergine Candlemas Network, 103–104

Moran, Herbert Michael, 187, 189, 191–192

Morocco, 120, 237, 238

Morris, Jan (travel journalist), 7

Mother Slave. See *Mamma Schiavona* (Black Madonna/Mother Slave)

Mount Vesuvius. See Vesuvius, Mount

Movimento del '77, 244, 249, 254n5

Movimento Identità Trans (MIT) (2017–). See MIT

Movimento Identità Transessuale (MIT) (1999–2017). See MIT

Movimento Italiano Transessuale (MIT) (1981–1999). See MIT

MtF (male-to-female): transitions, 127, 230, 248, 299

Muscella, 44–45

Muxé (from Zapotec society in Mexico), 76

muxes (two spirits), 119

name changes: acceptance of, 320–321; focus on, 233, 234; gender transition and, 66–69, 320–321; without gender reassignment surgery, xviii, 347n18

Nana (nymph), 92

Naples: Candelora (sacred festival), 15; coffee is friendship, 44, 56; evolution of, 76, 95–96, 97n4; as female city, 91–92, 117; history of, 85; moving to from small towns, 118; mythical story of, 318–319; *popolino* (local underclass), 13, 76, 97n4; Sacred Gender Collaboration, pilgrimage to Naples, 329, 330–331; Spanish Quarter, 87, 88, 89, 98n18, 98n19; la Tarantina, 344–345; traditions, 55–56; transvestites/trans women, 36, 41, 42, 57, 116; tricks, turning, 54, 55; vicoli (narrow streets), 48, 60n4, 75. See also *femminielli (femmenelle/femminelle)*; Neapolitan

National Observatory of Gender Identity. See Osservatorio Nazionale sull'identità di genere

Nazism, 162, 246, 347n15

Neapolitan: art of getting by, 48; cultural history, 12–13, 75, 101, 118, 344–346; dialect, 42, 45, 56, 60n13–14, 97n11, 322, 339;

Neapolitan *(continued)*
  folklore, 12, 120, 122n18, 322; gender-variant community, 41, 288, 317, 321–322, 324, 329, 345; luck, importance of, 58, 80, 308; numbers, importance of, 45, 56, 59, 60n6; Spanish Quarter, 87, 88, 89, 98n18, 98n19; urban context, 95–96. See also *femminielli (femmenelle/femminelle)*; Naples

Neapolitanness *(napoletanità)*, 89
Netflix, 16
Neumann, Erich, 90, 94
New York: civil rights uprising after police raid on Stonewall Inn (1969), xv, 6, 256n15; gay bars, 6, 11, 15, 286–287; homosexual rights bill (1986), 7; Pallotta's photographs, 280–281, 280f; Rivera, Sylvia (trans activist), 6, 19n32, 35–36, 39n8, 161, 179n2. See also Italian Americans
New Zealand: Crawford, Harry, 14, 181, 187–188; Immigration Act (1901), 188
Nilo (god), 89
Nina, 107
1977 liberation movement, 8–9, 10
ninety (novanta) *(la paura / fear)*, 60n6
nomadism, 164–165
"Non siamo nat@ ieri" ("We Were Not Born Yesterday") (Botteghi), 13–14
Non una di meno (Not One Less), 341
normalization process, 165–167
norms, gendered. See gendered norms
Not One Less. See Non una di meno (Not One Less)
numbers: *femminielli* use of, 45, 56, 59. See also *specific numbers (e.g., forty-four, ninety)*

offences, public, 134, 136
Oltre le monocolture del genere, 232
ommo 'e mmerda (active pederast), 80–81, 82
ONIG. See Osservatorio Nazionale sull'identità di genere (ONIG)
orejones, 87
Osservatorio Nazionale sull'identità di genere (ONIG), xvi–xvii, 159
Other Feminisms. See *Altri femminismi (Other Feminisms)* (Marcasciano); Marcasciano, Porpora (trans activist)
Other Transitions (Vesce). See *Altri transiti* (Vesce)
Ottaviano, Giulia (filmmaker), 345
OUT!. See Fronte Unitario Omosessuale Rivoluzionario Italiano (FUORI!)
Out-Takes archive (Cangelosi). See Archivio Out-Takes (Cangelosi)
Ovid, 177

pageants. See "Miss Italia Trans" pageant
Pallotta, Lina (photographer): Marcasciano, Porpora, friendship with, 15, 275–281; photo of, 280f; *Porpora* photo exhibition, 274
pansexual, 8
Pappagone, 57, 60n14
Paris: Cecconi, Romina in, 8, 133, 136–141; nightclubs, 167, 170; trans community, 205, 206
Paris Is Burning (documentary), 11, 21n62
Partenio (now Montevergine), 92, 93. See also Montevergine
Parthenope (siren), 90, 117, 319, 322, 326n3
Partito Comunista Italiano (PCI), 246
Partito Radical (Radical Party), 9, 250, 257n23

Partito Socialista Democratico Italiano (PSDI), 246
Partito Socialista Italiano di Unità Proletaria (PSIUP), 246
Pasolini, Pier Paolo (director): *Comizi d'amore (Love Talks)*, 1–2, 16, 337; Communist Party, 246; on history, 338; murder of, 37, 131n5; Piazza dei Cinquecento, 128–129; Rome, 244
patriarchy: binaries, 243, 304; and gender diversity, 1–2, 85–86, 92; and homosexuality, 82, 85–86; language, limitations created by, 2–3, 83
Patrizia, 106–107
"Pazza idea" ("Crazy Idea") (Pravo), 31
pederasts: active *(l'ommo 'e mmerda)*, 77, 80–81, 82, 97n11, 134, 137; passive *(ricchione)* (fairy), 82
Pelosi, Pino, 128, 131n5
Peloso, Riccardo, 130
pertenezza, 302, 313n3
"Perverse Polymorphs Proto T*" (Velena), 14
Petri of Orvieto, Margherita, 184
Pezzana, Angelo (FUORI! cofounder), 9, 245, 255n8, 255n10
The Pharaoh's Awakening (Mieli). See *Il risveglio dei faraoni* (Mieli)
Philadelphia, 294–296, 329
Piazza dei Cinquecento (Rome): description of, 126, 127; initiation ritual, 127–128; people who frequented, 128–130; Volturno cinema, 126–127
pink triangles, 162, 179n4, 347n15
Pinto, Samuel. See Pugñales, Lola
Plancus, Janus. See Bianchi, Giovanni (anatomy professor)
Plato, 177; on androgyne, 90

Poidimani, Nicoletta: on cross-dressing, 176; on first time, 173; trans experience, 4; "vetero-sexual" order of Western society, 32, 39n6
Poison Girls, 251, 257n27
police: gay bars, 287; harassment, 8, 50–51, 205–206, 227; informers (canaries), 129. See also Stonewall riots (1969)
polymorphous, 8
polysexual, 8
popolino (local underclass, Naples), 13, 76, 97n4
Poppea (Roman drag queen), 111
Porpora (film 2021), 47, 273
Porpora (photo exhibition 2018), 274–275, 275f, 276f, 278f, 280f
Porta Saragozza (Bologna), xvi, 10, 196, 197, 256n17, 266. See also Cassero (Bologna)
Pravo, Patty, 31
prejudice, 161–162, 187, 292
la presa del Cassero (the storming of Cassero), 10, 14, 195–197, 247. See also Cassero (Bologna)
Pride: Bologna, 196, 247, 262; Euro Pride, xviii; LGBT Pride Day, 179n2, 256n15; participation of trans people, 164, 226–227; San Francisco, 226–227; World Pride (Rome 2000), xvii, 225
Primordial Mother. See Great Mother
Prince Romaloff, 109
Progetto Moonlight (community-based project), 11
pronouns: challenges with, 191, 229, 231; *femminielli* use of, 43; gender neutral, 47, 236, 239; use of, 228–229, 231, 236, 340
prostitution: as a choice, 204–205; as means of survival, 164; trans women, 167–169; tricks, turning,

prostitution *(continued)*
  48, 49, 50, 51, 54–55; violence, street, 57–59
Prostitution in Naples. See *La prostituzione in Napoli* (Di Giacomo)
Proto, 182
Prussi, 196
Psychopathia Sexualis (Krafft-Ebing and Ellis), 173
pucchiacca (female genitalia), 117, 122n7
Pucci, Cavaliere, 185
Pugñales, Lola, 196, 244, 249, 255n6
punk scene, 243, 250, 251, 252
pyr (fiery), 117, 122n7

Radical Party. *See* Partito Radical (Radical Party)
raffle *(riffa)* (public bingo), 80
"rainbow cities," 6
Rando, Flavia, 287, 288
Raymond, Janice, 269–270
rebirth, 63–64
Red Brigades. *See* Brigate Rosse (Red Brigades)
reflux. *See riflusso* (reflux) period
religion: Catholicism, 234, 245–246, 247–249, 286, 331, 333; and transvestitism, 86. *See also* Madonnas; *Mamma Schiavona* (Black Madonna/Mother Slave)
Republic (Plato), 90
ricchione (passive pederast/fairy/femminiello), 82, 86–87, 98n17
riffa (raffle/public bingo), 80
riflusso (reflux) period, 251, 252–253, 257n28
Rifondazione Comunista: election of Luxuria, Vladimir (2007), xvii
Rio (Sacred Gender Collaboration pilgrimage), 330, 333, 336n3
Rio de Janeiro: Carnival, 202–203; gang culture, 201–202; samba, 201, 203–204; trans people, 204

Rivera, Sylvia (trans activist): Stonewall riots (1969), 6, 19n32, 35–36, 39n8, 161, 179n2; Transiti (2000), xvii; World Pride (Rome, 2000), xvii
Roberta, 278–279, 278*f*
Robson, Stewart (Sergeant), 189–190
roles: active (sexual relations), 80–81, 82, 85–86; gender, 82–83, 86, 87–88, 102; passive (sexual relations), 82, 85–86; sexual, 84
Roma, 111, 114n34
Romaloff, Prince, 109
Romanina. *See* Cecconi, Romina (Romanina)
Romano, Gabriella, 341–342
Romanov, Aunt Anastasia, 197
Rome: Campo de' Fiori, 245; Piazza dei Cinquecento, 126–130; World Pride (2000), xvii, 225
Rossella (Neapolitan transvestite), 106–107, 113n21
Rossi, Loredana (*femmenella* / activist): communications skills, 115; documentary on, 345; as *femmenella*, 115, 116, 324, 345; on *femminiello* history, 116–117, 120–121, 324; interview with, 13, 342–325; on LGBTQ+ community, 117–120
Rossi, Mario, 176
Rothblatt, Martine Aliana, 94

Sacred Gender Collaboration (pilgrimage to Naples), 329, 330–331
Saionara, 44
Salani, Lucy, 162, 163, 179n4, 341–342
Salvini, Matteo, 119, 122n17
samba, 201, 203–204
same-sex civil unions, 6
San Francisco, Pride, 226–227
Sanremo, xv–xvi, 9, 29, 36, 245–246
Santa Maria (church in Trastevere), 184, 185

Santa Maria della Scala (Siena church), 182
Santo Spirito, 134
Sasà. *See* Messalina (Sasà)
Satariano, Regina, 170–172, 173
Scarinci, Francesca, 267
Schinaia, Cosimo, 96
schwa (ə), 239n6, 339, 347n8
Sciò Sciò Ciucciuvè (tombola game), 104, 112n12
self-castration, 92, 94
self-emasculation, 92, 94
Serano, Julia, 7
seventy-one (*tortore* / man), 45
seventy-two (astonishment), 56, 59
sex: biological, xv, 29, 76, 97n3, 191, 249, 341; changes, Law 164, xvi, 10, 133, 231, 347n18
Sexology International Congress on Deviant Behaviors of Human Sexuality, xv–xvi, 9, 245–246, 255n12
sex reassignment surgery. *See* gender reassignment surgery
sexual deviant. *See* deviants, sexual
sexual inversion, 17n4, 172–173
sexual orientation, xviii, 82, 323, 343
Sienna, 182
silicone injections, 171, 179n10, 207–208
Simonelli, Pino (anthropology professor), 41, 42, 83–84, 105, 109
sirens (myth of), 90, 117, 318–319, 322
Sister Giulia. *See* Giulia, Sora
sixteen (the ass / *'o vascio*), 45
Smorfia, 60n6, 104, 113n15
sodomites, 85
sodomy, 82
Sokolov, Frances. *See* Subversa, Vi
Sora Giulia. *See* Giulia, Sora
Spanish Quarter (Naples), 87, 88, 89, 98n18, 98n19

Spiranza, Salviatore (Hope, Salvia), 297, 298
Spolato, Mariasilvia, 245
Sportello Trans CGIL (job help desk for trans people), xvi, 11, 229
spusarizio (wedding): *femminielli*, 80–81, 83–84, 105–110, 113n18; Neapolitan tradition of, 118; rite, description of, 80–81, 83–84
Staiano, Jo, 128
stilettos, 165–166
Stone, Sandy, 230, 240n8, 269
Stone Butch Blues (Feinberg), 6
Stonewall, 166
Stonewall Inn (NY), xv, 6
Stonewall riots (1969), xv, 6, 19n32, 35–36, 161, 256n15
storytelling, as instrument of transformation, 2–3, 30
street walking: initiation ritual, 50, 127–128. *See also* prostitution
Stryker, Susan, 18n17, 19n31, 25
Subbiondo, Frances Rose: Acorn (partner), 295, 296, 332, 336n3; childhood (NY), 292–293; community (queer and trans), 294–296; family's immigration to NY, 291–292; immigrant experience, 293–294; *N'Dakinna* (central Vermont), 297, 298; Philadelphia, 295–296; Sacred Gender Collaboration, 329–330, 331, 336n3; Spiranza, Salviatore (Hope, Salvia, child), 297, 298
subjection: history of, 172–173
subjectivation, 172–173, 178
subjectivities: definition used in this book, 17n6; trans, 4, 175, 178, 233
Subversa, Vi, 251, 257n27
subversion, 4, 244, 255, 274, 281
suicide, 82, 212–213
Summer Within (Minerva): on belonging, 325–326; *femminielli*,

378 | Index

Summer Within (Minerva) *(continued)*
  322–324; Montevergine, pilgrimage
  to, 323, 324–325; name, preferred
  and given, 319–321; *nonna*
  (grandmother), 321–322, 325;
  research for, 115; sirens, 318–319,
  322; summary of, 15, 317–318
superstitions, 58–59, 150, 258n34
Switzerland: acceptance of culture,
  142–144; gender reassignment
  surgery, xv, 145–148; Ginevra, 161
Sylvia Rivera Steering Committee,
  225–226
"Sympathy for the Devil" (Jagger), 31
Symposium (Plato), 90

T*. *See* "Perverse Polymorphs Proto
  T*" (Velena); Velena, Helena
  (musician)
Taccarelli, Valérie (trans activist), xvi,
  197, 197n3, 243, 247, 255
Tally-Ho, 188. *See also* Crawford,
  Harry
tammurriata (dance or song with
  drum), 79, 97n9, 332
la Tarantina, 12, 32n65, 344–345
TGEU. *See* Transgender Europe
  (TGEU)
thirty-eight (a beating), 56
Three Essays on the Theory of Sexuality
  (Freud), 17n4
tickets, public offences, 134, 136
Tiresias (seer), 62, 63, 177–178
tombola (game), 13, 56, 60n6, 102–
  104, 119
tombolelle, 103. *See also tombola* (game)
Tonino, 337
Toraloff, Duchess of, 104, 109, 110
Torre Annunziata: *femminielli* wedding,
  108, 109; *figliata* (birthing ritual),
  110–112; moving to Naples from,
  118

Torre del Greco: *figliata* (birthing
  ritual), 118; *spusarizio* (wedding),
  80–81
Towards a Gay Communism (Mieli). *See
  Elementi di critica omosessuale* (Mieli)
Tra le rose e le viole (Marcasciano):
  cross-dressing, 49–50, 51–54;
  femminielli traditions, 55–57;
  history of trans people, 165–166;
  prostitution, 48, 49–51, 55;
  violence, street, 57–59
trans: definition used in this book, 4,
  17n6, 19n24; Italian use of term,
  113n22
trans*, 5, 19n24
Transgender Day of Remembrance
  (TDOR): celebration of (1999), xvii
Transgender Europe (TGEU): Bologna
  meeting (2016), xviii; foundation
  of, 226, 239n4; MIT on steering
  committee (2016), xviii
transgenderism: explained, 97n3; and
  femminielli, 76, 91, 92, 116
Transiti (Transitions) (Bologna), xvii
transitions: FtM, 172, 173, 181, 211,
  214, 230, 248; MtF, 127, 230, 348;
  process, 165–167, 171–172
Transitions. *See* Transiti (Transitions)
trans people: Brazil, 204–205; history,
  reappropriation of, 160–166; and
  LGBTQ+ movement, 6–7, 117–
  119, 165–166, 340–341; memory
  (collective), 341; as nomads, 164–
  165; Pride celebrations, 164
transsexual: defining oneself as, 52;
  femminiello as modern, 119; Mieli's
  use of the term, 8, 247–248; term,
  coining of (1949), xv. *See also*
  transsexualism; trans women
Transsexual Association of Naples. *See*
  Associazione Transessuale Napoli
  (ATN)

Index | 379

The Transsexual Empire: The Making of the She-Male (Raymond), 269–270
Transsexual Identity Movement (Movimento Identità Transessuale). *See* MIT
transsexualism: and Cybele myth, 94; and *femminielli*, 92, 96, 116; and gender identity, 96; history of, 173, 232; as medical condition, xv; as mental illness, 162; social groups, formation of, 162–163; stigma about, 161–162; transition path, 177; what is, 178. *See also* transsexual; trans women
The Transsexual Phenomenon (Benjamin), xv, 177
Trans Steering Committee Sylvia Rivera. *See* Coodinamento Trans Sylvia Rivera
trans subjectivities, 4, 175, 178, 233
transvestites: Naples, history of in, 83; Piazza dei Cinquecento (Rome), 127; Stonewall riots (1969), xv; as a term, 6, 36
transvestitism, 48, 52; female (being and feeling), 96; Naples, unique to, 91; religious, 86, 94. *See also* cross-dressing
trans women: and feminism, 165–166; Law 164, 231; media, 234; Piazza dei Cinquecento (Rome), 127; prostitution, 167–169
Trastevere: Santa Maria church, 184, 185
triangles. *See* pink triangles
tricks, turning, 48, 49, 50, 51, 54–55. *See also* prostitution
Trump, Donald, 119
tumbulella (tombola) (game). *See tombola* (game)
Turin: FUORI! foundation of, 255n8; LGBT service, 228; Maurice (LGBTQ+ association), 225, 226–227, 229, 239n3
turning tricks. *See* prostitution; tricks, turning
Tuscany: transsexual community, 170–171
twenty-nine (the phallus), 45
twenty-one *(tombola / femminielli)*, 45
twenty-three (madman), 59
twenty-three (meaning of), 252, 258n34
two spirits, 119

Ulysses, 131n4, 319, 325, 326n4
Una nobile rivoluzione (A Noble Revolution) (Cangelosi), 261–266, 268–269
"Un asterisco sul genere" ("An asterisk on gender") (Paolo), 339
United Italian Homosexual Revolutionary Front. *See* Fronte Unitario Omosessuale Rivoluzionario
United States: conflicts (ethic and racial), 286; immigrant experience, 285–286; LGBTQ+ narrative, 269; music, 253. *See also specific cities (e.g.,* New York, Philadelphia, San Francisco)
Ursula (German transvestite), 140
Usi e costumi dei camorristi (Habits and customs of the Camorrists) (De Blasio), 80–81

Valentina (social worker at Lunatica), 209
Valerian, Emperor Publius Licinius, 182
"Valérie" (song by Cohen), 247
Valerio, Paulo, 159, 178
vasetto / vasetti (little vessel), 81, 98n13
Velena, Helena (musician): Cassero, 247, 249, 252; Convention against

Velena, Helena (musician) *(continued)* Repression, 244; FUORI!, 244–245; homosexuality laws, 246, 249–250; Mieli on transexuality, 247–249; music and culture, 250–251, 252–254; "Perverse Polymorphs Proto T*," 14, 243
the "Venetian," 135
Venus, 90, 91, 92
Very (friend of Cecconi), 136
Vesce, Maria Carolina: *Altri transiti (Other Transitions)*, 13; *figliata* (birthing ritual), 110–112; *tombola*, 101, 102–105; wedding, *femmenielli*, 105–110, 113n18
Vesuvius, Mount: *femminielli*, presence of, 96, 117; *figliata* (birthing ritual), 110; wedding, *femminielli*, 108
"vetero-sexual" order of Western society, 32, 39n6
vicoli (narrow streets in Naples), 48, 60n4, 75
Viewless Winds (Moran), 187
Vigna, Pier Luigi, 36, 39n11
violence: against *femminielli*, 119–120; street walking and, 58–59
Vivinetto, Giovanna Cristina: *Dolore minimo (Minimum Pain)*, 61–69; *Dove non siamo stati (Where We Haven't Been)*, 69–72; gender transition, 12, 63–66; name change, 66–69, 320
Vizzani, Caterina (Catterina), 14, 181, 184. *See also* Bordoni, Giovanni

Vizzani, Pietro, 184
Voli, Stefania, 10, 341
Volturino: Cecconi, Romina, confinement of, xv, 8, 36, 133
Volturno cinema (Rome), 126–127

wedding. *See spusarizio* (wedding)
Wegener, Einar (Danish painter), 16n2
The Well of Loneliness (Hall), 173, 175
Westphal, Karl, 172–173
"We Were Not Born Yesterday." *See* "Non siamo nat@ ieri" (Botteghi)
Where We Haven't Been. *See Dove non siamo stati (Where We Haven't Been)* (Vivinetto)
Whipping Girl (Serano), 7
Wiegman, Robyn, 342
Wilson, Elizabeth, 342
Wim (Sacred Gender Collaboration pilgrimage), 330, 336n3
Wittig, Monique, 32
Wonder, 196
World Pride: Rome (2000), xvii, 225
World Professional Association for Transgender Health (WPATH), xvii
WPATH. *See* World Professional Association for Transgender Health (WPATH)

Zangheri, Renato (mayor of Bologna), 197, 244, 247
Zan Law. *See* Legge Zan (Zan Law)
Zero, Renato, 250–251, 257n26